Public Sector Housing Law

Second edition

D.J. Hughes, LLB (Liverpool), LLB (Cantab)
Senior Lecturer in Law
University of Leicester
Honorary Legal Consultant to the National Housing and
Town Planning Council

London
Butterworths
1987

United Kingdom	Butterworth & Co (Publishers) Ltd, 88 Kingsway, LONDON WC2B 6AB and 61A North Castle Street, EDINBURGH EH2 3LJ
Australia	Butterworths Pty Ltd, SYNDNEY, MELBOURNE, BRISBANE, ADELAIDE, PERTH, CANBERRA and HOBART
Canada	Butterworths, A division of Reed Inc., TORONTO and VANCOUVER
New Zealand	Butterworths of New Zealand Ltd, WELLINGTON and AUCKLAND
Singapore	Butterworth & Co (Asia) Ptd Ltd, SINGAPORE
South Africa	Butterworth Publishers (Pty) Ltd, DURBAN and PRETORIA
USA	Butterworths Legal Publishers, ST PAUL, Minnesota, SEATTLE, Washington, BOSTON, Massachusetts, AUSTIN, Texas and D & S Publishers, CLEARWATER, Florida

© Butterworth & Co (Publishers) Ltd 1987

British Library Cataloguing in Publication Data

Hughes, D.J. (David John), *1945–*
   Public Sector housing law.——2nd ed.
   1. Public housing——Law and legislation——England
   I. Title
   344.204′636358   KD1179

ISBN 0–406–60062–7

Preface

Truly does Scripture say: 'Of making many books there is no end.' A senior local government officer said to me when I was writing the first edition of this book 'you won't be able to finish it. The law changes too often.' I did finish 'it', but the law has continued to change – and change too often. The 1980 Housing Act was succeeded by the 1984 Housing and Building Control Act, and though all must be grateful for the consolidation of the vast majority of housing legislation in the Housing Act 1985, The Housing Associations Act 1985 and the Landlord and Tenant Act 1985, almost predictably the ink is hardly dry before we are faced with the imposition of yet more change in the Housing and Planning Act 1986. This forces us once more to have to read two statutes together with all the attendant problems of comprehension this brings. This last named statute still awaited the Royal Assent at the time of writing, but the book has been written as if it is in force.

The *aims* of the book remain as stated in the first edition, and though its coverage has been expanded to include housing associations, I have struggled hard to prevent my own 'middle age spread' from being mirrored in its bulk!

I must, gladly, once more record my thanks to: Mrs B J Goodman and her staff in the Leicester Faculty of Law Office; my Leicester colleagues; those officers of central and local government who have continued to aid my researches, and my students. I must, equally gladly, add my thanks to: my colleagues at The National Housing and Town Planning Council and Hanover Housing Association for all their help, advice and encouragement; my publishers for commissioning this second edition; and my wife for her patient acceptance of being a 'law library widow'. This book remains dedicated to all of them, and to the proud and happy memory of Muriel May Hughes, November 16 1916–June 27 1982. '*Justorum Animae In Manu Dei Sunt.*'

David Hughes
Leicester
9 October 1986.

Contents

Acknowledgements

Grateful acknowledgement is made to the following authorities and publishers for permission to reprint material from their publications:

The Controller of Her Majesty's Stationery Office for the various statutory provisions reproduced, the passages from MOHLG Circular 55/54, the report 'Council Housing: Purposes, Procedures and Priorities', and the report of the Housing Services Advisory Group 'Report on the Housing of One Parent Families';

Longman Group Ltd for a passage from *Slum Clearance and Compensation* by Professor J Garner;

The passage from *Local Government* by R J Buxton (Penguin Education 1970) pp. 71–72, copyright © R J Buxton, 1970, reproduced by permission of Penguin Books Ltd.

Commencement

The Housing and Planning Act 1986

DoE Circular 22/86 gives information on the commencement of this Act.

Sections 1–4 (the right to buy etc)
Sections 10–11 (management agreements etc)
Section 14 (housing the homeless)
Section 16 (housing management grants)
Section 19 (housing association agency services)
Section 20 (disposal of new town housing)

and certain of the minor amendments and repeals, inter alia, came into force on 7 January 1987 and the necessary appointed day orders and associated regulations by 1 April 1987.

Table of Statutes

References in this Table to *Statutes* are to Halsbury's Statutes of England (Fourth Edition) showing the volume and page at which the annotated text of the Act may be found.

List of cases

List of cases

List of cases

List of cases

Addendum

At a late stage in the House of Lords the Government introduced many amendments to the Housing and Planning Act 1986. The generosity of my publishers has allowed me to incorporate this material at proof stage, so, while the main text represents the law at the end of September 1986, this addendum contains certain changes since then. The provisions of the 1986 Act are largely subject to Appointed Day Orders for their commencement.

1. Under section 69A of the Housing Associations Act 1985 an association is not entitled to HAG, revenue or hostel deficit grants in respect of properties comprised in management agreements within sections 27(2) and 27B(4) of the Housing Act 1985 (see Chapter 3 below).

2. Section 57A of the New Towns Act 1981 makes it clear that the provisions relating to the transfer of dwellings from a new town to a district council do not restrict the use of other powers under sections 36 and 64 of the 1981 Act to dispose of dwellings to 'any person'. Indeed it is policy that new town housing should, by the early 1990s, be increasingly transferred to housing associations and trusts.

3. Under section 1 of the Housing and Planning Act 1986, following a government defeat in the House of Lords, a new para. 11 will provide that RTB shall not arise where a dwelling (a) is particularly suitable for occupation by persons of pensionable age having regard to (i) its location, and (ii) its size, design, heating and other major features so far as those were provided by the landlord, a predecessor of the tenant, or a person qualified to succeed under Part IV of the Housing Act 1985; (b) was let to the tenant, or his predecessor in title, for occupation by a person of pensionable age or a physically disabled person. In determining the above question of suitability regard has to be had as to whether the dwelling is easily accessible on foot, is on one level, has no more than two bedrooms, has a heating system serving the living room and at least one bedroom, and, where the dwelling is a flat located above the ground floor, whether access by lift is available.

4. Section 155 of the Housing Act 1985 previously laid down a five year repayment period; the change will be introduced under section 2 of the Housing and Planning Act 1986.

5. Section 137(2) was inserted by Schedule 5 to the Housing and Planning Act 1986.

6. Section 20A of the LTA 1985, as inserted by Schedule 5 to the Housing and Planning Act 1986, will provide that where relevant costs for the purpose of computing a service charge are incurred in connection with works grant-aided under Part XV of the Housing Act 1985, e.g. an improvement grant, the amount of the grant is to be deducted from the costs and the service charge accordingly reduced, and appropriate information must be given to tenants.

7. Section 6 of the Housing and Planning Act 1986 inserts section 106A and Schedule 3A into the Housing Act 1985 to regulate the duties of local authorities proposing to dispose of *dwellings subject to secure tenancies*, and those of the Secretary of State in considering whether to give his consent to such disposals. These provisions, which replace the normal consultation requirements of section 105 of the 1985 Act (see Chapter 3 below) in relation to questions of disposal, require regard to be had to the views of tenants likely to lose secure tenant status in consequence of the disposal. Where a local authority disposes of an interest in land as a result of which a secure tenant of theirs will become the tenant of a private sector landlord that is a person *other than* a body falling within section 80 of the 1985 Act, the Secretary of State must not entertain an application for consent under section 32 to the disposal unless certain consultation requirements have been complied with. These requirements are that the authority must have served written notice on the affected tenant giving appropriate details of the proposed disposal, including the identity of the person to whom disposal will take place, the likely consequences of the disposal *for the tenant* the preservation of RTB (see main text page 77) and the effect of the provisions of Schedule 3A. The tenant must also be informed of his right to make representations to the authority within a specified reasonable time. Any representations received must be considered, and further notice served on the tenant informing him of any significant changes to the proposal, and of his right to object to the Secretary of State. The tenant must also be informed that consent must be withheld if it appears that a majority of relevant tenants oppose the proposal. The Secretary of State may require further consultation to take place, but must not give consent if it appears to him that a majority of the tenants of relevant dwellings do not wish the disposal to proceed, though he may, of course, refuse consent for other reasons. In coming to his decision the Secretary of State may have regard to any information available to him. However, consent to a disposal is not invalidated by a failure by the Secretary of State or the local authority to comply with the requirements of Schedule 3A, and so the purchaser(s) of the affected dwellings would be protected in cases of irregularity. Presumably in circumstances where tenants believed, for example, that consultation requirements were not being fulfilled they would have to seek judicial review *before* the giving of consent or face being left effectively without a remedy. The consultation provisions cover in effect only secure tenants in occupation. They could not apply where housing had already been *cleared* of tenants.

8. The termination of a landlord's interest in a qualifying dwelling does not *generally* affect PRTB unless there is:
  (a) a failure during the process of termination to register PRTB according to the requirements of para 6 of Schedule 9A to the 1985 Act;
  (b) termination by acquisition of the landlord's interest as a result of which acquisition an authority or body within section 80 of the 1985 Act becomes the landlord;
  (c) the occurrence of some event determining the landlord's estate or interest, or a re-entry on breach of condition or forfeiture;
  (d) in the case of a leasehold interest, notice given by the landlord, or a superior landlord, on the expiry or surrender of the term;
in which case the right to buy ceases to be preserved, though the terminations mentioned in (c) and (d) supra will entitle the person deprived of PRTB to compensation from the landlord where the events in question were caused by the landlord. See section 171E.

Section 171F provides that a qualifying person may not be dispossessed of a qualifying dwelling under section 98(1)(a) of the Rent Act 1977, on the understanding that suitable alternative accommodation is available, unless the court is satisfied that PRTB will continue to be available with regard to the dwelling offered as alternative accommodation, *or* that the landlord of the new dwelling will be an authority or body within section 80 of the 1985 Act, e.g. a local housing authority. Periods where a secure tenant enjoyed PRTB will count towards qualification to exercise the right to buy etc., under Schedule 4 para. 5A of the 1985 Act as inserted by the 1986 Act.

9. Under such a 'management agreement' the terms on which the new manager is to exercise the authority's functions, whether under statute or by virtue of being the freeholder of the affected land, are to be set out. Ministerial approval is required for both the terms of the agreement, and the identity of the manager, and may be given conditionally. Section 27A requires that authorities proposing to enter into such schemes must serve written notice of the proposal on affected tenants informing them of the details of the proposal, the identity of the proposed new manager, the likely consequences of the management agreement for tenants, and the effect of section 27A, which further allows tenants to make representations, which must be considered by the authority within a specified reasonable time. Further notices to tenants must specify any significant changes in proposals, and inform them of their right to object to the Secretary of State. Tenants must also be informed that the Secretary of State may not approve a proposal if he concludes that a majority of affected tenants do not wish the proposal to proceed, though he may refuse consent on other grounds also, having regard to any information available. The Secretary of State may not even entertain the application for approval unless the authority certifies that the consultation requirements have been complied with, and he may require it to carry out further consultation, though an agreement made with approval of the Secretary of State is not invalidated by a failure on his part, or by the authority, to comply with the requirements of section 27A. These consultation requirements supersede in the case of secure tenants those of section 105 of the 1985 Act (see main text pages 107–108) in relation to making management agreements: a similar consultation requirement applies to Redevelopment Schemes under Ground 10A and Part V of Schedule 2 to the 1985 Act, though in that case there is no ability for a majority of tenants to block a proposed redevelopment. (See main text page 104.)

It is thought that housing associations and trusts will be the most commonly appointed managers under these provisions introduced by the Housing and Planning Act 1986. Those few management transfers made under earlier powers to 'housing co-operatives' are, however, *in general* preserved, see section 27B of the 1985 Act as introduced in 1986.

10. Sections 91 to 108 of the Housing Act 1985, which relate to assignments and sublettings, repairs, improvements, variation of terms, provision of information, consultation, inter alia, do not apply to tenancies from co-operative housing associations, see section 109. Section 109A, added by the Housing and Planning Act 1986, will provide that where a body falling within section 80 of the 1985 Act, for example a local housing authority or registered housing association, becomes landlord of a dwelling subject to a statutory tenancy under the Rent Act 1977, the tenancy is to be treated as contractual and the provisions relating to secure tenancies and the rights of secure tenants applied to it.

11. The powers and obligations to make contributions to the Housing Revenue Account were reviewed in *Hemsted v Lees and Norwich City Council* (1986) 18 HLR 424. An authority *must* make a rate fund contribution to its housing revenue account at the end of the financial year to prevent a deficit, but they may make other contributions throughout the year. Furthermore, Schedule 14, Part IV, para. 1(1) of the Housing Act 1985 states that where benefits or amenities arise from the provision of houses by an authority, and these are shared by the community as a whole, for example the provision of public open space, the authority shall make a rate fund contribution to the Housing Revenue Account to reflect the community's share of the benefits. The general principle remains, however, that authorities are entitled to fix their rent on the basis of social policy, and need not charge market rents, nor make a profit on their housing operations.

12. Section 7 of the Housing and Planning Act 1986 will amend section 69 of the Rent Act 1977 by inserting subsection (1A) which will allow, inter alia, local authorities to apply to rent officers for certificates of fair rent in respect of dwellings of which they wish to dispose, either in their current state or after works of improvement, conversion or repair.

13. Section 14 of the Housing and Planning Act 1986 amends section 58 of the Housing Act 1985 by inserting subsections (2A) and (2B). These will provide that a person is not to be treated as having accommodation *unless* it is accommodation which it would be reasonable for him to continue to occupy, *and* regard *may* be had in determining the issue of such reasonableness to the general circumstances prevailing in relation to housing in the district of the authority applied to for aid. It would seem appropriate for other issues relating to the reasonableness of continued occupation to be considered, for example, the condition and location of the accommodation, as has been done under the similarly worded section 60 of the 1985 Act.

'Accommodation' must be such as it would be reasonable for the applicant to continue to occupy, *not* such that it would be reasonable for him to leave, and this equates to similar wording in relation to intentional homelessness (see main text page 171 et seq). The effect of the new provision will be that an applicant will be classified as homeless if the only accommodation he has is such that it would *not* be reasonable for him *to continue to occupy it*. The general housing circumstances, inter alia, in a district *may* have been considered in determining the issue. It may thus be considered reasonable for someone to continue to occupy inappropriate premises, and so 'have' accommodation in a district's area where others are living in even more adverse circumstances.

14. Section 14 of the Housing and Planning Act 1986 substitutes a new section 69(1) of the Housing Act 1985. This will provide that a local housing authority may perform any duty to a person found to be homeless, etc., to secure that accommodation becomes available for his occupation by making available *suitable* accommodation from their normal housing stock (or stock held under other legislation), or by securing that he obtains such suitable accommodation from some other person, or by giving him such advice and assistance as will secure that he obtains such suitable accommodation from another person. In determining whether accommodation is 'suitable' (*not* 'appropriate') regard must be had to the provisions of the 1985 Act dealing with slum clearance, over-crowding and multi-occupation. The exact effect of this new requirement awaits judicial clarification. Arguably authorities should not unthinkingly place homeless persons in the future in any accommodation that is overcrowded or in contravention of the multi-occupation provisions, or unfit for human habitation. An authority must make an honest effort to find accommodation for homeless persons that is not overcrowded etc. However, a requirement to 'have regard to' the provisions of the law is not a requirement to adhere to them slavishly, and, for example, an authority that did its honest best is an area of high housing stress and demand with little available public sector stock, would be justified in placing a homeless person in bed-and-breakfast multi-occupied accommodation on a *temporary* basis if that is all they could find at the time of the application. It could be, however, a failure to perform obligations under the Act to 'forget' such a person thereafter, leaving him in the accommodation first found, and to fail to make continuing efforts to find him something better, with the ultimate objective of providing decent permanent housing. Presumably authorities must still continue to consider other issues relevant to suitability, such as the health of applicants, in relation to accommodation found, and must not perform any obligation in a perverse or absurd fashion. Authorities should also remember that the general purpose of the law is to ensure that homeless families are kept, or brought, together, for accommodation secured for a person must be available for occupation by him and those who might reasonably be expected to reside with him.

In determining the question of who can reasonably be expected to reside with an applicant factors such as the nature of a person's family unit and its relationships and dependencies should *always* be considered. In a case of doubt as to whether co-residence is reasonable other factors, such as the practicability of providing accommodation, or the possibility of dividing a family unit, their readiness to separate, and their geographical locations, before and after the authority's decision, may be considered. In *R v Lambeth London Borough Council ex p Ly* (1986) Independent 15 October, the applicant was a Vietnamese woman of 74. Her son and his family lived together before fleeing Vietnam in 1978 when they separated. By 1984 the son and his children were together at a hotel but this had no room for the mother who made an application as a homeless person. The authority made her an offer of accommodation some two miles away from the hotel for herself and four of the older grandchildren. It was held that the offer was not unreasonable as the eleven members of the family had not arrived in this country together, and were separated at the time of their various arrivals. The family had been separated for some years and the older children were old enough to move away from their parents. It was reasonable to regard the eleven people as capable of forming separate sub-units who would then be accommodated as close as possible to each other.

15. Section 21 of the Housing and Planning Act 1986, which came into force on 7 November 1986, inserts section 259A into the 1985 Act. This provides that the general rule is that a resolution declaring an area to be a HAA, excluding land from a HAA, terminating a HAA, declaring an area to be a GIA, excluding land from a GIA or terminating a GIA, comes into force on the day the resolution is passed. However, a resolution declaring an area to be a GIA *may* be expressed to have effect from a future date, not later then four weeks after the passing of the resolution, at which point the whole, or part, of the area in question will cease to be, or form part of, a HAA.

Introduction

The purpose of this introduction is to familiarise the reader with the content of the book, to say what it is about and also what it does not cover. As this is a 'law' book it cannot deal in great detail with the history, economics and philosophy of housing as an aspect of social policy. Nevertheless as housing law cannot be studied in a traditional 'black letter' fashion but can only be understood in its wider social, political and economic context some initial mention must be made of the policy issues and debates that have done so much to form and, some would say, *deform* the law. These wider policy issues will be discussed in some detail subsequently in this Introduction. The *economics* of public sector housing will not be dealt with in great detail as the present author is neither an accountant nor an economist. The use of central government subsidies and loan sanction powers as means of *control* over local authorities will be discussed, and there is a later chapter on rent for public sector housing, but beyond that I have not thought it safe to go. Likewise there is a geographical limitation on the ambit of the book in that it relates to municipal housing functions in England and Wales. Scotland and Northern Ireland have their own housing systems and their own housing problems which are better dealt with by those having first-hand experience of local situations.

As the title states this is a book about the rôle public and voluntary bodies play in relation to housing. Accordingly this work will *not* deal with the private rented sector, nor, in general, with the law relating to the private owner-occupier, nor with the building societies.

Unlike the first edition the second will deal with housing associations, the 'third force' in the housing market filling the gap between the private and the local authority landlord. The housing association movement has developed greatly in the last twenty years, and especially since the changes introduced by the Housing Act 1974 and now consolidated in the Housing Associations Act 1985. It is increasingly central policy to favour associations as the providers and managers of rented homes and low cost housing for ownership rather than to view these tasks as,

1

unquestionably, the proper preserve of local authorities. However, many, if not most, housing associations, would say they are given insufficient resources to meet the burdens increasingly laid upon them. The concern of this book then is with the powers and duties of public and voluntary bodies with regard to housing. These will be considered generally under two main headings: first, the functions of authorities and associations as *providers* of homes and the relationships between them and the persons who look to them for accommodation, and second, the task that has been committed to local authorities to oversee housing repair and public health standards, not just in relation to their own properties but also with regard to owner-occupied and rented dwellings. This division is mirrored in the structure of the work which consists of two parts. The first deals with the housing provision powers of authorities and associations, their general rôle as landlords, and the responsibilities of authorities with regard to the homeless. The second part deals with local authority responsibilities to enforce housing and public health standards with regard to sub-standard properties, though I have been somewhat pragmatic and included in this part local authority and housing association repairing obligations arising out of their capacity as landlords.

Local authorities are presently one of the two great sources of accommodation in this country. At the end of the First World War about 90 per cent of the housing stock was privately rented, and nearly all the rest was owner-occupied, with very little local authority housing. The *Housing and Construction Statistics 1978–84* revealed in 1986 that Great Britain has 21,715,000 homes, of which 60.9 per cent overall are owner-occupied (the figures for England and Wales are, respectively, 62.9 per cent and 65.9 per cent). 27.9 per cent overall are rented from public authorities (England 25.6 per cent and Wales 24.0 per cent). 2.4 per cent overall are rented from housing associations (England 2.5 per cent, Wales 1.5 per cent). 8.7 per cent overall are 'other' tenures, principally the private rented sector (England 8.9 per cent, Wales 8.5 per cent). Shelter's 1983/84 survey of *English* local authority waiting lists showed that there were additionally some 1.2 million applicants for municipal housing.

The law as the child of policy

The law relating to the provision of public sector accommodation, and also to the other housing functions of local authorities, is the child of housing policy, and also housing politics. It is sadly a truism that housing is a political football in this country, though, speaking of analogies, the present author prefers the symbolism of a clock whose pendulum has come to describe an ever increasing arc with the passage of time and the widening divergence of views between the major political parties. In the years since the end of the Second World War the Conservative Party has come increasingly to stand for owner-occupation as the dominant housing tenure and the philosophy of the 'property owning democracy'. There are also a number of Conservatives who would like to see a revival in the fortunes of the private landlord. This preference for a mixture of private renting and for increasing owner occupation, if necessary by the widespread sale of public sector housing, tends to lessen the housing rôle of local authorities and even to reduce it to what is essentially a welfare service designed to meet the needs of those who cannot afford to be owner-occupiers. The traditional stance of the Labour Party has been to see public sector housing as having a wider social rôle to play. Traditional Labour policy, especially in the post-war years of the Atlee Government, has seen such housing as being for all who want it and not just for one particular social class, a policy embodied in the Housing Act 1949. The Labour Party has also tended to favour municipalisation of houses, especially at the expense of the private landlord.

The political issues surrounding housing have been made more complex by the fact that both major parties while in power have tended to veer between dogmatism and pragmatism on housing issues. Pragmatism has been particularly evident under Labour administrations, especially as they have tended to be dominated by the right wing of the Labour Party which has come to accept the Conservative view of owner-occupation as the normal and natural form of land tenure to the exclusion of all others. Indeed there are some commentators who would argue that a Labour administration in this country has yet to pursue a truly left-wing socialist housing policy: see Stephen Merrett, *State Housing in Britain* Chap. 11. However, leaving aside the rights and wrongs of left versus right housing policies, an even more serious allegation can be made against governments of all political colours, and that is the failure to devote sufficient resources, in both sectors, to providing the homes the nation needs. In 1979–80 *public* spending on housing was 2.2 per cent of Gross Domestic Product, compared with 3.3 per cent in 1960–67, 3.5 per cent in 1968–73 and 3.2 in 1974–81 (averaged figures). By 1985–86 public investment was down to 0.8 GDP. The *Inquiry into British Housing* showed how public expenditure on housing has *decreased* by 54.6 per cent between 1979/80 and 1984/85. Much of the current housing stock is ageing, with 30 per cent of the total built before 1919, and such old houses require considerable amounts of public and private investment if they are to continue to provide acceptable accommodation, and the cost of eradicating disrepair in both sectors could amount to between £30bn and £40bn, according to the Audit Commission. [See further Malpas, *The Housing Crisis* Chap. 1.]

The wider debate on housing

The debate on housing has not been confined to the political parties. Over the past few years we have lived through a remarkable period in which the basic philosophy of municipal housing law, policy and practice has come under increasing scrutiny and attack. The debates have been drawn from a wide spectrum of political opinion and from an equally wide range of academic and vocational disciplines. The debate has not just been confined to public sector housing and has ranged across housing policy generally, but it has been at its most fierce in relation to council housing.

The argument on tenure

There has been a fear that there could be a growth of class distinction based on the tenurial difference between owner-occupiers and council tenants. A number of commentators, see, for example, B.T. Robson in *Urban Social Areas* at p. 41, have pointed out that owner occupation and council tenancies have been exclusive tenure types into which people have moved and have stayed, with very little flow between the tenures. Concern over this feature of our society was further voiced in *The Inquiry into British Housing* which pointed out the need to avoid segregation of communities by virtue of housing type or location. It is clearly obvious to anyone with eyes to see that there is a very real measure of segregation in many parts of this country between the owner-occupied suburbs and the large council estates and especially where these contain large numbers of unpopular and 'hard to let' types of dwellings such as high rise or deck access blocks of flats (see generally Coleman, *Utopia on Trial*). However, the distinction is not just between suburban and council estate dwellers; there is a further distinction between richer and poorer owner-occupiers. Some commentators argue that many less well off people, particularly in inner urban areas, have been led into owner-occupation, either by its fashionability or because they have no other choice, given the diminishing pool of rented housing. In a time of recession and high unemployment, with mortgage interest rates being much higher than they have historically been, many such owner-occupiers are very precariously placed in the housing market, being unable to meet their mortgage commitments or face major repair bills should they fall out of work, or reach retirement with low pensions and few savings.

Mortgage arrears are rising, with both local authorities and the building societies pointing to low incomes, unemployment, short time working, relationship breakdown and financial over-commitment as being major causes of arrears. In 1981 5 per cent of families made homeless were in mortgage arrears, in 1986 the figure was 10 per cent. Local authorities in the metropolitan areas were owed £14.5m in mortgage arrears in 1985, a 36 per cent increase from 1983. Building society arrears and repossessions have also increased, in 1979 societies repossessed 2,530 houses. This rose year by year, from 3,020, 4,240, 5,950, 7,400, 10,950 to 16,770 in 1985. Actions for possession increased from 35,471 in 1981 to 54,754 in 1984. By 1985 there were 60,390 building society mortgages with more than six months' arrears. In relation to the total size of the housing market these figures are not actually large, but the upward trend is a cause for concern for both local authorities and building societies. There are, clearly, numbers of people for whom the financial burdens of owner occupation are too great. (See further: *Behind with The Mortgage*, National Consumer Council; Building Societies Association Bulletin No. 43, July 1985; Malpas, *The Housing Crisis* Chap. 5; 'Financial Times' Monday 28 April 1986, 'Sunday Times' Sunday 27 July 1986, and 'The Times' Monday 29 September 1986).

At the lowest level of the housing market there are those who experience great difficulty in finding, or paying for, accommodation of any sort. The *Inquiry into British Housing* revealed a Department of the Environment estimate of a third of a million 'hidden' households, that is persons with no homes of their own living with others, about half of whom would like independent accommodation. Additionally there are the homeless, with over 83,000 families being accepted as homeless in 1985. The young single and young families find accommodation hard to find and hard to pay for; in parts of London rents of £70–£100 a week for single bedsitters are charged. Even when accommodation is available many people need assistance with meeting housing costs. In 1983–84 housing benefits cost £2.6bn and two-thirds of council tenants needed assistance with housing costs.

The picture is of a housing system not just divided by tenure but by poverty and location. The 'haves', i.e. better off owner-occupiers enjoy the best housing, and public sector tenants in secure employment and in favoured locations are not far behind them in terms of housing advantages. The disadvantaged (the 'have nots') are the homeless, less well-off owner-occupiers in financial difficulties because of, e.g. age or unemployment, the young who cannot find housing they can afford, and tenants of council housing in unpopular areas or of unpopular types. There is frequently geographical segregation between the 'haves' and the 'have nots'. It is against this background that the changes in housing law over the past fifteen years or so must be examined and assessed. The first point to note is that by the end of the 1970s it was generally accepted that some fundamental re-examination of the legal and tenurial position of public housing was essential, but why?

First, local authorities are collectively the greatest landlords in the country. The two largest groups of housed people in this country are those living in owner-occupied property and those living in council owned property – yet the rights and liabilities of these two groups are very different. In 1962 Professor Lafitte said, 'within ten years we shall urgently need new forms of housing tenure combining the advantages, but not the drawbacks, of the owner-occupation and the council tenantry between which we are becoming increasingly divided', see 'Social Policy in a Free Society', reprinted in *Social Welfare in Modern Britain* (Ed. by Butterworth and Holman) (Fontana, 1975) p. 55. Housing associations and the Housing Corporation may go some way to providing those new forms of tenure, but we must not expect too much of them, see *Municipal and Public Services Journal*, 4 July 1975, pp. 875–876. I have already referred to the importance of the form of tenure in formalising and sustaining social divisions, and so if we wish to move towards a society free from divisions, and if we cannot look to housing associations to provide a real 'bridge' between owner-occupiers and council tenants, then it would seem essential to examine modifications of the law relating to council housing so as to give its occupiers a greater say in the determination of decisions relating to their homes, without necessarily handing over to them the fee simple.

Second, vis-à-vis his local authority a tenant or potential tenant is in a very weak position legally. In general terms no one has the *right* to be housed just as he wishes. The insertion of one's name on the housing list is likewise no guarantee of housing. When council housing is being allocated, or a tenant requests a transfer to another council house the broad general discretionary powers of the local authority come into play. It is, of course, well known that local authorities use a variety of schemes to help them in the exercise of this discretion, and these will be examined in greater detail in due course. But it should be a matter for public concern that there are often odd policy biases in these schemes which seem to be subject to no legal control or central governmental direction. There can be little doubt that some local authorities have graded tenants and potential tenants, and placed them in houses according to their social desirability. [The allegations come from too many sources to be ignored – see B.T. Robson, *Urban Social Areas* pp. 48–49 (quoting D.A. Kirkby (1971) 42 Town Planning Review

250–268 and J. Tucker, *Honourable Estates* (1966); Colin Ward, *Tenants Take Over* pp. 16–18; and Norman Lewis, 'Council Housing Allocation: Problems of Discretion and Control' in (1976) Public Administration, vol. 54, p. 147.] And of course there is a considerable body of evidence as to the discriminatory attitudes adopted in the past by some housing authorities towards black people. Not only is this undesirable, leading as it can to a concentration of socially inadequate families and individuals in particular areas, it is a method of proceeding which bears no resemblance to allocation according to need. [See: Ernest Krausz, *Ethnic Minorities in Britain* (Paladin, 1971) Chap. 4; W.W. Daniel, *Racial Discrimination in England* (Penguin, 1968) Chap. 11; Deakin, *Colour Citizenship and British Society* (Panther, 1970) Chap. 6; Lester and Bindman, *Race and Law* (Penguin, 1972); David J. Smith, *Racial Disadvantage in Britain* (Penguin, 1977) Part III; and Smith and Whalley, *Racial Minorities and Public Housing* (P.E.P., 1975).] To be fair, it must be stressed that many, if not indeed most, local authorities *now* adopt liberal and progressive administrative policies with regard to their tenants. Nevertheless, attention must be drawn to the often paternalistic and, sadly, sometimes negligent ways in which housing powers have been used.

A heritage of poor law thinking that produces a paternalistic use of legal powers, coupled with the British habit of thinking and governing *for* the people, rather than *through* them, further coupled with a degree of public parsimony that has ensured there never has been production of the right *quantity* of housing of the right *quality*, and allied, particularly since the end of the Second World War, with a blind adherence to each new architectural fad for providing 'units of accommodation', has resulted in the public sector tenant being seen as a second class citizen, with no right to be consulted about the sort of dwelling he/she would like to live in, and the burdening of the land with unlovely, unloved and unwanted estates and blocks of system built housing. There are over 4,000 tower blocks of flats in this country, many of them amongst the most unpopular housing ever built. [See further Gauldie, *Cruel Habitations*; Berry, *Housing: The Great British Failure*, Coleman, *Utopia on Trial*; and Esher, *A Broken Wave*.]

Turning to maintenance the evidence mounted throughout the period under discussion that a great deal of council housing – much of it new or recent – was declining into poor condition as a result of the failure of local authorities to maintain it. In some cases the decline has been so serious as to render the premises 'prejudicial to health or a nuisance' contrary to section 92(1)(a) of the Public Health Act 1936. One must sympathise with the economic plight of local authorities, and realise the effect of government restrictions on maintenance programmes, but the sad fact remains that all over the country council owned property has declined in condition at an alarming rate, and until the use of section 99 of the Public Health Act 1936, there seemed little hope of legal redress for tenants. Even when it was established that a *criminal* sanction under the public health legislation is available to individuals against a defaulting local housing authority, the courts, as we shall see, have been wary of granting contractual remedies to tenants. It is easy to say that tenants should resort to self help, but the problem is often too large for the resources of individuals, and why, it can reasonably be asked, should they bother to do anything about the problems when they have no real degree of control over their own environment, and the local authority frequently seems remote, unwilling to listen, or even intransigent?

To sum up so far, for a variety of reasons the law relating to public sector housing has become subject to numerous criticisms. First of all its tenurial basis may confirm the mythical divisions between the supposedly 'subsidised' council tenant and the 'poor mortgaged' ratepayer. In truth mortgage interest relief to owner-occupiers totalled £3.5bn in 1984/85, an increase of 219.8 per cent on the figure of £1.1bn for 1978/79, and this should be set alongside the £2.3bn spent on housing benefits in 1983/84, the £636m in exchequer housing subsidies to local authorities for 1983/84 and the £656m general rate fund subsidies for council housing in 1983/84, see the *Inquiry into British Housing* Chap. 4. Second, the law subjects potential and actual council tenants to the discretionary selection and allocation powers of the local authority which are subject to little legal control. Third, the law subjects the council tenant to the great managerial powers of his local authority with, in the past, few opportunities for the redress of grievances. Fourth, despite the official central government lip service given to the notion of public participation, council tenants have been given very little say in the control and management of their homes and their immediate environment. Fifth, local housing authorities have been subject to very little central control in relation to these great discretionary powers of selection, allocation and management. *Housing Policy*, Cmnd. 6851, the consultative paper on future developments in housing, accepted that there would have to be changes in both law and practice, and the then government accepted the need for a 'tenants' charter'.

The Housing Act 1980

It was against this background of increasing debate and dissatisfaction that the Housing Act 1980 emerged. However, it is the present writer's belief that the 1980 Act only dealt with some of the problems. The provisions of the 'tenants' charter', conferred a number of new and important rights on individual public tenants, but did not go nearly as far as many critics would have wished in relation to tenant involvement and participation in housing management. With regard to selection and allocation procedures the new law made no radical changes. The truly wide reaching alterations were the 'right to buy' provisions. The Conservative Government committed themselves to a major new departure in both legal and policy terms by introducing a form of 'compulsory purchase in reverse'. This forced sale of public sector assets is a most controversial issue and, whether one agrees with it or not, it has to be seen as a piece of dogmatic and overtly politically motivated legislation. It is most odd that the years of debate about the tenurial basis of municipal housing should have produced a sadly simplistic governmental response which could not lead to the development of the longed-for new land tenures, but rather serves only to strengthen the ranks of the dominant land-holding group within society, i.e. the owner-occupiers. The 1980 Housing Act enshrined the current housing orthodoxy that owner-occupation is self-evidently good and desirable for as many as can afford it, coupled with the government's determination to effect a massive transfer of wealth from the public to the private sector. It seems somewhat sad that the opportunity was missed for attempting at least a degree of tenurial experimentation.

The danger remains that only the most pleasant and socially desirable council houses will be purchased under the terms of the law, leaving authorities and associations with less attractive properties with which to meet the needs of those who cannot, or do not wish to, become owner-occupiers. This can only lead to an increase in that undesirable social polarisation according to tenure and poverty referred to earlier. It is, moreover, in less desirable council houses, the older properties, those situated on socially stigmatised estates, and in the tower blocks where the largest number of repair problems and design and construction defects are likely to occur.

It is hard to escape the conclusion that the provisions of the Housing Act 1980 were, with some exceptions, *exactly the wrong response* to the mounting criticisms of housing law and practice heard over the preceeding years. However, the policies enshrined in the 1980 Act were continued and developed in the Housing and Building Control Act 1984, both now consolidated in the Housing Act 1985, and in the Housing and Planning Act 1986. The law continues to favour the continued prescription of doses of owner-occupation as the treatment for the nation's housing ills.

The erosion of local housing autonomy

The last fifteen years have seen the definite, if gradual, erosion of local autonomy in housing matters and its replacement by an ever increasing degree of control. This process was implicit in the Act of 1980 despite its cosmetic removal of certain minor controls. It is arguable that the forced sale of council houses is the greatest imposition of central policy on local discretion to date.

The Housing Finance Act 1972, which was an attempt to introduce new 'fair' rents for council houses everywhere, was undoubtedly a major inroad into local discretion. Though this legislation was largely repealed by the Housing Rents and Subsidies Act 1975, those provisions relating to rent rebates were left in force, and so there remained a mandatory requirement for all local authorities to operate a rent rebate scheme for their tenants. [See Chapter 4 below.] Some people also viewed the Housing (Homeless Persons) Act 1977 as a further erosion of local autonomy in that it placed a statutory duty on local authorities to provide accommodation for certain groups of homeless persons. Another 'legal' reduction in local discretion was introduced by section 105 of the Housing Act 1974 which provided that local authorities should not incur expenditure in connection with the provision of dwellings by conversion or the carrying out of improvements and associated repairs without the approval of the Secretary of State. The object of this provision was to introduce a strategic system of control whereby the Secretary of State could direct local investment *away* from the improvement of existing council houses and *towards* the conversion and improvement of acquired properties. [See now section 431 of the 1985 Act.]

These reductions in the amount of discretion enjoyed by local authorities are, however, of comparatively little importance when contrasted with central requirements as to municipal house building standards and control over housing finance.

Capital for local authority house building

Local authorities require loan sanction from the Secretary of State before raising money for housing purposes. The detailed rules on borrowing generally are now found in Schedule 13 to the Local Government Act 1972. Section 428 of the Housing Act 1985 (which must be read subject to the terms of the above Schedule) is also relevant in this context. Section 428 grants a general power to local authorities to borrow in so far as that relates to the execution of repairs and works by them, and also with regard to clearance and re-development. Local authorities also have power to borrow for the purposes of providing housing accommodation, housing grants and mortgages.

Approval for loan finance may be withheld or given subject to restrictions whenever central government feels it necessary to reduce or contain public spending. Indeed, control over local authority borrowing has become an important part of the government's general economic managerial rôle.

The vast majority of money used in the construction of council housing is in fact borrowed, and loan finance rather than money raised from taxation is an enduring feature of our municipal housing system.

For our present purposes, however, the important point to make is that new council house construction is dependent on finance being raised, for which central loan sanction will be required, and, as has been said above, central control over local borrowing has become an important feature of the economic policy of successive governments.

The system of capital expenditure control

Part VIII of the Local Government, Planning and Land Act 1980 introduces legal limits on the capital *expenditure* powers of local authorities. For the present not just the power of local authorities to borrow is controlled – the power to spend what has been borrowed is controlled. Housing authorities fall within the scope of this new legislation under section 71 and Schedule 12. The 'meat' of the system of control is contained in S.I. 1983/296, S.I. 1984/223, S.I. 1984/257, and DoE Circulars 23/82, 9/83, 6/84 and 9/85.

The basic scheme under the legislation is that 'prescribed expenditure', including acquisition of land, construction of dwellings, their maintenance and repair and making grants and advances of capital, is controlled, with borrowing approval ('loan sanction') also required whenever such capital expenditure is to be paid for out of borrowed money. This statutory system is supplemented by appeals from the Secretary of State that authorities should further voluntarily restrict capital expenditure, see Circular 9/85 para. 3. In each financial year authorities are given an allocation made up of 'blocks' of permitted expenditure for each of their various services, of which housing is one. These 'blocks' may be aggregated together so that the technical allocation for housing does not have to be spent on housing. The amount of the allocation may be increased by an authority by adding: up to 10 per cent of the aggregated allocation for the year, for example derived from allocation unused in the previous year (this is known as 'tolerance'); additional allocations within the year, or transferred from other authorities; specified proportions of the authority's 'net capital receipts' under sections 72 and 75 of the Local Government, Planning and Land Act 1980; an amount equal to the profits from the authority's trading undertakings, if any. 'Net capital receipts' in the housing context are now specified as *proportions* of the net receipts of capital received by authorities, and *generally* authorities may use only 20 per cent of the money received on the sale of council houses and 30 per cent of their other housing receipts in order to supplement capital expenditure allocations, see Circular 9/85 para. 11. Because of these restrictions on using capital receipts to supplement expenditure, money received as such receipts is building up unused, and the *Inquiry into British Housing* computed the sum 'in the bank' as some £6 billion, growing at a rate of between £1 and 1.5 billion p.a.

Where an authority's permitted expenditure is to be financed by borrowing, and most of it is in relation to housing, Annex A of Circular 9/85 gives block borrowing approval under para 1(b) of Schedule 13 to the Local Government Act 1972 for an amount equal to the capital expenditure allocation. The approval extends to borrowing for non-housing purposes, and for housing purposes, save that it does *not* apply, unless the Secretary of State gives particular approval, to the acquisition of land under the Housing Acts for new building, or for *certain types* of 'municipalisation' of housing. It is convenient to note at this point that 'municipalisation' is the acquisition of existing housing by an authority for continuing use. Certain minor municipalisations are allowed to fall within the general approval of borrowing for housing purposes, and these are listed in Annex B of Circular 9/85 and cover matters *such as* acquisitions where the authority is under a specific statutory obligation to buy a dwelling, or acquisitions by agreement from defaulting mortgagors of dwellings mortgaged to authorities. With regard to the acquisition of land for new house-building Circular 23/82 argues that the cost of acquiring land for new building and the admissibility of such projects for subsidy justifies continuing the pre-1980 system of approving borrowing on project by project basis (see below).

Consequently in what Bucknall in *Housing Finance* terms 'the housing capital expenditure cycle' there may be up to three stages. In the first place an authority will submit a Housing Investment Programme (HIP) as its 'bid' for expenditure allocation under the Local Government, Planning and Land Act 1980. HIPs were introduced in 1978–79 and represent assessments by authorities of their housing need and their proposals for meeting such needs. The 'core' of a HIP is the request for capital expenditure allocation and this is based on the figures of the previous year's programme, estimates of current spending and proposals for the next two years. The HIP will identify projects in new house-building (especially identifying programmes for those with special housing needs) slum clearance, renovation of existing council stock, municipalisation programmes, insulation and renovation grants, mortgage finance and finance for housing associations. As the second stage the bid, along with others from the rest of the housing authorities, will be moderated nationally in consultations between the Department of the Environment and the representative local authority associations. Thereafter actual allocations of permitted expenditure will be made for each authority and these will form part of the blocks of permitted capital expenditure, which will carry block borrowing approval equal to the capital allocation.

Certain housing projects are generally treated as being within the block borrowing approval without more ado, for example, unless the Secretary of State notifies authorities to the contrary in particular instances, the construction of new buildings and hostels, and the renovation of local authority dwellings, see Circular 23/82 paras. 6 and 24, and municipalisation falling within Annex B of Circular 9/85. However, acquisition of land for new house-building and general municipalisation of housing are subject to a third stage of control, individual project control and approval by the Secretary of State, and only after a project has been individually considered will the Department of the Environment inform the relevant authority whether or not the block borrowing approval may apply. Where approval is withheld the Department will inform the authority of the reasons. [See further Bucknall *Housing Finance* Chap. 3, to which the present author acknowledges his indebtedness.]

The controls over capital expenditure on housing, and the associated controls over capital borrowing, have been subject to criticism. The *Inquiry into British Housing* pointed to the continual restriction in capital allocations for housing (in 1983 it was announced that HIP allocations for 1985–86 and 1986–87 would be, respectively, 80 per cent and 70 per cent of the 1984–85 allocations), and the fact that a system of capital finance based on year to year calculations is incompatible with long term planning for housing expenditure which must relate to developments that inevitably take a number of years to come to fruition. The year by year system inhibits the making of rational long term investment decisions. The increasing degree of control over housing capital investment has led to a major decline in public sector house-building. In 1967 213,000 public sector dwellings were constructed, the figure fell to 37,200 in 1981, rose to 53,000 in 1982 but declined again to 33,600 in 1985. As a proportion of Gross Domestic Product public expenditure accounts for only 0.8 per cent. The private sector has not been able to compensate for the public sector's decline, see 'Why we need a building boom' (Smallwood) 'Sunday Times', 10 August 1986. However, the present system of capital controls represent, for central government, one of two very effective ways of exercising the 'power of the purse' over local government, the other means of control to which we must now turn are housing subsidies.

The control of recurrent housing expenditure: the role of housing subsidies

Housing subsidies were introduced by the Housing, Town Planning &c. Act 1919 and have remained an essential feature of public housing provision ever since, though the form and nature of those subsidies has varied greatly with the years. Subsidies were just as important to the continuing health of the municipal housing stock as loan capital was to its creation. This can be readily understood when the classic composition of local authority housing expenditure is examined. A local authority's housing operations, as brought to account in the 'Housing Revenue Account', have had as their income rents and subsidies, and as their expenditure interest on loans, and the costs of repair, maintenance and management. As we have seen above the money for actually *building* houses is capital expenditure and so forms no part of the housing revenue account. However, the *interest* payable on such borrowed capital forms a large part of a local authority's recurrent expenditure and so of the historic need for subsidisation.

Before 1967 subsidies were given as fixed annual payments over a number of years for each completed house, irrespective of its cost. The amounts payable were simply varied by legislation, though the Housing Act 1961 did introduce some allowance for variations between local authorities with extra subsidies for those who faced especially high housing costs. The Housing Subsidies Act 1967 introduced a new system of subsidies to cover not only the special costs associated with building on expensive sites or in areas of subsidence, but also to provide local authorities with a 'cushion' against high interest rates by having the subsidies related to the interest rates actually payable.

The new subsidy system proved extremely complex to operate, sometimes wasteful in its operation and inequitable in its distribution. The 1970 Conservative Government introduced another subsidy system in the Housing Finance Act 1972. Local authorities were placed under an obligation to pay rent rebates to their more needy tenants, and were expected, in the first instance, to find that money from their own resources. Subsidies were payable to cover rent allowances payable to *private* sector tenants, slum clearance programmes, and in respect of rising costs to those local authorities whose expenditure was outstripping their income. These new subsidies were coupled with the introduction of 'fair' rents for council houses – and these were generally rather higher than the old 'reasonable' rents. The measure was one of the most politically controversial introduced by what was a generally controversial government. Another new subsidy system, designed to undo what the 1972 Act had done, was introduced by the Housing Rents and Subsidies Act 1975. This Act was designed also to be an interim measure. It restored the power of local authorities to charge 'reasonable' rents, and on the subsidy side made the following major subsidies payable:

1) An annual lump sum representing a consolidation of the *actual* subsidies paid for 1974–75 under the 1972 Act;

2) a sum to meet 66 per cent of loan charges on new expenditure on house building, the acquisition of houses or land, or improvements;

3) a sum to cover 33 per cent of the extra costs incurred since 1974 on refinancing earlier borrowing; and

4) a sum to meet 75 per cent of the cost of rent rebates.

The new subsidy system

The Housing Act 1980, Part VI introduced yet another new housing subsidy system which replaces the interim system of the 1975 Act. The system is based on deficit financing. Local authorities are expected to balance their books with regard to housing expenditure and any short-fall will have to be borne by income from increased rents and rates. The 1980 Act [now Part XIII of the Housing Act 1985] also gave the Secretary of State much greater discretion than he had before to determine subsidy levels. The heart of the system is the equation contained in section 422 of the 1985 Act whereby the amount of subsidy payable depends upon the sum of the 'base amount' (BA) (i.e. the previous year's subsidy, if any) *plus* the 'Housing Costs Differential' (HCD) (which is a sum to be determined annually by the Secretary of State) minus the 'Local Contribution Differential' (LCD) (another sum largely to be determined by the Secretary of State).

The definition of HCD is found in section 424 of the 1985 Act and is the amount by which an authority's 'reckonable' expenditure for the year in question exceeds their 'reckonable' expenditure for the previous year, and, according to Bucknall's *Housing Finance* 'reckonable' expenditure are loan charges on 100 per cent of admissible *capital* housing costs up to 31 March 1981 and the notional loan charges on 75 per cent of those costs entered into since 31/3/1981. The definition of LCD is found in section 425 and is the amount by which their reckonable income for the year in question exceeds that for the preceding year, and 'reckonable income' is a *deemed* figure determined by the Secretary of State, but *including* any rate fund contributions made by an authority, and subsidies payable in respect of housing benefits. [Readers seeking further detail are referred to Bucknall *op cit* Chap. 5, and the *Housing Subsidies and Accounting Manual 1981* HMSO.]

The formula BA + HCD – LCD has been used to reduce general exchequer subsidies since its introduction in 1980/81, such subsidies declining from £2,029 million in 1980/81 to £656 million in 1983/84 (not allowing for inflation). Few authorities now receive general subsidy, so that by 1985 only 50 out of the 319 English and Welsh authorities still received subsidies, and most of that subsidy was devoted to London boroughs. The consequences of this are:

1) The general rate fund has, in some cases, borne a slightly greater burden of assistance towards housing costs, the amount so devoted rising from £523m in 1980/81 to £636m in 1983/84;

2) unrebated rents for local authority dwellings have generally risen considerably, with it being central policy that local authority rents should at least rise annually in line with inflation;

3) Because, however, of the local discretion either to subvent rents by making a contribution from the general rate fund to the housing rent account, or to budget for a surplus on the latter account so making a transfer *to* the general rate fund possible, rent levels vary considerably between authorities of different political colours. Weekly rents may vary, within a few miles, from £20 p.w. down to £14.30 p.w. in the North West to £24.66 p.w. down to £16.30 p.w. in the South East;

4) Subsidies given in respect of 'bricks and mortar' have, however, been replaced by subsidies to individuals in the form of housing benefits, with some 65 per cent of council tenants receiving such benefits in 1985;

5) It is still arguable, however, that average weekly council rents are too low to generate a sufficient surplus of income over other expenditure to provide for repairs and renovations; this reflects a national reluctance to devote both public and private resources to housing.

The following figures illustrate the above points.

Gross weekly unrebated rents (average) for council dwellings

1978/79	1982/83	1984/85	1985/86
£5.9	£13.58	£14.83	£15.66
			[provisional]

[See Table 3.9.15, Cmnd. 9702-11].

Selected items of income for Housing Revenue Accounts 1980/81 and 1985/86

	1980/81 (Actual)	1985/86 (Estimate)
Net Rents	£1709m (36.6%)	£1823m (31.2%)
Housing Benefits	£519m (11.1%)	£2011m (34.4%)
Housing Subsidy	£1459m (31.2%)	£315m (5.6%)
[CIPFA Housing Revenue Account Statistics]		

What is chiefly notable is the 287.5 per cent *increase* in housing benefits and the 77.4 per cent *decrease* in general exchequer subsidies over the years surveyed.

Whither local housing autonomy?

By now it should be clear that the current housing and local government legislation marks a further, and most important, stage in a process whereby the effective control over both capital and recurrent expenditure on housing has passed from local to central government. In 1973 Richard Buxton in *Local Government* drew attention to the increasing control exercised by Whitehall over the town hall. He wrote at pp. 71–72: '. . . a wide range of capital projects, the essential vehicles of policy change, can be, and are, controlled by Whitehall by means of the power to prevent the borrowing of money. . . . The need for ministry consent effectively deprives . . . councillors of much of their influence. . . . In recent years it has not been unknown for house or school-building programmes to be altered at very short notice, and for local authorities to be required to provide Whitehall with answers on priority and policy questions with a rapidity which has made it difficult for the issues even to be submitted to committees and councils, let alone to be properly considered by them. . . . The erratic nature of the relations between central and local government is in a large part explicable by the use which has been made of the loan sanction system as a means of controlling spending in the economy as a whole'.

In the years that have passed since these words were written some attempts, such as the introduction of HIPs, have been made to restore some freedom of action to local authorities, but in the main they have been cosmetic. The control of finance and capital has passed increasingly from local to central bodies, something that is more than confirmed by the latest legislation. The result is not happy. We have a municipal housing system which is much more amenable to the dictates of central government than to the desires of local communities and individuals. The common criticisms made of council housing stand: with regard to the individual the local housing authority is in a powerful, perhaps over powerful, position. However, as between local and central government the latter has far too much power.

It would be easy here to go on and decry all levels of government and to state that what will be found in the following chapters will be a handbook for those who are the defenders of tenants' rights. It is hoped that the book will be useful for such people but it is not intended *just* for them. Champions of underdogs frequently attack middle dogs rather than directing their attention to the real villians of the dog fight. There *is* a great deal to criticise in local authority housing practice and in the way in which housing law is administered. But it must not be forgotten that much of that law and practice is determined by central government, and that the mind of central government changes in confusing and contradictory ways. Local authorities are caught between the legitimate wants and needs of communities and the dictates and directives of an over-powerful central administration. Over the last few years local authorities have been made subject to increased statutory duties while not being given resources commensurate to these new responsibilities.

Finance for housing association developments

Like local authority housing the stock of housing associations is constructed using borrowed capital, such capital coming to associations in the form of loans principally from the Housing Corporation and local authorities (effectively district councils and London boroughs). To meet the cost of these loans the Department of the Environment makes a capital grant (Housing Association Grant – HAG) in respect of individual projects, and this grant is paid to the body making the loan. This grant is paid under section 41 of the Housing Associations Act 1985 (HAA 1985) in respect of *registered* housing association expenditure under an approved development programme (ADP). Projects qualify for grant where they are to provide: dwellings for letting (including shared ownership leases); hostels; improvements or repairs to dwellings or hostels; ancillary land or buildings; dwellings subject to improvement for sale, see sections 42 to 45 of the HAA 1985. The following costs, inter alia, are generally within the statutory provisions: acquisition of land and buildings, subject to certification by the district valuer; site development costs; works of new building or rehabilitation or of major repair or other remedial measures; professional costs, e.g. legal fees; administrative costs in respect of developments, and interest on bridging finance borrowed to meet the capital cost of a project before HAG is paid and rental income begins to flow in. [See further Bucknall,

Housing Finance Chap. 11.] Grants may be made subject to conditions (see section 50 of the HAA 1985) and registration of fair rents is normally such a condition.

HAG is intended to cover that part of the cost of a dwelling which rental income will not meet – in other words the loan on approved expenditure is reduced to such a level that the relevant association can service the mortgage securing the loan from its fair rent income etc., after having made allowance for costs of maintenance, management, income lost on empty dwellings (voids) and bad debts (arrears) etc. In the year 1984/85 HAG generally approached between 80 and 90 per cent of the total costs of providing a qualifying dwelling.

Grant is only paid in respect of *approved* development and under the ADP system registered associations seeking grants must develop according to a programme prepared by the Housing Corporation or a local authority and approved by the Secretary of State. Grant approval is automatic provided this condition is met. Once the Housing Corporation, or local authority, as the case may be, has agreed an ADP with the Department of the Environment, projects approved by the Corporation etc. within the ADP will require no further scrutiny by central government before HAG is payable, though the grant will not be *paid* until the relevant building is completed.

HAG is actually calculated by taking, first, the rental income on a fair rent basis that can arise from the development. This is then discounted by deducting management and maintenance allowances which are fixed annually and which are designed to cover *routine* maintenance and repairs and an association's costs of housing management and administration. Further discounting follows in respect of voids and bad debts. The balance that is left is the sum available to service the mortgage on the borrowed capital, and the maximum mortgage capable of being met by this sum is calculated. HAG will make up the difference between the mortgage charged on the development and its actual allowable cost, see section 47 of the HAA 1985.

Overall control over the development programmes of the Housing Corporation, and so effectively over the projects of associations, is secured by the Corporation's annual cash limit for lending as fixed by the government. Within the limits imposed by government the Housing Corporation has to decide its priorities for lending. The current policy, as agreed with ministers, is to concentrate resources within inner city areas. Special attention also has to be given to the sorts of project the Corporation is prepared to fund, e.g. sheltered housing for the elderly, and the types of associations to be favoured, e.g. large national associations or smaller more locally based ones.

The Secretary of State has discretion under section 54 of the HAA 1985 to pay a 'revenue deficit grant' to a registered association which

incurs a deficit on its revenue account (which will be provided for under
the association's rules) for any period. Such a deficit occurs where
relevant expenditure, i.e. that expenditure attributable to housing
activities which the Secretary of State considers reasonable and appropriate, exceeds relevant income, i.e. such income which the Secretary of
State concludes the association could reasonably receive in respect of its
housing activities, including sums by way of grant or subsidy. Such
grants are thus capable of being made where an association, though
behaving perfectly probately, does not have sufficient income to pay
for proper management and maintenance of its housing, for example
where increases in rental income have had to be 'phased' under the fair
rent provisions of the Rent Act 1977, and the rate of increase has been
insufficient to bring in sufficient funds to meet outgoings. It is central
policy to reduce the payment of such grants. Similar grant aid is payable
in relation to shortfalls of income in respect of hostels managed by
associations, see section 55 of the HAA 1985.

Under section 56 applications for deficit grants must be made within
fifteen months of the period in which the deficit fell, and must contain
such information as the Secretary of State specified, including, in the
case of a Revenue Deficit Grant, the audited accounts of the association
for the relevant period. [*See Addendum 1*].

Under section 53 of the HAA 1985 registered associations that have
at any time received HAG must show separately in their accounts any
surpluses arising from increased rental income from housing projects in
connection with which HAG was made. The surpluses are to be shown
as The Grant Redemption Fund, and this is to be included in accounts in
accordance with the Secretary of State's directions. The method of
calculating surpluses is to be determined by the Secretary of State after
consultation with organisations - representing housing associations.
Money in the Grant Redemption Fund must be retained and the
Secretary of State may give notice to an association requiring it to pay
to him, with interest if demanded, sums outstanding in the fund, or to
apply or appropriate them for other purposes specified by him, for
example money in such a fund could be directed to meet a shortfall on
income otherwise qualifying for a deficit grant.

It is an obvious truism to state that this country's housing problem
will not be solved until society devotes the necessary social, political and
economic resources to the problem, and that it is impossible to solve the
issue merely by putting laws on the statute book. Nevertheless the
lawyer can play some real part in trying to bring about better housing
conditions. In the first place he can expose the political policy biases
implicit in much of our housing law and practice, and he can show how
extremes of policy, be they from the right or the left, work confusion.
Second, he can work for a system of laws that will produce a just and

equitable division of housing resources within society, though it must be admitted that the debate on what is 'just and equitable' will probably, and quite rightly, never be ended. That is no bad thing for the law must adapt itself to the ever-changing needs of society. Finally he can discharge the traditional lawyer's rôle of seeking justice for individuals in individual situations. It is the author's hope that the present work can make some contribution with regard to the tasks outlined above.

Further reading

Arden, A., and Partington, P., *Housing Law* (Sweet & Maxwell, 1983, 1st Supplement 1985).
Arden, A. (Ed), *Encyclopedia of Housing Law and Practice* (4 Vols.) (Sweet & Maxwell).
Pollard, D. (Ed), *Encyclopedia of Social Welfare Law* (2 vols) (Oyez Longman).

Journals

Regular reference should be made to *Housing* and *Inside Housing* (both published by the Institute of Housing). *The Housing Revue, Voluntary Housing* (Published by the National Federation of Housing Associations), and *Roof* (published by Shelter) in addition to the usual 'legal' journals such as *Legal Action, The Conveyancer* and *The Journal of Social Welfare Law*, and the *Housing and Planning Revue* published bi-monthly by the National Housing and Town Planning Council.

On finance and policy

Balchin, P.N., *Housing Policy and Housing Needs* (Macmillan, 1981).
Ball, M., *Housing Policy and Economic Power* (Methuen, 1983).
Berry, F., *Housing: The Great British Failure* (Charles Knight, 1974).
Bucknall, B., *Housing Finance* (CIPFA, 1985).
Burnett, J., *A Social History of Housing 1815–1985* (2nd edn, University Paperbacks, 1986).
Coleman, A., *Utopia on Trial* (Hilary Shipman, 1985).
Dunleavy, P., *The Politics of Mass Housing in Britain 1945–1975* (Oxford U.P., 1981).
English, J., (Ed) *The Future of Council Housing* (Croom Helm, 1982).
Esher, L., *A Broken Wave* (Allen Lane, 1981).
Malpass, P. (Ed), *The Housing Crisis* (Croom Helm, 1986).
Malpass, P., and Murie, A., *Housing Policy and Practice* (Macmillan, 1982).

Merrett, S., *State Housing in Britain* (Routledge and Kegan Paul, 1979).

Short, J.R., *Housing in Britain* (Methuen, 1982).

Cowan, R., 'Co-op or Cop-out' *Roof*, July/August 1986, p. 19.

Gibson, J., 'Block Grant and Subsidies', *Roof*, July/August 1981, p. 19.

Matthews, R., 'Housing Investment – a programme in search of a policy' *Roof*, July/August 1982, p. 11.

Lansley, S., 'Private Concern', *Roof*, July/August 1983, p. 10.

Fielding, N., 'Who is Subsidising Whom?', *Roof*, March/April 1984, p. 11.

Reports

The Inquiry into British Housing (Chaired by H.R.H. The Duke of Edinburgh, published by The National Federation of Housing Associations, 1985).

Part I
The public and voluntary provision
of housing

Chapter 1

Housing, housing authorities and housing associations

Historically the provision of housing, until well into the 20th century, was primarily the function of private landlords, but public and voluntary bodies have also provided housing for a considerable length of time. The housing association movement can arguably trace its origins back to the provision of almshouses which began in the 12th century, especially where these were provided by trade guilds and associations. Local authorities were given power to build lodging houses for working people by the Lodging Houses Act 1851, but made little use of the other housing powers they were given over the next seventy years. However, philanthropic housing provided by charitable trusts, such as the Peabody and Guinness, and Sutton foundations, was provided during the 19th century, and this continued into the 20th as numbers of persons banded together, under the legal form of Industrial and Provident Societies, to provide housing for those with special needs. At the same time local authorities were given increased housing powers, and were made subject to certain housing duties throughout the 1920s and 30s, a time when it was established that central exchequer subsidies would be paid towards meeting the loan charges on capital raised to build municipal housing.

The modern period in housing can be said to date from 1949 when the Housing Act of that year widened local authority housing responsibilities to include all members of the community and not just the working classes. The need to provide houses to replace those lost due to enemy action, and those unsuitable for occupation by reason of their condition or location, was recognised centrally, and authorities were assisted to construct large numbers of new homes; 229,305 houses in 1953 and 223,731 in 1954, figures they have never attained since. At the same time whole new communities were centrally planned and created under The New Towns Act 1946. The Housing Act 1961 encouraged new building of cost rent houses by housing associations using unsubsidised public loans, but the real expansion of voluntary housing came after the Housing Act 1974 when a new governmental structure and a system of public funding for housing associations was introduced, though associations have still continued largely to concentrate on housing rehabilitation schemes, and providing appropriate housing for the elderly and for others with special physical and/or social needs.

Since 1980 the emphasis under the Conservative government has been on the privatisation of housing, first through the provisions of the 'right to buy', but of late increasingly involving the privatisation and re-development of local authority housing on a block, area or estate basis, and the privatising of municipal housing management functions, very often by encouraging their transfer to housing associations. However, not only has the Labour Party accepted the need for the continuance of some sort of 'right to buy', but Labour housing policy favours the take-over of management of council estates by their tenants, though obviously such arrangements would have to be served by qualified professional staff. Labour housing policy favours tenants having consultative rights in relation to new developments, access to allocation and transfer systems and some access to their files as kept by housing departments. [See 'The Times' 18 September 1986.] It is essential to understand the policies that lie behind the law, and of which the law is only the ritual expression, for otherwise the consolidating Housing Act 1985 with its 625 sections and 24 Schedules, as passed, is no more than a bewildering maze of intertwined provisions. And even the pristine condition of the 1985 Act has been sullied by the legislative incursions of the Housing and Planning Act 1986 which represents once more the continued influence of policy upon law. As a final introductory point it should be noted that authorities and associations do not exercise their functions in isolation from each other. Reciprocal arrangements for the discharge of certain functions, for example finding housing accommodation, are made, either informally at officer level, or formally after approval by members.

Before considering the functions of the authorities and associations who operate subject to the body of housing law, it is worthwhile to pause and consider what the law contemplates as housing. A number of provisions in the Housing Act 1985 define 'house', 'flat' and 'dwelling' for a variety of purposes, for example sections 53, 56, 183, 205, 207, 237, 252, 322, 343, 345, 399, 401, 417, 457, 525, 575, 602, 623; but there is no one unified definition, and the approach of the courts seems to be to take a common sense approach to deciding whether as a matter of fact any given set of premises can be reasonably called, for example, a 'house' and then to decide further, as a matter of law, if it falls within the particular provision of the Housing Act in question; see *Reed v Hastings Corpn* (1964) 62 LGR 588 and *Okereke v Brent London Borough Council* [1967] 1 QB 42, [1966] 1 All ER 150. In *Gravesham Borough Council v Secretary of State for the Environment* (1984) 47 P & CR 142 McCullough J. pointed out, in a case under planning law, that an important factor to consider is whether any given set of premises provides facilities required for daily private domestic existence. As a general rule premises constructed as a house will continue to be treated as such unless they are drastically reconstructed, as for example, where premises are reconstructed as a block of self-contained flats, see *R v Kerrier District Council, ex p Guppys (Bridport) Ltd* (1985) 274 Estates Gazette 924, though whether the process of reconstruction goes far enough in any given case to warrant holding that the character of the original house has been lost must be a question of fact; see *Pollway Nominees Ltd v Croydon London Borough Council* [1986] 2 All ER 849, [1986] 3 WLR 277.

The housing authorities

Outside Greater London the principal local housing authorities are the district councils, see section 1 of the Housing Act 1985. County councils have only certain reserve powers under section 28 of the Act of 1985, such as to undertake the provision of housing on behalf of a district or districts within their area, following a request from such councils, provided the Secretary of State gives his approval. County councils have power under section 29 of the Housing Act 1985 to provide homes for persons employed or paid by them, for example school caretakers. In the Greater London area the Common Council is the housing authority for the City of London. In the rest of the metropolis the London Boroughs are, under section 1 of the Housing Act 1985, the principal housing authorities within their areas. London Boroughs are not permitted to exercise their powers to provide housing under Part II of the Housing Act 1985 outside Greater London without ministerial consent (see section 16), but they may, under section 15 agree amongst themselves to rehouse persons on each others behalf, and make appropriate financial contributions in such cases.

The former housing land and functions of the Greater London Council, which was abolished by the Local Government Act 1985, are now generally in the hands of the London Boroughs who operate their own inter-borough mobility scheme, The London Area Mobility Scheme. G.L.C. housing was transferred to the boroughs under section 23 of the London Government Act 1963, and section 89 of the Local Government Act 1985 confers miscellaneous powers on the Secretary of State in relation to such transferred housing, including the power to nominate tenants to such transferred housing.

Part XVI of the Local Government, Planning and Land Act 1980 provides for the creation of new corporations to regenerate urban areas, for example London's docklands. The powers of such corporations are to be modelled upon those of new town development corporations. Under section 153 of the Act the Secretary of State may provide by order that such a corporation may assume total and exclusive or shared housing powers under the Housing Acts within its area or in any part thereof.

The duty to provide housing

This is contained in Part II of the Housing Act 1985. (All references hereafter are to this Statute unless otherwise stated.)

Section 8 provides that it shall be the duty of every local housing authority to consider the housing conditions in and the needs of their district with respect to the provision of further housing accommodation.

The housing needs of a district are not confined to the needs of its inhabitants. In *Watson v Minister of Local Government and Planning* [1951] 2 KB 779, [1951] 2 All ER 664 where the appellant claimed that the local authority had no power to make a compulsory purchase order on his land because they required it partly to house persons from *outside* their area, Devlin J said, at p. 783: 'It cannot be right . . . that in considering the needs of a district a local authority should stop short at a street which is immediately beyond their district and which is badly overcrowded and the inhabitants of which might more conveniently be rehoused on the other side of the boundary. It seems to me that a local authority must, when considering the needs of their district look at the districts immediately adjacent'. Thus the needs of persons in adjacent districts who could conveniently be housed within a local authority's area may also be taken into account.

Local authorities must themselves review from time to time the housing information with which they have been presented about their district, whether that has been provided by their own officers or otherwise, and in particular information obtained under section 605 following surveys of unfit housing, area needs and houses in multiple occupation, etc.

Under section 9 accommodation may be provided by erecting houses, or by converting buildings into houses, on land acquired by the authority, or by the acquisition of existing houses. These powers may also be used where the houses to be provided are subsequently to be disposed of, and housing land may also be disposed of to persons intending to provide housing on it, see section 9(3). Under these powers authorities may, inter alia, proceed to acquire older properties on an 'improvement for sale' basis, or may acquire land for the purpose of providing accommodation for first time buyers under low cost home ownership initiatives, possibly in conjunction with housing associations.

Any house so erected, converted or acquired may subsequently be altered, enlarged, repaired or improved. Supplementary powers to fit out and furnish section 9 accommodation are granted by section 10, and powers to provide meals, refreshments, including the sale of alcoholic liquors for consumption with meals, laundry facilities and services are granted by section 11.

Section 12 provides that the local authority may, with ministerial consent, provide along with housing accommodation, shops, recreation grounds and other land or buildings which the minister considers would benefit the occupants of the housing provided, a power wide enough, according to the opinion of Peterson J in *Conron v LCC* [1922] 2 Ch 283 at 297, to cover the provison of public houses so long as they are 'conducted on the most improved lines'.

Section 23 permits the making of byelaws with respect to the use of any land held under section 12, and *not* covered by buildings or within the curtilage of a building or forming part of a highway, and for the management and regulation of local authority housing.

The London Boroughs also have power to provide and maintain commercial premises along with housing accommodation, under section 15(1). Section 13 grants powers to lay out public streets, roads and open spaces on land acquired for housing purposes. In *Meravale Builders Ltd v Secretary of State for the Environment* (1978) 36 P & CR 87 it was held that this power only entitles a local authority to build such roads as fairly and reasonably relate to the provision of housing accommodation, and not to create new major roads, inter-changes and extensions which have a purpose independent of housing. Section 607 requires local authorities to have regard to 'the beauty of the landscape or countryside, the other amenities of the locality, and the desirability of preserving existing works of architectural, historic or artistic interest' when proposing to provide housing.

The power to provide section 9 accommodation may be used outside an authority's district, but only after they have given notice to their county council, and also, where they propose to act outside their county, to the council of the county where they propose to act, see section 14. The obligation to provide housing cannot, in effect, be transferred to private shoulders by attaching a condition to a grant of planning permission that the developer must grant the first right to occupy dwellings he wishes to build to persons on the local authority waiting list, see *R v Hillingdon London Borough Council ex p Royco Homes Ltd* [1974] QB 720, [1974] 2 All ER 643.

To deal with the problem of a restrictive covenant standing in the way of the conversion of, for example, a large old house, into smaller units of accommodation, a local authority may use section 84 of the Law of Property Act 1925 under which the Lands Tribunal may discharge or modify restrictive convenants affecting freehold land. With regard to leasehold properties acquired by a local authority, section 610 of the Act confers power on the county court to vary the terms of the lease if, they prohibit or restrict conversion of the property. The local authority *must* prove either that, because of changes in the character of the neighbourhood of the house it cannot be readily let as a single house, but could be if it were, for example, divided into two or more flats or bed sitting rooms, or that planning permission has been granted for such a conversion into separate dwellings.

Section 26 provides that where a tenant of a local housing authority moves to another house, whether or not it is one of theirs, the authority may meet his removal expenses, and, where the tenant is purchasing the house, may pay his expenses incurred in connection with the purchase, except, of course, the purchase price!

The acquisition of land for housing purposes

Section 17 allows local housing authorities for the purposes of Part II to acquire land as sites for the erection of houses, or to acquire houses or buildings which may be made suitable as houses, to acquire land to provide facilities under sections 11, 12 and 15 in connection with housing, and to acquire land in order to carry out on it works for the purpose of, or in connection with, the alteration, enlargement, repair or improvement of an adjoining house. Section 17(2) allows for the acquisition of land where the purpose is to dispose of houses to be built on it, or for the purpose of disposing of the land to a builder. Land may be acquired under section 17(3) by agreement or, with ministerial confirmation, compulsorily, even where the land is not immediately required for housing purposes, though compulsory acquisition may not be authorised unless the Secretary of State concludes the land is likely to be required within ten years of the confirmation of the compulsory purchase order, see section 17(4).

A number of points should be noted about this section. First, the power is very wide. In *H E Green & Sons v Minister of Health (No 2)* [1948] 1 KB 34, [1947] 2 All ER 469, a building company had acquired land in 1938, on which they laid down sewers and roads and built 22 houses. The Second World War stopped further work and shortly after peace returned the local authority made a compulsory purchase order on the site. This was held to be within the words of the statute. In *Andresier v Minister of Housing and Local Government* (1965) 109 Sol Jo 594 it was held that a local authority may use its power to acquire houses with a view to improving them as housing accommodation, even if that work does *not* result in a net increase in the amount of available accommodation.

Section 18 provides that where a local authority acquires a building which may be made suitable as a house, they are forthwith to secure that the building is made suitable, either by doing work themselves, or by selling or leasing it to some other person on condition that he does the work. In those cases where they acquire a house or a building which may be made suitable as a house and they do the work themselves they are under a further duty to ensure, as soon as practicable after the acquisition or the completion of the necessary work as the case may be, that the house or building is used as housing accommodation. Such buildings are often acquired as a consequence of use of local authority powers to deal with unfit housing (see Chapters 8 and 9 below). In some cases such buildings are used for accommodation purposes, for example as short life housing, see Bob Widdowson, 'Short Life Ghettoes', *Roof*, March 1977, pp. 42–45. But in some areas older houses, once acquired, are simply boarded up and left unused, or subjected to the process known as 'prior demolition' and the properties have been demolished and the sites left vacant for many years before redevelopment, see Ron Bailey, 'Grabbing the Smashers', *Roof*, July 1978, p. 99. Over the years the courts have interpreted section 18 so that it cannot be used to prevent such a waste of housing resources.

In *Uttoxeter UDC v Clarke* [1952] 1 All ER 1318 a local authority made a compulsory purchse order on an estate which contained a large old house converted into a private hotel. They then used the house for administrative and social service purposes. It was held that there was no obligation on the local authority to convert the old house into suitable dwellings. That obligation was said to arise only where a local authority acquires a house for *conversion*, and does not arise in relation to houses merely acquired as part of an estate. In *Attridge v LCC* [1954] 2 QB 449, [1954] 2 All ER 444 a local authority compulsorily acquired a site for the purposes of building a housing estate. There was already a bungalow on the land which could have been used as housing accommodation, but they wished to demolish this in order to construct a road giving access to the housing estate. It was held that where a local authority acquires a site, the fact that there are already buildings on it which might be used as dwellings does not in any way restrict the local authority in the proper development of their estate plans. Finally in *A-G ex rel. Rivers-Moore v Portsmouth City Council* (1978) 36 P & CR 416 the local authority had acquired a number of old houses using their compulsory purchase powers. It was alleged that due to the council's neglect these houses became unfit. The local authority subsequently declared the area a clearance area and proposed to demolish the houses. It was alleged, inter alia, that the local authority were in breach of their duty under section 18 to secure the speedy use of acquired premises as housing accommodation. The court held the various duties imposed by section 18 are not of infinite duration, and a local authority is bound to deal with houses as they are and not as they once were. Even though the houses had become unfit as a result of municipal inaction, provided the council could honestly say that they were in bad condition and unfit for human habitation, having outlasted their reasonable life by years, they could be properly included in a demolition area.

Section 19(2) provides that, where a local authority have acquired or appropriated land for the purposes of Part II of the Act, they may not put any part of the land consisting of a house, or part of a house, to any other purpose without ministerial consent. The relationship of this provision to section 18 should be noted. The new requirement is that where land has been appropriated or acquired for housing purposes, houses on that land shall not be put to any other purpose without ministerial consent. It is *not* a requirement that such houses shall not cease to be used as accommodation. This provision does not overturn the decisions in *A-G ex rel. Rivers-Moore v Portsmouth City Council*, where houses were simply left empty; in *Uttoxeter UDC v Clarke* where the property acquired was not at the time of acquisition a house but a hotel; nor in *Attridge v LCC* where the house was acquired so that it could be demolished prior to the building of other houses. See also DoE Circular 12/85 – on the use of empty property.

Compulsory purchase of land

Reference has already been made to the power to acquire land compulsorily under section 17(3) and (4). Section 578 directs that the Acquisition of Land Act 1981, the Compulsory Purchase Act 1965 and the Land Compensation Act 1961 generally apply to compulsory acquisitions for housing purposes. [Special provisions apply with respect to procedures in clearance areas, see Chaps. 8 and 9 below.] It is the Acquisition of Land Act 1981 which governs the procedures for making and confirming compulsory purchase orders.

Very briefly this means that the local authority has to make the compulsory purchase order in draft, describing the land to be acquired by reference to a map. Thereafter the authority must serve notice on owners, lessees and occupiers except tenants for a month or less, of the land stating times and places where the order and map can be seen, and granting at least 21 days for the making of objections. Additionally the same information must be advertised in the local press for two successive weeks. If any objections are received, unless they are such as can be dealt with when the issue of compensation is being settled, they must be heard either at a public local inquiry, or, more rarely, at a hearing before an inspector appointed by the Secretary of State. The procedure at any inquiry is governed by the Compulsory Purchase by Public Authorites (Inquiries Procedure) Rules (S.I. 1976/746). After the inquiry or hearing the inspector will make his report and this will be considered by the Secretary of State when he decides whether or not to confirm the order. The Secretary may confirm the order with or without modification, or refuse to confirm it. By section 12 of the Tribunals and Inquiries Act 1971 the Secretary of State must state the reasons for his decision in any case where an inquiry has been, or could have been, held. Where an order is confirmed notice must again be given in the local press, and further notices must be served on those owners, lessees and occupiers who were previously notified. These notices must state the times and places where the confirmed order and maps can be inspected. The order will normally come into operation on the day on which the announcement of its confirmation first appears in the local press. The validity of the order can then be challenged during a six week period, but not otherwise, in the High Court by a person aggrieved on the grounds either that the order is ultra vires or that the procedure followed in its making has been faulty. If no challenge is made the acquiring authority may then proceed to serve notice to treat on the affected landholders and thereafter proceed to take possession.

(Readers requiring a fuller exposition of compulsory purchase procedure are referred to Keith Davies, *The Law of Conpulsory Purchase and Compensation* (4th edn.) Chaps. 3 and 4.)

Confirmation by the Secretary of State of a compulsory purchase order will normally be dependent on the necessary planning permission being obtained for the proposed development. Section 40 of the Town and County Planning Act 1971 provides:

'1) Where the authorisation of a government department is required by virtue of an enactment in respect of development to be carried out by a local authority . . . that department may, on granting that authorisation, direct that planning permission for that development shall be deemed to be granted. . . .'

In practice local authorities are expected to obtain planning permission. [Readers requiring further information on how local authorities obtain planning permission in such circumstances are referred to Telling, *Planning Law and Procedure* (7th edn.) pp. 243 to 245.] Perhaps even more relevant in the present context to the question of confirmation of an order is the overall attitude of central government towards compulsory acquisitions. Central policy on such issues is declared in DoE Circular 13/81 pointing out that compulsory acquisi-tions should only be used where there is a clear compelling case to do so in the public interest, and urging that where a CPO is made that it should be proceeded with expeditiously. Acquiring authorities should be certain to have the case for acquisition well prepared, and should have clear estimates of the cost of achieving the purpose for which they wish to acquire the land. Orders are not likely to be confirmed where they relate to the acquisition of private housing in good order. DoE Cir-cular 23/82 goes further and indicates central concern that land should not be acquired where insufficient thought has been given to an authority's ability to use it, and use it within a reasonable time, or the effect of the acquisition on the ability of other developers to acquire land. There is a general policy bias against acquisition of new land unless the stock of land already held by the acquiring authority is unsuitable for new house building, or is badly located, or is inadequate to meet immediately forseeable demands. [See also *Introduction* above on the related capital controls on new schemes.] Further guidance is contained in DoE Circular 6/85 which further counsels expedition in making compulsory acquisitions, and also points out the need to consider using the power to acquire land by agreement contempora-neously with compulsory powers of acquisition.

The acquisition of ancillary rights

On the whole the procedure for acquiring land compulsorily and then obtaining the necessary planning permission to develop it though some-what attenuated is not over complex. But it can contain pitfalls of an unexpected nature. In *Sovmots Investments Ltd v Secretary of State for the Environment* [1979] AC 144, [1977] 2 All ER 385 such a pitfall was encountered. This case arose out of the disquiet that has surrounded the tower block known as 'Centre Point' ever since it was completed in 1967. The development has three parts: a tall tower meant to be used as offices; a bridge block intended for use as shops and showrooms; and a wing block consisting of a basement car-park surrounded by four floors of offices and shop units which itself supports stilts which in their turn support a six storey block of 36 maisonettes, access to which was pro-vided by lifts and staircases. The services for the whole of this wing block were common, and the electricity, water and sewerage services were all shared and incapable of separation. The local authority, Camden LBC, wishing to alleviate the housing shortage in their area, made a compulsory purchase order on the maisonettes in 1972 as they were unoccupied. This was in due course confirmed, and was said to include all the access ways to the dwellings.

The question then arose of whether the local authority had also acquired all the ancillary rights necessary for them to make use of the maisonettes, for example use of emergency fire escapes, use of goods lifts and rubbish chutes, a right support from the unacquired shop units and stilts below the maisonettes, a right to use the service facilities, and a right of access to the outside of the building in order to allow window cleaning and repair. The House of Lords held that the powers of a local authority, being strictly limited by statute, did not allow them to compel the grant of ancillary rights over land which was not being acquired. Before the attempted compulsory purchase Centre Point was a single unit held in entirety by Sovmots Investments Ltd. The purported acquisition would have divided the block and given the local authority a 'flying leasehold'. This would have been utterly useless to them unless its acquisition carried with it the ancillary rights mentioned above. As they had, apparently, no power to compel the grant of such rights they could not use the maisonettes for housing purposes, and as they only had power to make the compulsory purchase order to acquire property for housing accommodation, they could not acquire the block of maisonettes at all. The House of Lords added that even if a local authority have power to force the grant of ancillary rights, any such rights required must be clearly specified in the compulsory purchase order.

In these circumstances local authorities should rely on section 13 of the Local Government (Miscellaneous Provisions) Act 1976 which provides that where a local authority is authorised to purchase land compulsorily that the Secretary of State may also authorise them by such an order to purchase compulsorily such 'new rights' as are specified in the order. 'New rights' are rights which were not in existence when the order specifying them was made, but otherwise they are not defined by the Act, though easements and those rights of a like kind which caused the trouble in the *Sovmots* case are within the meaning of the phrase. DoE Circular No. 6/85, Appendix K points out that when reliance is placed on this provision:

1) Each new right should be separately referenced and made easily identifiable in the order, as relating to relevant parcels of land.

2) Orders may provide for the acquisition of land and new rights for the same purpose.

3) Where an order is made for the acquisition of land and new rights for different, though usually connected, purposes, the purposes should be clearly and separately described in the compulsory purchase order.

4) In any case it must be made clear which land is being acquired and which is being made subject to the acquisition of rights, and a statement

of the need for new rights, their nature and extent, should be given in the order whereunder acquisition of such rights is sought.

Supplementary provisions

Section 583 permits a local authority who have acquired the right to enter and take possession of a house following its compulsory purchase to authorise any person in occupation of the house at that time to continue his occupation, subject of course, to the rights of the local authority. Section 19(1) allows the appropriation for the purpose of providing housing accommodation, of any land which is for the time being vested in a local authority or at their disposal.

The provision of housing in new areas

Many of our older large towns and cities, particularly before the creation of the large new districts by the Local Government Act 1972, had insufficient land within their areas to provide all the new housing they required. This led to the development of the concept of 'overspill' whereby the surplus population from older urban areas was rehoused in new developments in rural areas reasonably adjacent to their former home towns. Such large scale movements of population have been resisted by employers, by the host areas and sometimes by those to be rehoused themselves. Local authorities have power as we have seen to provide housing outside their areas under section 14 of the 1985 Act, but the immediate post war years saw the development of two policies designed to provide much more comprehensive powers to develop housing in new areas, as part of general central policy to effect a material rise in the health and housing standards of urban dwellers. One policy was to expand existing smaller towns, the other was to create entirely new communities in rural areas.

The policy of expanding already existing smaller towns was contained in the Town Development Act 1952. While the creation of new urban centres was originally undertaken under the New Towns Act 1946, see now The New Towns Act 1981. Readers requiring a deeper treatment of the powers available under these Acts than this edition of this work contains are referred to the first edition, pp. 46 to 53. The legislation, though still in force, has been overtaken by policy. House-building is currently seen as, primarily, the responsibility of the private building industry, and such public sector initiatives as are being under-taken are generally in the hands of housing associations or on existing urban land held by local authorities, see generally DoE Circular 15/84 'Land for Housing'. So far as the new towns are concerned the current thrust of legislation is towards the disposal of their housing stock. [*See Addendum 2.*]

The new towns: history and current status

The first modern new towns legislation was, as stated above, the New Towns Act 1946. The first 'new town' was Stevenage which was designated on 11 November 1946, followed shortly by Crawley, Hemel Hempstead, Harlow, Hatfield, Welwyn Garden City (which had been previously begun by Ebenezer Howard the originator of the 'garden city' concept), Basildon and Bracknell. These were the ring of new towns around London. Newton Aycliffe and Peterlee in Durham were founded about the same time to meet local housing needs and to diversify industry. Corby was designated a new town in 1950, and then several years elapsed before the designation of Skelmersdale in 1961, Telford, 1963, Redditch, 1964, Runcorn, 1964, Washington, 1964, Milton Keynes, 1967, Peterborough, 1967, Northampton, 1968, Warrington, 1968 and Central Lancashire in 1970. There are other new towns in Wales, Scotland and Northern Ireland. It will be noted that in many cases the towns were not 'new' at all. Peterborough and Northampton in particular are centuries old as urban centres, but in all cases a massive expansion of housing and opportunities for employment was planned, together with, in nearly all cases, a great reconstruction of the old inner urban areas and central shopping zones.

Section 1 of the New Towns Act 1981 provides for the designation of new towns by the Secretary of State, and section 3 places him under a duty to establish a development corporation for each town designated. The object of such corporations, under section 4 of the 1981 Act, is the laying out and development of the new town, and, to this end, inter alia, they are given powers under section 4(2) to acquire, hold, manage and dispose of land, powers that, under section 10, may be exercised by agreement or compulsorily following ministerial approval. A power to dispose of land, subject to ministerial oversight, is given by section 17 of the 1981 Act. Part II of the Act establishes the Commission for the New Towns by virtue of section 35. Its function is to take over, hold and manage property previously vested in a development corporation, and transferred to the Commission by order under the legislation, see sections 36 and 41. These provisions were designed to further a policy of winding up the development corporations where it could be shown that the purposes for which they had been achieved had been, town by town, achieved.

Section 42 of the 1981 Act provides generally for the transfer of new town housing and associated property to relevant district councils.

Section 43 elaborates upon this by allowing the Secretary of State to make certain directions where:

1) An order has been made before 15/11/1976 with respect to the new town under section 41 of the New Town Act 1965 transferring its development corporation's property to the Commission for the New Towns; or

2) The new town's site was first designated not less than fifteen years before the date of the section 43 directions; or

3) The Secretary of State has, after consulting the development corporation, formed the opinion that its task is substantially complete.

These directions, given to the new town development corporation and relevant district councils, require the opening of consultation with a view to the transfer of housing stock from the corporation to the relevant district or districts. Section 44 proceeds to allow the Secretary of State to give directions after the consultation process requiring the making of transfer schemes specifying dwellings and other property involved in the transfer, together with other relevant rights and obligations. The procedure for making a transfer scheme is contained in section 46 of the 1981 Act which makes the whole process subject to ministerial oversight, and the effect of a scheme, under section 47, is to vest in relevant districts the interest of the new town corporation in the transferred land, together with all other relevant rights, liabilities and obligations. Sections 44 and 48 of the Act originally provided for new town corporations to have rights to nominate tenants for dwellings transferred to district councils.

The policy of winding up the new towns programme was furthered by the New Towns and Urban Development Corporations Act 1985. Section 1 of this Act empowers the Commission for the New Towns to dispose of property transferred to it from new towns as soon as it considers it expedient to do so, and the Secretary of State is further empowered to wind up the Commission itself, under Section 2, when its purposes have been substantially achieved. Section 3 of the 1985 Act modifies the nomination rights of new town corporations under sections 44 and 48 of the 1981 Act, the latter section being repealed in 1985. Transfer schemes may confer on new town corporations a right to nominate tenants of 'Housing Act dwellings', i.e. dwellings provided under Housing Act powers by the relevant district, or treated as provided by them by virtue of the transfer, see section 47(6) of the 1981 Act. This power to nominate exists only for a specified length of time, see section 44(7B) of the 1981 Act as amended. While, however, the new towns continue to own housing stock both development corporations and the Commission for the New Towns are 'housing authorities' for the purposes of the Housing Act 1985, see section 4, and are generally subject to, inter alia, the provisions relating to secure tenancies and the right to buy.

Housing associations

Brief mention was made earlier of the history of voluntary housing, and further details may be found in *Committee Members Handbook* (1984) published by the National Federation of Housing Associations (NATFED), to which the author acknowledges general indebtedness, and *Housing Associations* by C.V. Baker, Chap. 1. The NATFED is a voluntary banding together of associations. It has representative, advice giving, service providing, research organising, educational and consultancy functions to aid member associations. The NATFED is recognised by the Secretary of State under section 33 of the Housing Associations Act 1985 for grant aid purposes so that it may better pursue the functions outlined above. In the 1984 *Handbook* the NATFED reported the existence of some 4,500 associations, the majority of which were registered with the Housing Corporation. Many of these were small, and over 80 per cent of them had less than 250 units of accommodation, and few employees each, with one-third being run entirely by volunteers. Some few associations are very large with thousands of dwellings and over 100 staff. In 1983 associations were renting 500,000 dwellings, there were 20,000 units in co-ownership and 24,600 units owned by almshouses. Most of the housing association stock dates from post 1970. Associations basically exist to meet special needs. In 1984 30 per cent of their lettings were to the elderly, 16 per cent to young single persons, 10 per cent to single parent families; 50 per cent of tenants were non-earners and of those in work 87 per cent received less than the national average wage; the majority of association tenants were movers from other rented accommodation, some of it in poor condition; one third of those housed were homeless or threatened with homelessness; 15 per cent of those accommodated by associations needed extra social services or support, or some form of special accommodation. The rest of this chapter is concerned with the legal structure of the voluntary housing movement.

The Housing Corporation

This exists under Part III of the Housing Associations Act (HAA) 1985, and its tasks, under section 75, are to promote the development of associations, and their proper functioning; to maintain a register of associations (which must be open to the public, see section 3) and to supervise those that are registered; to act as agent for the Secretary of State with regard to the making of grants to registered associations, and to undertake the provision of dwellings and hostels, their management, and sale, as the case may be. The Corporation must, under section 76 of the HAA 1985, act in accordance with directions given by the Secretary of State, and may, under section 77, offer legal, architectural and other technical advice to associations, or those contemplating forming an association. Section 78 imposes a duty on the Corporation to make an annual report.

The Corporation has power to lend to registered housing associations under section 79 of the HAA 1985, and may lend to individuals for the purpose of assisting them to acquire dwellings for their occupation from the corporation or an association. These powers are additional to the right to a mortgage provision in relation to the right to buy, see Chapter 2 below. Section 83 gives a power to guarantee, with the Secretary of State's consent, the repayment of the principal and interest on sums borrowed by registered housing associations. The aggregate amount of loans guaranteed must not exceed £300m, though the Secretary of State may increase this to up to £500m. Section 92 of the HAA 1985 empowers the Corporation to borrow from the Secretary of State, and from other sources including the European Investment Bank or the Commission of the European Communities, or on the open money market, but these powers are subject to an aggregate limit under section 93 of £2,500m, which may be increased to up to £3,000m with Treasury consent. The Treasury may, under section 94, guarantee in such manner or on such conditions as they think fit, the repayment of the principal of and interest on any sums borrowed by the Corporation from any source other than the Secretary of State. The Corporation may turn its resources to account in so far as they are not required in the exercise of its functions, and may thus invest portions of its funds, see section 96 of the HAA 1985, and may, under section 98, acquire securities (that is stocks and shares etc.) in bodies corporate. Proper accounts and audits are required by section 97, and grants in aid of administrative expenses may be paid to the Corporation by the Secretary of State under section 95. [The detailed organisation of the Corporation is contained in Schedule 6 to the HAA 1985.] Despite the range of its powers, the Corporation is not, as its annual reports make clear, a trading body seeking to make a return on its capital. Its policy is that the money it advances to associations as loans is charged at a rate of interest sufficient to meet that on its own borrowings. [See *Introduction* above for how loans and grants 'mesh' together in housing association finance.]

In addition to its powers to lend to registered housing associations it has been noted that the Corporation also has general supervisory powers over such bodies. Supervision is exercised vis-à-vis individual associations by monitoring visits which take place, generally, on a two year basis. Section 28 of the HAA 1985 empowers the Corporation to conduct inquiries into the affairs of registered housing associations, and the person who is appointed, who may not be an actual or former member of the Corporation's staff, may require the production of books, accounts and other documents relating to the association's business for the purpose of conducting the inquiry. A special audit of an association's accounts for the purposes of the inquiry may be undertaken under section 29. Where the Corporation are satisfied as a result of their inquiries that there has been misconduct or mismanagement in an association's affairs, they may, under section 30, remove or suspend those responsible from membership and/or office, order banks or others holding an association's money or securities not to part with them without Corporation approval, and generally restrict the powers of the association to enter into transactions. Due notice of an intention to remove a person from office, etc. must be given to the person and the association, and the person has a right of appeal to the High Court. The exercise of powers under sections 28 to 30 is limited in relation to an association which is also a registered charity in that they may only be exercised where the association has received a grant or loan under the principal grant aiding powers of the 1985 Act, e.g. section 41 relating to Housing Association Grant, or section 79 (loans by the Corporation).

Where an inquiry or audit has uncovered mismanagement or misconduct in the administration of a registered association which is also a society registered under the Industrial and Provident Societies Act 1965 (see below), *or* that the management of the association's land would be improved if transferred to another association, the Corporation may direct the land to be transferred to another registered housing association, though where the delinquent association is a charity the transfer may only be to another registered association which is a charity having objects akin to those of the delinquent.

Section 88 of the HAA 1985 empowers the Corporation to acquire land by agreement, or compulsorily if so authorised by the Secretary of State, for the purposes of selling or leasing it to registered housing associations, or to provide hostels or dwellings for rent or sale itself. The land may be acquired notwithstanding that it is not immediately required. The procedure for compulsory acquisition is that under the Acquisition of Land Act 1981. Section 89 further empowers the Corporation to provide or improve dwellings or hostels on its land, and they may clear land, and prepare it as a building site by, inter alia, laying out streets and open spaces and providing mains services. They may insure and repair their buildings and manage them, doing all such things as are conducive to faciliating the provison or improvement of dwellings or hostels on the land, including the provision of ancillary developments for commercial, recreational or other non-domestic purposes. Section 90 authorises the disposal of land on which no dwellings have been provided to a limited range of bodies, principally registered associations or subsidiaries of the Corporation. Where dwellings have been provided, they may be disposed of to registered associations, local authorities, new town corporations, the Development Board for Rural Wales or Corporation subsidiaries. The Corporation may sell or lease individual dwellings to persons for their occupation. Certain disposals require the consent of the Secretary of State, see section 90(3) to (6) of the HAA 1985. In the context of the HAA 1985 generally 'hostel' is defined by section 106(1) as a building in which is provided for persons generally, or for classes of persons, residential accommodation *not* in separate and self-contained sets, *and* either board, *or* facilities for the preparation of food adequate to the needs of those persons, or both.

The types and structures of housing associations

The initial point to note is that associations are voluntary bodies, not generally subject to the rules of judicial review appropriate to a local housing authority, so that even where they receive public funds which they are obliged to apply in particular ways, that does not turn *their* normal and essential functions as landlords into the exercise of a reviewable statutory power, see *Peabody Housing Association Ltd v Green* (1979) 38 P & CR 644.

Housing associations are further defined by section 1 of the HAA 1985 (section 5 of the Housing Act 1985). They are societies, bodies of trustees or companies established for the purpose of providing, constructing, improving, managing, facilitating or encouraging the construction or improvement of housing accommodation, *and* which do not trade for profit, or whose constitution or rules prohibit the issue of capital with interest or dividend exceeding such a rate as may be prescribed by the Treasury. This covers a multiplicity of forms.

Associations which are 'societies' will in general exist under the terms of the Industrial and Provident Societies Act 1965. They will be run by a Committee of Management and may have charitable status, depending on their constitution, or they may be self-help bodies such as co-operative or self-build organisations. Charitable status applies to those associations who act to relieve 'aged, impotent and poor people'. These words must be read disjunctively, for the aged need not be necessarily also impotent or poor, nor the poor aged, etc. What is required is that the body alleviates need attributable to the aged, impotent, or poor condition of the recipient of relief, and that that need is one which those persons could not alleviate, or would find it hard to alleviate, from their own resources, see *Joseph Rowntree Memorial Trust Housing Association Ltd v A-G* [1983] Ch 159, [1983] 1 All ER 288. The rules of a '1965 Act' society determine its legal entity, its powers, and the internal relationships of its members. Such societies may only do what their rules permit them to do. [See further the NATFED *Handbook* Chap. 9.]

Associations which are charitable trusts derive their powers from their trust deeds and will come under the jurisdiction of the Charity Commissioners under the Charities Act 1960. '1965 Act' societies are outside this jurisdiction, whether or not 'charitable', as they are supervised generally by the Registrar of Friendly Societies and the Housing Corporation. [See NATFED *Handbook* Chap. 18.] An association which is a company will derive its powers and functions from its memorandum and articles of association under the terms of the Companies Acts. It is not uncommon to find associations forming part of a group of institutions founded by the same persons wishing to take maximum advantage of the variety of legal and financial advantages peculiar to each type of legal entity capable of being a housing association. Each of these institutions must, of course, adhere strictly to its constituent rules and the laws applicable to it, but within those parameters may pursue a particular housing object.

The right to buy does not arise where a housing trust or a housing association which is a charity is the landlord, but under section 45 of the HAA 1985 other registered housing associations may arrange for the acquisition of dwellings and, without taking the conveyance, grant or assignment as the case may be, may dispose of their interest to tenants of charitable associations etc. Such acquisitions qualify for grant aid. The tenant will qualify for discount and all the other incidentals of the right to buy, see further Housing Corporation Circulars HC 16/84 and 35/85.

Associations which are 'fully mutual' are those with rules that restrict membership to persons who are tenants or prospective tenants of the association and which preclude granting or assigning tenancies to persons other than members. Co-operative housing associations are those that are both fully mutual and societies registered under the 1965 Act.

The next point is that an association may be registered or unregistered with the Housing Corporation under section 3 of the HAA 1985. Registered associations are eligible for loan and grant aid, but, of course, are supervised by the Housing Corporation. The distinction also has consequences for tenants, for the 'landlord condition' for secure tenant status under the Housing Act 1985 is, for present purposes, that the landlord is a housing association which is a registered housing association *other than a co-operative housing association* (see above), or an unregistered housing association which is   a co-operative housing association, see section 80(2) of the Housing Act 1985. An association may be registered under section 4 of the HAA 1985 if it is a registered charity, that is a charity registered under section 4 of the Charities Act 1960, (and that will apply to companies wishing to register with the Corporation), or if it is a '1965 Act' society fulfilling certain conditions. These are that it must not trade for profit, i.e. it does not make a profit extractable by its members, and must be established for the purpose of, or have among its objects or powers, the provision, construction, improvement or management of houses to be kept available for letting, or houses for occupation by members of the association where it is fully mutual, or hostels. Where an association has additional purposes etc. they must fall within the following:

1) providing land or buildings for purposes connected with the requirements of occupants of houses provided or managed by the association;

2) providing amenities or services for such persons;

3) acquiring, repairing or improving houses to be disposed of by sale or lease;

4) building homes to be disposed of on a shared ownership basis;

5) encouraging and giving advice on the formation of other registrable associations;

6) providing services for registered associations;

7) effecting transactions under section 45(1) of the HAA 1985 (see above);

8) providing services of any description for owners or occupiers of houses in arranging or carrying out works of maintenance, repair or improvement. [This last head was added by section 19 of the Housing and Planning Act 1986.] See generally *Goodman v Dolphin Square Trust Ltd* (1979) 38 P & CR 257.

Registration is at the discretion of the Housing Corporation under section 5. They consider the financial soundness of the association, its management and development abilities and what part it has to play within its proposed area of operation. The Corporation is a statutory body and so here, as elsewhere, is open to judicial supervision. Deregistration may take place under section 6(1) where the Corporation conclude a registered body is no longer a housing association eligible for registration, or has ceased to exist or does not operate. The Corporation must give the body a least fourteen days notice before removing it from the register. Registered bodies may request deregistration under section 6(4) where they have not at any time received housing association grants, revenue deficit grants or certain grants under para. 2 or 3 of Schedule 1 to the HAA 1985. A body aggrieved by a decision to deregister it may appeal under section 7 to the High Court. The Housing Corporation also has power under section 16 to remove a member of a registered association's committee of management if he is bankrupt, or incapable of acting because of mental disorder, or he has not acted, or cannot be found or does not act and his absence or failure to act impede its proper management. Due notice must be given of action under this section. New members may be appointed in place of those removed, or where there are no committee members, or where it is necessary for the proper functioning of an association, by the Corporaton under section 17. The powers under sections 16 and 17 may only be exercised in respect of an association which is a registered charity where the association has been granted aid under specified provisions. See section 18 of the HAA 1985. Where a registered association is a company incorporated under the Companies Acts, or is a '1965 Act' society to which the winding-up provisions of the Companies Act apply under section 55(a) of the Industrial and Provident Societies Act 1965, the Housing Corporation may petition for it to be wound up on the ground that it is failing to carry out its purposes or objects properly.

Without prejudice to the right to buy provisions of the Housing Act 1985, section 8 of the HAA 1985 grants a general power to registered housing associations to dispose of their land, but this is subject to the consent of the Housing Corporation under section 9. Such consent may be given generally or to a particular association or associations, or in relation to particular land and may be given subject to conditions. To dispose in this context includes selling, leasing, mortgaging, charging or otherwise disposing of land. General consents have been given to various types of disposal, for example, low cost home ownership initiatives. Where a discount is given to a purchaser from a housing association or where the house in question is in a National Park, area of outstanding natural beauty or a rural area designated under section 157 of the Housing Act 1985, Schedule 2 to the HAA 1985 applies to impose requirements for the repayment of discount in certain cases of early disposal, and restrictions on redisposals. [See Chapter 2 below for the general scheme of such restrictions under the right to buy.] Disposals made without consent are avoided by section 12 unless the disposal in question is to an individual and does not extend to more than one house.

Current or past members of registered housing associations, members of their families, companies of which they, or members of their families, are directors may not, under section 13 of the HAA 1985, be made gifts or paid sums by way of dividend or bonus by a registered association. Payment of interest on capital lent to an association in accordance with its rules is allowed. Sums paid in contravention of this provision may be recovered, and the Housing Corporation has power to direct the taking of proceedings to make such a recovery. The Corporation also has power to specify under section 14, the sums which a registered association which is also a '1965 Act' Society may give by way of fees or remuneration of expenses to an association's officers and · employees, and the reimbursement of a committee member's expenses. Committee members are, of course, not allowed to profit from their membership, and section 15 prohibits registered associations which are '1965 Act' societies from making payments or granting benefits to, committee members, officers and employees, their close relatives and concerns trading for profit of which any such person is a principal proprietor or manager save as allowed. What are allowed are inter alia payments made to officers and employees under contracts of employment and reimbursement of a committee member's expenses.

Certain other actions by registered associations which are also '1965 Act' societies are also subject to control by the Housing Corporation, these are changes of rules, see section 19, and proposals to amalgamate with another society, or to dissolve, see section 21. Where a '1965 Act' society is dissolved under the 1965 Act, section 23 of the HAA 1985 directs that so much of its property as remains after its liabilities have been met is transferred to the Housing Corporation, or to such other registered associations as the Corporation specifies. [The accounting requirements for associations are laid down in sections 24 to 27 of the HAA 1985. The requirements, most of which are contained in regulations made under the Act, are so complex as to be beyond the scope of this work. The interested reader is referred to Bucknall, *Housing Finance*, Chap. 11.]

Local authorities and housing associations

Section 58 of the HAA 1985 empowers local authorities to promote the formation or extension of associations, and to assist them. In particular they may make grants or loans to associations, subscribe for share or loan capital in an association, guarantee sums borrowed by associations on such terms as they think fit, save that they may not limit the aggregate of rents payable in respect of relevant dwellings, nor specify a limit which the rent of a dwelling is not to exceed. The giving of such grants, loans and guarantee is generally restricted to registered housing associations under section 60. Authorities may make use of these powers to promote the work of associations within their areas, and may seek rights to nominate tenants to association developments in consequence, sometimes up to 50 per cent of the lettings.

Housing trusts

A housing trust under section 2 of the HAA 1985 (section 6 of the Housing Act 1985) is a corporation or body of persons which is required by its constitutive instrument to use all its funds, including surpluses arising from its operations, to provide housing accommodation, *or* is required to devote all, or substantially all, its funds to charitable purposes and *in fact* uses all, or substantially all, such funds to provide housing. Such a trust may be a registered charity, and registered also under section 4 of the HAA 1985. Housing trusts may, under section 35, sell or lease to the local authority houses provided by the trust, or make over the management thereof to the authority; this power does not apply to registered housing associations. Section 36 empowers the Secretary of State, where of the opinion that legal proceedings are required with respect to any housing trust property or that any such proceedings be expedited, to certify the case to the Attorney General who may institute, or intervene in, proceedings as he thinks fits. A housing trust which is a charity may grant secure tenancies. Housing trusts may be initiated and partly funded by central government bringing together local authorities with run down estates and sources of private finance so that non-profit-making trusts are set up to take over the estates. In such circumstances some sitting tenants may purchase their homes, while others will be charged fair rents under the Rent Act 1977, see 'Sunday Times' 17 August 1986.

Further reading

Arden, A., and Partington, P., *Housing Law* (Sweet & Maxwell, 1983), Chaps. 1 and 17.
Baker, C.V., *Housing Associations* (Estates Gazettes Ltd, 1976).
Pollard, D., (Ed) *Encyclopedia of Social Welfare Law* (Oyez Longman) paras. B101 to B450.
National Federation of Housing Associations, *Committee Members' Handbook* (1984).
Halstead, P.H., 'To be or not to be (a house), that is the question' [1984] *The Conveyancer* 121.

Chapter 2

The disposal of public sector housing

Introduction

The sale of council houses has been an issue ever since municipalities first began to provide housing. It is no new subject for debate both nationally and locally, and central and local policies have varied greatly from time to time and place to place. It has been the subject of fierce and often bitter controversy in town halls and at Westminster.

Over the years the main planks in the arguments used by both the Conservative and Labour parties for and against the sale of council houses remained fairly constant. The principal difference seems to be that the Labour party was prepared to allow the sale of council houses, provided that such sales were not to the disadvantage of the community, and provided that they did not impair the ability of housing authorities to meet their other obligations, while the Conservatives favoured the idea that local authorities should be under an obligation to give tenants the right to buy. During most of this period of debate the form of the law remained constant, in that local authorities had a *power* to sell their houses subject to ministerial consent. That consent was varied from time to time but the basic law, which was to be found in section 104 of Part V of the Housing Act 1957, remained fundamentally unchanged for many years. What was dramatically new in the debate after 1980 was the new law giving certain persons the *right* to purchase council houses and stating that local authorities should be unable to prevent the exercise of that right. The *power* to sell was transformed into a *duty* to sell, and the *privilege* of being able to purchase was transmuted into a *right*.

Readers seeking the history and development of the law from 1957 to 1980 are referred to the first edition of this work pp. 54 to 60. It is sufficient here to note that the new right to buy (RTB) was extended by the Housing and Building Control Act 1984, now consolidated in the 1985 Act, and the Housing and Planning Act 1986. The sale policy enshrined in law applied to housing associations as well as council housing. RTB was, and is, the right of an individual to acquire a particular dwelling, and considerable numbers of dwellings have accordingly changed hands. Sales of public sector dwellings (including sales under RTB, other sales to tenants and disposals of vacant dwellings, etc.) rose from 55,400 to a peak of 204,600 in 1982–83, and were provisionally stated to be 105,500 for 1985–86 in Cmnd. 7902–II. The millionth dwelling disposed of in the U.K. under the RTB provisions was reported as having changed hands in Scotland, see 'Sunday Times', 7 September 1986. Most of these were disposals by local authorities, though housing associations disposed of 19,000 dwellings in 1982–83, 18,100 in 1984–85 and 9,900 (provisional figures) in 1985–86. The vast majority of sales of local authority dwellings since 1980 have been to sitting tenants, 97,055 in 1981, 196,680 in 1982, 133,820 in 1983 and 98,300 in 1984. Purchases on a shared ownership basis, see further below, were introduced, *as of right* by the 1984 Act, and, though few such sales have yet taken place, overall the 1984 Act did increase the numbers; 550 such purchases were made in 1979, 910 in 1980, 915 in 1981, 885 in 1982, 750 in 1983 and 1,270 in 1984 (source B.S.A. Bulletin No. 45 January 1986). The discounts on such sales (see further below) have also increased as a result of changes in the law. In 1979 the average percentage discount given on the sale of a council dwelling under the old 1957 Act powers was 27 per cent of the value, this rose to 38 per cent in 1980, 41 per cent in 1981, 43 per cent in 1982, hovered around that figure for 1983 and 1984 and began to rise to 46 per cent in 1985 (source B.S.A. Bulletin No. 45). Those purchasing public sector houses with the highest discount entitlements have been able to do so with comparatively small mortgages, and in 1984 the average mortgage in such cases was £15,000.

The pattern of sales, however, under RTB has not been even – unsurprisingly houses have been more popular purchases than flats. The 1984 Greater London Council Survey, 'The implications of council house sales for local authority housing in London', indicated that 94 per cent of sales had been of houses, and that three-quarters of sales had taken place in the outer London Boroughs. There is evidence to suggest that it is the better houses on the more desirable surbaban estates that have in the main been purchases under RTB, leaving local authorities with a stock of less desirable housing types, for example high rise flats, and less favoured housing locations, for example in inner city areas or on socially stigmatised 'hard-to-let' estates. (See further *Roof* November/December 1982, p. 19 and January/February 1984, p. 7). It should not be assumed that for purchasers an automatic housing utopia has followed the exercise of RTB. Sudden changes in financial circumstances, consequent for example on short time working and redundancy, have led to some purchasers being unable to meet their mortgage commitments. (See further *Roof* November/December 1983, p. 23 and 'Sunday Times' 13 January 1985). Owner occupation may be desirable for many people, but there are some who should be seriously counselled not to exercise their technical right to buy. This is especially so where tenants are being allured by the prospect of generous discounts: house purchase is an expensive business involving not just mortgage repayments, but also the payment of rates and maintenance costs.

RTB, and its derivative, the right to shared ownership, however, exist against the wider background of *powers* to dispose of council housing. The future direction of the law is likely to be increasingly towards the privatisation of *areas* of local authority housing or indeed whole estates, paralleling the privatisation of management functions considered below in Chapter 3. In some cases such blocks of housing will be cleared of tenants before sale, but in others they will be sold with their tenants *in situ*, as was the case with the first council estate to be put up for sale, Strinesdale in Oldham sold in 1984, see 'The Times' 12 December 1984. The changes in the law made by the Housing and Planning Act 1986 will greatly facilitate these developments.

The 'right to buy' under the Housing Act 1985 (as amended)

RTB is enshrined in Part V of the 1985 Act, and unless otherwise stated all subsequent references are to the legislation.

Section 118 grants a secure tenant (see Chapter 3 for the definition of 'secure tenant') the right to acquire the freehold of his dwelling where it is a house, and the landlord owns the freehold, or, where his dwelling is a flat, or where the landlord does not own the freehold, to take a long lease of it. Dwelling-houses and flats are defined by section 183 so that:

(a) where a building is divided horizontally the units into which it is divided are *not* houses;

(b) where a building is not structurally detached from its neighbours it is *not* a house if a material part of it lies above or below the remainder of the structure (this covers maisonettes and flats built over municipal shop developments);

(c) where a building is divided vertically the units may be houses so a dwelling in a terrace is a house, provided it is otherwise a structure reasonably so called.

Any dwelling which is not a house must be treated as a flat for sale purposes. Any land used for the purposes of the dwelling may be included in the disposal by agreement between the parties (section 184(2)) and any land let with a dwelling is to be treated as part of the dwelling unless it is agricultural land exceeding two acres (section 184(1)).

This right to buy only arises after the secure tenant has enjoyed the status of a public sector tenant for a period of not less than two years, or for a number of shorter periods amounting together to two years. During that period neither the landlord nor the dwelling-house need have been the same throughout so a secure tenant can build up his entitlement to buy, for example, during a time in which he moves from one secure tenancy with a local authority to another, see section 119 and Schedule 4.

In support of a claim to have complied with the qualification period a tenant may have to make a statutory declaration, particularly where he has moved around the country from one local authority dwelling to another and has no other proof of residence. Such declarations may be accepted as sufficient evidence of the matters contained in them by virtue of section 180.

A period qualifies towards exercise of RTB where the secure tenant, or his spouse (provided they are living together at the relevant time) or a deceased spouse of his (provided they were living together at the time of death) was a public sector tenant, or was the spouse of such a person and occupied the house of which that person was the tenant as his only or principal home. A joint tenant is deemed to fulfil these requirements provided he occupied the dwelling as his only or principal home. Likewise where the public sector tenant of a dwelling has died, or has otherwise ceased to be a public sector tenant of the relevant dwelling, and thereupon a child of his who before occupied the dwelling as his only or principal home becomes the new public sector tenant of the dwelling, a period during which that new tenant, since reaching the age of sixteen, occupied as his only or principal home a dwelling-house of which a parent of his was sole or joint public sector tenant, counts towards qualifying to exercise RTB, *provided* that that period was the portion of time at the end of which the new tenant became the public sector tenant or it was a portion of time ending not *more* than two years before that date. Time spent by the secure tenant or his living or deceased spouse in accommodation provided for the regular armed forces of the Crown also counts towards qualification. Similar provisions apply in respect of any periods during which the tenant enjoyed the Preserved Right to Buy, see further below. The periods may be aggregated together where applicable and necessary. The essential point is that though RTB attaches to the dwelling of which a qualifying person is the tenant, it is those periods spent as a public sector tenant in the circumstances outlined above that qualify him to exercise the right.

For the above purposes a public sector tenant is a tenant of a local authority (e.g. counties, districts and London Boroughs), a new town development corporation, the Development Board for Rural Wales, an urban development corporation, the Housing Corporation, a registered housing association which is not a co-operative housing association.

Section 120 and Schedule 5 lay down certain exceptions where the right to buy does not apply. These are as follows:

1) Where the landlord is a housing trust or is a housing association *and* is a charity.

2) Where the landlord is a co-operative housing association.

3) Where the landlord is a housing association which at no time received public funding under certain specified statutes.

4) Where the landlord does not own the freehold or some other interest sufficient to grant a lease, in the case of a house, for a term exceeding 21 years, or, in the case of a flat, for a term of not less than 50 years.

5) Where the dwelling-house is comprised in a building held by the landlord mainly for non-housing purposes *and* consisting mainly of non-housing accommodation, or is situated in a cemetery, *and* the dwelling was let to the tenant or his predecessor in consequence of his, or that predecessor's, employment by the landlord or the local authority, etc.

6) Where the dwelling has features substantially different from ordinary dwellings, and designed to make it suitable for occupation by physically disabled persons, *and* it has had those features since construction.

7) Where the dwelling has features substantially different from ordinary dwellings designed to make it suitable for occupation by physically disabled persons, *and* it is part of a group which it is the landlord's practice to let for occupation by such persons, *and* social services or special facilities are provided in close proximity to assist those persons.

8) Where the landlord, or its predecessor, has carried out one or more of the following alterations for the purpose of making the dwelling suitable for occupation by physically disabled persons, that is to say –
    (a) the provision of not less than 7.5 square metres of additional floor space,
    (b) the provision of an additional bathroom,
    (c) the installation of a lift.
[In this context it should be noted that in *Freeman v Wansbeck District Council* [1984] 2 All ER 746 the Court of Appeal held that the special features referred to above comprise matters such as ramps instead of

staircases, special doors, cooking surfaces at special heights, etc., and *not* facilities such as additional downstairs lavatories. Thus the special features will be 'designed' to make a dwelling suitable for occupation by a disabled person where, e.g. the building is built with those features, merely to add special features to an ordinary dwelling with the *intention* of having a disabled person reside there is not enough.]

9) Where the dwelling is one of a group of houses which it is the landlord's practice to let for occupation by persons who are suffering, or have suffered, from mental disorder, *and* social services or special facilities, are provided to assist those persons.

10) Where the dwelling is one of a group of houses particularly suitable, having regard to their location, size, design, heating systems and other features for occupation by persons of pensionable age, *and* which it is the landlord's practice to let for occupation by such persons, or for occupation by such persons *and* physically disabled persons, *and* special facilities consisting of, or including, warden alarm and common room facilities are provided for such persons in close proximity.

11) Previously the Secretary of State could determine on the application of the landlord that RTB was not capable of being exercised in relation to the dwelling, which the Secretary of State could only do where satisfied that the dwelling was particularly suitable for occupation by persons of pensionable age having regard to its location and to its size, heating system and other features, *and* that the dwelling was let to the tenant or his predecessor in title for occupation by a person of pensionable age or a physically disabled person. [*See Addendum 3.*]

12) Where the dwelling is held by the landlord on a Crown tenancy, subject to certain exceptions.

Neither can the right to buy be exercised where either:

1) the tenant is, or will be, obliged to give up possession of the house in pursuance of a court order, or

2) where a bankruptcy petition is pending against the person to whom the right to buy belongs, or where he has a receiving order in force against him, or where he is an undischarged bankrupt, or has made a composition with his creditors, see section 121. Where a possession order in respect of a council house or flat is obtained by the landlord *after* the tenant has served notice claiming to exercise RTB, the tenant is precluded from continuing with the purchase, because exercising RTB is a continuing process until the sale is completed, and so the tenant can be prevented from exercising the right at any time before completion if

any of the circumstances mentioned above occur, see *Enfield London Borough Council v McKeon* [1986] 2 All ER 730, [1986] 1 WLR 1007.

Where a secure tenancy is a joint tenancy section 118(2) states that the right to buy belongs to all the joint tenants or to such of them as they may agree between them (provided at least one of them occupies the house as his only or principal home). In any case a secure tenant may, under section 123, join up to three members of his family in the right to buy even if they are not joint tenants with him provided those members of the family joined in the right to buy, occupy the dwelling as their only or principal home , and are either:

1) the tenant's spouse, or

2) have been residing with the tenant throughout the period of twelve months preceding the notice claiming the right to buy, or

3) the landlord consents.

The claim to join members of a family in the purchase must be made in the notice claiming to exercise the right to buy.

By virtue of section 186 a person is a member of a tenant's family if he is his spouse, parent, grandparent, child, grandchild, brother, sister, uncle, aunt, nephew or niece: relationships by marriage count as relationships by blood; half-blood counts as whole blood, and step-children count as ordinary children, with illegitimate children being treated as legitimate, and also treating persons living together as man and wife as being members of a family.

The price to be paid for the house or flat

By section 126(1)(a) the price to be paid is the 'value at the relevant time' which is the price, under section 127, the dwelling would fetch on the open market at that time, that is the date, under section 122(2), on which the tenant's notice claiming to exercise the right to buy was served, on a willing vendor basis but subject to certain assumptions:

1) the vendor was selling for an estate in fee simple, or was granting a lease, for the appropriate term defined in Schedule 6 paragraph 12, *generally* 125 years, at a ground rent of not more than £10 per annum, *with vacant possession* (i.e. the existence of a sitting tenant is not to depress the value of the house);

2) neither the tenant nor a member of his family residing with him wished to acquire the property (i.e. the desire of the tenant to buy is not to increase the price in any way);

3) any improvements made by the tenant or his predecessors in title, or by a member of his family who immediately before the present secure tenancy was granted was the secure tenant of the dwelling together with any failure by them to keep the property in good internal repair are to be disregarded;

4) that the conveyance, or grant of the lease as the case may be, is on the terms laid down in Part V of the Housing Act 1985.

But this price must be discounted according to section 126(1)(b). Modifications to discounts will be made under section 2 of the Housing and Planning Act 1986. The discount is, under section 129, in the case of a house, will be 32 per cent plus one per cent for each complete year by which the qualifying period of entitlement exceeds two years up to a maximum of 60 per cent, and, in the case of a flat, 44 per cent plus two per cent for each complete year by which the qualifying period exceeds two years, up to a maximum of 70 per cent. Under section 129(2A) the Secretary of State may provide by order for the maximum and minimum discounts and the amount of percentage increase per annum to be *increased*, and, under section 129(2B) such orders may make different provision with respect to different cases or types of case. The qualifying period for discount entitlement is calculated, as is the period for determining qualification to exercise RTB, by reference to Schedule 4 (see above). Thus, briefly, discount entitlement is built up where the secure tenant, or his spouse (provided they are living together at the relevant time, see section 122(2) supra), or a deceased spouse of his (provided they were living together at the time of death was a public sector tenant (see above)) or was the spouse of a public sector tenant and occupied as his only or principal home the dwelling of the spouse was such a tenant. A person who, as a joint tenant under a public sector tenancy, occupied a dwelling house as his only principal home, is treated as having been the public sector tenant under that tenancy. Likewise entitlement will be built up by the child of a public sector tenant of a dwelling where that tenant has died or otherwise ceased to be such a tenant, and thereupon the child, having occupied the dwelling as his only or principal home becomes the new public sector tenant. A period during which that new tenant, since reaching the age of sixteen, occupied as his only or principal home a dwelling house of which a parent of his was the public sector tenant, provided that period was the period at the end of which the child became the new public sector tenant *or* it was an earlier period ending *two years or less* before that period, is to be treated as a period during which the child was a public sector tenant.

The housing legislation since 1980 has been retrospective in so far that time spent, for example, as a local authority or housing association etc., tenant before 1980 counts towards discount entitlement and qualifying to exercise RTB. The discount entitlements apply to both full purchases and shared ownership transactions, see below.

Where two joint tenants exercise the right to buy, Schedule 4 is to be so applied so that for the secure tenant is substituted that one of the joint tenants whose discount entitlement is greatest.

These somewhat complex rules are best explained by some examples:

1) Bill is a secure tenant of 20 years' standing – he is presumptively entitled to a 50 per cent discount irrespective, for example, of whether he has moved from one municipal house to another, or has made moves between local authorities.

2) Ben has been a secure tenant for five years since he married his wife Ada who was the widow of Charles who had been, until the time of his death, a secure tenant for ten years. The period for discount purposes is fifteen years, if Ada lived in the house as her only or principal home with Charles for the ten years.

3) Dick has been a secure tenant for five years and is married to Ethel who was the widow of Frank who before his death had been a secure tenant for ten years. However, before Dick served his notice wishing to buy his dwelling Ethel left him. The discount is only five years.

4) Gus has been a secure tenant for five years, and is now married to Helen who at one time was married to Ivan, also a secure tenant, but whom Helen divorced after five years of marriage during which time they had never lived together. The discount period is only five years.

5) Jack is a secure tenant of eighteen years' standing. He has just married Kay who, before their marriage, was a secure tenant herself of twenty years' standing. After their marriage the local authority granted them a joint tenancy of a house into which they moved from their previous homes. Jack and Kay now wish to buy their house, the discount period will be calculated by reference to Kay and will be 20 years.

There is to be deducted, under section 130, from the discount an amount equal to any previous discount qualifying because it was given before the relevant time on a conveyance or lease by a public sector landlord, or on a shared ownership transaction, *and* was given to the person, or one of the persons exercising RTB, *or* to the spouse of that person (provided they are living together at the relevant time) or to a deceased spouse of that person (provided they were living together at the time of death). Furthermore, under section 131, except where the Secretary of State so determines, the amount of discount may not reduce the purchase price below the amount which, in accordance with his determination, represents so much of the costs incurred in respect of the dwelling after 31 March 1974, and if the price before discount is below that amount there can be no discount. In any case discount may not reduce the price by more than such a sum as is prescribed by the Secretary of State. The current limit is £25,000, see S.I. 1980/1342. Where the price of a dwelling is discounted section 155 requires that the purchaser shall covenant to repay on demand to the landlord a specified amount of the discount, if within a period of three years he further conveys, or leases, or assigns as the case may be, the dwelling he has acquired. The amount of discount repayable under this covenant is the discount reduced by one-third for each complete year elapsing after the date of transfer to the purchaser. [*See Addendum 4.*]

Liability to repay arises in respect of 'relevant disposals' as outlined above, see further section 159 and later material on restrictions on the resale of dwellings in rural areas. However, liability to repay does not arise if the disposal is 'exempted' under section 160. This will be considered in greater detail below, but it should be noted that it exempts disposals under wills and intestacies, under the terms of the family provision and inheritance legislation, certain disposals within families and disposals of dwelling houses under section 24 of the Matrimonial Causes Act 1973, that is property adjustment orders in connection with matrimonial proceedings. This was considered in *R v Rushmoor Borough Council, ex p Barrett* (1986) Times, 5 September. Here a married couple had purchased their council house at a discount, and the conveyance to them required the repayment of discount should they dispose of the property within the period specified by law. Just over one year later the marriage was dissolved and within three months the court made an order requiring the home to be sold and the proceeds divided equally. This order was made under *section 24A* of the 1973 Act. It was held that an 'exempted disposal' under section 24 of the 1973 Act is not one where a dwelling is sold and the proceeds divided, but rather is one, for example, where a house is transferred between former spouses so that one of the parties to the former marriage continues to live in the house after the transfer, gaining no liquid cash advantage thereby. Accordingly the sale of the house in the present case was *not* an exempted disposal and there was liability to repay the discount.

Exercising the right to buy

The procedure for initiating the process of transfer is contained in section 122(1). The tenant must serve on the landlord a written notice claiming to exercise the right to buy. If this notice is not withdrawn the landlord must, under section 124, serve a written counter notice *generally* within four weeks which either admits the tenant's right, or denies it, stating the reasons why, in the landlord's opinion, it does not exist. Disputes as to the tenant's right to buy are to be determined by the county court, see section 181. Once the right to buy has been established the landlord must serve, under section 125, within eight weeks where the right is to acquire the freehold, or within twelve weeks where it is to acquire a leasehold interest, a further notice on the tenant. This will describe the dwelling-house and state:

1) the price at which, in the landlord's opinion, the tenant is entitled to take the freehold/leasehold as the case may be, and, in order to show how the price has been arrived at, shall further state the value of the dwelling at the relevant time, any improvements disregarded under section 127 in determining value;

2) the appropriate discount, stating further the discount period taken into account under section 129;

3) the provisions which the landlord concludes should be included in the conveyance/lease; [and, under section 4 of the Housing and Planning Act 1986];

4) where the notice states provisions which would enable the landlord to recover service charges or improvement contributions, that notice must also contain the estimates and other information required by sections 125A (service charges) and 125B (improvement contributions); and

5) a description of any structural defect known to the landlord affecting the dwelling or the building in which it is situated. [Schedule 5 of the 1986 Act.]

Under section 125A as inserted in 1986 the landlord's section 125 notice must state as regards service charges the landlord's estimate of the average annual amount (at current prices) which would be payable in respect of each head of charge in the 'reference period' and the aggregate of those estimated amounts, and shall also contain a statement of the reference period adopted for estimate purposes. For the purposes of sections 125A and 125B (see below) the 'reference period' is effectively a period of five years beginning on date specified reasonably by the landlord as a date by which the conveyance/lease etc. will be completed, such date not to be more than six months after the section 125 notice is given. With regard to *flats* certain charges must be separately itemised under section 125A(2), which provides that the notice must, as regards service charges in respect of repairs (including works to make good structural defects) contain:

(i)   in respect of works itemised in the notice, estimates of the amount (at current prices) of the likely cost of, and of the tenant's likely contribution in respect of, each item, and the aggregates of those costs and contributions;

(ii) for non-itemised works, an estimate of the average annual cost (at current prices) which the landlord considers it likely to be payable by the tenant;

(iii) a statement of the reference period adopted for the purpose of the estimates;

(iv) a statement of the effect of paragraph 16B of Schedule 6 (see below) and

(v) a statement of the effect of section 450A (see below).

Paragraph 16B of Schedule 6 provides that where the lease of a flat requires the tenant to pay service charges in respect of repairs (including works to make good structural defects) his liability to pay in respect of costs incurred in the 'initial period' (see later) is restricted, so that he is not required to pay in respect of works itemised in the estimates contained in the section 125 notice any more than the amount shown as his estimated contribution in respect of that item, together with an allowance for inflation. In respect of works not itemised he is not required to pay at a rate exceeding:

(a) as regards parts of the 'initial period' falling within the reference period (see above) for estimates contained in the section 125 notice the estimated average amount shown in the estimates;

(b) as regards parts of the initial period falling outside the reference period, the average rate produced by averaging over the reference period all works for which estimates are contained in the notice, together with, in each case, an allowance for inflation. Such inflation allowances are to be calculated according to methods prescribed by the Secretary of State under paragraph 16D of Schedule 6. The 'initial period' of a lease is effectively five years from the date of its grant.

Section 450A will provide that the Secretary of State may provide by regulations that where the lease of a flat has been granted in pursuance of RTB and the landlord is the *housing authority (which includes housing associations within section 80) who granted the lease, or another housing authority*, the tenant shall have the 'right to a loan', to be charged on the security of the flat, see section 450C, in respect of certain service charges. These are charges in respect of repairs (including works for making good structural defects) payable in the period beginning with the grant of the lease, and ending, generally, with its tenth anniversary. The right may be specified by the regulations only to arise in respect of specified amounts of a service charge. Where the landlord *is a housing association* the right is to a loan from the Housing Corporation. In any other case it is a right to leave the whole or part of the service charge outstanding. [Section 450B creates a *power* to grant loans etc. in circumstances falling outside the right to a loan.]

'Service charges' are defined by section 621A to be amounts payable by purchasers or lessees of premises which are payable directly or indirectly for services, repairs, maintenance or insurance or the vendor/lessor's costs of management, and which vary in whole or part according to 'relevant costs'. These latter are the costs or estimated costs incurred, or to be incurred, in connection with the matters for which the charge is payable, including overheads.

Under section 125B the landlord's notice in respect of a flat will also, as respects 'improvement contributions', contain a statement of the effect of paragraph 16C of Schedule 6 (see below) and estimates in regard of works in respect of which the landlord considers that costs may be incurred in the reference period (see above). The works in question must be itemised, and the estimates must show the amount (at current prices) of the likely cost of, and the tenant's likely contribution in respect of, each item, and the aggregate of these costs and contributions. In this connection section 187 (as amended) provides inter alia that improvement means in relation to a dwelling any alteration in or addition to the dwelling, including additions or alterations to the landlord's fixtures and fittings or to ancillary services, the erection of wireless or television aerials and carrying out external decoration. 'Improvement contribution' means a sum payable by a tenant of a flat in respect of improvements carried out to the flat, the building in which it is situated, or any other building or land, other than works carried out in discharge of obligations under paragraph 16A of Schedule 6 (see below) to repair or reinstate property etc.

Paragraph 16C of Schedule 6 provides that where the tenant of a flat is required to pay such contributions, his liability in respect of costs incurred in the initial period (see above) of the lease is restricted so that he is not required to make any payment in respect of works for which no estimate was given in the landlord's section 125 notice, and he is not to pay in respect of works for which an estimate was given in that notice any more than the amount of his estimated contribution in respect of that item with an allowance for inflation (see above).

The section 125 notice must further inform the tenant of his right to a mortgage (see below); about the effect of a landlord's notice to complete, failure to comply therewith and the right to defer completion; about the right to a shared ownership lease, and the right under section 128 to have the value of the dwelling determined by the district valuer. He must follow the procedure laid down in section 128 and serve written notice within three months of having received the section 125 notice, requiring the district valuer to determine the value of the property at the 'relevant time', that is the date on which notice claiming to exercise RTB was served. The three month period is extended if there are proceedings pending on the determination of any other question arising under Part V of the 1985 Act. In such a case the notice may be served at any time within three months of the final determination of those proceedings. Where such proceedings are begun *after* a determination made by the district valuer, a redetermination may be required under section 128(3) of the Act by either of the parties within four weeks of the conclusion of the proceedings. The district valuer must consider any representations made to him by either the landlord or the tenant within four weeks from the service of a notice under section 128. It is the duty of the local authority under section 128(5) to inform the tenant of the outcome of any determination or redetermination made by the district valuer. The jurisdiction of the district valuer in such valuations is exclusive.

Completing the transfer

Once all the above steps have been taken, the matters relating to the transfer and the arrangements as to mortgage finance, etc., have been completed, section 138(1) binds the landlord to convey or lease, as the case may be, the dwelling to the tenant. On completion the secure tenancy comes to an end; section 139(2). The landlord is not bound to complete while the tenant is found to be in arrears with his rent or other tenancy outgoings for a period of four weeks after the money due has been lawfully demanded from him (section 138(2)). This provision prevents tenants who are in arrears from proceeding with the purchase of their homes. If there are no impediments to the transfer the landlord must go ahead with it, and the duty is enforceable by way of an injunction (section 138(3)).

The actual transfer to the purchaser takes place according to the registered conveyancing procedure under section 123 of the Land Registration Act 1925. This is so, by virtue of section 154, whether or not the dwelling is in an area subject to registered conveyancing. In those cases where the dwelling is not within a registered conveyancing area, the selling landlord must certify their right to sell.

The right to a mortgage

The 'right to a mortgage' is guaranteed by section 132. This phrase, however, is somewhat misleading. It means that the purchasing tenant has the right to leave the whole or part of a sum fixed in accordance with section 133 outstanding on the security of the dwelling. Some purchasers will look to the building societies for mortgage assistance. For those who are not able to rely on building society assistance the 'right to a mortgage' is an essential part of the 'right to buy'. Those sales taking place in reliance on this right will involve little or no capital changing hands at the time of sale for the purchaser will leave the price outstanding secured on the dwelling and will pay it off, with interest, over a period of years.

The amount to be left outstanding

Section 133(1) states that the amount which a secure tenant exercising the right to a mortgage is entitled to leave outstanding on the security of the dwelling is the aggregate of:

1) the purchase price

2) the costs chargeable under section 178(2), i.e. those incurred by the landlord, or the Housing Corporation as the case may be, in connection with the tenant's exercise of the right, subject to such limit as may be specified by the Secretary of State, see S.I. 1984/1174.

3) any costs incurred by the tenant and defrayed on his behalf by the landlord.

[Where the landlord is a housing association the right is to have the aggregate sum advanced by the Housing Corporation on the security of the dwelling.] This aggregate sum is subject, under section 133(2) to a limit; namely that it does not exceed the sum produced by multiplying the amount to be taken into account as the tenant's available annual income by a certain factor. Under section 133(3) the Secretary of State is empowered to make regulations to make provision for calculating in any given case what figure should be taken into account as a tenant's available annual income, and also to specify a multiplying factor appropriate to that amount in order to arrive at the limit for the given individual. The regulations may provide for a person's available annual income to be calculated on the basis that sums related to his needs and commitments are to be excluded from the calculation. They may also specify different amounts and factors in different circumstances. See S.I. 1980/1423. Where the right to a mortgage belongs to more than one person section 133(2)(b) states that the limit is the aggregate of the amounts for each of them produced by taking their individual available annual incomes and multiplying them by the appropriate multiplyer. Where the appropriate limit in any given case is *less* the aggregate otherwise produced under section 133(1), section 133(4) empowers the landlord, if they think fit, and if the tenant agrees, to allow the tenant to leave all or part of the difference between the limit and aggregate outstanding on the security of the dwelling.

Exercising the right to a mortgage

By section 134 the right to a mortgage must be exercised by serving written notice on the landlord not later than three months after the tenant has himself been served with notice under either section 125 or section 128, whichever is appropriate (see above). (Though this period may be extended under section 134(2) and (3).) As soon as practicable after the service of the tenant's notice claiming mortgage entitlement the landlord must serve, under section 135, a written counter notice which contains:

1) the amount which, in their opinion, the tenant is entitled to leave outstanding;

2) a statement of how that amount has been arrived at;

3) the provisions which they consider should be contained in the mortgage deed.

The notice must be accompanied by a form for the tenant to use should he be entitled to defer completion, and wish to do so, under section 142 (see further below), and, where the tenant is not entitled to a full mortgage, a statement of the provisions governing shared ownership transactions, and there must be an accompanying form for the tenant to use if he wishes to avail himself of that right. [See further below.] Where the landlord is a housing association these requirements are to be undertaken by the Housing Corporation.

Under section 138 where a secure tenant has claimed to exercise the right to buy and that right has been established, the landlord is bound to complete the conveyance or lease, as the case may be, subject to, inter alia, agreement on those matters connected with the right to a mortgage.

Under section 140 the landlord may at any time serve written notice on the tenant requiring him, if all relevant matters concerning the grant and finance have been agreed or determined, to complete the transaction within a specified reasonable period of at least 56 days, *or*, if any relevant matter is outstanding, to serve on the landlord a written notice specifying the matter to be settled. This is the 'first notice to complete' and it must inform the tenant of the effect of the notice, and of the landlord's power to serve a 'second notice to complete'. Such a 'first notice' may not be served earlier than whichever of the following is applicable:

1) where there has been no claim to a mortgage, nine months after the end of the period in which notice claiming to exercise that right could have been served;

2) where that right has been claimed, but there is no entitlement to defer, nine months after the service of notice under section 135;

3) where there is an entitlement to defer (see below), three years after

the service of the section 122 notice claiming to exercise RTB, or nine months after the service of notice under section 135 if that is later.

Notice may not be served where requirements as to valuation of the dwelling by the district valuer have not been complied with, or where relevant matters have not been settled or disposed of. In this connection a tenant is entitled to defer completion under section 142 where he has claimed the right to a mortgage, but is not entitled to a full mortgage, and has, within three months beginning with service on him of the section 135 notice, served notice on the landlord claiming to be entitled to defer completion, and has, within that same period, deposited the sum of £150 with the landlord. A tenant who is entitled to defer completion may, at any time before a first notice to complete is served on him, serve a further section 134(1) notice claiming to exercise the right to a mortgage. Deferring purchase fixes the price at which the tenant can buy, while allowing the tenant time to find the purchase money, or to hope for an improvement in his circumstances justifying higher mortgage entitlement. Where the £150 deposit is made this counts towards the purchase price on final completion.

Under section 141 where the tenant does not comply with the first notice to complete, the landlord may serve a second notice requiring him to complete within a specified reasonable period of at least 56 days, and informing him of the effect of the notice. Where the tenant fails to comply the notice claiming to exercise RTB is deemed withdrawn at the end of the specified period.

The terms of the mortgage

Where a tenant claims to exercise the right to a mortgage the mortgage deed, unless the parties agree otherwise, must, under section 139(3) and Schedule 7.

1) provide for the repayment of the amount secured in equal instalments of principal and interest combined; and

2) provide that the period over which repayment is to be made shall be 25 years (at the option of the mortgagor it can be a shorter period) but this period is capable of being extended by the mortgagee.

Other terms may be included by agreement, or on the order of the Secretary of State. For rates of interest see below.

Miscellaneous points

Where a former secure tenant has given notice claiming to exercise the right to buy and he is superseded by a new secure tenant under the same secure tenancy (otherwise than on an assignment made as an exchange under section 92), or under a periodic tenancy arising after the end of such a tenancy under section 86, the new tenant is in the same position *as if the notice had been given by him*, see section 136. The new tenant will have the right to a mortgage, and, even if notice of the purchase price and terms of the sale has already been served on the former tenant, another form to enable him to claim a mortgage must be supplied, following which he will have three months in which to claim the mortgage. For the purposes of entitlement to exercise the right to buy and also discount entitlement it is the new tenant's circumstances that must be considered.

On the other hand where there is a change of landlord, by transfer of the freehold, after the service of notice claiming to exercise the right to buy, section 137(1) lays down that all parties shall be in the same position as if the acquiring landlord had been landlord before the notice was given and had taken all steps which the former landlord had taken. However, if any of the circumstances after the change differ in any material respect, as where, for example, an exception to RTB becomes applicable, then section 137(2) requires that all concerned must, as soon as possible, take such steps as are necessary for securing that the parties are, *as nearly as may be*, in the same position that they would have been in had those circumstances previously obtained. [*See Addendum 5.*]

A tenant who has claimed to exercise the right to buy may, in general, withdraw it by serving written notice at any time on his landlord (section 5(1)).

A tenant who exercises the right to buy, but *not* the right to a mortgage, cannot be obliged to bear any part of his landlord's costs in connection with the sale, and any agreement to that effect is void (section 178).

The terms of the freehold sale or long lease

Section 139(1) and Schedule 6 contain the terms on which the transfer of dwellings takes place. Most reflect common conveyancing practice, but some are deserving of comment.

Leasehold terms: Schedule 6, Parts I and III

1) The lease must be, *in general*, for a term of not less than 125 years at a ground rent of not more than £10 per annum. But if in a building containing two or more dwellings, for example a block of flats, one has already been sold on a 125 year lease since August 8 1980, any subsequent long lease granted under the right to buy provisions may be made

for a term of less than 125 years so as to expire at the same time as the initial 125 year term.

2) Following the transfer the purchaser will continue to enjoy the common use of any premises, facilities or services enjoyed previously as a secure tenant unless both parties agree otherwise. This ensures not only that the purchaser will retain the use of and access to the common parts of any buildings in which his flat is situated, but also that he will continue to be able to receive the benefit of any services and facilities previously enjoyed in his capacity as a tenant along with other tenants.

3) The landlord is made subject to quite onerous repairing covenants:
   (a) to keep in repair the structure and exterior of the dwelling, and also of the building in which it is situated (including drains, gutters and external pipes) and to make good any defect affecting that structure; 'structure' can include roofing tiles and external wall rendering, see *Granada Theatres Ltd v Freehold Investments (Leytonstone) Ltd* [1959] Ch 592, [1959] 2 All ER 176;
   (b) to keep in repair any other property over or in respect of which the tenant has any rights by virtue of Schedule 6, for example any common parts which the purchaser has the right to use;
   (c) to ensure, so far as practicable, that any services which are to be provided by the landlord and to which the purchaser is entitled (either alone or in common with others) are maintained at a reasonable level, and also to keep in repair any installation connected with the provision of such services;
   (d) to rebuild or reinstate the dwelling and the building in which it is situated in the case of destruction or damage by fire, tempest, flood or any other normally insurable risk.

It will be seen that these covenants go far beyond those implied in short lettings under the Landlord and Tenant Act 1985 (see Chapter 7). But the landlord's liability will not be absolute. They will not be liable for any breach of covenant unless they are given notice of the defect, and the standard of repair required will depend on the age, character and locality of the dwelling, see *Lurcott v Wakely* [1911] 1 KB 905.

Mention has been made above of the requirements of paragraphs 16B and 16C of Schedule 6, but it should be noted that under paragraph 16A a lease may require a tenant to bear a reasonable part of the landlord's costs in discharging, or insuring against, the obligations to repair, make good structural defects and also to provide services mentioned above, or in insuring against the obligation to rebuild or reinstate. Where the lease requires a tenant to contribute towards insurance, the tenant is entitled to inspect the policy at reasonable times. Where the landlord does not insure against the obligations imposed by the covenant to rebuild or reinstate, the lease may require the tenant to pay a reasonable sum in place of the contribution he could be required to make if there were insurance. Paragraph 16A has effect subject to 16B which, as we have seen, limits certain costs payable by a tenant during the initial period of his lease.

Paragraph 18 of Schedule 6, as substituted, will make it clear that a provision in a lease, or an agreement collateral thereto, is void in so far as it purports either to authorise the recovery of contributions in respect of those repairs, etc., mentioned in paragraph 16A otherwise than in accordance with paragraphs 16A and 16B, or to authorise the recovery of any charge in respect of the landlord's costs incurred in discharging the obligation to rebuild or reinstate, or the recovery of an improvement contribution otherwise than as allowed by paragraph 16C.

Schedule 6 also makes void any term of the lease purporting to prohibit or restrict assigning or subletting the dwelling. To make sure that the bargain is not entirely one-sided the schedule imposes an obligation on the tenant, unless the parties agree otherwise, to keep the interior of the dwelling in good repair, including good decorative repair. Even so the purchasers of municipal flats buy on very favourable terms as can easily be seen.

Those who purchase long leasehold interests in flats may also rely on the provisions of sections 18 to 30 of the Landlord and Tenant Act 1985. In most cases such purchases will arise out of the 'right to buy'. The provisions only apply to 'flats', that is separate sets of premises, constructed *or* adapted (*and* occupied) as private dwellings, *and* forming part of buildings, *and* divided horizontally from other parts of such buildings. There may be two or more such flats on one floor of a building. See section 30 of the Landlord and Tenant Act (LTA) 1985.

A 'service charge' is an amount payable by a tenant of a flat, as part of or in addition to the rent, in respect of services, repairs, maintenance or insurance or the landlord's costs of management and which amount varies or may vary according to the costs or estimated costs incurred or to be incurred in any period by the landlord in providing the service. These costs are known as 'the relevant costs' and include overheads. See section 18 of the Landlord and Tenant Act 1985.

Section 19 of that Act controls the extent to which costs can be recovered as service charges by a test of reasonableness. The tenant will only have to pay where costs can be shown to have been reasonably incurred and where they are for services or works only if the services or works themselves are of reasonable standard.

Section 20 of the LTA 1985 places a limit on costs incurred in carrying out works on buildings which can be recovered without getting estimates. This amount is £25 multiplied by the number of flats in the building or £500 whichever is the greater. The Secretary of State may specify other figures. Any costs incurred in excess of this amount cannot be regarded as relevant costs unless these requirements are satisfied:

1) At least two estimates for the work must be obtained, one from a person wholly unconnected with the landlord;

2) A notice with copies of the estimates must be forwarded to the tenant concerned or displayed in the building and, if one exists, forwarded to the relevant tenants' association. The notice must describe works to be carried out and invite observations by a date not earlier than one month after the date of service or display of the notice;

3) The landlord must consider observations received and must not commence works before the date specified in the notice unless required urgently.

In proceedings relating to a service charge, the county court, if satisfied that the landlord acted reasonably, may dispense with all or any of the requirements set out above.

The landlord must supply, on written request by a tenant or secretary of a relevant tenants' association, a written summary of costs incurred and from which service charges are determined. This information must be provided, under section 21(4) of the LTA 1985 within six months of the end of the previous accounting period or within one month of the request whichever is the later. Where a building has more than four flats or where the costs relate also to other buildings, the summary must be signed by a qualified accountant to the effect that it is a fair summary supported by appropriate documentation. For accountancy qualifications see section 28 of the LTA 1985. The landlord must if requested allow a tenant or appropriate secretary facilities to conduct his own inspection of the particulars upon which the summary is based.

Any question as to whether costs have been reasonably incurred or whether services or works are of a reasonable standard may only be determined by a county court or by arbitration agreement under section 32 of the Arbitration Act 1950. Any agreement purporting to allow for other determinations is void, see section 19(3) LTA 1985. Similar provisions apply to service charges on houses under sections 46 to 51 of the Housing Act 1985. [*See Addendum 6.*]

Terms common to freehold and leasehold sales

Schedule 6, paragraph 2(1) provides, inter alia, that as regards any rights to support or access of light and air, the passage of water, or sewage or of gas or other piped fuel, smoke and fumes, to the use or maintenance of pipes or other installations for such passage, or to the use or maintenance of cables or other installations for the supply of electricity, the disposal to the purchaser is subject to certain conditions. These are that the purchaser will acquire rights of usage and maintenance equivalent to those enjoyed under the secure tenancy or under any collateral agreement or arrangement on the severance of the dwelling from other property then comprised in the same tenancy, and second that the dwelling will remain subject to all such rights for the benefit of other property *as are capable of existing in law* and are necessary to secure to the person interested in the other property as nearly as may be the same rights against the purchaser as were available when he was a secure tenant, or under any collateral agreement or arrangement made on severance. This provision must be read along with paragraph 9 of Schedule 6 (freehold sales only) which states that the conveyance to the purchasing tenant may be subjected to burdens 'in respect of the upkeep or regulation for the benefit of any locality of any land, building, structure, works, ways or water course'.

Restrictions on resale

One of the chief fears of those who have opposed the indiscriminate sale of council houses has been that the most attractive houses only will be purchased leaving local authorities with the less desirable homes. This argument has been also heard in relation to *areas* of houses. It has been argued that there is a danger that houses in rural areas may be purchased by their tenants and then sold to wealthy city dwellers looking for second or holiday homes, thus further eroding the already limited stock of dwellings available to people living and working in rural areas. Section 157 goes some way towards allaying such fears by placing restrictions on the resale of certain public sector houses.

Where a transfer is made by, inter alia, a district council, a London Borough council, a county council or a housing association, of a dwelling situated in a National Park, an area designated under section 87 of the National Parks and Access to the Countryside Act 1949 (area of outstanding natural beauty) or an area designated by order of the Secretary of State as a rural area, [see S.I. 1980/1375, 1981/397, 940, 1982/21, 187] covenants may be imposed limiting the freedom of the purchaser and his successors in title to dispose of the dwelling.

The limitation is that until such time as is notified by the landlord to the tenant, there may be no 'relevant disposal' which is not an 'exempted disposal' without the landlord's written consent, though such consent may not be withheld if the disposal is to a person who has throughout the period of three years immediately preceding the application for consent had his place of work in a region designated by order of the Secretary of State which is wholly or partly comprised in the National Park or area, *or* has had his only or principal home in such a region *or* has had the one in part or parts of that period and the other in the remainder, though the region need not have been the same throughout the period. This enables rural workers and dwellers to move from one designated region to another over a short period and yet retain the ability to purchase houses otherwise subject to resale restrictions. A 'relevant disposal' is, under section 159, a conveyance of the freehold or assignment of the lease, or the grant of lease for more than 21 years, otherwise than at a rack rent. An 'exempted disposal' is under section 160:

1) a disposal of the whole of the dwelling and a further conveyance or assignment to a 'qualifying person', i.e. a person, or one of the persons, by whom the disposal is made, or the spouse or former spouse of that person, or one of those persons, or a member of the family of that person(s) who has resided with him throughout the period of twelve months ending with the disposal; or

2) a vesting of the whole dwelling under a will or on an intestacy; or

3) a disposal under section 24 of the Matrimonial Causes Act 1973 or section 2 of the Inheritance (Provision for Family and Dependants) Act 1975;

4) a compulsory disposal, as under a compulsory purchase order;

5) a disposal of property consisting of land let with or used for the purposes of the dwelling house.

Disposals in breach of covenant are void.

With the consent of the Secretary of State or the Housing Corporation where the landlord is a housing association the covenant may be that until the end of the period of ten years beginning with the initial disposal there will be no further sale or long lease, etc. other than an exempted disposal, unless:

    (a) the tenant or his successor in title first offers to re-transfer the dwelling to the original landlord, and

    (b) they refuse the offer or fail to accept it within one month of its being made.

The purchase price to be paid in such cases will be, under section 158, the price agreed between the parties or determined by the district valuer, reduced to take account of any liability to repay discount.

The powers of the Secretary of State

The sale of public sector houses to their sitting tenants is a fundamental plank of government housing policy. The government has shown its determination to pursue that policy by granting in sections 164 to 170 most extensive powers of intervention to the Secretary of State in cases where landlords individually or collectively, attempt to resist or hinder the sales policy.

Where it appears to the Secretary of State, presumably on reasonable evidence, that a tenant or tenants of a particular landlord or of a description of landlords are finding it difficult to exercise the right to buy effectively and expeditiously, he may, by giving written notice of his intention to do so, intervene in the given situation, under section 164. Once such notice is in force, and it is deemed to be given 72 hours after it has been sent, he may do *all* such things as appear to him necessary or expedient to enable the exercise of the right to buy and the right to a mortgage. The Secretary of State's notice has the effect of preventing further action by a vending landlord with regard to the right to buy, and nullifies any previous action they may have taken. The rights and obligations of the landlord are vested in the Secretary of State though he is not bound to follow the exact sales procedure required of a landlord in the exercise of RTB. See on this provision *R v Secretary of State, ex p Norwich City Council* [1982] QB 808, [1982] 1 All ER 737.

For the purpose of making a transfer of a dwelling, section 165 empowers the Secretary of State to make a Vesting Order which has the effect of:

1) vesting the property in question in the tenant on the appropriate tenurial basis; and

2) binding the landlord and the tenant and their successors in title by the covenants it contains.

A vesting order, on presentation to the Chief Land Registrar, requires the registration of the tenant as proprietor of the title concerned.

Under section 166 where the Secretary of State receives money due to a landlord in consequence of using his powers, he may retain it, while the section 164 notice is in force, and the interest thereon. He may furthermore recover his costs, with interest, as a debt from a landlord against whom he is exercising his powers, and may do this by withholding any sums due from him to the landlord. Section 167 gives the Secretary of State power to direct landlords not to include certain covenants in conveyances or grants of dwellings where it appears to him the inclusion of such covenants would lead to inconformity with the requirements of Schedule 6. Such a direction can have a retrospective effect under section 168, discharging or modifying existing covenants included in conveyances etc. executed before the section 167 direction to such extent or in such manner as the notice provides. Section 169 grants the Secretary of State extensive powers to obtain documents, copies of documents and other information where that appears necessary or expedient for the purpose of determining whether his powers under sections 164, 166, 167 or 168 are exercisable, or for, or in connection with, exercising those powers. This power is exercised by written notice to the landlord. Any officer of the landlord designated in the notice or having custody of documents or possessing information must, without instructions from the landlord, take all reasonable steps to ensure that the notice is complied with. Finally section 170 gives the Secretary of State powers to grant assistance to a party to proceedings in connection with RTB, other than valuation proceedings, who applies to him for assistance. Assistance may be granted on grounds that the case raises an issue of principle, or that it is unreasonable, having regard to the complexity of the issues, to expect the applicant to deal with the matter unaided. The assistance may take the form of giving advice, or procuring, or attempting to procure, a settlement, arranging for legal advice and/or representation, or any other form of aid considered appropriate.

Shared ownership sales

Where a secure tenant has claimed to exercise RTB and the right has been established, and his notice of claim remains in force, and he has claimed the right to a mortgage, but is not entitled to a full mortgage, and he is entitled to defer completion under section 142 (see above), section 143 grants the right to a shared ownership lease. This is a system whereunder the tenant purchases a long lease of his dwelling for a premium calculated by reference to part of its then assessed value, and the lease contains the right for him to 'staircase' his interest in the dwelling by acquiring further leasehold 'tranches', with the ultimate intention of acquiring the whole.

Under section 144 the tenant must claim to exercise the right to a shared ownership lease (RTSOL) by serving written notice on the landlord stating the 'initial share' he proposes to acquire (see below). On the service of such notice any notices served by the landlord requiring completion are deemed withdrawn, and such notices may not be served while a notice under section 144 remains in force, but RTSOL only exists while the tenant is not entitled to a full mortgage. The tenant's 'initial share' under section 145 must be a multiple of the 'prescribed percentage' (12.5 per cent) and may not be less than the 'minimum initial share' (50 per cent); these percentages may be varied by the Secretary of State.

Once a notice claiming to exercise RTSOL has been served, the landlord must within four weeks serve written notice admitting the right, or denying it with reasons, see section 146, Once the right claimed has been established, the landlord must serve further written notice on the tenant stating the amount which the landlord considers should be the consideration for the grant of the lease considering the amount of the initial share and the effective discount available. The notice must also state the provisions the landlord considers should be included in the lease. The consideration for the grant of the shared ownership lease, that is the amount of the tenant's initial contribution, is determined under section 148 by the formula:

$$C = S\frac{(V - D)}{100}$$

where C is the tenant's initial contribution, S is his initial share expressed as a percentage, V is the value of the dwelling at the relevant time under section 127 and D is the discount which would be available if the tenant were exercising RTB. The effective discount is determined by:

$$E = \frac{S \times D}{100}$$

where E is the effective discount, S (see above) and D (see above). Where all the issues relating to a claim to RTSOL have been settled, the landlord is under a duty to grant a shared ownership lease under section 150, though the landlord has powers similar to those in relation to ordinary RTB transactions to require the tenant to complete under sections 152 and 153.

The lease must conform with the requirements of Schedule 6 Parts I and III (see above) and with Schedule 8 which contains the terms of shared ownership leases. The most important requirement is that the lease must enshrine provisions enabling the tenant to acquire additional shares in his dwelling; these shares may be acquired in individual tranches of 12.5 per cent or in multiples thereof. That right is exercisable at any time during the term of the lease (generally 125 years) on the tenant serving written notice on the landlord. Where such a notice is served the landlord must as soon as practicable serve a counter notice stating the amount payable as consideration for the share(s) to be acquired and the effective discount. The consideration and discount and calculated once more by reference to the formulae $C = S\frac{(V - D)}{100}$ and $E = \frac{S \times D}{100}$, but in this case C is the additional contribution to be paid, S is additional share in percentage terms, V is the value of the dwelling, as agreed by the parties or determined by the district valuer *at the time the notice claiming the right to acquire an additional share was served*, and D is the discount calculated on the assumptions that the shared ownership lease has not been granted and that the tenant's former secure tenancy continues and that the tenant was claiming to exercise RTB.

Where the dwelling is a house of which the landlord owns the freehold, and the tenant acquires such additional shares in·it as take his interest in the dwelling up to 100 per cent, the tenant is entitled to require the freehold to be conveyed to him or to such other person as he directs.

While the tenant's total share in the dwelling is less than 100 per cent he must pay rent, determined by the formula

$$R = \frac{F(100 - S)}{100}$$

where R is the rent payable, F is the amount determined by the landlord as the rent which would have been payable under the tenant's former secure tenancy, though excluding elements attributable to rates and services provided by the landlord, and S is the tenant's total share expressed as a percentage. For any period for which the tenant's total share is 100 per cent the rent payable under the lease is £10 p.a.

If at any time when the tenant's total share is less than 100 per cent and there is a relevant disposal (see above) which is not an exempted disposal (see above) or a compulsory disposal (see above), under a covenant, which must be included in the lease, the tenant must pay to the landlord on demand a sum in respect of the outstanding share. That sum is calculated by the formula

$$P = \frac{V(100 - S)}{100}$$

where P is the sum payable, V is the value of the dwelling at the time of disposal, and S is the tenant's share already held in percentage terms. Where a tenant satisfies liability under this covenant the rent payable under the lease becomes £10 p.a., and, where the dwelling is a house owned freehold by the landlord, any person in whom the tenant's interest in the dwelling is vested is entitled to require the freehold to be conveyed to himself. Furthermore there is a prohibition, under a covenant which must be included in the lease, on relevant disposals, other than compulsory disposals, of *parts* of dwellings at any time when the tenant's interest is less than 100 per cent. Liability to repay discount may arise on an early disposal.

Thus dwellings subject to shared ownership leases may be transferred on the open market, but only on the basis that the incoming purchaser will be the 100 per cent shareholder and so, where the dwelling is a free-hold house, entitled to the freehold.

Under section 151 the shared ownership lease must conform with the requirements of Schedule 7 as to mortgage terms, and must comply with Schedule 9 which enshrines the tenant's right to require further sums to be advanced to him to enable him to pay for the 'staircasing' of his interest in the dwelling. The limit on this right is that the aggregate of the amount to be advanced and the amount already secured by the mortgage on the dwelling must not exceed the amount determined by multiplying his available annual income by a factor specified in regulations, see S.I. 1985/758.

Shared ownership leases are not protected tenancies under section 5A of the Rent Act 1977 (as inserted by the Housing and Planning Act 1986) and are excluded from the operation of the Leasehold Reform Act 1967 by virtue of section 33A and Schedule 4A to that Act (again inserted by the 1986 Act).

General powers of disposal

The 'right to buy' is not the only plank in sales policy. Not every tenant will wish to buy the house he occupies, and there will be a number of people who are not existing tenants who may wish to purchase houses offered for general sale.

Section 32 of the Housing Act 1985 gives power to local authorities to dispose of land which they hold for the purposes of Part II of the 1985 Act. In general disposals other than by way of a secure tenancy or under the right to buy provisions require the consent of the Secretary of State. Section 34 makes provision for the giving of either general or individual consents. Sales may also take place at a discount as provided for by section 34(4). The provisions in section 35 relating to the payment of discount on an early disposal mirror those of section 155 of the 1985 Act.

Section 33 allows local authorities limited freedom to impose such covenants or conditions as they think fit on a disposal. But certain covenants and conditions may only be imposed with ministerial consent. These covenants, etc., are:

1) those limiting the price or premium which may be obtained on a further disposal of the dwelling;

2) in the case of a sale those requiring the first purchaser and his successors in title to grant pre-emption rights to the local authority before allowing any other form of sale;

3) in the case of a lease those precluding the lessee and his successors in title from assigning or sub-letting the dwelling.

Section 37 applies similar restrictions on the resale of houses situated in National Parks, areas of outstanding natural beauty and other designated rural areas, to those contained in section 57.

The Secretary of State, in exercise of his powers under section 34, has issued general consents that equate, in so far as possible, disposals of individual houses under the power of sale with those under RTB, see the Ministerial Letters of 2 and 4 June 1981 to the English and Welsh authorities and DoE Circular 21/84.

However, the power to dispose of housing land goes far further than the power to dispose of individual houses, and, as was stated earlier in this chapter, it is a power being used by some authorities to dispose of whole estates, with or without sitting tenants. Mention has already been made of the disposal of the Oldham Strinesdale estate, but, as Jones and Hillier point out in 'Privatising Local Authority Housing' *Housing and Planning Review* Vol. 41 No. 4, August 1986, p. 20, up to mid-1986 53 privatisation schemes comprising 6,000 untenanted dwellings, and two schemes with 3,000 tenanted properties had been centrally recorded, while schemes for a further 15,000 dwellings were proposed. Schemes may be small or large and are spread across the nation – Salford, Portsmouth, Westminster, Bradford, Leeds, Liverpool, Knowsley, Wandsworth, Preston, South Tyneside, Burnley and Thamesmead all have, or are considering, privatisation schemes. Schemes may involve the rehabilitation of existing stock, the units of which are subsequently sold for owner occupation, and may take place on the basis that the company acquiring housing land and stock from an authority does work on other local authority housing as consideration rather than making a capital payment to the authority.

The fear, however, is that the provisions of the Housing and Planning Act 1986 may herald a major policy incentive to privatise many more areas of local authority housing. Thus the new Ground of Possession, 10A, in Schedule 2 to the Housing Act 1985, will allow for recovery of possession of dwellings subject to re-development schemes centrally approved under the new Part V of Schedule 2, following due tenant consultation, see further Chapter 3 below. Likewise section 69(1A) of the Rent Act 1977 will allow 'public sector bodies' with a view to disposal of an interest in a dwelling, to apply to the Rent Officer for a certificate of fair rent in respect of the dwelling either in its present condition, or after the completion of works of improvement, conversion or repair. In this context 'public sector body' means a local authority, new town corporation, urban development corporation, or the Development Board for Rural Wales. Effectively this allows districts and London Boroughs to apply for certificates of fair rent for their houses before they are disposed of to the public sector. Tenants transferred from the public to the private sector in this way will be transferred from secure tenant status to regulated tenant status under the Rent Act 1977, see the DoE Consultation Paper of 29/11/85 and *Legal Action*, March 1986, p. 32. This provision will, inter alia, facilitate the transfer of municipal or new town housing to housing associations, for example, because the latter bodies have fair rents in nearly all cases on their tenanted dwellings. [*See Addendum 7.*]

RTB will, however, continue to apply to dwellings transferred out of the public stock as Preserved Right to Buy (PRTB) by virtue of section 171A to 171H of the Housing Act 1985. The RTB provisions continue to apply where a person ceases to be a secure tenant by reason of the disposal (a 'qualifying disposal') by the landlord of *an interest* in the dwelling to a person who is *not* an authority or other body within section 80 applying to local authorities and most housing associations. The provisions accordingly refer to the 'former secure tenant' and the 'former landlord'. PRTB does not apply where the former landlord was a body falling within Schedule 5, paragraphs 1, 2 and 3 to the 1985 Act, that is charities and certain housing associations, against whom RTB could not be exercised, *or in any other case provided for by order of the Secretary of State.* Under section 171B a former secure tenant has PRTB so long as he occupies the 'relevant dwelling', see below, as his only or principal home, but this is subject to, inter alia, the requirements of paragraph 6 of Schedule 9A whereunder PRTB is a registrable interest under the Land Registration Act 1925, and so requires registration to be protected, such registration to be effected by the Chief Land Registrar on the disposal of relevant housing stock, the disposing body to ensure that the Chief Land Registrar is informed of the necessary particulars to enable him to proceed.

PRTB is exercisable only by a 'qualifying person', that is the former secure tenant, a person to whom a tenancy of a dwelling is granted jointly with a person having PRTB in relation to that dwelling, and a 'qualifying successor', that is either:

1) a person who on the death of the former secure tenant becomes the statutory tenant of the dwelling, in relation to which the deceased had PRTB, under paragraphs 2 and 3, Part I, Schedule 1 of the Rent Act 1977, that is a surviving spouse or member of the tenant's family; or

2) a person who becomes the tenant of the dwelling in place of the former secure tenant by virtue of orders under the matrimonial legislation.

PRTB is also exercisable only in respect of a qualifying or 'relevant' dwelling. Such dwellings are:

1) in relation to the former secure tenant, the dwelling subject to the disposal under which he ceased to be secure;

2) in relation to a qualifying successor, the dwelling of which he became the statutory tenant; and

3) in relation to a person to whom a tenancy of a dwelling is granted jointly with a person who has PRTB in relation to it, that dwelling.

However, if a person having PRTB becomes tenant of another dwelling, and the landlord is the same as the landlord of the previous dwelling, or, where the landlord is a company, is a connected company, the new dwelling is the relevant dwelling for the purposes of PRTB, and the right is also not generally affected by the disposal of the landlord's interest in the dwelling. 'Connected Companies' are, under section 736 of the Companies Act 1985, subsidiary or holding companies. PRTB is accordingly not lost on transfers between dwellings of the same landlord.

Section 171C empowers the Secretary of State to make regulations to modify the provisions of the 1985 Act with regard to PRTB, so that, for example, where PRTB is exercised the right to a mortgage is exercisable against the former landlord, and that the RTSOL provisions do not apply. [*See Addendum 8.*]

All this flows from the section 32 power to dispose of housing land and stock in any manner, subject to ministerial consent, and, subject generally to such covenants and conditions as the local authority think fit. In *R v Hammersmith and Fulham London Borough Council, ex p Beddowes*, (1986) HLR 458, (1986) Times, 26 August the Court of Appeal held that this allows an authority to dispose of land subject to covenants binding its own future use of land retained for the time being, provided that it can be said that the authority's overall policy for the land is the provision of housing accommodation for its district. This is so even where the accommodation is to be provided on the basis of owner-occupation, as opposed to renting, provided the accommodation is to be available at reasonable prices, for such a policy can be a statutory object under the housing legislation. Authorities thus seem to have a choice in relation to their housing land. They may dispose of it for private sector development, and if they do they may restrict the use of any land retained, or they may retain land for the purpose of providing publicly rented accommodation. Making an option between the choices is not a fetter on the discretionary powers available for the course of action *not* followed, and will not be interfered with by the court provided an authority's policy option is honest and reasonable, bearing in mind all the circumstances of the case such as any managerial and economic problems implicit in retaining a given area of land for rented accommodation.

The consent of the Secretary of State is required for the disposal by a local authority, other than in relation to RTB, of houses let on secure tenancies but which have not been acquired or appropriated by the authority for the purposes of Part II of the 1985 Act, for example houses held by county councils for educational purposes. Disposals made without the consent required by sections 32 and 43 are, under section 44, void unless the disposal is to an individual, or two or more individuals, and is only related to a single dwelling.

Local authority mortgage powers

The vast majority of local authority mortgage lending, apart from monies secured under RTB, is now conducted under section 435 of the 1985 Act. Local authorities, including counties, districts and London Boroughs, may advance mortgage finance to any persons for the purposes of acquiring or constructing houses, or converting buildings into houses, or altering, enlarging, repairing or improving houses. They may make advances to enable the mortgagor to discharge a previous loan made in order to facilitate house purchase or improvement, or where some part of the premises will not be used as a dwelling, provided they conclude that the primary effect of the advance will be to meet the housing needs of the mortgagor. The power to make an advance to pay off a previous loan on a house enables a local authority to allow re-mortgaging of property. This power is very useful where houses have been purchased jointly by husband and wife and the wife has given up or lost her job making repayment of the mortgage difficult. The new mortgage will provide for a longer mortgage period and lower monthly outgoings.

These powers exist in respect of houses both inside and outside the local authority's area, though some authorities are reluctant to lend on houses outside their areas. The range of property capable of forming the subject of a local authority mortgage is also wide, and includes free-hold and leasehold property, though in such a case authorities *must* require that the unexpired portion of the term should be at least ten years more than the period of the mortgage, see section 436(2).

The range of potential borrowers is also great. The Act says money may be advanced 'to a person' but authorities tend to give preferential treatment to various categories of people such as their own tenants, or persons on, or eligible for, the housing waiting list, first time buyers living or working within their areas, those who are homeless and those who wish to convert or improve older large properties with a view to relieving overcrowding.

In the allocation of mortgage finance, local authorities should not, of course, discriminate on racial or sexual grounds. Before advancing money the local authority must be satisfied, under section 439 that the house in question is or will be made fit for human habitation. They must then proceed to have the property duly valued to ascertain its *market* value. Thereafter they may proceed to advance the money, up to the value ascertained, see section 436(3), and secure both capital and interest on the house by way of mortgage.

Local authority mortgage interest rates

Section 438 and Schedule 16 to the Housing Act 1985 lay down the formula for determining interest rates. Those looking to local authorities for mortgage finance in connection with house purchase, improvement or conversion, etc. (whether or not they acquire their houses from the local authority) pay as their rate of interest *whichever is the highest* of:

1) The standard national rate, i.e. the rate declared from time to time by the Secretary of State after taking into account rates of interest charged by United Kingdom building societies, or

2) The applicable local average rate, i.e. a rate to be determined and declared by each local authority on a six monthly basis and tied to the amount the authority has itself to pay to service its loan charges plus ¼ per cent. These rates apply to all local authority mortgages, including those in connection with the 'right to buy' provisions of the 1985 Act.

3) A rate specified by the Secretary of State in a written notice to an authority.

The notice will direct the authority to treat the specified rate as the highest, and therefore the one to be applied. Where a variation in the interest rate occurs a local authority may allow a variation of the mortgage repayments, and must do so if the period over which the repayment of the principal sum is to be made would otherwise be reduced below the period fixed when the mortgage was effected. When an interest rate is varied the local authority must serve on the person liable to pay the interest written notice of the variation not later than two months after the change. Thereafter the variation will take effect in relation to his liability on the first payment of interest due after a date specified in the notice, which

1) if the variation is a reduction, must be not later than one month *after* the change, or

2) if it is an increase , must be not *earlier* than one month nor *later* than three months *after the service of the written notice.*

Where certain conditions are satisfied section 441 of the Housing Act 1985 allows local authorities to waive or reduce the interest payable on a mortgage, and also to dispense with the repayment of any of the principal sum, for a period of five years. The conditions are:

1) The loan must be made to a person acquiring a house in need of repair or improvement, whether from them or some other person;

2) The person acquiring the house must enter into an agreement with the local authority to carry out within a specified period specified works of repair or improvement;

3) The mortgage assistance must be given in accordance with a scheme conforming with the requirements of, or approved by the Secretary of State.

Section 436(5) provides for the repayment of the principal of the mortgage either by way of instalments – as is the usual practice – or by way of a single payment at the end of a fixed period or on the happening of some specified event before the end of that period. This latter provision enables local authorities to grant maturity loans. Maturity loans are a useful form of advancing money which is, in effect, only to be repaid on the death of the mortgagor, usually from the proceeds of sale of the property in question. Such loans are most helpful as a means of assisting elderly owner occupiers to meet the cost of major repairs on their homes. Generally maturity loans are offered to applicants who are in receipt of supplementary benefits, subject to an assurance from the local offices of the Department of Health and Social Security that they are prepared to meet the interest payments on the loan. The mortgagor is then assured of sufficient capital to repair his house while not having to make any payments himself during his life. After death the mortgage will be a debt on the estate to be settled during administration, but the value of the house as repaired will be able to meet this burden. The use of maturity loans in this way can obviate any need for the premanent rehousing of elderly house owners.

Local authority mortgage guarantee powers

Section 442 of the 1985 Act allows a local authority, with the approval of the Secretary of State, to enter into an agreement with a building society whereby, in the event of the mortgagor's default, and subject to the terms of the initial agreement, the authority will be bound to indemnify the society in respect of:

1) The whole or part of the outstanding mortgage debt, and

2) Any loss consequent on the default.falling on the society.

This power is exercisable by county and district councils, the London Boroughs, and the Common Council of the City of London.

The form of the agreement may provide for the authority to take a transfer of the mortgage, together with the benefit and burden of all preceding acts, omissions and events, so that the building society is entirely discharged of its obligations, provided the mortgagor is a party to the agreement. See DoE Circular 5/81.

Other local authority mortgage powers

Section 228 of the Housing Act 1985 places local housing authorities under a duty to offer home loans to persons made subject to compulsory improvement notices, or who have entered into improvement undertakings. Before making such an offer a local authority must be satisfied:

1) that an applicant for a loan is capable of repaying it;

2) that an applicant's interest in the dwelling concerned consists either of the fee simple, or is a leasehold term which will not expire before the date of the final repayment of the loan; and

3) that the amount of the principal of the loan does not exceed the value which it is estimated the mortgaged security will bear after the requisite works of improvement have been carried out.

No loan is to be made for any part of the necessary expenditure that can be met by a grant payable under the Act. Applications for loans under this provision must be made in writing within a period of three months beginning with the date when the compulsory improvement notice becomes operative, or the improvement undertaking is accepted, as the case may be. A local authority may, in writing, allow a longer period for applications.

Local authority and housing association powers as mortgagees

A mortgagee's power of sale as it applies to such a body is modified by section 452 of the Housing Act 1985. In *Williams v Wellingborough Borough Council* [1975] 3 All ER 462, [1975] 1 WLR 327 a local authority sold a council house to a sitting tenant, and the purchase price was secured by a legal charge on the property. The mortgage conferred the power of sale contained in section 101(1) of the Law of Property Act 1925 on the local authority in case of a default on repayment. The mortgagor defaulted and the local authority purported to 'sell' the house to themselves. It was held that the local authority had no power to do this. There was no power to re-take the property in a case of default. This decision will now for certain purposes be set aside. Section 452 provides that where an authority or registered association has sold a relevant house *and* they are mortgagees of the house, and the conveyance or grant contains a pre-emption provision in their favour, and the mortgagees' power of sale in respect of the dwelling under section 101 of the Law of Property Act 1925 becomes exercisable during the pre-emption period, they may, if given leave by the county court, vest the dwelling in themselves by deed under Schedule 17, but subject to the payment of compensation to affected parties. A pre-emption provision is a covenant imposing a condition or limitation of the kind mentioned in section 33(2)(b) or (c) i.e. a right of pre-emption imposed under *powers* of sale, or in section 157(4), i.e. the restriction on the disposal of dwellings in national parks etc., see above.

Local authority home purchase assistance powers

Section 445 of Housing Act 1985 enables the Secretary of State to make advances to 'recognised lending institutions' to enable them to provide assistance to first time house buyers. County and district councils, London Borough councils, the Common Council of the City of London, and new town development corporations are among the recognised institutions. The assistance is only available where mortgage finance for house purchase is obtained by way of a secured loan from the lending institution, subject to the purchase price of the property being within the limits specified from time to time by the Secretary of State.

In addition the recipient of the assistance must satisfy certain conditions before being aided.

1) He must be a 'first time buyer'. Paragraph 24(2) of the Home Purchase Assistance Directions 1978, states: 'A person is not to be treated as a first-time purchaser if he has previously been the beneficial owner (whether individually or jointly with others) of [the freehold or the interest of the tenant under a lease granted for a term of more than 21 years] in a house in the United Kingdom in which he made his home'.

2) He must intend to make the property he is purchasing his home.

3) He must have been saving with a recognised savings institution for at least two years proceeding the date of his application for assistance, and

also throughout the twelve months proceeding the date of his application he must have had at least £300 worth of such savings. Also by the date of his application he must have accumulated at least £600 worth of such savings, though the Secretary of State has power to relax or modify this requirement in particular cases. Recognised savings institutions include building societies, local authorities, Trustee Savings Banks, certain banking companies, Friendly Societies, the Director of Savings and the Post Office.

Assistance under the Act may take the following forms.

1) The secured loan may be financed by the Secretary of State to the extent of £600, that amount being normally additional to that which the lending institution would have lent, but the totality of the loan is not to exceed the loan value of the property, which is stated by paragraph 37(1) of the Home Purchase Assistance Directions 1978 to be the purchase price of the property, or its estimated value, whichever is lower.

2) £600 of the total loan may be made free of interest and of any obligation to repay that sum of the principal, for up to five years from the date of purchase.

3) The lending institution may provide the purchaser with a tax free bonus on his savings up to a maximum of £110, payable towards the purchase or expenses arising in connection with it.

Exactly *what* assistance is available to any individual applicant is determined by section 446(2) of the Act, a complex provision whose effect is:

1) the £600 assistance is available to an applicant who has accumulated £600 of savings, has saved for two years, and has maintained a minimum balance of £300 in his savings for the year before his application. Such a borrower can also qualify for the bonus.

2) the bonus *only* is available to an applicant who has satisfied all the above conditions, save that he has not managed to accumulate savings worth £600.

3) No one qualifies for assistance unless he is borrowing at least £1,600, and the sum he is borrowing amounts to at least a quarter of the purchase price.

4) the amount of bonus payable in any case is determined by paragraph 35 of the Home Purchase Assistance Directions 1978. A sliding scale is established whereby the greater the amount saved, the greater is the bonus payment. To qualify for the full £110 bonus the minimum

amount of savings held in the twelve months proceeding the date of application for assistance must be not less than £1,000.

Further reading

Arden, A., and Partington, P., *Housing Law* (Sweet & Maxwell, 1983) Chap. 21.

Pollard, D. (Ed), *Social Welfare Law* (Oyez Longman) Paras. B.1391–B.2300.

Friend, A., 'A Giant Step Backwards: Council House Sales and Housing Policy', CHAS Occasional Papers No. 5, 1980.

English, J. (Ed), *The Future of Council Housing* (Croom Helm, 1982) Chap. 2, 3, 4, 5 and 8.

Forrest, R., and Murie, A., *Right to Buy? Issues of Need, Equity and Polarisation in the Sale of Council Houses* Working Paper No. 39, University of Bristol School for Advanced Urban Studies, 1984.

Forrest, R., and Murie, A., *Monitoring the Right to Buy 1980–1982* Working Paper No. 40, University of Bristol School for Advanced Urban Studies.

Forrest, R., and Murie, A., 'The Great Divide', *Roof*, November/ December 1982, p. 19.

Knight, M., 'When Owning Becomes a Nightmare', *Roof*, November/ December 1983, p. 23.

Forrest, R., and Murie A., 'If the Price is Right', *Roof*, March/April 1986, p. 23.

Jones, P., and Hillier, D., 'Privatising Local Authority Housing', *Housing and Planning Review*, Vol. 41, No. 4 August 1986, p. 20.

Chapter 3

Public sector housing: its allocation and the rights of its tenants – management I

Allocation policies (council housing)

Section 21 of the Housing Act 1985 vests the general management, regulation and control of municipal housing in the local authority, and gives them power to pick and choose their tenants at will. It is true that section 22 states that the authority shall secure that in the selection of tenants a reasonable preference is given to persons who are occupying insanitary or overcrowded houses, have large families or are living in unsatisfactory housing conditions and to persons towards whom they are subject to a duty under the homelessness provisions. But this requirement is far from specific and creates no *duty* towards those mentioned. Apart from specific statutory obligations, such as that under section 39 of the Land Compensation Act 1973, the general selection and allocation powers of local authorities are subject to very little legal supervision, see per Lord Porter said in *Shelley v LCC* [1949] AC 56 at 66, [1948] 2 All ER 898 at 900.

This does not mean that authorities have total *carte blanche* to allocate as they will, they must behave reasonably, and are subject to the general principles of administrative law. In *R v Canterbury City Council, ex p Gillespie* (*Housing Aid*, July 1986, unreported, QBD) [1986] *Legal Action* 136, a woman and her child lived in overcrowded and unsatisfactory situations following a relationship breakdown. The authority refused for almost three years to rehouse her, or even place her on a housing 'waiting list' unless she relinquished the joint tenancy she technically held with her former co-habitee. But the landlord authority for that tenancy would not accept the surrender because of rent arrears, and she could not take proceedings against the man as that could render their other child living with him homeless. It was held that the authority were rigidly adhering to a policy of not rehousing a person who had a share in joint tenancy, and had fettered their discretion in not considering the applicant's peculiar circumstances.

From a strictly *legal* point of view local authorities have virtually complete control over the process whereby they select their tenants.

They do not have to observe limits as to income, social class or length of residence, though they may not discriminate in the allocation of their houses on either racial or sexual grounds.

In nearly every district there is more demand for housing than the local authority can supply, and so their allocation powers operate as a way of 'metering out' or sharing round a scarce resource amongst an over-large number of potential beneficiaries. Until sufficient resources are allocated to the creation of a *surplus* of good quality municipal housing then the municipal housing system will always be open to two major criticisms:

1) that it is no more than a welfare net designed to 'catch and accommodate' the worst off and most underpriviledged section of society;

2) that even within the context of welfare, it fails to take account of, and be responsive to, various forms of housing needs.

On the other hand most local authorities do the best they can with severely limited resources. In any given year the number of persons who can be housed is limited by the number of houses falling vacant, or created by new building or acquisition. Against this authorities receive requests for housing from an increasingly large and diverse number of people such as: those living in houses due for demolition; the homeless; other households wishing to move into municipal accommodation, for example young married couples living with in-laws; existing municipal tenants wishing to transfer houses; persons from outside the district wishing to move into it, for example those in search of work, and a miscellaneous group, consisting mainly of young single people wishing, or having, to leave their parental homes for various reasons.

The frequently contradictory and mutually exclusive claims of these various groups have to be met in some way by local authorities and they have evolved various administrative procedures for dealing with the problem. These schemes have been subject to criticism. When a resource is in short supply no system for its rationing out can ever be fully accepted as fair, for any sort of rationing inevitably means disappointment for someone – a disappointment that can easily be viewed as unfair treatment. Furthermore it must be admitted that some authorities have adopted practices and procedures that leave much to be desired from the point of view of equitable fair dealing.

Residence qualifications

To operate allocation procedures local authorities maintain what are officially termed 'housing registers' but which are more colloquially, and correctly, referred to as 'waiting lists'. Some authorities go beyond this and impose conditions for the entry of an applicant's name on the waiting list: for example a condition that an applicant must be living in the district at the time of his application; or that he has lived in the district for the previous two years, and has not lived elsewhere for more than five years; or that he has been working in the district for ten years. Other authorities achieve the same result by operating two waiting lists, the first a 'live' list made up of applicants with a real chance of being housed and the second a 'deferred' list made up of those considered not to be in serious need. Such pre-conditions for inclusion on the housing waiting list have been repeatedly criticised.

Waiting list restrictions were criticised by the Central Housing Advisory Committee in 1949, 1953, and 1955, and in the 1969 report, *Council Housing Purposes, Procedures and Priorities*, and in the 1978 Housing Services Advisory Groups Report *Housing for People*. However, since then other restrictions of various sorts have been discovered in various localities. In some authorities there has been pressure to introduce an 'income bar', with those earning in excess of a certain sum being 'advised' to consider house purchase rather than council accommodation. Other authorities have very strict residence qualifications, coupled with income criteria, and the test that the applicant for housing is able to show 'housing need'. Some authorities additionally exclude single people from their normal allocations procedures, unless they are over a particular age, or have some special medical need. Even where an 'open' policy is adopted with regard to allowing anyone to register on a housing waiting list, actual *consideration* of an application made may still be affected by restrictive considerations. 'London Housing' (January 1984) revealed that, at that time, nineteen London Boroughs restricted consideration by reference to a residence requirement, five boroughs had restrictive age considerations, and one had an income criterion bar. Several boroughs did not consider an application until the applicant's name had been on the waiting list for a specified time. The residence requirements could be either that an applicant had lived in a particular borough for a set time, or had been resident in the Greater London area. The report criticised such policies for failing to take into account people's need to be able to change accommodation in order to be able to take up employment in new areas.

That last point is particularly important in a time of high unemployment when many may wish to move from older, declining industrial areas to other parts of the country where new industries are creating employment opportunities. Home ownership may not always be open to such would-be migrants on grounds of cost, and so it is necessary to have some public sector housing available. Under section 107 of the Housing Act 1985 the Secretary of State has power to make grants or loans towards the costs of arrangements to facilitate moves to and from homes whereby a secure tenant voluntarily transfers to a secure tenancy with another landlord, or where each of two or more tenants of dwellings, at least one of which is subject to a secure tenancy, becomes the tenant of the other, or one of the other, dwelling or dwellings. Since 1981/82 local authorities, new town development corporations and housing associations have participated in the *voluntary* National Mobility Scheme. The scheme is open to the tenants of the participating bodies, and to others high on the waiting lists of those bodies, or in pressing need to move to a new area. Such people may apply to move under the scheme provided: they have obtained permanent employment beyond reasonable travelling distances from their existing homes; or they need to move on social grounds, for example the need to move closer to family support. The scheme operates at both the county and national levels. At the county level, a number of lettings are made available by the participating local authorities on a quota basis designed to ensure that the number of moves *into* an area within a county is approximately equivalent to the numbers *from* that area rehoused elsewhere in the county. Nationally each participating authority makes available 1 per cent of its annual lettings for persons needing to move to its area from beyond its county, and also makes available further lettings equal to the number of persons *from* its area who are rehoused by authorities *beyond* its county. Housing associations may also join the scheme, and this allows their tenants to participate alongside local authority tenants.

The scheme is operated bilaterally by each receiving and nominating authority, and receiving authorities apply their normal eligibility criteria to those wishing to move into their areas under the scheme, minus, of course, residence requirements. The scheme is overseen by a steering committee made up of representatives of the participating bodies and the Department of the Environment; there is also an advisory group of housing officers, and a National Mobility Office which is responsible, inter alia, for monitoring and publicising the scheme nationally. The scheme was initially funded under section 107.

Critics of the scheme point out that: a nomination under the scheme takes anything between up to four weeks or two months to be processed, too long a time when an applicant is anxious to take up a new job, especially where an immediate offer of a house does not follow on acceptance by the receiving authority; the scheme explicitly only applies to those with jobs to go to, rather than those anxious to move to a new area to seek for work; not enough houses are available under the scheme, and that the scheme is under publicised. It is also the case that authorities may reject a transfer without giving reasons, and that acceptance practices vary greatly from authority to authority.

Owner-occupiers do not seem to be popular potential transferees, nor are some disabled applicants with some authorities, nor those with rent arrears. See *Roof*, November/December 1983, p. 4; and *A Job to Move*, Conway and Ramsay, Chap. 5.

Selection schemes

Even after an applicant's name is on a housing waiting list there is no guarantee of speedy rehousing taking place. Some authorities allocate their houses according to date order on a 'first-come-first-served' basis. According to such schemes housing will be offered, as it becomes available, to those whose names appear at the top of the list. A small number of authorities use merit schemes to allocate houses. Here tenants are selected according to the knowledge of councillors as to individual applicants. Such schemes have been criticised in the past, for example by the Housing Services Advisory Group in *Housing for People* (1978), and in *Council Housing: Purposes Procedures and Priorities*, which stated at paragraphs 122 and 123: 'Without [a clearly defined and publicised selection policy] it is difficult to achieve fairness and even more difficult to demonstrate it: particularly in small authorities and, in scattered rural areas members will be subject to pressure from applicants and officers will be subject to pressure from individual members'.

It remains perfectly lawful for a local authority to allocate their houses according to such a 'merit' scheme. Indeed there is a virtual absence of control and supervision over the means whereby municipal housing is allocated. See Murie, Niner and Watson in *Housing Policy and the Housing System* p. 119.

Most authorities allocate their houses according to some sort of points system. Once an applicant is registered on the waiting list the speed with which he is housed will depend on the number of points he can amass.

That general statement about points schemes obscures their vast diversity in practice. Their working varies, often quite dramatically, according to the factors selected for 'pointing' and according to the number of points actually allocated under each head of entitlement. An applicant may do well under the points scheme operated by one local authority, whereas he could do badly, on exactly similar facts, according to the scheme operated by the neighbouring district. This possibility of variation has been a cause of considerable concern to the critics of municipal housing practice. Factors frequently selected for 'pointing' include:

1) The date of application;

2) The number of bedrooms needed by an applicant;

3) The size of the family involved;

4) Whether the applicant is living in rooms as opposed to a self-contained house or flat;

5) Whether the applicant has a separate living room;

6) Whether the applicant, having children, occupies only a bed sitting room;

7) The existence of illegal overcrowding;

8) The enforced splitting-up of a family because of accommodation difficulties;

9) Sexual embarrassments arising out of unsatisfactory sleeping arrangements;

10) Ill-health or disability;

11) Lack of amenities;

12) Sharing of kitchen facilities;

13) Being forced to occupy badly located accommodation;

14) The age of the applicant;

15) The length of time the applicant has been registered on the waiting list;

16) The suitability of the applicant for the accommodation sought;

17) Other factors, such as hardship, or the desire of the applicant to be accommodated near to friends or relatives.

Some local authorities retain a discretion to simply 'add on' extra points in individual cases, or otherwise to vary the points awarded so as to promote or retard an applicant's progress up the waiting list. Points schemes have been criticised for giving too much weight to factors which have no real relevance to housing *need*, for example length of residence in a district, or length of time on the list, while other factors, such as disrepair or harassment by a landlord, are not considered 'pointable'.

It is probably impossible to create one national housing allocation scheme because the needs and resources of local authorities vary so much. Likewise some matters, such as cases of severe ill-health, or illegal eviction, or where the social services authority is involved, etc., cannot be dealt with by the routine points system, but must be considered separately under special allocations procedures.

When a person has qualified to be housed by amassing a sufficiently large number of points, or by falling within the rehousing obligations of the local authority, he will not be offered a free choice amongst the available municipal housing. A completely free choice is impossible because factors such as the numbers of bedrooms needed have to be taken into account in the allocation process. Some authorities, however, base their allocations on the reports of housing department officials who pay visits to potential tenants before the offer of a municipal house is made. These reports are frequently used to grade applicants, and, in general, the better the grade the applicant receives the better will be the choice of housing offered to him. See Murie, Niner and Watson in *Housing Policy and the Housing System* pp. 125 to 126.

In Merrett's *State Housing in Britain* at p. 224 its author demonstrated the sort of judgmental comments made in grading assessments by housing officers, for example 'Poor type, will need supervision'. There is an obvious danger that a report based on the professional and social values of an officer may be detrimental to an applicant whose standards and values are different from the officer's. Grading will not just determine the type and location of house offered to an applicant, it will consequently segregate those seen as 'less desirable' tenants from those living in more favoured council dwellings and estates.

Thus the discretionary powers conferred on local housing authorities can be used in a wide variety of ways. When Parliament confers discretionary power it intends local authorities to make decisions. It would be wrong to argue that discretion should be entirely replaced by rigid legal rules which would be too inflexible to meet the wide variety of circumstances with which local housing authorities have to cope. Nevertheless there is room for centrally laid down guidelines and/or model allocation schemes designed to iron out the most extreme variations that may be caused as a result of the adoption of differing selection and allocation practices.

The Housing Act 1985 takes a few tentative steps in this direction. Section 106 of the 1985 Act states that every landlord authority (i.e. local housing authorities and most housing associations) must publish summaries of their rules for determining priorities between applicants in relation to the allocation of housing, and governing cases where secure tenants wish to move (whether or not by way of exchanging dwellings) to other dwellings let under secure tenancies by that landlord or another body. An authority is not required to give an indication of how long an applicant may have to wait to be housed. Sets of allocation rules must be maintained by such bodies and made available for public inspection, though to comply with this obligation housing associations must instead send copies of their rules to the Housing Corporation and to the councils of any districts or London Boroughs in which there are houses let, or to be let, by the association on secure tenancies, and in such cases it is the council's duty to make the rules available for public inspection. These rules are to be sold at a reasonable fee to the public, and copies of the summaries made available free of charge.

The reasoning behind this provision is that 'publicity is control'. As local authorities are democratically elected bodies their electors may reject them at the polls should they disapprove of policies and procedures made public for discussion and comment. That is the theory; whether local elections are conducted quite in that way is open to doubt! It can also be argued that public disquiet over a particular policy or procedure, especially as aired in the local press, *might* lead to a change on the part of the local authority or a particular housing association.

So far as an individual applicant for housing is concerned, section 106(5) of the 1985 Act provides:

'At the request of any person who has applied to it for housing accommodation, a landlord authority shall make available to him, at all reasonable times and without charge, details of the particulars which he has given to the authority about himself and his family and which the authority has recorded as being relevant to his application for accommodation'.

This provision enables an applicant to check that the landlord authority have recorded the relevant details of his application as he has supplied them correctly. It does *not* entitle the applicant to see any other facts, opinions, assessments or gradings recorded about him. Neither does it confer any right to change or challenge any particulars other than those which '*he* has given to the authority'.

Reform

The courts have often stated their unwillingness to intervene in the exercise of a local housing authority's discretion unless the very heavy burden of proving an act contravening the general principles of administrative law can be discharged (*Bristol District Council v Clark* [1975] 3 All ER 976, [1975] 1 WLR 1443 and *Cannock Chase District Council v Kelly* [1978] 1 All ER 152, [1978] 1 WLR 1). Reform comes better from the legislature. The following principles should be enshrined in housing law and practice.

1) Elected members should concern themselves with the formulation of

policy and should, in general, be excluded from day to day housing administration and allocation.

2) There should be *national* guidelines for the creation of local allocation, transfer and exchange schemes.

3) In the processing and consideration of housing applications, etc., wherever possible, anonymity for the applicant should be the rule so as to reduce any possibility of bias.

4) There should be an obligation on local authorities to inform disappointed applicants why their requests have met with no success. This should be coupled with a provision requiring greater disclosure of the contents of an applicant's file to him than the 1985 Act requires.

5) Local authorities should be encouraged to set up systems whereby disappointed applicants may appeal against housing allocations, and the contents of housing files.

Housing allocation is a highly judgmental process. Inevitably some of the judgments reached must give rise to feelings of real or imagined grievance. Where the local authority have committed an act of maladministration there will be a remedy via the offices of the local ombudsman (see Chapter 5, below). The creation of an appeals system would, however, be a useful and speedy supplement to the local ombudsman.

At present it is possible for those who 'know' the housing allocation system to make an informal 'appeal' either by contacting a superior officer in the housing department, or maybe by approaching a member of the local authority, especially one known to be a member of the housing committee. Thereafter a process of internal discussion and evaluation may lead to the applicant's case being differently resolved, but the workings of that process will not be patent, and may act to the disadvantage of other applicants for the sort of housing initially sought by the appellant. See further *Housing Allocation Policy and its Effects*, Corina, p. 17.

Something more structured and formal than this is required. It should involve senior officers and elected members and there should be the possibility of legal or other representatives having rights to address the appellate body on behalf of the disappointed applicant.

Allocation policies (housing associations)

Housing associations who are 'landlord authorities' within section 114 of the 1985 Act, i.e. registered housing associations (other than co-operative associations) and housing trusts that are charities fall within the ambit of section 106 as to the publication of information about housing allocations, see above. But additionally associations have to have their own selection and allocation rules, bearing in mind Housing Corporation advice on such matters, and counsel from the National Federation of Housing Associations that it is important for associations to make their selection criteria clearly public as they are not democratically answerable bodies yet are in receipt of considerable public funding. Of course the objects which an individual association was set up to achieve will constrain its selection and allocation policies. For example, associations may concentrate on housing the elderly or young single people, those below particular income levels, or those with special ethnic or religious needs; but within such constraints policies must be fairly and lawfully applied.

Housing associations have their own Housing Association Liaison Office (HALO) to provide further opportunities for housing mobility for their tenants. This was created in 1978 and since 1982 HALO has been a participating authority in the National Mobility Scheme, acting as an agent for member associations in relation to the scheme. HALO is more flexible in that the national scheme, assisting job seekers as well as those with work, however, it principally concentrates on the Greater London area, and is not able to assist many families to move because of the nature of the housing stock of the participating associations.

Racial and sexual discrimination in housing allocation

There is no lack of evidence that black people fare badly in relation to housing in both sectors. The Commission for Racial Equality's 1984 report *Race and Council Housing in Hackney* confirmed this, finding in particular that white applicants for housing were more likely to be housed in houses and maisonettes than blacks, who were more likely to be placed in flats, very often on the sixth floor or higher. White applicants were also much more likely to receive new properties from the local authority than blacks. The inequality of treatment could only be attributable to racial discrimination. The earlier report *Allocation of Council Housing with Particular Reference to Work Permit Holders* (C.R.E. November 1982) found discriminatory practices in providing housing for short stay foreign workers on work permits by the G.L.C. and two London Boroughs.

Black people suffer for a variety of reasons: language problems and a lack of knowledge, experience and negotiating ability in applying for public sector housing; poor existing housing leading to low expectations of what the public sector can offer, both factors tending to lead authorities to offer less desirable housing; allocation systems disadvantaging ethnic groups, for example rules barring owner-occupiers from eligibility for rehousing which can operate against Asians many of whom live in small, poor quality houses in inner city areas; the housing construction system which provides units apt for western 'nuclear families' but not large enough to house the extended families found particularly in the Asian community.

In a multi-racial society, both the law and administration of municipal housing must operate so as to minimise housing disadvantage arising because of a person's colour, race, or sex, etc. Section 71 of the Race Relations Act 1976 makes it the general duty of local authorities to work towards the elimination of discrimination and to promote good race relations and equal opportunities for all. Other provisions are even more relevant to housing. Section 21 of the 1976 Act provides:

'(1) It is unlawful for a person, in relation to premises . . . of which he has power to dispose, to discriminate against another –
   (a) in the terms on which he offers him those premises; or
   (b) by refusing his application for those premises; or
   (c) in his treatment of him in relation to any list of persons in need of premises of that description.

(2) It is also unlawful for a person, in relation to any premises managed by him, to discriminate against a person occupying the premises –
   (a) in the way he affords him access to any benefits or facilities, or by refusing or deliberately omitting to afford him access to them; or
   (b) by evicting him, or subjecting him to any other detriment'.

Such unlawful discrimination can happen in two ways.

Direct discrimination

This is the act of treating another less favourably on grounds of colour, race, nationality or ethnic or national origins, see sections 1(1)(a) and 3(1) of the Race Relations Act 1976. Thus, for example, it is unlawful to refuse an applicant's name for rehousing because he is black, or to affect his priority on the waiting list because of his colour, or to allocate him a house in a particular area solely because of his race.

This can have serious consequences for local authorities. Racial minorities tend to be found in a definite number of localities where they form tightly knit communities. Members of minority groups who have moved into municipal housing have tended to move as close as possible to houses occupied by members of their own race or nationality for mutual support and aid, and because of family ties amongst extended families. The danger is that white families can panic and leave leading to the creation of ghettoes isolated from, and embattled against, the outside world.

Faced with this problem the City of Birmingham operated a policy of 'discrete dispersal' whereby a black/white balance ratio was kept on all estates, within streets and in blocks of flats. In *Housing Policy and the State*, Lambert, Paris and Blackaby relate, at p. 54, that the keys of council dwellings were marked as vacancies occurred to ensure that the racial balance programme could be maintained. The Race Relations Board declared this practice to be discriminatory and it was abandoned. Even where it is operated with the well-motivated desire of preventing the creation of ghettoes a dispersal policy is illegal.

Good housing practice will reflect the requirements of the non-discrimination notice issued by the C.R.E. to Hackney LBC under section 58 of the 1976 Act:

1) authorities should record the ethnic origin of all applicants for housing, and those they house, and monitor the records regularly in relation to the quality, type, age and location of properties offered and allocated to the applicants;

2) there should be a review of procedures, practices and criteria used in allocation and transfer matters, and such procedures, etc should be clearly relevant to housing need and applied equally;

3) housing staff should be trained to avoid discriminatory practices, to inform applicants for housing of all the options available to them, to consider the special needs and preferences of applicants, and to apply only criteria relevant to housing need in their allocation decisions, particularly where a number of applicants are effectively competing for an available dwelling.

It is also wise for authorities to know the racial composition of their communities, provide facilities for communicating with members of minority groups in their own languages, understand the cultural and family patterns of ethnic groups, and, where possible, to provide appropriate accommodation within their housing stock for extended families. Similar consideration apply to the work of housing associations.

Indirect discrimination

This is the act of applying to a person a requirement or condition which applies equally to persons of *other* racial groups but which is:

1) such that the proportion of persons of the *same* racial group as that of the person affected who can comply with the condition is

considerably smaller than the proportion of persons not of that group who can comply;

2) not justifiable irrespective of the colour, race, nationality or ethnic or national origins of the person to whom it applies; and

3) is to that person's detriment because he cannot comply with it. See section 1(1)(b) of the 1976 Act.

In 'Indirect Discrimination and the Race Relations Act' (129) New Law Journal 408, Geoffrey Bindman argues that the following are instances of indirect discrimination in housing:

1) A requirement that applicants for local authority housing must have been resident in the authority's area for a specified period because fewer numbers of ethnic minority groups could comply with the residence requirements than could members of the host community, or

2) A requirement that housing points can only be given for children actually living with an applicant, as this works to the detriment of any immigrant, part of whose family has yet to join him.

Those authorities who apply residence qualifications should certainly review them to ensure that they do not result in indirect discrimination.

Similar provisions apply to discrimination on grounds of sex under sections 1 and 30 of the Sex Discrimination Act 1975.

Tenure of council houses

The rights of secure tenants are contained in Part IV of the 1985 Act. Sections 79 to 81 define a secure tenancy as being one where the following conditions are satisfied:

1) the dwelling must be let as a separate dwelling-house; there must be no sharing of 'living accommodation' (for example kitchens, but *not* bathrooms or lavatories) with other households, see *Neale v Del Soto* [1945] KB 144 and *Cole v Harris* [1945] KB 474;

2) the landlord must be a local authority, that is a county or district council, a London Borough council, the Commission for the New Towns, or a new town or urban development corporation, or the Housing Corporation or a housing trust which is a charity, or a *registered* housing association, other than a co-operative housing association, or an *unregistered* housing association which is a co-operative housing association.

3) the tenant must be an individual, or in the case of a joint tenancy each joint tenant must be an individual, and he, or in the case of joint

tenants at least one of them, must occupy the dwelling as his only or principal home;

4) the tenancy must not fall within the excepted classes as laid down in Schedule 1. These are:
  (a) long tenancies, that is a tenancy granted for a term certain exceeding 21 years;
  (b) premises occupied by a tenant as a requirement of his contract of employment directed to the better performance of his duties;
  (c) where (i) the tenant is a member of the police and the dwelling is provided rent and rate free under the Police Act 1964, or where (ii) the tenant is a fire authority employee *and* his contract of employment requires him to live close to a particular fire station, *and* the dwelling was let to him by the fire authority in consequence of that requirement, or where (iii) within the period of three years immediately preceding the grant of the tenancy the police, or fire authority conditions above, or the conditions in (b) above have been satisfied with respect to *a* tenancy of the dwelling, *and* before the grant the landlord notified the tenant in writing of the circumstances, stating that the tenancy would fall within this exemption. But in this case the tenancy is only non-secure until the periods during which the conditions are not satisfied with regard to the tenancy amount, in aggregate, to *more* than three years.
  (d) where the house stands on land acquired for development and is only being used as temporary housing accommodation;
  (e) where accomodation has been provided temporarily for a homeless person under sections 63, 65(3), or 68(1) of the 1985 Act, the tenancy cannot become secure before the expiry of a period of twelve months beginning with the date on which he receives notification of the local authority's findings as to his homelessness, unless he is notified otherwise within that period;
  (f) accommodation *specifically* granted to a person who was immediately before the grant not resident in the district and having employment or the offer thereof, within the district or its adjoining districts, to meet his need for temporary accommodation, in order to work there and also to enable him to find permanent housing, cannot be subject to a secure tenancy before the expiry of one year from the grant unless the tenant is otherwise notified within that period;
  (g) where the landlord has taken only a short term lease from a body incapable of granting secure tenancies, for example a private individual, of a dwelling for the purpose of providing temporary accommodation, on terms including one that the lessor may

obtain vacant possession from the local authority on the expiry of the specified period or when he requires it, there is no secure tenancy for *their* lessees;

(h) a tenancy is not secure if it is of a dwelling-house made available for occupation by the tenant while works are being carried out at his own former home, *and* provided the tenant was not a secure tenant of that former home;

(i) where the tenancy is of an agricultural holding under the Agricultural Holdings Act 1948 and the tenant is a manager;

(j) where the tenancy is of licensed premises;

(k) where the tenancy is one granted specifically to a student to enable him to attend a designated course at a university or further education establishment;

(l) where the tenancy is of business premises falling within Part II Landlord and Tenant Act 1954;

(m) where the licence to occupy the dwelling was granted by an alms-house charity.

Provided the above conditions are satisfied the tenant is 'secure'. By section 79(3) and (4) it applies to a licence to occupy whether or not granted for consideration, provided it was not granted as a mere temporary expedient to a person who originally entered the dwelling or any other land as a trespasser.

The rights of secure tenants

Under section 86 of the 1985 Act where a secure tenancy consisting of a certain term comes to an end, a periodic tenancy arises automatically unless the tenant is granted another secure tenancy of the dwelling. Thus a secure tenant at the end of his tenancy enjoys rights equivalent to those of a statutory tenant under the Rent Act 1977. Most secure tenancies will, however, be periodic and so more important rights for secure tenants will be those of succession conferred by sections 87 to 89 of the Act.

Where a secure tenancy is a periodic tenancy, on the death of the tenant it will vest in one of the following as a successor tenant:

1) the tenant's spouse;

2) any other member of the tenant's family who has resided with him throughout the period of twelve months prior to the tenant's death,

provided, in either case, that the successor occupied the dwelling as his only or principal home at the time of the tenant's death. If more than one person is qualified to succeed, the spouse is to be preferred to all others. If there is no spouse those qualified may agree amongst themselves who is to succeed; if they cannot agree the choice is to be made by the local authority.

Sections 87 and 88 only provide for a tenancy by succession to arise once. Section 88 classifies the following also as successor tenants for this purpose:

1) a joint tenant who becomes a sole tenant;

2) a tenant holding a periodic tenancy under section 86 of the Act where the former fixed term tenancy was granted either to another person or to him and another;

3) a tenant who holds by virtue of an assignment, save where the assignment is made under section 24 of the Matrimonial Causes Act 1973, provided the assignor was *not* himself a successor tenant or save the assignment was made under section 92 of the 1985 Act (see below) provided the assignor was *not* himself a successor;

4) a tenant who has the tenancy vested in him on the death of a deceased previous secure tenant. The effect of section 88(4) of the Act should be noted. This provides that where, within six months of the coming to an end of a secure periodic tenancy (Tenancy I), the tenant takes up another secure periodic tenancy (Tenancy II), and

  (a) the tenant was a successor tenant in relation to Tenancy I, and
  (b) under Tenancy II *either* or *both* the dwelling-house and the landlord is or are the same as under Tenancy I, the tenant will be a successor tenant in relation to Tenancy II, unless the tenancy agreement provides otherwise.

Thus, if the widow of a secure tenant succeeds to the dwelling, and then within six months moves, with her children, into a smaller house owned by the same landlord, she will continue to have in relation to the new house the status of a successor tenant, so that on her death her children will not be qualified to succeed to that tenancy.

The definition of 'family' under section 113 of the Act should be noted. The term includes spouses, parents, grandparents, children, grandchildren, brothers, sisters, uncles, aunts, nephews and nieces; treating relationships by marriage as by blood, the half-blood as the whole blood, and stepchildren as full children. Illegitimate children are to be treated as the legitimate children of their mothers and reputed fathers, and persons living together as husband and wife are also to be regarded as members of a family. In *Harrogate Borough Council v Simpson* [1986] 2 FLR 91, the Court of Appeal held that two lesbians living together, even in a committed monogamous relationship, cannot be regarded as living together as husband and wife.

Security of tenure

The basic rule contained in section 82 of the Housing Act 1985 is that a secure tenancy cannot be brought to an end without an order from the court (that is the county court by virtue of section 110). The court may not entertain proceedings for such an order unless the landlord has first served on the tenant a notice in correct ministerially specified form specifying the ground on which the court will be asked to give possession, but the ground may be altered with the leave of the court, see sections 83 and 84. In the case of a periodic tenancy the landlord's notice, which will have a currency of twelve months, must also specify a date after which possesion proceedings may be begun. That date must not be earlier than the date on which the tenancy could, apart from the Act, be brought to an end by notice to quit given on the same day as the landlord's notice.

The grounds on which possession may be given are contained in Schedule 2 to the Housing Act 1985. Their substance is as follows:

Ground 1

Where any rent lawfully due from the tenant has not been paid, or where any obligation of the tenancy has been broken or not performed.

Ground 2

Where the tenant or any person residing in the dwelling has been guilty of acts of nuisance or annoyance to neighbours, or has been convicted of using the house for illegal or immoral purposes. However, there is no implied term in a secure tenancy obliging the landlord to enforce the tenant's obligation not to commit a nuisance, the remedy is an action in nuisance on the part of those aggrieved, see *O'Leary v Islington London Borough Council* (1983) 9 HLR 81. A local authority landlord is not *in general* liable for a nuisance committed by a council tenant, see *Smith v Scott* [1973] Ch 314, [1972] 3 All ER 645.

Ground 3

Where the condition of the dwelling-house or any common parts of a building comprising the dwelling-house have deteriorated as a result of the tenant's waste, neglect or default, or as a result of the acts of any person residing in the dwelling-house whom the tenant (if that person is a lodger or sub-tenant) has unreasonably failed to remove from the dwelling.

Ground 4

Where the condition of any furniture provided by the landlord for use under the tenancy (or in any common parts of a building as the case may be) has deteriorated as result of ill treatment by the tenant or any person residing in the dwelling.

Ground 5

Where the tenant obtained his tenancy knowingly or recklessly by false statements.

Ground 6

Where the tenancy was assigned to the tenant, or to his predecessor in title being a member of his family and residing in the dwelling, by virtue of exchange under section 92 *and* a premium was paid in connection therewith.

Ground 7

Where the dwelling is comprised within a building held by the landlord mainly for non-housing purposes and consisting mainly of non-housing accommodation, *and* the dwelling was let to the tenant in consequence of his employment by the landlord, or the local authority etc., *and* the tenant, or a person residing in the dwelling, has been guilty of conduct such that, having regard to the purpose for which the building is used, it would be wrong for the tenant to remain in occupation.

Ground 8

Where the tenant, being a secure tenant of another dwelling which is his home and which is subject to works, has accepted the tenancy of the dwelling of which possession is sought on condition that he would move back to his original home on completion of the works in question, and where the works have been completed.

Ground 9

Where the dwelling-house is illegally overcrowded.

Ground 10

Where the landlord intends within a reasonable time to demolish, or reconstruct or carry out works on the dwelling, etc., and cannot do so without obtaining possession.

Ground 10A (Introduced by the Housing and Planning Act 1986)

Where the dwelling is in an area subject to a ministerially approved redevelopment scheme under Part V of Schedule 2 and the landlord intends to dispose of the dwelling under the scheme within reasonable time of obtaining possession.

[Under Part V of Schedule 2 approval may be given for schemes of disposal and redevelopment of areas of dwellings. Landlords must first serve notice on affected tenants stating the main features of the scheme, that they intend to apply for approval, the effect of approval in relation to possession proceedings, and giving the tenants at least 28 days to make representation. Landlords must not apply for approval before considering representations made. In considering whether to approve a scheme the Secretary of State must particularly consider the effect of the scheme on housing accommodation in the area, the proposed time scale of the scheme, the extent to which housing to be provided under the scheme is to be sold or let to existing tenants and other representations made to him or brought to his notice. Approval may be given subject to conditions. Home loss payments under section 29 of the Land Compensation Act 1973 are available in respect of orders made under grounds 10 and 10A, and, of course, suitable alternative accommodation must be available.]

Ground 11

Where the landlord is a charity and continued occupation by the tenant would conflict with its objects.

Ground 12

Where the dwelling is comprised in a building held by the landlord mainly for non-housing purposes and consisting of mainly non-housing accommodation, *and* the dwelling was let to the tenant in consequence of his employment by the landlord, or the local authority etc., *and* that employment has ceased *and* the landlord reasonably requires the dwelling for some other employee.

Ground 13

Where the dwelling has features which are substantially different from those of ordinary houses so as to make it suitable for occupation by a physically disabled person, and where there is no longer such a disabled person living in the house, while the landlord requires the dwelling for occupation by such a person.

Ground 14

The landlord is a housing association or trust which lets dwellings to persons whose non-financial circumstances make it difficult for them to satisfy their housing need, and *either* there is no longer such a person residing in the dwelling, *or* the tenant has received an offer of a secure dwelling from a local authority, *and* the landlord requires the dwelling for occupation by a person with special needs.

Ground 15

Where the dwelling is one of a group which it is the practice of the landlord to let for occupation by persons with special needs, and also:

1) a social service or special facility is provided in close proximity to the dwellings in order to assist those with the special needs;

2) there is no longer a person with those needs residing in the house, and

3) the landlord requires the house for someone with those needs.

Ground 16

Where the tenant, being a successor, by virtue of being a member of the deceased previous tenant's family, is underoccupying the dwelling, in that it is too large for his reasonable requirements. But notice of intention to commence possession proceedings must be served *more* than six months but *less* then twelve months after the date of death of the original tenant. (This does not apply to spouse-successors.) In determining whether to make an order under this ground the court must consider, inter alia, the tenant's age, the period of occupation of the dwelling and any financial or other support given by the tenant to the previous tenant.

The court is not to make a possession order on Grounds 1 to 8 unless it considers it reasonable to do so; on Grounds 9 to 11 unless it is satisfied that suitable accommodation will be available for the tenant on the order taking effect, and on Grounds 12 to 16 unless *both* the above conditions are satisfied.

What is to be regarded as 'suitable accommodation' for the purposes of granting possession is defined by Schedule 2 Part IV of the 1985 Act.

The accommodation is suitable if it is to be let as a separate dwelling under a secure or protected tenancy, and the court considers the accommodation is reasonably suitable to the needs of the tenant and his family. In reaching such a conclusion the court must consider: the nature of the accommodation usually let by the landlord to persons with similar needs; the distances between the accommodation and relevant places of work or employment and the home of any member of the tenant's family if closeness between the parties is essential to the well being of either; the needs and means of the tenant and his family; the terms on which the accommodation is available; where furniture was provided in the former tenancy, whether furniture will be provided in the new accommodation. Where the tenant is *not* the tenant of a local housing authority, a certificate from the local housing authority for the district containing the dwelling, possession of which is sought, that they will provide suitable accommodation is conclusive evidence that such accommodation will be available.

Under section 85 of the Act the court has extended discretion as to ordering possession.

Where possession proceedings are brought under Grounds 1 to 8 and 12 to 16 above, the court may adjourn the proceedings for such periods as it thinks fit. Where a possession order is made under any of the above grounds its execution may be stayed, suspended or postponed for such period as the court thinks fit. Where the court exercises this discretion it must impose conditions with regard to the payment of any arrears of rent, etc., unless it considers that to do so would cause exceptional hardship to the tenant or would be otherwise unreasonable. Other conditions may be imposed. Where these conditions are fulfilled the court may rescind or discharge the order. A tenant's spouse or former spouse having rights of occupation under the Matrimonial Homes Act 1983, and in occupation of a dwelling, the tenancy of which is terminated by possession proceedings, has the same rights with regard to suspensions and adjournments, etc., as if his or her rights of occupation were not affected by the termination. In connection with those cases where the court must be satisfied that it is reasonable to make a possession order, *Woodspring District Council v Taylor* (1982) 4 HLR 95, an action under Case 1, should be noted. The tenants had maintained a satisfactory rent record for over twenty years, and then ran up arrears as a result of unemployment and disability. The court held that it is for the landlord to show why it would be reasonable to grant possession, which, in the circumstances of the case, they had not done. In proceedings for rent arrears the landlords notice should be sufficiently specific to show amounts claimed, see *Torridge District Council v Jones* (1985) 276 Estates Gazette 1253. Landlords should not assume that a tenant vacating a dwelling while owing rent is evidence of a surrender of the tenancy, evidence of absence for a substantial period while in arrears is required, see *Sutton London Borough Council v Swann* (1985) Times, 30 November. In such circumstances landlords should seek possession on the statutory grounds, see *Preston Borough Council v Fairclough* (1982) 8 HLR 70. Where under Case 1 possession is sought by a local or public authority against a tenant with arrears of rents, he may defend the action in the county court by challenging the validity of their decision to increase the rents which led to the arrears, see *Wandsworth London Borough Council v Winder* [1985] AC 461, [1984] 17 HLR 196.

Where the court makes a possession order on grounds where the reasonableness of the issue is not a deciding factor, discretion is limited by section 89 of the Housing Act 1980 (still in force). So far as secure tenancies are concerned this provision is relevant where recovery of possession is sought under Grounds 9 to 11 above. In such circumstances the giving up of possession cannot be postponed (whether by the order itself, or any variation, suspension or stay) to a date later than fourteen days after the making of the order unless it appears to the court that exceptional hardship would be caused by requiring possession to be given up by that date. In such cases the giving up of possession may be suspended for up to six weeks from the making of the order but for no longer. This provision also applies to non-secure tenancies.

Tenant participation in housing management

Section 105 of the 1985 Act requires that certain authorities shall, maintain such arrangements *as they consider appropriate*, to enable secure tenants who are likely to be substantially affected by matters of housing management to be informed of proposed damages and developments, and also to ensure that such persons are able to make their views known to the authority within a specified time. Matters of 'housing management' are defined by section 105 to include those matters which, *in the opinion of the authority*, relate to the management, maintenance, improvement, or demolition of municipal dwellings, or are connected with the provision of services or amenities to such dwellings, *and* which represent new programmes of maintenance, improvement or demolition, or some change in the practice or policy of the authority, *and* which are likely to affect substantially all an authority's secure tenants or a group of them. A 'group' is defined as tenants forming a distinct social group, or those who occupy dwelling-houses which constitute a distinct class, whether by reference to the kind of dwelling, or the housing estate or larger area in which they are situated. However, see *Short v Tower Hamlets London Borough*

Council (1985) 18 HLR 171 where the Court of Appeal held that a decision taken 'in principle' to market the sale of certain council properties was not a matter of 'housing management' requiring consultation. The obligation to consult arises where there is a real question of *implementing* a change.

A matter is *not* one of housing management in so far as it relates to rent payable or to any charge for services or facilities provided by the authority. It is the duty of an authority to *consider* any representations made by secure tenants before making any decisions on a matter of housing management.

Landlord authorities must publish details of their consultation arrangements. A copy of any published material must be made available for free public inspection at their principal offices during reasonable hours. Copies must also be available for sale at reasonable charges. 'Landlord authorities' for the purposes of this provision *include* local housing authorities, i.e. district and London Borough councils and registered housing associations other than co-operative associations, but an association is to comply with its obligations by sending a copy of its consultation arrangements to the Housing Corporation and the council of any district or London Borough where it grants secure tenancies, and that authority must then undertake the publicity arrangements.

Practice varies greatly as to the involvement of tenants in management. Some authorities have set up joint estate management committees to transfer a measure of power to tenants, or have created area or district committees of tenants, members and officers to discuss relevant housing issues. Consultation rights and procedures may or may not be mentioned in tenancy agreements (see below) or tenants' handbooks, see *Roof* July/August 1983, p. 5.

It was possible from 1975 to transfer management powers to housing co-operatives, but little progress was made in this respect. Section 27 of the 1985 Act, as substituted by the Housing and Planning Act 1986, will enable local housing authorities to transfer specified housing management functions over specified property, subject to ministerial consent which may be given subject to conditions, to 'another person'. [*See Addendum 9.*] Under section 27C where a qualifying tenants' association serves written notice on the local housing authority proposing that the authority should enter into a management agreement with the association with regard to specified houses and land, or offering to acquire specified houses and land, the authority must consider the proposal. Where the proposal is not accepted in principle by the end of six months the authority must give the association a written statement of reasons for non-acceptance. 'Qualifying' associations must be housing associations where at least half the members are tenants of dwellings specified in the written notice, which have at least 50 such members, or are registered under the Industrial and Provident Societies Act 1965, and where at least half the tenants of the specified dwellings are members of the association.

Under section 429A of the 1985 Act the Secretary of State may make grants to persons managing such public sector housing, or to persons providing services for those managing such houses, or in connection with the provision of educational or training courses in housing management. This provision can be used to grant aid to those seeking to educate tenants in participatory management or control. However, it is thought that the main result of the 1986 Act amendments will be that Housing Associations and Housing Trusts (see section 6 of the 1985 Act) will take over the management of a proportion of local authority housing.

Other rights of secure tenants

a) Subletting

Section 93(1)(a) of the Housing Act 1985 makes it a term of every secure tenancy that the tenant may allow any persons to reside as lodgers in his dwelling. Section 93(1)(b) goes on to state that tenants must not, without written consent, sublet or part with possession of a part of their dwelling-houses. Such consent is not to be unreasonably withheld, see section 94. In any dispute over the withholding of consent it is for the local authority to show that its refusal was not unreasonable. The county court has jurisdiction in such matters. Possible overcrowding, and also any proposed carrying out of work on the house in question may be taken into account when determining whether a refusal of consent was unreasonable. Consent may not be given conditionally. If the tenant applies for consent in writing the local authority must give their consent within a reasonable time or it is deemed to be withheld. If they withhold consent they must give a written statement of reasons for the refusal.

Secure tenancies cannot be assigned, neither can a secure tenant part with possession of or sublet the whole of a dwelling let on a secure tenancy, without the tenancy ceasing to be secure. See sections 91 and 93(2) of the Act of 1985. To this there are three exceptions:

1) where the tenancy is assigned under section 24 of the Matrimonial Causes Act 1973; or

2) where the assignment is to a person who would be qualified to

succeed the tenant if the tenant had died immediately before the assignment; or

3) where the assignment is by way of exchange under section 92. Every
secure tenant may, with the landlord's consent assign his tenancy to
another secure tenant, provided that other has his landlord's written
consent to the operation. Consent, which may not be given conditionally (save as to conditions requiring the payment of rent arrears or the
performance of tenancy obligations) may only be withheld on the
grounds set out in Schedule 3 of the 1985 Act. These are that the tenant
or proposed assignee is subject to a possession order; possession
proceedings under Grounds 1 to 6 of Schedule 2 have begun; the proposed assignee would unreasonably under occupy the dwelling; the
dwelling is not reasonably suitable in extent to the assignee's needs; the
dwelling is comprised within a building held mainly for non-housing
purposes and was let to the tenant in consequence of his being in the
landlord's (etc.) employment; the assignee's occupation of the dwelling
would conflict with the landlord's charitable status; the dwelling has
features substantially different from ordinary dwellings designed to
make it suitable for occupation by a physically disabled person, and the
result of the assignment would be that such a person would no longer
reside there; the landlord is a housing association or trust letting
dwellings to persons whose non-financial circumstances make it difficult for them to satisfy their housing needs, and if the assignment were
made such a person would no longer reside in the dwelling; the dwelling
is one of a group normally let for occupation by persons with special
needs and close to a social service or special facility provided therefor,
and if the assignment were made such a person would no longer reside
in the dwelling, the dwelling is subject to a management agreement with
a qualifying tenants' association and the proposed assignee is unwilling
to be a member of the association. To rely on any of these grounds the
landlord must serve notice specifying and particularising the ground in
question on the tenant within 42 days of the tenant's application for
consent. [The final ground of refusal is added by the Housing and
Planning Act 1986.]

b) Improvements

It is a term of secure tenancies under section 97 that a tenant may not
make any improvement without the landlord's written consent, though
such consent is not to be unreasonably withheld. 'Improvement' is
defined as any alteration in, or addition to a dwelling and includes additions to or alterations in the landlord's fixtures and fittings, and alterations, etc., to the services to the house; the erection of wireless or
television aerials, and the carrying out of *external* decoration. If a

dispute arises over the withholding of consent it is for the landlord to show, under section 98 of the 1985 Act, that it was reasonable. The county court may consider any of the following in determining the issue:

1) whether the improvement would make the dwelling or any other premises less safe for the occupier;

2) whether it would be likely to involve landlords in expenditure which they would otherwise be unlikely to incur; or

3) whether it would be likely to reduce either the price of the house if sold on the open market, or the level of the rent at which it could be let.

Where a tenant applies in writing for the necessary consent the landlord must give it within a reasonable time, otherwise it is deemed to be withheld and must not give it subject to an unreasonable condition, otherwise consent is deemed to be unreasonably withheld. A refusal of consent must be accompanied by a written statement of the reasons for the refusal. Consent that is *unreasonably* withheld is treated as being given.

Consents may be given retrospectively to work already done, and may be given conditionally, though it is for the landlord to show the reasonableness of any condition imposed. Under section 99 a failure to comply with a reasonable condition is to be treated as a breach of a tenancy obligation. This may render the tenant subject to possession proceedings, as also will any carrying out of improvements without consent.

Where a secure tenant begins and makes an improvement to a dwelling after 3 October 1980 and this (a) has received the landlord's consent, and, (b) has added materially to the dwelling's sale or rental value, section 100 of the Act gives the landlord power to make such payments to the tenant as they consider appropriate at the end of the tenancy. The amount payable must not exceed the cost or likely cost of the improvement *after* deducting the amount of any grant paid under Part XV of the Housing Act 1985. Under section 101 of the Housing Act 1985 the rent of a dwelling let on a secure tenancy is not to be increased on account of a tenant's improvements where he has borne the *whole* cost himself, or would have so borne that cost but for a grant paid under Part XV of the Act. If irrespective of grant aid, only part of the cost is borne by the tenant, a pro rata increase in rent can be made. [For the 'right to repair' see chapter 7 below.]

Under section 108 of the 1985 Act secure tenants of dwellings supplied with heat from a heating installation by a heating authority (that is a housing authority, effectively district councils and London Borough councils) may have rights under regulations which may be made by the Secretary of State in respect of the amount they may individually be reasonably charged for heat, and to be given information by the authority as to heating costs and charges. No such regulations have *yet* been made, but consultation is taking place about regulations.

Variation of terms and publicity

Under section 102 of the 1985 Act the terms of a secure tenancy, other than those implied by statute, and *other* than with regard to rent etc., may be varied, deleted or added to by agreement between the parties. (For variation of rents see Chapter 4, below.) In the case of a periodic tenancy terms may also be varied under section 103 by the landlord serving notice on the tenant. Such a notice must specify the variation in question, and the date on which it will take effect. The period between service and the coming into effect of the change must not be shorter than the rental period of the tenancy, nor shorter than four weeks. Before a notice of variation is served, the landlord must serve a preliminary notice on the tenant informing him of the proposed changes and their effects and inviting his comments within a specified time. Any comments received must be considered. When the variation is made it must be explained to the tenant. A variation will not take effect where the tenant gives a valid notice to quit before the arrival of the date specified in the notice of variation. A change in the premises let under a secure tenancy is *not* a variation.

Section 104 of the 1985 Act imposes a duty to publish, and thereafter to update, information about secure tenancies. This must explain in simple terms the effect of the express terms (if any) of secure tenancies, the provision of Parts IV and V of the Housing Act 1985, and of sections 11 to 16 of the Landlord and Tenant Act 1985 (implied covenants of repair). Every secure tenant must be supplied with a copy of this information, and also with a written statement of the terms of his tenancy so far as they are not expressed in a lease or tenancy agreement or implied by law. This written statement must be supplied on the grant of the tenancy or as soon as practicable afterwards. [*See Addendum 10.*]

Further reading

Arden, A., and Partington, M., *Housing Law* (Sweet & Maxwell 1983), Chaps. 17, 20, and 22.
Lambert, Paris and Blackaby, *Housing Policy and the State* (Macmillan, 1978), Chap. 3.
Merrett, S., *State Housing in Britain* (Routledge and Kegan Paul, 1979), Chap. 8.

Murie, Niner and Watson, *Housing Policy and the Housing System* (George Allen and Unwin, 1976), Chap. 4.

Malpas, P., and Murie, A., *Housing Policy and Practice* (Macmillan, 1982), Chap. 7.

Social Welfare Law (Ed. by D.W. Pollard) (Oyez Longman) paras. B. 451–B. 771.

On racial discrimination

Daniel, W.W., *Racial Discrimination in England* (Penguin, 1968), Part 4.

Deakin, N., *Colour, Citizenship and British Society* (Panther, 1970), pp. 148–170.

Krausz, E., *Ethnic Minorities in Britain* (Paladin, 1971), pp. 88–94.

Lester and Bindman, *Race and Law* (Penguin, 1972), pp. 57–61.

Smith, D., *Racial Disadvantage in Britain* (Penguin, 1977), Part 3.

Smith and Whalley, *Racial Minorities and Public Housing* (P.E.P., 1975).

Simpson, A., *Stacking the decks* (Nottingham CRC, 1981).

Housing in Multi-racial Areas (Community Relations Commission 1976).

Race and Housing – Still a cause for concern (National Federation of Housing Associations, 1983).

Race Relations and Housing, Cmnd. 6252.

Race and Council Housing in Hackney. (Commission for Racial Equality, 1984).

Harrison, P., 'How Race Affects Council Housing'. *New Society* 12 January 1984, p. 43 [see also *Roof* May/June 1982, p. 20, March/April 1983, p. 19 and May/June 1983, p. 11].

On allocation

Corina, L., *Housing Allocation Policy and its Effects* (Department of Social Administration, University of York, 1976).

Matthews, R., *Restrictive Practices* (Shelter, 1983).

Vincent, J., *The Housing Needs of Young Single Mothers* (Social Policy Research).

Hughes and Jones, 'Bias in the Allocation and Transfer of Local Authority Housing' (July 1979) Journal of Social Welfare Law 273 to 295.

Lewis, N., 'Council Housing Allocation: Problems of Discretion and Control' (1976) Public Administration, Vol. 54, p. 147.

Conway, J., 'The Evidence from Waiting Lists' *Roof* May/June 1982, p. 14.

114   *Public sector housing: allocation and rights of tenants*

On tenant participation

Ward, C., *Tenants Take Over* (Architectural Press, 1974).
Franey, R., 'Making Tenants' Charters Work' *Roof*, January 1979, pp. 20–22.
Grosskurth, A., 'Bringing Back the Braddocks'. *Roof* January/February 1985, pp. 19–23.

On mobility

Conway, J., and Ramsay, E., *A Job to Move* (Shac Research Report 8, 1986).

Chapter 4

Rents and housing costs assistance for public sector houses – management II

Local authority housing

At the heart of an individual local authority's rent scheme for its houses lies the Housing Revenue Account (HRA) which local authorities were first required to keep by the Housing Act 1935. Section 417 of the Housing Act 1985 is now the governing provision, and requires the keeping of a HRA in respect of income and expenditure on, inter alia, all houses and buildings provided under Part II of the 1985 Act, unfit houses purchased under that Act, and land acquired or appropriated for the purpose of Part II of the 1985 Act.

'Expenditure' includes the following matters:

1) Supervision of and services to council houses;
   (a) general management costs, i.e. rent collecting, accounting, allocation and operational costs,
   (b) special costs, such as heating supplied to tenants under a common scheme, lighting and cleaning the common parts of flats, the upkeep of estate grounds, roadside verges, etc.,

2) Repair charges;

3) Charges on the capital debt undertaken to provide housing (inevitably the largest single item of expenditure);

4) Other expenditure, such as debt management expenses, revenue contributions to capital outlay, i.e. revenue temporarily treated as capital for building purposes, and a proportionate part of salaries paid and overheads incurred in connection with housing capital works.

'Income' will include:

1) Rents from dwellings;

2) Rents from municipally provided amenities such as common heating schemes;

3) Rents from other properties such as shops on housing estates and garages provided for tenants;

115

4) Exchequer subsidies;

5) Contributions from the General Rate fund;

6) Other miscellaneous income.

Income and expenditure as a general rule should balance, and so a local authority's *total* rent income should in general be equal to its total current expenditure on housing less the amount of subsidies. Where at the end of a year the HRA is found to be in deficit it must be made to balance by means of a contribution from the local authority's general rate fund under Schedule 14, Part IV, Para. 4(1) to the Housing Act 1985. There is no general duty, however, on a local authority to make a *fixed* annual contribution out of the general rate fund to the HRA, though authorities *may* credit their HRAs with such sums as they think fit, see Schedule 14, Part IV, Para. 4(2) of the 1985 Act. As we shall subsequently see this discretion has led to wide variations in rent levels across the nation for what are similar houses as some authorities have chosen to make general rate fund contributions to their HRAs while others have not. [*See Addendum 11.*]

Schedule 14, Part V of the 1985 Act allows working balances in HRAs. Furthermore section 419 allows local housing authorities to establish Housing Repairs Accounts. To such an account are credited the following:

1) contributions from the HRA;

2) income arising from the investment or other use of money credited to the account; and

3) sums received by the authority in connection with the repair and maintenance of any of their housing stock, either from its tenants, or from the sale of scrapped or salvaged materials.

This account, if established, is to be debited with the following:

1) all expenditure (including loan charges) incurred in connection with the repair or maintenance of the local council housing stock, and

2) such expenditure as is incurred in connection with the improvement or replacement of any of the municipal housing stock as is from time to time determined by the Secretary of State.

If an authority decide to establish a Housing Repairs Account they must ensure that sufficient sums are credited to it to prevent it ever going into deficit. If an authority consider that any credit balance in the repairs account at the end of a year will not be needed for the purposes of that account, they may carry some or all of that balance to the credit of the HRA.

Rent pooling

What falls to be paid collectively by municipal tenants is that part of their municipal landlord's costs which have been incurred in providing and maintaining housing and which is not otherwise met by central government subsidies or local contributions from the general rate fund. But an individual tenant does not pay a sum representing those actual costs in relation to the particular house in which he lives. Instead the arrangement is that the gross rents of a local authority's houses are set at such a level that their total sum meets the local authority's costs less subsidies and other contributions. This is known as 'rent pooling'. This is an equitable arrangement. As we have seen, the largest items of expenditure in the provision of housing are the loan charges on the capital debt, and these are much higher on post-war houses than on those built pre-1939. Rent pooling allows the burden of loan charges to be spread across all an authority's housing. So far as an *individual* dwelling is concerned, its gross rent will be based on the concept of 'relative use value', which takes into account factors such as the number of rooms in the dwelling, its total floor area, its age, whether it is a house or a flat, the quality of fixtures and fittings, its location and general condition etc. As a guide many authorities use the gross rateable value of their properties as estimated by the rating valuation officer.

Rents for municipal housing have risen considerably over the years, despite 'rent freezes' imposed by central government from time to time, as, for example, by statute in 1974. The reason for these increases is that housing costs have risen even faster than the general rate of inflation over the last decade because of:

1) the high cost of land and house–building costs;

2) the increasing costs of management, maintenance and administrative support services;

3) the rapid rise in interest rates;

4) The change in the period 1978/79 to 1983/84 in the proportion of exchequer subsidies and rent income. In 1978/79 Exchequer subsidies for housing were £1323m, falling to £351m in 1983/84; Rent income was £1242m in 1978/79 rising to £2953m in 1983/84. Rents, including certificated housing benefits (see below) in 1983/84 contributed 55.3 per cent of total income of the HRAs of the English and Welsh local authorities.

Municipal rents have varied greatly from one part of the country to another. One reason for this variation has been mentioned already, namely policy variations between local authorities as to the exercise of their discretion in making contributions to their HRAs from their general rate funds, but there are other reasons. These include:

1) the age and character of any given authority's housing stock: the newer the stock, the more, in general, it cost to build, and that leads to higher rents;

2) regional variations in construction, maintenance and improvement costs which have been so marked, particularly in the London area, that subsidies have been unable to even them out;

3) the fact that subsidies have been generally related to the historic costs of providing houses, not to any given authority's *current* needs, nor to the needs and/or resources of its tenants.

Thus between 1981 and 1983 the *average* net rent (unrebated) for a council dwelling varied between £12.82 (1981) and £16.00 (1983) in London boroughs, and £11.19 (1981) and £13.88 (1983) in non-metropolitan districts, *but* the *range* from the lowest to the highest rents in those areas was from £10.05 (to) £19.84 (1981) to £12.38 (to) £28.23 (1983) in London boroughs and from £7.15 (to) £15.67 (1981) to £9.17 (to) £19.13 (1983) in non metropolitan districts. Rent levels do thus vary greatly, with those in the South East of England being highest, while Yorkshire and Humberside have the lowest rents. See further Bucknall, *Housing Finance*, Chap. 4 and Table 7.

Reasonable rents

The principal provision is section 24 of the Housing Act 1985, under which authorities may make such reasonable charges for the occupation of their houses as they determine, but must from time to time review their rents. This does not give an absolute discretion to local authorities as to the fixing of rents for it was held in *Belcher v Reading Corpn* [1950] Ch 380, [1949] 2 All ER 969 that a local authority must maintain a balance between the interests of their tenants on the one hand and the interests of the ratepayers as a whole on the other. Authorities are entitled to pursue social policies in fixing rent levels, provided they do not behave unreasonably, see *Manderville v Greater London Council* (1982) Times, 28 January and *R v Greater London Council, ex p Royal Borough of Kensington and Chelsea* (1982) Times, 7 April. The courts are unwilling to interfere with an authority's policy, and will only intervene where an authority comes to a clearly perverse decision on its policies and what it considered material and immaterial policy matters. Certainly an authority can consider the existence of a subsidy when fixing rent levels, see *R v Secretary of State for Health and Social Security, ex p City of Sheffield* (1985) 18 HLR 6. A local authority also are not entitled to indulge in expenditure having no relation to their housing stock for which they propose to pay by increasing the rents paid by their tenants. Apart from those requirements there are few other restrictions on the exercise of their powers. Thus:

1) An authority may spread the cost of their housing over all their properties, and need not take each house or estate separately, they need not limit the rent by reference to the initial cost of providing the house or flat, and may charge different tenants different rents for the same accommodation, see *Summerfield v Hampstead Borough Council* [1957] 1 All ER 221, [1957] 1 WLR 167;

2) Rents may be assessed on the basis of gross rateable values, *Luby v Newcastle-Under-Lyme Corpn* [1965] 1 QB 214, [1964] 3 All ER 169, or by means of comparison with economic rents charged in the private sector, *Evans v Collins* [1965] 1 QB 580, [1964] 1 All ER 808;

3) Apart from the statutory obligation to grant rent rebates there is no legal requirement that a differential rent scheme be operated, *Luby v Newcastle-Under-Lyme Corpn* though if a local authority wish to operate such a scheme they may do so, and they may take into account the differing means of their tenants, *Leeds Corpn v Jenkinson* [1935] 1 KB 168 and *Smith v Cardiff Corpn (No 2)* [1955] Ch 159, [1955] 1 All ER 113.

It can thus be appreciated that the courts exercise little effective supervision over the day to day administration of local authority rent policies and will only intervene in extreme circumstances. Moreover in *Smith v Cardiff Corpn* [1954] 1 QB 210, [1954] 2 All ER 1373 great obstacles were placed in the way of a group of tenants wishing to bring a representative action on behalf of themselves and all their fellow tenants. Here the local authority proposed to increase the rents of their houses on a differential basis according to the incomes of the tenants, with the better-off subsidising the less well-off, while the lowest paid tenants were to be subject to no rent increase at all. There were four plaintiffs who sought to bring a representative action on behalf of themselves and all other tenants of the local authority to attack the proposal. It was held by the Court of Appeal that to bring a representative action it must be shown: first, that all the members of the class have a common interest; second, that they all have a common grievance, and third, that the relief sought will in its nature benefit them all. It was held that the plaintiffs in this case did not satisfy the second and third conditions. The very nature of the local authority's scheme was to produce two classes of tenant whose interests, far from being identical, were in conflict, and so the relief sought by way of a declaration to impugn the rent scheme could not benefit *all* 'the tenants. The plaintiffs were allowed to continue their action as four individuals but, as we have seen from *Smith v Cardiff Corpn (No 2)*, they were unsuccessful.

Increasing rents

By section 24(2) of the Housing Act 1985 'the authority shall from time to time review rents and make such changes, either of rents generally, or of particular rents, as circumstances may require'. The Secretary of State has a reserve power under section 31(1) of the Landlord and Tenant Act 1985 to make orders 'restricting or preventing increases of rent for dwellings which would otherwise take place or restricting the amount of rent which would otherwise be payable on new lettings'. An order may make provision generally or in relation to any specified description of dwelling.

With regard to *secure* tenancies (other than housing association tenancies) sections 102 and 103 of the Housing Act 1985 allow variations of rent and payments in respect of rates or services to be made either by agreement between landlord and tenant or in accordance with any terms in the lease or the agreement creating the tenancy. In the case of periodic tenancies variations may also be effected by the landlord serving a notice of variation on the tenant. This notice must specify the variation it makes and the date on which it takes effect; and the period between the date on which the notice is served and the date on which it takes effect must not be shorter than the rental period of the tenancy nor in any case shorter than four weeks. Where such a notice is served and, before the arrival of the date specified in it, the tenant gives a valid notice to quit, the notice will not take effect unless the tenant, with the landlord's written consent, withdraws his notice to quit before the relevant date.

Tenancies which are *not* secure tenancies fall to be dealt with under section 25 of the Housing Act 1985. This provision gives local authorities power to increase rents for their houses let on weekly or other periodical tenancies by means of the service of a 'notice of increase' instead of a notice to quit.

Rent arrears

Despite the existence of a statutory housing benefit scheme many local authority tenants still get into arrears with their rents either because of an unforeseen financial problem, such as unemployment, desertion by a spouse, illness, or general poverty, or, much less probably, because of

unwillingness or incapacity to manage their financial affairs in a satisfactory way. It is very difficult to assess how many municipal tenants
are in rent arrears. In December 1984 *London Housing* reported that
the inner London boroughs were owed £56,019,000 in current rent
arrears, and £21,626,000 by ex-tenants. The outer boroughs were owed
£24,617,000 in current arrears, and £10,178,000 by ex-tenants. The
estimated *total* arrears were well over £112m for the Greater London
area, while the September 1983 figure was assessed by the Audit Commission as £92.3m. 'The Times' 11 December 1985 reported that over
£60m rent was unpaid in inner London, some £140 for every council
dwelling. Local authorities generally were owed over £2000m, the
equivalent of 5.8 per cent of collectable rent. *Rate* arrears could amount
to another £100m.

In 1983 Duncan and Kirby's *Preventing Rent Arrears* pointed out
that *serious* rent arrears, i.e. at 1980/81 levels, £50 or more, affected
one in twenty local authority tenants, but arrears were not evenly
distributed among authorities, being concentrated in metropolitan
areas, with the most deprived 'Inner Urban' districts having the
greatest number of tenants in arrears. However, in 1986 the Audit
Commission considered the rising trend in arrears in the metropolitan
and large shire districts to have ceased. Serious arrears are found in
cases where there is a low income, a sudden income drop, e.g. as a
consequence of unemployment, or unexpected heavy demand on
finances. Families with dependent children and single parent families
are the most likely households to be in arrears, with a crisis, such
as the departure of a wage earner, precipitating arrears. Tenants in
arrears often live in flats and masionettes and are dissatisfied with
their housing, and the highest rates of arrears are often found on
unpopular 'difficult to let' estates, especially where the rents are
above average. Tenants in arrears frequently experience other
budgetting problems, experiencing fuel and other forms of debt, yet
rarely do such tenants live extravagantly or possess cars and other
expensive commodities.

The Duncan and Kirby Report, and the Audit Commission's 1986
Report *Managing the Crisis in Council Housing* between them recommended:

1) authorities should ensure, by campaigns and other informative processes, that tenants take up as many benefits as possible and that
monetary counselling is available for tenants with many debts, with
housing staff receiving training to identify those in need of such
counselling;

2) authorities should consider using door-to-door collection of rent, as
this reduces arrears, and consider tenant representations about

methods of rent payment, trying to ensure that, consistent with economy, it is an easy as possible for tenants to pay rent;

3) the use of 'rent-free' weeks helps to prevent arrears, as tenants in arrears can be visited then and back rent collected from them;

4) efficient data services should be employed to identify tenants with mounting arrears and in respect of whom action is, or ought, to be taken, and likewise tenants should be clearly told how much they owe;

5) accounting practices should be examined to prevent the creation of 'technical arrears', e.g. accounting periods which close mid-week when many tenants pay on Fridays, thus making themselves apparently in arrears, and rent collecting and accounting should be undertaken by one department;

6) authorities should fix specific levels at which action in respect of arrears is taken, allocate sufficient staff to deal with arrears, [in 1986 the Audit Commission criticised the Inner London Boroughs particularly in this respect] should give tenants more information about rent payment options, and how to cope with arrears, should monitor performance in dealing with and reducing arrears, and members should set clear policy guidelines on control and recovery of arrears;

7) good staff training, initially and in service, in dealing with arrears and those in arrears is most important and specialist staff may be needed;

8) effective liaison with the courts and local offices of the DHSS can help in dealing with tenants against whom action has to be taken;

9) early, firm and fair action over arrears is useful in reducing arrears, though no action should be threatened that an authority is not prepared to follow up. Interviews with tenants in serious arrears are also useful in such circumstances;

10) distraint should only rarely be used (see below);

11) court proceedings should be taken only as a last resort, and only after a tenant has been interviewed and the tenant's entitlement to state benefits has been investigated, with authorities seeking suspended possession orders in most cases, and only resorting to eviction where the tenant fails to comply with the court's order on payment of arrears;

12) policies on the allocation of dwellings and on transfers by tenants should reflect the need to prevent, or reduce existing, arrears, with tenants being informed in advance of the likely cost of running a dwelling, and the least well off not being placed, or required to stay, in the most expensive to run housing [see also City University Housing

Research Group *Could Local Authorities Be Better Landlords?* Chap. 5, 5.2.].

The taking of the administrative steps outlined above may well help prevent arrears problems from arising in a number of cases. If such problems do arise, however, local authorities have a number of powers to deal with them.

An action for the rent ('rent action')

This can be brought in the county court under Part II r. 8, Ord. 24 County Court Rules 1981 (S.I. 1981/1687). Where the tenant or former tenant is still in occupation application is made to the county court for the district in which the house in question is situated and a summons for the arrears will issue. The hearing then follows and judgment is given whether or not the tenant appears, unless he files some substantial defence. After judgment has been entered the defendant can pay money into court either on account of the claim or in satisfaction of it. Should he fail to pay the local authority may take enforcement proceedings. Satisfaction of the debt can be achieved by an attachment of earnings order under the Attachment of Earnings Act 1971. Department of the Environment Circulars No. 83/72 and No. 18/74 counselled the use of this method of dealing with arrears. *Preventing Rent Arrears* (Duncan and Kirby) discovered, however, that few authorities seem to use this method of proceeding, the argument being that a Notice Seeking Possession under section 83 and Ground 1 of Schedule 2, Part 1 of the Housing Act 1985 is just as efficacious, even though it puts the tenancy at risk, and informs the tenant that possession is being sought on grounds of arrears, see further Chapter 3 above, Arden and Partington, *Housing Law*, paras. 3–110 to 3–118 and Pollard, *Social Welfare Law*, paras. G.3149 to G.3167.

Distress

In *Abingdon RDC v O'Gorman* [1968] 2 QB 811, at 819, [1968] 3 All ER 79 at 82. Lord Denning MR said: 'It is very rarely that we have a case about distress for rent. It is an archaic remedy which has largely fallen into disuse. Very few landlords have resort to it'. Indeed within the private rented sector section 147 of the Rent Act 1977 provides: 'No distress for the rent of any dwelling-house let on a protected tenancy or subject to a statutory tenancy shall be levied except with the leave of the county court'. But in the local authority sector no such restriction applies and there is evidence that an increasing number of authorities do levy distress as a means of recouping rent arrears. The recent use of distress as a way of recovering unpaid rent was examined in the journal *New·Society* on 16 February 1978. Shortly thereafter Shelter published Steve Schifferes' *In Distress over Rent* which contained a list of 106 housing authorities who in March 1978 stated they used distress in rent arrears cases. [See further 'Finding New Ways to Beat The Bailiff' (Fielding), *Roof* May/June, 1984, p. 23, *Bringing Council Tenants' Arrears Under Control* The Audit Commission, March 1984, HMSO, and *Managing the Crisis in Council Housing* The Audit Commission, March 1986, HMSO.] But what is distress?

Distress is a common law remedy enabling the landlord to secure the payment of rent by the seizure of goods and chattels found upon premises in respect of which the rent is due. It need not be expressly created by the lease or tenancy agreement. The basic common law rules have been much modified by statutory intervention over the years, and so though at common law the right to levy distress only entitles the landlord to seize and hold goods until his debt is satisfied, section 1 of the Distress for Rent Act 1689 as amended by section 5 of the Law of Distress Amendment Act 1888 allows the sale of the goods seized as a satisfaction of the debt. Before distress can be levied the relationship of landlord and tenant must exist between the parties, both when the rent becomes due and when the distress is levied, and the rent must also be in arrear. Therefore there can be no distress until the day after rent becomes due, and if the landlord allows the tenant 'days of grace' to pay the rent these must also expire before distress can be levied.

Distress may only be levied on certain goods and personal chattels found on the demised premises. So far as municipal tenants are concerned the chief exemptions from distress are the wearing apparel and bedding of a tenant and his family and the tools and implements of his trade. The protection is, however, limited to such goods to a total value of £100 (in the case of wearing apparel and bedding) and £150 (in the case of tools and implements), see the Protection from Execution (Prescribed Value) Order 1980 (S.I. 1980/26). In the case of municipal tenancies furniture other than bedding, i.e. bedsteads and mattresses, is the usual item upon which distress is levied. Distress itself may not be levied at night, which is the period between sunset and sunrise, nor on a Sunday. Furthermore a tender to the landlord, or his agent, by the tenant, or his agent, of the rent in arrear *before* the seizure of goods extinguishes the right to levy distress and the levying of distress is, in general, a bar to the levying of distress a second time for the *same* rent.

The procedure for levying distress

Local authorities, in common with other corporations, levy distress by bailiffs who must be authorised to carry out this function by their employers. This authorisation is normally put into writing when it is known as a distress warrant, but it is not essential that there be an authorisation in writing. Nevertheless before a person may act as a bailiff he must be certificated under the Law of Distress Amendment Act 1888 by the county court, such certification being for periods of twelve months at a time.

Bailiffs employed by local authorities can rely on the general rule that there is no need to issue a prior demand for the rent in arrear before levying distress, but they have to observe a number of rules in the performance of their duties. They may enter the premises in question to levy distress, but they must not break in nor enter by force. They may enter via an outer door that is closed but not fastened, and they may even unlock a door where the key has been left on the outside of the lock. Once inside, however, inner doors may be broken open during the levying process. Bailiffs may enter via *open* windows and may climb over walls and fences from adjoining premises. Once a bailiff has made a legal entry upon the premises he may obtain the assistance of the police and use force to break open outer doors if he is forcibly expelled from the house by violence on the part of the tenant.

The actual process of levying distress is completed by the bailiff making a seizure of goods. A bailiff levying distress must deliver to the tenant, or leave on the premises where the distress is levied, a memorandum setting out the amounts for which the distress is levied and the fees, charges and expenses to which the bailiff is entitled, together with an inventory of the goods seized, see generally the Distress for Rent Rules 1983 (S.I. 1983/1917). (For a detailed statement of the law of distress the reader is referred to *Halsbury's Laws of England* (4th edn) vol. 13, paras. 105–390.)

Various calls have been made over the years for the abolition of distress for rent culminating in Shelter's 1978 report. There can be no doubt that the remedy is archaic, over-technical and cumbersome. There are many other arguments against its use:

1) it is, as we have seen, a remedy effectively available only against municipal tenants because of statutory restrictions in the private sector;

2) its incidence is unevenly geographically situated, and it seems to be most used in rural areas;

3) some authorities refuse to countenance the use of distress, while others use it only to administer a 'sharp shock' where they feel that the tenant is wilfully withholding the rent. It seems odd that tenants' rights

should vary so much according to mere geographical locations and the administrative practice of individual authorities;

4) the remedy is medieval and if used can damage the development of good landlord/tenant relationships;

5) the *threat* or actual levying of distress can be, and sometimes is, used against tenants who are in real financial difficulties through no fault of their own, as such it militates against the idea that local housing authorities should attempt to help such people through their difficulties;

6) the bailiffs employed by local authorities are frequently not public employees but are in private practice;

7) the evidence is that distress does not solve the problem of rent arrears, especially where these are the result of misfortune and unavoidable low income.

Duncan and Kirby surveyed authorities who used distress where there was an *unwillingness* to pay, but where a household enjoyed a high income. However, the resale value of goods distrained is never high and so to recoup arrears in this way requires early action before 'serious arrears' develop, and this makes it all the more necessary to use such action with discrimination so that genuinely vulnerable tenants are not subjected to distress. This involves housing staff selecting and supervising the certificated bailiffs who distrain with real care. In *Distress for Rent* Association of District Council Circular 1980/204, it is recommended, inter alia, that bailiffs should be carefully vetted before appointment, and instructed to refer back to the authority cases of genuine hardship. The use and effectiveness of distress should also be regularly monitored.

Those authorities who do *not* use distress very often refrain from the practice because they find that the value of the property seized will be insufficient to satisfy the debt owed. In such circumstances the only persons who stand to gain from the distress are the bailiff retained by the local authority and the auctioneer employed to sell the goods seized.

Housing association rents

Part VI of the Rent Act 1977 applies to 'housing association tenancies', i.e. tenancies (other than co-ownership) where the landlord's interest belongs to a housing association, or housing trust or the housing corporation, *and* where the tenant would be 'protected' but for sections 15 and 16 of the 1977 Act (which exclude such tenancies from protection and Rent Act security of tenure) and where the tenancy does not fall within Part II of the Landlord and Tenant Act 1954. Section 87 goes on to lay down that there shall be a part of the register under Part IV of the 1977 Act in which rents may be registered for dwelling-houses let under housing association tenancies and that sections 67, 69, 70, 71, 72 (save for (3)) and Schedules 11 and 12 apply to that part of the register. (See further below.) Under section 88 a rent limit exists for housing association tenancies, excess rent above the limit being irrecoverable from the tenant. That limit (subject to section 89, which is concerned with the phased increase of rent on registration) is, where a rent is registered, the registered rent [together with a sum for rates borne by the landlord], or, where there is no registered rent, whichever of the following applies is the limit:

(a) where the lease or agreement creating the tenancy was made pre 1 January 1973, the rent recoverable thereunder;
(b) where the lease or agreement was made after 1 January 1973, *and* not more than two years before the tenancy began the dwelling was subject to another tenancy, the rent is that recoverable under that other tenancy's last rental period;
(c) otherwise the rent originally payable under the lease or agreement is that which is recoverable.

Under section 94 where a tenant has paid 'irrecoverable' rent, that tenant is entitled to recover the relevant amount from the landlord, and may do this by deduction from rent payable, though no such amount is recoverable at any time after the expiry of two years from the date of payment. Housing association periodical tenancy rents may be increased, without the tenancy being terminated, from the beginning of a rental period by a written notice of increase, specifying the date on which the notice is to take effect and given by the landlord to the tenant not later than four weeks before that date; but the increases may not be above the rent limit, see section 92(1) and (5). The county court has jurisdiction in relation to rent limit disputes, see section 96(3).

Under section 67 of the 1977 Act application for registration of a rent may be made to a rent officer by either landlord or tenant, or jointly. Applications must be in prescribed form, and must specify the rent it is sought to register, sums payable in respect of services and such other particulars as are prescribed. In general once a rent is registered, no application *by either party alone* for registration of a different rent for the dwelling may be entertained before two years have expired from the date on which a registered rent took effect, or, where a registered rent has been confirmed, the date on which its confirmation took effect, unless there has been such a change in the condition of the dwelling (including improvements), the terms of the tenancy, the quantity, quality or condition of furniture provided under the tenancy, or any other circumstances taken into account when the rent was registered, as to make the registered rent no longer fair. However, a *landlord* alone may make an application within the last three months of the period of two years.

The procedure in respect of determining a rent is laid down in Schedule 11. Where an application to register is received the Rent Officer may obtain information relevant to the application from the parties. On a joint application the Rent Officer may register the rent specified in the application without more ado if he considers it fair. In other cases the Rent Officer invites the parties whether they wish him, in consultation with them, to consider what rent ought to be registered. The party who did not make the application must be served with a copy of the application. Where no response is made in due form to the Rent Officer's invitation, he may consider what rent ought to be registered, and register a rent, or new rent, or confirm the existing as the case may be, or serve notice of intention to fix a rent. Where the officer's invitation results in a written response from either or both parties that he/they wish the rent to be considered, the officer must serve notice of the time and place at which he proposes in consultation with the parties, or such of them as appear, to consider what rent ought to be registered etc., for the dwelling. At the consultation the parties may be represented. Thereafter the officer may determine, or confirm, as the case may be, the rent and register it, informing the parties by notice. They then have 28 days to lodge an objection, and the matter is then referred by the officer to a rent assessment committee.

The rent assessment committee may obtain further information from the parties, and must allow them to make representations to the committee, either in writing or orally. It is the committee's duty to make such inquiries as they think fit and to consider information supplied and representations made, and then to determine whether the rent officer reached a correct fair rent, or whether his rent was not fair, in which case they determine the fair rent. Their decision is notified to the parties and the officer, who makes an appropriate entry in the register of fair rents.

Section 69 of the 1977 Act allows a person intending to let a house not subject to a tenancy and which has either no registered rent, or has such a rent but not less than two years have elapsed since it took effect, to apply to the rent officer for a certificate of fair rent in which the officer specifies a rent which he considers would be fair. Such certificates are used to support applications for registration of a rent once a tenant has accepted the offer of a dwelling, see Rent Act 1977, Schedule 11, Part III. [*See Addendum 12.*]

In determining a fair rent under section 70 regard has to be had to all the circumstances, other than personal circumstances, and in particular to the age, character, locality and state of repair of the dwelling, and the quantity, quality and condition of any furniture provided under the tenancy. The 'scarcity value' of dwellings may not, however, be taken into account, nor may improvements or defects attributable to the tenant affecting the dwelling or furniture provided under the tenancy. The amount to be registered as rent under section 71 must include any sum payable for the use of furniture or services, whether or not those sums are separate from the sum payable in respect to occupation of the dwelling, or are payable under a separate agreement. Where any sums payable include sums varying according to the cost from time to time of services provided by the landlord, or works of repair carried out by the landlord, the amount to be registered as rent may, where the rent officer, or rent assessment committee as the case may be, is satisfied that the terms as to variation are reasonable, be entered as an amount varying in accordance with those terms.

Under section 72 the registration of a rent takes effect, where determined by the rent officer, from the date of registration, and, where determined by the committee, from the date of their decision, and similarly for confirmation of existing rents. [For further detail on the procedures etc. to be followed see *The Encyclopedia of Housing Law and Practice* paras. 1–1913 to 1–1933 and 1–1967 to 1–1987.]

Not only do the great majority of housing association tenancies fall within the terms of Part VI of the 1977 Act, but most tenancies will also have a registered rent as a condition of receiving Housing Association Grant (HAG) for HAG is a grant of capital against the cost of providing housing association dwellings, so that the amount of that cost left outstanding can be serviced by fair rents received on the property, see further Bucknall, *Housing Finance* pp. 125, and 135 to 137. It is rare also for an association to charge *less* rent than the maximum legally recoverable because of grant conditions etc.

Rent assistance

Before 1972 there was an attempt to introduce rent rebates contained in section 113(3) of the Housing Act 1957: 'the local authority may grant to any tenants such rebates from rent, subject to such terms and conditions, as they may think fit'. But this scheme was discretionary and was replaced by a mandatory national scheme under section 18 of the Housing Finance Act 1972, as amended by Schedule 15 to the Housing Act 1980. A completely new 'housing benefits' scheme was introduced by Part II of the Social Security and Housing Benefits Act 1982. This is to be replaced under the Social Security Act 1986. This Act provides a general framework for a detailed scheme to be made by way of regulations. However, the principal features of the new scheme will be that there will be as 'housing benefits' rate rebates, funded and administered by rating authorities, rent rebates, funded and administered by housing authorities in respect of payments, other than of rates, made to them, and rent allowances, funded and administered by local authorities, to cover other cases. The new scheme is expected to be introduced in April 1988.

The proposal in the 1985 Green Paper on Social Security (Cmnd. 9517, 9518, 9519) was that there should be for both supplementary benefits and housing benefits a common system of assessing income based on an applicant's 'net income' with all those whose net income is below the 'income support' level qualifying for maximum benefit levels. Benefits will taper off according to the rate at which the 'income support' level is exceeded [see further McGurk and Raynsford, *Guide to Housing Benefit* Chap. 1, to which the author acknowledges indebtedness.] Accordingly the 1986 Act provides for 'prescribed schemes' to provide for, inter alia, housing benefit as an income related benefit. A person will be entitled to this if he is liable to make payments (that is such payments as are prescribed, but excluding mortgage payments) in respect of a dwelling in Great Britain occupied as his home, *and* there is an appropriate maximum housing benefit in the case, such maximum benefit to be fixed by regulations, *and either* he has no income, or such as does not exceed the 'applicable amount' (again to be prescribed) in which case the amount of benefit is the appropriate maximum housing benefit in his case. A person may also be eligible for housing benefit where his income exceeds the 'applicable amount', but the amount of benefit shall be what remains after deducting from the appropriate maximum housing benefit prescribed percentages of the excess of his income over the applicable amount.

Authorities will have a discretion in determining income for the purposes of benefits to disregard the whole or part of any war disablement or war widow's pension payable to a person, and may modify the benefit scheme to such other extent as may be prescribed, but so as not to allow the total of rebates/allowances granted in any one year to exceed the permitted total of such benefits for that year. This permitted total is to be calculated in the manner specified by the Secretary of State. Determinations of claims for benefit must be notified to claimants, and the scheme will make provision for reviews of determinations.

The Secretary of State will pay rate rebate, rent rebate and rent allowance subsidies to relevant authorities, such subsidy to be calculated in the manner specified by the Secretary of State, though, in the case of rent rebates, authorities will have to make a rate fund contribution to meet any shortfall between rent rebate subsidy and the cost of rebates granted, together with the cost of administering rebates. Provision is made for the supply of information in relation to benefits between the Secretary of State and authorities, and to require authorities to bring the existence of benefits to the attention of those who may be entitled to them.

In view of the likely changes to be made to benefits under the 1986 Act, what follows is a *brief* survey of the principal features of the schemes under the 1982 Act. Readers requiring more details are referred to Pollard, *Encyclopedia of Social Welfare Law* paras. F.3001 to F.3600.

In 1984 the government announced that 6,970,000 households received some form of housing benefit, of whom 3,729,000 were council tenants, and 4,130,000 were pensioners. In March 1985 it was further announced that the cost of housing benefits to all *tenants* was currently £2.6bn p.a. These benefits were payable under a scheme whose chief feature is the division of claimants into two groups ('standard' and 'certificated', the latter generally those in receipt of supplementary benefits) with the scheme administered by local authorities, subject to rigid cost constraints, coupled with administrative complexity which has led to the scheme being greatly criticised, officially and unofficially. See, for example, Shac Policy Paper No. 8, *Housing Benefit: Is This the Promised End?*, and National Audit Office, *Department of Health and Social Security: Housing Benefits Scheme* HMSO 1984.

The present scheme exists under section 28 of the Act of 1982, and is subject to review under section 29. The national scheme is made by the Secretary of State, though local authorities have a certain discretion to introduce local schemes under section 30. Before making regulations under section 28, the Secretary of State is under an obligation under section 36 to consult with organisations appearing to him to be representative of the authorities concerned. Such consultation must be genuine, allowing consultees reasonable time to formulate their views. Consultees must also be given all material information, see *R v Secretary of State for Social Services, ex p Association of Metropolitan Authorities* [1986] 1 All ER 164, [1986] 1 WLR 1. Authorities granting benefits under schemes are under a duty to publicise them by virtue of section 31. Subsidies are payable by the Secretary of State in respect of schemes under sections 32 and 33, though a rate fund contribution may be payable by authorities themselves in respect of rent rebate benefits paid, see section 34 of the Social Security and Housing Benefits Act 1982.

The 'meat' of the scheme is contained in S.I. 1985/677, which provides for both the national 'statutory' and local schemes, the former being described in what follows.

Eligibility

Regulation 4 imposes a general ban on anyone being eligible for benefit in respect of more than one dwelling. The requirements for particular benefits are:

1) for rate rebates, that the person is liable to pay rates on the dwelling, or, though not liable, makes them as if he were, being either the partner of the person liable, or some other person whom the rating authority consider it reasonable to treat as eligible;

2) for rent rebates, that the person is liable to make payments other than rates to a housing authority (i.e. effectively district and London Borough councils) in respect of the dwelling, or makes payments as if liable, etc.;

3) for rent allowances, that the person is liable to make payments, other than of rates, and otherwise than to a housing authority in respect of the dwelling, or makes payments as if liable.

Certain persons are excluded in whole, or partly, from benefit, e.g. owner-occupiers and long leaseholders may receive benefits in respect of rates only, while Crown tenants, boarders and non-householders in receipt of supplementary benefit and certain overseas students are excluded wholly, see further McGurk and Raynsford op cit Table 2.1.

Eligible payments

Housing benefits are not payable in respect of all housing costs. Eligible rates are defined by Reg. 17, and include general rates paid to a rating authority, whether directly or indirectly, but only in so far as the rates refer to residential accommodation occupied as the rebatee's home; water rates are not eligible save in some 'certificated cases', see McGurk and Raynsford, para. 3.3.8. Eligible rents are defined by Reg. 18, 'rent' having been widely defined by Reg. 2, but, of course, including payments in respect of the use and occupation of a dwelling. However, the *eligible* rent is such amount as the applicant is liable to pay *less* any amount fairly attributable to the inclusive payment of rates, charges for water, etc. and the provision of board, *or*, where the rent includes charges for fuel for heating, water, lighting or cooking in respect of the dwelling, the eligible rent is what is paid, less an amount calculated under Schedule 3 of the Regulations. This amount will generally be (save in certificated cases) where the fuel charge is readily identifiable, the amount of that charge, and in other cases such amount as the appropriate authority considers is fairly attributable to such a charge. In certificated cases a deduction specified in the regulations is made. [See further McGurk and Raynsford Table 2.2.]

Reg. 19 allows authorities to reduce to an amount appropriate in the circumstances eligible rents and rates where they consider that the eligible person is occupying a dwelling larger than he reasonably requires, or the eligible person's dwelling by reason of its location has rates and/or a rent unreasonably high by comparison with other rates/rents payable in respect of suitable alternative accommodation in the area. But such a reduction is not to be made where it is not reasonable to expect the eligible person to seek cheaper accommodation having regard to the availability of suitable alternative accommodation *and* the circumstances of the occupiers of his dwelling, the eligible person's prospects of retaining or obtaining employment and the effect on the education of any dependent children if a change in accommodation were to result in a change of school.

Rebates and allowances may be reduced in respect of non-dependents within the applicant's household, see Reg. 20, which applies *fixed* deductions, and see McGurk and Raynsford, paras. 2.2.9 to 2.2.12. Rent and rates received from sub-tenants may also reduce benefits, see Schedule 3, paras. 10 and 11.

The classes of beneficiary

Certificated cases

Under Reg. 9 where a person, other than someone ineligible, has claimed and is entitled to supplementary benefit, the Secretary of State's duty is to issue to each appropriate authority a certificate in respect of that person stating the date on which benefit became payable, and on receipt of that certificate the appropriate authority must treat him as a person eligible for housing benefit in respect of the dwelling he occupies as his home, and thus to receive total assistance to meet eligible costs. The certificate is treated as a claim for benefit, see Reg. 31(2). Even a certificated claimant may find his entitlements reduced in respect of matters such as receipts from sub-tenants, or the presence in his household of non-dependants etc., see above and McGurk and Raynsford, paras. 3.3.1 to 3.3.9, and Reg. 24. The benefit period begins on the date specified in the certificate as that on which the supplementary benefit in respect of which it was issued became payable, see Reg. 28(1)(b). Where the beneficiary is a local, or other public, authority tenant benefit is received as a rebate from liability to pay rent and rates, and this may mean 'nothing to pay', but not where there are housing costs ineligible for benefit. The position is similar in respect of rebates on rates for certificated owner occupiers. Notification of determinations on benefits must be made under Reg. 50, and such notifications should state, inter alia, in certificated cases the amount of any charges ineligible for benefit still to be collected. Where the beneficiary is the tenant of a private landlord or housing association, benefits are payable by way of an allowance, and this should cover eligible housing costs, see Regs. 24 and 32(1)(b).

Under Reg. 44 rent allowances are not to be paid to a person other than the beneficiary. However, payment *may* be made direct to the landlord where the beneficiary consents or has requested such a payment; where the beneficiary is at least thirteen weeks in arrears with his rent, and *must* be made where the appropriate authority are notified by the Secretary of State that a weekly amount of the beneficiary's supplementary benefit is being paid to his landlord to meet arrears of rent. The Court of Appeal has held that where a tenant in receipt of housing benefit fails to pay his rent, it may be appropriate, to protect the landlord, and prevent abuse of the benefits system, to grant the landlord an ex parte injunction requiring the tenant to pay his benefit into court pending determination of the landlord's claim for arrears of rent, see *Berg v Markhill* (1985) 17 HLR 455.

Standard cases

Standard benefits cover all eligible persons not certificated. Claims for benefits have to be made, under Reg. 31, in writing to the appropriate authority, and they must, under Reg. 32, determine the claimant's entitlement. To enable them to do this they must request the claimant to produce evidence of inter alia the amount of his rent/rates; income consisting of rent payable to him or any partner of his; the number and identity of other occupiers of the dwelling; the income of the claimant and any partner of his, and the capital on which the claimant receives interest. Claims must be determined within fourteen days of reception of such evidence, or so soon as reasonably practicable thereafter, see Reg. 32(5).

Standard benefits are computed as weekly amounts having regard to an amount to be allowed for the needs of the claimant, any partner of his and any dependent child (the 'needs allowance'); the weekly income of the claimant and any partner, disregarding certain sums under Schedule 2; in the case of rate rebates the amount of eligible rates, and in the case of rent rebates and allowances the amount of eligible rent; amounts to be deducted for non-dependants and the minimum and maximum amounts of rebate, see Reg, 23. The actual equation for determining benefit in any given case is contained in Reg. 22. The first step is to determine a figure equal to 60 per cent of eligible rent/rates, and from this any deduction in respect of 'non-dependants', i.e. members of the claimant's household (other than his partner or dependant children) or his lodgers, required under Reg. 20 must be made. This produces a figure, positive or negative, known as £X. The second step is to compare the weekly income of the eligible person under Reg. 16, allowing for disregards, with the relevant needs allowance as contained in regulations. Where weekly income is equal to the relevant needs allowance, the weekly benefit will be £X as previously computed. Where income and needs allowances are not equal the weekly amount of benefit is £X minus/plus specified percentages of the amount by which weekly income either exceeds, or is less than, the relevant needs allowance. The specified percentages are known administratively as tapers, and different percentages are applied in different circumstances, the object being to ensure that someone, for example, with a weekly income *below* the relevant needs allowance receives £X plus a percentage of the amount whereby weekly income falls short of the needs allowance as his benefit. [For the special form of supplementary benefit known as housing benefit supplement, see McGurk and Raynsford, paras. 4.7 to 4.7.4, and Pollard, *Encyclopedia of Social Welfare Law* paras. F.3451 to F.3468.]

Where a beneficiary's circumstances change, either before a claim is determined, or during the benefit period, in such a way that a person may reasonably be expected to know that it may affect eligibility for benefit, it is his duty to inform the appropriate authority, see Reg. 33.

One feature of the scheme of benefits new to local authority practice, and to be continued, at least in some form, under the Social Security Act 1986, is provision for reviews of benefit determinations. Under Reg. 51 a person may make representations to an authority concerning a determination on benefit made in relation to him. Where an authority receives such representations in writing from a person within six weeks of notification to him of such a determination, it must consider the representations, review the determination and alter or confirm it according to the circumstances, and notify the person in question, informing him of their decision and giving reasons therefor, and informing him of his right to require a further review under Regs. 52 to 54. A person who has thus made representations under Reg. 51 (an interested person) may then within twenty days of being given notification by the authority of their decision require, in writing, a further review, stating the grounds on which it is required.

The further review is conducted by a review board consisting of not less than three persons qualified under Schedule 5 of the regulations. For a local authority these persons will be its councillors. Within six weeks of receiving a requirement for a further review the review board must hold a hearing on the initial determination. Reasonable notice of the time and place of the hearing must be given to the interested person, and if he makes written representations these must be considered. The interested person is entitled to be present at the hearing, other than the time set aside for arriving at a decision, and is also entitled to be heard, to call and cross-examine evidence, and may be represented; otherwise the review board may regulate their procedure and receive evidence from such persons as they consider appropriate.

It is for the review board to decide whether to confirm or alter the authority's determination, applying the regulations. They must record their decisions in writing, also recording their findings on materials questions of fact, and giving reasons for their decision. Within seven days of a decision a copy of this record of the decision must be sent to the authority and the interested person. Authorities must alter their determinations in accordance with decisions of review boards.

To enable claimants to avail themselves of these rights every determination on a benefit under Reg. 50 must inform the claimant of his right to make representations under Reg. 51. Furthermore under Reg. 50(5) a person may request a statement from an authority showing how his entitlement to benefit, or lack of it, has been calculated, and the authority must provide that within fourteen days.

Illustrative examples of practice before review boards may be found in 'LAG Bulletin', November 1983, p. 135; 'Legal Action' January 1984, p. 4; 'Housing Aid', January 1985, No. 31, p. 7; and 'Housing Aid' April 1985, No. 32, p. 13. Review boards are subject to the supervisory jurisdiction of the High Court, see *R v Ealing London Borough Council Housing Benefit Review Board, ex p Saville* (1986) 18 HLR 349, (1986) Times, 6 May.

Further reading

Harvey, A., *Remedies for Rent Arrears* (Shelter, 1979).
Schifferes, S., *In Distress over Rent* (Shelter, 1979).
Behind with the Rent (National Consumer Council Discussion Paper, 1976).
Franey, R., 'Punishment for Rent Arrears' *Roof* May/June 1980, p. 80.
Could Local Authorities be better Landlords? (Housing Research Group, The City University, 1981).
HMSO *Housing Subsidies and Accounting Manual* 1981.
Duncan, S., and Kirby, K., *Preventing Rent Arrears* (HMSO, 1983).
Fielding, N., 'The housing benefit fiasco' *Roof* Nov/Dec. 1983, p. 19.
Timmins, N., and Walker, D., 'Anatomy of a bureaucratic jungle' *The Times* 20 January 1984.

Ermisch, J., *Housing Finance: Who Gains?* (Chap. V) (Policy Studies Institute, 1984).

Fielding, N., 'Finding new ways to beat the bailiff' *Roof* May/June 1984, p. 23.

National Audit Office, *Department of Health and Social Security: Housing Benefits Scheme* (HMSO, 1984).

Shac, 'Housing Benefit: is this the promised end?' (Shac Policy Paper 8).

Bucknall, B., *Housing Finance* (Chap. 4, 6, 11 and 15) (CIPFA, 1985).

McGurk, P., and Raynsford, N., *Guide to Housing Benefit* (Shac and the Institute of Housing, June 1986).

National Audit Office, *Managing the Crisis in Council Housing* (HMSO, 1986).

Pollard, D., *Encyclopedia of Social Welfare Law* (Oyez Longman) paras. B.291 to B.318, B.1101 to B.1109, and F.3001 to F.3561.

Arden, A., and Partington, P., *Housing Law* (Chap. 3 and 6) (Sweet & Maxwell 1983).

Law Commission Working Paper No. 97, 'Distress for rent'.

Chapter 5

Matrimony and
maladministration – management III

The public sector house as the matrimonial home

Conveyancing practice has for many years tended, in the private sector, to treat joint ownership of the house as the norm where property is to be occupied as the matrimonial home. In municipal housing historic practice was to assume that where a married couple occupied a council house the husband would be the tenant. The 1976 National Consumer Council discussion paper *Tenancy Agreements* pointed out it cannot be assumed that the male partner of a couple should automatically be the tenant. In 1977 the Housing Services Advisory Group (HSAG) in its report on tenancy agreements argued that prospective tenants should be given the opportunity to choose between a joint and a sole tenancy. By 1978 the HSAG in its report on the housing of one parent families actually recommended the use of joint tenancies in municipal lettings: 'In council tenancies too there are strong advantages to joint tenancies . . . . For common-law wives there is a great advantage in having a joint tenancy. Unfortunately many authorities refuse to give tenancies to unmarried couples. Some even refuse to house them at all. We believe that such policies should be reconsidered'.

There are obvious advantages for the female if she has a joint tenancy of a house with the male:

1) In the event of his death or desertion there is no need for her to apply for a transfer of the tenancy to herself;

2) In any proceedings for divorce, nullity or judicial separation the court may make an order with regard to the transfer of the property under section 24 of the Matrimonial Causes Act 1973;

3) If the relationship breaks up she will be entitled to remain in occupation of the home by virtue of her legal estate.

4) Under section 9 of the Matrimonial Homes Act 1983 where *each* of two *spouses* is entitled by virtue of a joint legal estate to occupy a dwelling which is, or was, their matrimonial home, either may apply to the

court with regard to the exercise during the subsistence of the marriage of the right to occupy the dwelling for an order prohibitting, suspending or restricting its exercise by the other or requiring that other to permit its exercise by the applicant. This right also applies where the entitlement of the spouses arises by virtue of a contract or enactment. In the case of a *periodic secure* tenancy if any of the joint tenants gives notice to quit in due form the joint tenancy is determined, thus depriv-, ing the other(s) of security, see *Greenwich London Borough Council v McGrady* (1982) 6 HLR 36, and *Parsons v Parsons* [1983] 1 WLR 1390.

The disadvantage of a joint tenancy to a woman is that she can be held liable for any rent arrears accrued by the man before his death or desertion, etc.

The Housing Act 1985 recognises in a number of its provisions that local authorities may grant joint tenancies but goes no further in encouraging them to do so. One pre-1980 practice that is impossible under current law is that of issuing notice to quit to a deserted joint tenant before granting a new sole tenancy, unless, of course, the local landlord can show one of the grounds for possession. For the future it may be hoped that landlords will use joint tenancies when letting to couples. Administrative practice should reflect the legal situation and communications from the landlord should be sent to tenants jointly in both names. It should also be made clear in the tenancy agreement that the authorisation of either partner will be sufficient to authorise or agree to the doing of works and repairs by the landlord. Where joint tenancies are not possible and a single tenant is required, a couple being allocated a house should be given a choice as to which of them will be named as tenant. Before a choice is made between different kinds of tenancy it is obviously a matter of good housing management for a landlord to explain the implications of each to intending tenants.

The rights of a non-tenant female

A *wife* who is not a tenant has the right to occupy and use the matrimonial home because at common law she is entitled to maintenance by her husband.

Legislation goes further than this, for section 1 of the Matrimonial Homes Act 1983 provides that where one spouse is entitled to occupy a dwelling by virtue of a beneficial interest, contract or enactment giving him or her the right to remain in occupation, and the other is not so entitled, then that spouse has rights of occupation in the dwelling; in particular, if in occupation, the right not to be evicted or excluded from the dwelling except by court order, or, if not in occupation, the right to enter and occupy the dwelling by virtue of a court order. So long as one spouse has rights of occupation either may apply for a court order declaring, enforcing, restricting or terminating the rights, prohibiting, suspending or restricting the exercise by either spouse of the right to occupy the dwelling, or requiring either spouse to permit the exercise by the other of that right. The court has wide discretion, under section 1(3), in the making of orders and is to take into account the conduct of the parties, their needs and resources, the needs of any children and all other circumstances of the case.

The needs of children are not the only consideration, nor are they of paramount importance, in governing the exercise of this discretion, see *Richards v Richards* [1984] AC 174, [1983] 2 All ER 807, though most commentators agree that the courts will give great consideration to advancing the interests of that spouse with whom the children of the relationship are living, particularly if they are in bad or unsuitable housing while the other spouse occupies the former home alone. However, a wife who has behaved badly may find the court's discretion exercised against her. An order may be made under this provision even though violence has not yet broken out between the parties provided it is clear the marriage cannot continue, though mere tension is not enough, see *Phillips v Phillips* [1973] 2 All ER 423, [1973] 1 WLR 615. A court will not, however, make an order merely to aid a local housing authority to obtain posession of a dwelling in circumstances where it is clear the wife will not return to a dwelling if the husband is excluded, see *Warwick v Warwick* (1982) 1 HLR 139. The Matrimonial Homes Act 1983 is, however, considered by many to be a complete and exclusive code to regulate rights of occupation in relation to *matrimonial* homes during the currency of marriage, see 1983 LAG Bulletin (December) 145 (Rae), (1983) 133 NLJ 759 (Purdie) and (1984) Legal Action (March) 25 (Hamilton). The above rights only apply within marriage, not outside it. This is a very good reason why 'common law' wives should seek to obtain joint tenancies wherever possible as a way of obtaining at least some legal interest in the property.

Domestic violence

'Domestic violence' is the euphemism for the social phenomenon of wife-battering. The Select Committee on Violence in Marriage Report (H.C. 553, 1974–5) recognised the extent of this problem and recommended that special refuges be set up where women could go to get away from violent men, and that the initial target provision should be one family place per 10,000 of the population. Local authorities should assist in making this provision and the HSAG report *The Housing of One Parent Families* stated at pp. 15–16: 'The refuge need not be in the form of a hostel. In fact in rural areas and small towns it will probably be more appropriate to have mutual arrangements between the police, probation services, social services and housing departments for the provision of emergency accommodation and social work support where and when the need arises. In cities, there may be a strong case for hostel-type provision, but this should be only for short stay emergency accommodation and more satisfactory family accommodation should be provided as quickly as possible, even if this is an intermediate step before permanent rehousing. . . . The local authority should undertake to rehouse, if needed, women who leave these refuges having separated from their partners. Some authorities are now giving a general undertaking to rehouse all women who go through these hostels within six months of their arrival, whether or not they have any legal separation or custody order and whether or not they have previous arrears'.

There are now some 150 to 200 refuges nationwide, (one refuge place per 70,000 of the population) some municipally provided and administered, others provided by various support groups and often run on a cooperative basis. Refuges may be overcrowded, with limited facilities and an absence of privacy, and the refuge at first applied to may be full and only able to give the address of a further refuge that does have space, see further *A Woman's Place* (Witherspoon, published by Shac) pp. 41–42 and 'Are battered Women a lost cause in the 1980s?' Roberts, Sunday Times 17 August 1986.

To protect the woman in the home the Domestic Violence and Matrimonial Proceedings Act 1976 was enacted. This legislation was necessary because the existing law was inadequate. Previously a wife could commence assault proceedings against her husband, and this might result in the husband being bound over with, perhaps, some supervision by a probation officer. Likewise where a wife had commenced divorce or judicial separation proceedings she could also apply for an injunction to prohibit molestation, or even a mandatory injunction excluding the husband from the home. But faster and simpler legal machinery was needed. The 1976 Act therefore provides:

'1(1) Without prejudice to the jurisdiction of the High Court, on an application by a party to a marriage a court shall have jurisdiction to grant an injunction containing one or more of the following provisions, namely,

    (a) a provision restraining the other party to the marriage from molesting the applicant; [an 'anti-molestation' order]

  (b) a provision restraining the other party from molesting a child living with the applicant; [an 'anti-molestation' order]
  (c) a provision excluding the other party from the matrimonial home or a part of the matrimonial home or from a specified area in which the matrimonial home is included; [an 'ouster' order]
  (d) a provision requiring the other party to permit the applicant to enter and remain in the matrimonial home or a part of the matrimonial home; whether or not any other relief is sought in the proceedings.

(2) Sub-section (1) above shall apply to a man and a woman who are living with each other in the same household as man and wife as it applies to the parties to a marriage and any reference to the matrimonial home shall be construed accordingly'.

This provision was tested in *Davis v Johnson* [1979] AC 264, [1978] 1 All ER 1132. A young unmarried mother held a joint tenancy of a council flat with the father of her child. She left the flat with her child because of the father's violent behaviour towards her and applied to the county court under the 1976 Act for an injunction to restrain him from molesting her or the child and also excluding him from the flat. The House of Lords held that the county court has jurisdiction under section 1 of the Act to grant an injunction excluding a violent person from a home where he has lived, with a woman, irrespective of their marital status, and irrespective of any right of property vested in the person excluded, whether as owner, tenant or joint tenant. A further illustrative case is *Adeoso v Adeoso* [1981] 1 All ER 107, [1980] 1 WLR 1535. The parties began living together in a council flat in January 1975, and were subsequently moved into another flat consisting of one bedroom, a sitting-room, kitchen and bathroom. They did not marry, but Mrs Adeoso adopted her partner's name. By July 1979 the relationship had become unhappy and Mr Adeoso had begun to resort to violence. The parties slept in different rooms, and Mrs Adeoso ceased to cook or wash for Mr Adeoso. Their only communication was by notes. They locked the rooms they occupied individually. Mrs Adeoso applied for an order under the domestic violence legislation requiring Mr Adeoso to stop molesting her and also to leave the flat. Mr Adeoso argued that the 1976 Act did not apply as the parties were not in fact living together, and also because they occupied separate accomodation. The Court of Appeal rejected both contentions. Ormrod LJ said that looking at the Adeoso household from the outside it would be assumed that the parties were living together, and that the case fell within the rule in *Davis v Johnson*. Also it was impossible to say that the parties were living separately in a flat with only two rooms.

In practical terms exclusions are not permanent, but should be for such a period of time as will enable the applicant to make other arrangements for accomodation, or effect a reconciliation, or commence separation proceedings, as the case may be.

In *Wooton v Wooton* [1985] Fam Law 31 the court held that orders under the 1976 Act were temporary measures, designed to make stop gap provision in a situation where immediate protection is required pending a property adjustment by the court, and inappropriate where no such order is to be made. This was followed in *Collins v Freeman* (1983) 12 HLR 122. But an order lasting for a longer period may be granted where the evidence of continuing violence justifies it, see *Spencer v Camacho* (1983) 12 HLR 130 and *Fairweather v Kolosine* (1983) 11 HLR 61. It seems that where an order is sought under the 1976 Act the same considerations will apply as to its grant as apply to an order made under Section 1 of the 1983 Act (see above).

Section 2 of the 1976 Act provides extra enforcement proceedings for breach of injunctions.

'(1) Where on an application by a party to a marriage, a judge grants an injunction containing a provision . . .
- (a) restraining the other party to the marriage from using violence against the applicant, or
- (b) restraining the other party from using violence against a child living with the applicant, or
- (c) excluding the other party from the matrimonial home or from a specified area in which the matrimonial home is included,

The judge may, if he is satisfied that the other party has caused actual bodily harm to the applicant, or, as the case may be, to the child concerned and considers that he is likely to do so again, attach a power of arrest to the injunction'.

Where such a power of arrest is attached to an injunction, a police constable may arrest without a warrant any person whom he reasonably suspects of being in breach of the provisions detailed above included in the injunction. Again, this section applies both to married couples and to a man and a woman living together as man and wife. See *White v White* [1983] Fam 54, [1983] 2 All ER 51.

Section 16 of the Domestic Proceedings and Magistrates' Courts Act 1978 empowers a magistrates' court to make a personal protection order prohibiting a spouse from threatening, or using violence against, the other spouse, or any child of the family.

Either party *to a marriage* may apply to the magistrates under this section. Where the court is satisfied the respondent has used, or threatened to use, violence against the applicant, or a child of the family, *and* that it is necessary for their protection to make an order, one or both of the following 'personal protection' orders may be made; a) an order not to use or threaten to use violence against the applicant, b) an order not to use or threaten to use violence against a child of the family. Further, where satisfied that the respondent *has used* violence against the applicant or a child of the family, *or* that the respondent has threatened to use violence against the applicant or a child of the family *and* has used violence against some other person, *or* the respondent has threatened violence in contravention of a personal protection order, *and* that the applicant or a child of the family is in danger of physical injury by the respondent, the court may make an 'exclusion' order either requiring the respondent to leave the matrimonial home, or to prohibit the respondent's entry, or both.

Provision is made for extremely rapid hearings in such situations. Section 18 of this Act allows the magistrates to annex a power of arrest to an exclusion order where they are satisfied that the respondent has physically injured the applicant or a child of the family, and consider him likely to do so again.

Thus the magistrates in the exercise of their domestic jurisdiction now have powers approximating to those of the county court, but it must be remembered that their powers apply only within the context of marriage.

The rights of the parties on the break-up of a marriage

Section 24 of the Matrimonial Causes Act 1973 grants the court an extensive jurisdiction to adjust the property rights of the parties on the break up of a marriage, and to order one party to transfer property to the other. The assignment of a secure tenancy in pursuance of a property adjustment order made in connection with matrimonial proceedings is allowed under section 91(3)(b) of the Housing Act 1985. Thus in the case of a secure tenancy the court has wide powers to order its transfer between the parties to a divorce, decree of nullity or judicial separation. The court also has power to transfer, by its *own order*, secure tenancies. Section 7 and Schedule 1 of the Matrimonial Homes Act 1983 provide that where one spouse is entitled singly or jointly with the other to occupy a dwelling by virtue of, inter alia, a secure tenancy, then on a grant of a divorce, a decree of nullity or judicial separation, or at any time thereafter, the court may make an order transferring the tenancy, its benefits and burdens, from the spouse entitled to occupy to the other spouse, the transfer to take effect on the date specified in the order. Under section 22 of the Matrimonial and Family Proceedings Act 1984 the court has the same power to transfer a secure tenancy as it has under the Matrimonial Homes Act 1983, Schedule 1 on the grant of a divorce etc., where leave is given to apply for an order for financial relief, *provided* the dwelling-house has at some time during the marriage been a matrimonial home, this latter is also a *general* requirement under section 1(10) of the 1983 Act in proceedings under that Act.

But what of husbands who lose their homes as a result of court orders? A single man is unlikely to fall within the priority classes of homeless persons, but the husband may have formed another liaison, and children, other than those of the marriage may be involved. In this connection the findings and recommendations of the HSAG in *The Housing of One-Parent Families* should be remembered.

1) Local authorities should remember that on the break-up of a marriage two tenancies may be needed rather than one. This 'two for one' element should be remembered in computing the future housing needs of an area.

2) Where a man is living in the former matrimonial home with a woman who is not his wife, following the break-down of marriage, and the court makes an order against him in respect of that home, simple eviction merely leads to an increase in the number of homeless persons. An increasing number of authorities try to offer the displaced husband suitable alternative housing.

3) Where the husband has developed no new relationship and is alone following marital break-down, the local authority should attempt to *rehouse* him bearing in mind the following factors:
   (a) will the man be living near enough his children to be able to see them?
   (b) will he need to be able to have them to stay?
   (c) is he expecting to remarry?
   (d) is he emotionally upset and unable to cope with eviction on top of losing his wife and children?

The general tenor of the HSAG's findings is that, while local authorities have no desire to encourage marital break-ups by the premature allocation of separate tenancies to husband and wife, wherever possible housing should be provided for parties to a marriage leaving the matrimonial home. The group added (at p. 10 of their report): 'Though this may appear to be a far-reaching decision, we consider it essential if the local authority is to develop a routine policy towards marital break-ups rather than a policy of intervening when a crisis occurs. It is worth recalling the very large proportion of the homeless who are lone parent families and the very great cost to the authority of providing emergency accommodation for the homeless'.

Other housing problems arising after marital break-up

After marital break-ups where there are children the parent having custody of them will face other problems, in particular those of a financial nature. The HSAG have made recommendations with regard to local authority housing practice in relation to such one-parent families.

1) It is the best policy to house one-parent families in ordinary family housing in a mixed development, as such accomodation accords with their needs and helps prevent social stigmatisation.

2) Even where both former partners have been responsible for a build-up of rent arrears, it should be remembered that these may have arisen during a period of stress. Local authorities should make arrangements for the gradual repayment of arrears, but should not otherwise penalise the parties.

3) Liaison between housing and social service departments is essential in order to provide all-round support for the one-parent family. Though this is difficult where the services are administered by different tiers of the local government system, such co-operation is essential if financial and emotional distress amongst one-parent families is to be reduced.

4) A wife who retains, or is granted possession of, the former matrimonial home may not wish to stay there. Requests for transfers to housing closer to relatives, schools, places of work or nursery facilities, or to the area of another authority, should be treated sympathetically. A transfer request should not be made conditional on a woman paying off arrears of rent on the former matrimonial home for which her husband was solely responsible. Local authorities should also be prepared to make rapid housing exchanges in the case of any woman who fears violence from her former husband. Similar conclusions were reached in the Finer Report, Cmnd. 5629. See also DoE Circular No. 78/77.

Progressive authorities operate wherever possible, within the constraints of finance and the available housing stock, liberal policies with regard to the marital problems of their tenants. Unfortunately there are pockets of resistance to the introduction of such policies. Some authorities have adopted harsh, and indeed even illegal, practices with regard to lone parents. In such circumstances the best remedy is an investigation for maladministration by the local ombudsman. It is to the powers of the local ombudsman that we must now turn.

The Commission for Local Administration and housing

We have already seen how local authorities are the second main provider of homes in Britain, and that municipal housing is a scarce resource with an insufficient supply to meet the demands of society. Its allocation can therefore often give rise to disputes with feelings of anger at real or imagined injustices. It must be remembered that local authorities have an almost total discretion as to the disposal and transfer of their housing stock – a discretion with which the courts are reluctant to interfere. For this reason the existence of an independent body such as the Commission for Local Administration (the 'local ombudsman') is extremely important for those who rely on administrative discretion to obtain accommodation. It is now necessary to consider the role of that 'local ombudsman' principally in relation to housing authorities, though it is impossible to divorce housing from other aspects of the Commission's work. Housing authorities fall within the scope of that work under section 25(1)(a) of the Local Government Act 1974.

The creation of the Commission and its terms of reference

Established by the Local Government Act 1974, Part III, the Commission for Local Administration in England came into being in April 1974 and was modelled on the Parliamentary Commissioner, who had no jurisdiction over the actions of local government. The Commission is charged with investigating complaints from members of the public about injustice caused by maladministration in local government.

The Local Government Act 1974, s. 34(3) provides that nothing in the Act authorises or requires a Local Commissioner to question the *merits* of a decision taken without maladministration by an authority in the exercise of a discretion vested in it. This does not prevent the *investigation* of the merits of a decision, but it prevents the Commission from criticising a decision as *wrong in substance* when there was no procedural flaw in the process leading up to the decision. The maladministration must, by virtue of section 26(1) of the 1974 Act, arise 'in connection with action taken *by or on behalf of*, a local authority. This is wide enough to cover the acts and decisions of members, officers and other employees, and also agents of an authority.

It is possible to arrive at a working definition of 'maladministration' by reading the Commission's published decisions, and by assigning the subject matter of the complaint to a classified complaints system. It has to be admitted that in some cases this process is somewhat arbitrary as many reports raise multiple issues and allegations cutting across neat category boundaries. The most useful system of categorisation seems to be, so far as housing matters are concerned: delay; bias and victimisation including unfair treatment; complaints arising out of planning and building regulation powers and also related to housing; inefficiency, including bad or non-existent administrative procedures, failures to fulfil statutory obligations and broken promises; repair problems, including heating, and covering both public and private sector tenants; health complaints, especially with regard to cases arising out of failures to allocate council housing despite medical evidence of need; grant and home loss payment disputes; disputes arising under the right to buy and homelessness provisions; and, finally, miscellaneous. On this basis most complaints seem to arise out of allegations of general inefficiency, with problems relating to repairs and those arising from delay coming quite a close second and third respectively. On the other hand an examination of the reports shows that a complaint based on inefficiency has less chance of suceeding than one in either of the two other large categories.

The complainant must also claim to have sustained injustice in consequence of maladministration. 'Injustice' is not defined in the legislation but covers a wide range of matters from loss consequent upon a refusal to make a financial grant through to annoyance, disturbance or frustration caused by maladministration. No actual financial loss need be proven.

Procedure before the Commission

There is a strict procedure, laid down in section 26 of the Local Government Act 1974, to be followed before a complaint will be entertained and failure to comply with the procedure set out in the Act is responsible in some measure for the large number of complaints which are not accepted for investigation. The Local Commissioner will not investigate any complaint until it has been brought to the attention of the authority complained against, either by the person aggrieved (or his personal representative) or by a member of the authority on behalf of that person, and until the authority has had a reasonable time in which to reply to the complaint. A complaint intended for reference should be made in writing to a member of the authority complained against with a request that it should be sent to the Local Commissioner. It should state the action which it is alleged constitutes maladministration. If the member does not refer the complaint to the Commissioner, the person aggrived may ask the Commission to accept the complaint direct. A complaint should not be addressed directly to a Local Commissioner in the first instance.

When a complaint is received direct the Commission advise the complainant on the correct procedure. In appropriate cases the Commission will inform the Chief Executive of the Authority of the direct complaint regardless of whether it might be within a local ombudsman's jurisdiction if it were properly referred. The Chief Executive is asked to consider whether the complaint can be settled locally and it is known that local settlement is achieved in some such cases.

The actual procedure for an investigation is set out in the booklet published by the Commission, *Your Local Ombudsman* pp. 2 and 3.

When a complaint is received it is examined to see whether it is one that can be investigated. If the complaint is outside the local ombudsman's jurisdiction or there is clearly no evidence of maladministration the complainant will be told by letter why the local ombudsman has decided not to investigate the complaint. The councillor who referred the complaint will also be told of the local ombudsman's decision.

If the local ombudsman decides to investigate the complaint further, the council will be asked for their comments on the complaint. Unless the complaint is settled locally, the local ombudsman will then decide whether or not to carry out a formal investigation. During a full investigation, the complainant and everyone involved with the complaint will be interviewed. The council's files on the matter may also be examined. At the end of an investigation the local ombudsman will issue a report saying whether or not there has been maladministration by the council and whether this caused injustice to the complainant. The local ombudsman's report will not normally mention people's names. [The author wishes to acknowledge indebtedness to the staff of the Commission for Local Administration in England for their help in his work on this portion of this chapter.]

An investigation, once it has been undertaken, usually involves a visit by an officer of the Commission to the authority concerned where the relevant files are investigated and the officers, the complainant, members and any other person considered to have information bearing on the matter complained of will be interviewed. Interviews are held in private, and interviewees may be accompanied by a friend, a trades union adviser or a legal representative. Where a junior local government officer is involved chief officers are not allowed to be present, neither may an officer be represented by a lawyer in the employment of his local authority. These practices are followed to ensure candour in the investigative process. Before a report is issued on an investigation it is sent in a draft form to the complainant and the local authority for their comments.

Operating procedures

During 1979/80 the Commission reviewed their operating procedures with the aim of providing a fairer and more economic service to complainants and authorities. As a result certain changes were made in April 1980. Previously only about 20 per cent of all properly referred complaints were described as being 'investigated'. But about half the remaining complaints were subject to inquiries which went well beyond consideration of the material submitted by the complainant. These inquiries usually included a request to the Chief Executive of the Authority for preliminary comments on the complaint, or for some specific information, and may have included an interview with the complainant, or examination of the authority's files.

Currently the definition of 'investigation' includes all dealings with a complaint which is within jurisdiction and has been properly referred. As previously, the depth of investigation varies according to the particular complaint. The detailed procedures are:

1) in many cases the Chief Executive of the Authority will be asked for comments on a complaint on the understanding that these may be sent to the complainant;

2) if the Local Commissioner then feels, after considering the complaint submitted and the comments, that he should not investigate further, a copy of the letter giving the Chief Executive's comments will generally be sent to the complainant in support of that decision. The complainant will then be able to submit reasons why the investigation should continue;

3) in those cases where the investigation continues, the authority will be asked if they have any further comments to make on the complaint;

4) the Local Commissioner may decide not to investigate further at a later stage in the process (for example, after an authority's files have been seen it may become clear that there was no maladministration). In many such cases it will be possible to put this decision in a letter which will not require publication as a report, or in a short report discontinuing the investigation. In the remaining cases investigation will continue and a formal report will be issued;

5) the Commission's published statistics will show as investigations all those cases where some investigation has been made, including those where the Local Commissioner decided not to investigate to the point of a formal report.

Certain matters are excluded from the ambit of the Commission's investigations; for example the Commission cannot normally investigate the matter if the person has or had a right of appeal or a right to go to the courts but has not used it, Local Government Act 1974, s. 26(6). Similar exclusions apply where there is a right of appeal, reference or review to any statutorily constituted tribunal, or where there is a right of appeal to a minister. But all these exclusions are subject to the proviso that the Commission may conduct an investigation if satisfied that in the particular circumstances it was reasonable for the complainant not to have used his other legal remedies. The Commission will exercise their discretion where, for example, the cost of pursuing a remedy in the High Court would be prohibitively high. The Commission has a general discretion to investigate complaints. The circumstances of the exercise of that discretion were considered by the Court of Appeal in *R v Local Comr for Administration for the North and North East Area of England, ex p Bradford Metropolitan City Council* [1979] QB 287, [1979] 2 All ER 881.

The Court of Appeal's decision confirmed:

1) that although a Local Commissioner cannot question the merits of a decision taken without maladministration, he can investigate a complaint about the decision to see whether there was maladministration in the process of making it;

2) that the fact that a complaint is about the exercise of 'professional judgment' does not prevent investigation by the Local Commissioner to determine whether there was maladministration;

3) that the Local Commissioners should not be rigid in enforcing the section 26(4) requirement that a complaint should have been made to a member of the authority within twelve months from the date when the complainant first knew about the matter alleged in the complaint where justice requires that the time be extended and the complaint heard;

4) that a complainant (who of necessity cannot know what took place in the council offices) should not have to specify any particular piece of maladministration. It is enough if he specifies the action of the local authority in connection with which he complains there was maladministration;

5) that because the complainant might be able to voice the complaint in court proceedings, a Local Commissioner is not barred from investigating questions of injustice and maladministration which will not be directly at issue in those proceedings.

[This case arose out of an alleged failure by a local authority to use their statutory powers and resources to help a woman look after her children before they were taken into care.]

The Commission will not investigate an action which affects all or most of the inhabitants of the area of the authority concerned, section

26(7). Apart from these restrictions there are other drawbacks implicit in the procedure for referring complaints: the lack of direct access and the need to exhaust local complaints procedures (if they exist) mean that any complaint takes a long time to process. Where an investigation is continued to the issue of a formal report, the *average* length of the investigation was 43 weeks in 1983/84, 41 weeks in 1984/85 and 42 weeks in 1985/86, figures that are in line with those for the last ten years.

The effectiveness of the Commission in providing a remedy

There is no obligation for a local authority to heed a Commissioner's report. Indeed even when a report is heeded the Commission regularly records its concern at the length of time authorities take to remedy injustice satisfactorily.

On the other hand a complainant does not go to the Commission for *redress* as he would go to a court, he goes for a *finding* as to whether or not there has been maladministration. The Commission may find such maladministration but cannot insist on its being remedied. All they have power to do, under section 31 of the Local Government Act 1974, is to make a report of findings to the authority concerned, who must then consider it and notify the Commission of the action they have taken or propose to take. If no such notification is received, within a reasonable time, or if the Commission is not satisfied with the action taken or proposed they may make a second or further report indicating what they consider would be appropriate. Generally, therefore, the *absence* of a second report is good evidence that the problem complained of has been dealt with to the satisfaction of all the parties. In fact very few second reports have been issued in relation to housing complaints. Second reports do not have to be considered by local authorities and there is nothing that can be done if an authority resolves to do nothing after such a report has been issued. Between 1974 and 1984/85 *overall* the Commission have found maladministration and injustice in 1,619 cases, 1,442 of which have been settled satisfactorily, 85 of which were still awaiting settlement in 1985, and 92 of which had achieved no satisfactory outcome, only 6 per cent of all cases. Where a second report is issued their effect seems to be slight; since 1974 128 such reports have been made, leading to satisfactory outcomes in only 27 cases, a rate of one in five. These figures, of course, do not all relate to housing. It should also be remembered that sometimes though maladministration is found the Commissioner states that no injustice was caused, or that a mere apology on the part of the authority concerned would be sufficient. From the evidence to hand it would seem that most cases where maladministration causing injustice was found were remedied satisfactorily. The general rarity of further reports in housing cases indicates that the activities of the Commission have some effect on local housing authorities and may contribute to the better administration of discretion in this area of the law. Against this it should be said that some local housing authorities have from time to time been made the subject of multiple complaints by numbers of individuals. The evidence here suggests that there may well be pockets of resistance to the introduction of good housing administration policies.

Remedial action taken following the issue of a report in which maladministration causing injustice is found is likely to fall under one, or more, of the following four headings; the giving of an apology; the redressing of the actual grievance; the making of a compensatory payment; and the improvement of administrative procedures. Where an authority apologises to a complainant it is the easiest and cheapest form of redress which should, at least, appease ill feeling and make for better relationships without necessarily removing all cause for complaint. Where steps are taken that redress the cause of the complaint this will satisfy the complainant. However, there are times when correcting one wrong may well cause other problems. An example of this is where rehousing a complainant raises allegations of unfair treatment in relation to other persons awaiting municipal accommodation. In such circumstances a local authority would seem justified in considering the wider issues and their implications before deciding what response to make to the Commission's findings.

In some cases making a monetary payment may be the best course of action. Before the Local Government Act 1978 local authorities had, in the absence of express statutory permission, to seek the sanction of the Secretary of State to make *ex gratia* payments in those cases where such compensation was considered appropriate. Section 1 of the 1978 Act now allows a local authority subject to investigation by the Commission to make payments to or provide other benefits for persons who have suffered injustice because of maladministration. This, of itself, does not remove all the difficulties. It may not always be easy to satisfy the loss caused by maladministration. Legal costs and damage to property are easily reduced to cash terms, but injury to health, or inconvenience and discomfort are not so easily quantified. Some authorities have resorted to the services of an independent expert to quantify the amount of payments to be made. Such an independent assessment is likely to be fair and unbiased and acceptable to all the parties. An alternative solution is to make an analogy with damages in tort and to make such payments as will put the complainant in the position in which he would have been had the maladministration not taken place. Such an approach to the problem should not be pursued in too legalistic a fashion, otherwise the compensation payment might well approach the level of tort damages. In 'Local Authority Response to the Local Ombudsman' (1979) JPEL 441 Christine Chinkin reveals that sums of up to £20,000 have been paid as compensation. Before making a compensatory payment an authority must consider the general duty they owe to their ratepayers not to impose over heavy burdens on the general rate fund, and also the need to avoid uncomfortable precedents. Further advice on the making of payments under the 1978 Act is contained in Department of the Environment Circular No. 54/78. Recently the Commission has become more willing to make specific suggestions in reports as to the best way to satisfy it that the act of maladministration has been remedied.

The receipt of a finding of maladministration causing injustice may, of course, lead to a change or improvement in an authority's administrative workings so as to minimise the risk of future complaints. Such a response may be particularly appropriate where the complaint arose out of unjustifiable delay on the part of an authority. Some authorities have gone so far as to set up schemes to monitor their future performance in relation to their statutory functions, and others have created special subcommittees to deal with specific problems. But excessive caution in relation to administrative matters could bring the wheels of local government to a halt. Furthermore, local authorities are unlikely to be able to devote considerable resources to changing their practices at a time of general financial stringency. The Annual Report of the Commission for 1979 reports the findings of a survey of complaints carried out by Justice. This revealed that a substantial majority of complainants who had been subject to injustice caused by maladministration were dissatisfied with the remedial action taken by the authorities concerned. There is still, therefore, room for improvement on the part of local authorities in relation to their practices and procedures.

Another difficulty with the present system for investigations was highlighted in *Re a complaint against Liverpool City Council* [1977] 2 All ER 650, [1977] 1 WLR 995. A Commissioner requested the Council to produce certain relevant records for the purpose of the investigation. The Council refused to do so and the Commissioner issued a subpoena requiring production. The Council replied by serving a notice under section 32(3) of the Local Government Act 1974 claiming that it would be against the public interest for them to disclose the records (which related to action taken concerning children in the care of the Council) and applied to the court for the subpoena to be set aside. The court granted the application. The Commissioner had a further right under section 32(3) of the Act to apply to the Secretary of State to discharge the notice but decided not to do so on the basis that the logical solution would be to amend the Act to bring the procedure into line with that governing the Parliamentary Commissioner. Section 11(3) of the Parliamentary Commissioner Act 1967 provides that a minister may serve a notice claiming that it would be prejudicial to the safety of the State or against the public interest to disclose certain documents and the effect of such a notice is to prevent the Parliamentary Commissioner, communicating to any other person the information contained in such documents. Unlike the position under section 32(3) of the Local Government Act 1974 the Parliamentary Commissioner is therefore entitled to see the documents specified in the notice. In the *Bradford* case the Secretary of State's powers were, however, invokèd in order to secure production of local authority records.

An assessment of the work of the Commission

The general consensus of opinion as to the performance of the 'local ombudsmen' since 1974 would seem to be that there has been a worthwhile achievement both in terms of individual complaints remedied and in relation to general improvements in administrative practices. An example of such an achievement was the joint issue in 1978 by the Local Authorities Associations and the Commission of a Code of Practice for local authorities to adopt when dealing with complaints made to them. Amongst other matters this Code urges all local authorities to have a standard written procedure for dealing with complaints, irrespective of the particular department or action against which any given complaint is directed. The Code also counsels authorities to ensure that their members are fully aware of and conversant with the complaints procedure. It also makes the telling point that complaints and queries can be minimised if the public are given adequate information in advance about the activities and problems of local authorities. The complete text of the Code can be found in Appendix 9 of the Annual Report of the Commission for 1978. There is, however, no obligation on any authority to adopt and use the Code.

The significance of the Commission's work for local housing authorities

In conclusion it should be noted that there are certain sorts of failings and practices – sins of both omission and commission – that regularly result in findings of maladministration causing injustice. Authorities should beware of:

1) delay in processing grant applications, or applications for housing benefits, or claims to exercise the right to buy, or in transferring anti-social tenants to other accommodation or otherwise failing to deal with nuisances caused by such tenants, or in pursuing programmes of repair and modernisation, or in delaying housing applications under the National Mobility Scheme so that applicants fail to gain accommodation and so cannot accept offers of work in *new* locations;

2) failure to keep promises or to implement undertakings given in relation to housing matters, or to respond to complaints about dampness, or to compensate tenants for damage suffered as a result of an authority's fault in relation to their obligations, such as where a heating system fails to function for a considerable length of time;

3) not making their policies on housing issues clear, or giving misleading information in relation to a housing matter or failing to make clear the effect of obtaining alternative accommodation on a council waiting list application;

4) failing to consider medical or overcrowding evidence in relation to rehousing applications;

5) general inefficiency in processing housing applications etc., or in providing services where stipulated in a contract of letting, for example the provision of caretaking or warden facilities, or in securing the proper cleaning of a house before it is re-let, or in failing to give a tenant an opportunity to reply to complaints made about his behaviour by other tenants;

6) behaving inappropriately in cases of relationship breakdown. In view of the subject matter of the first part of this chapter, it is necessary to expand on this last named head. When an authority deal with the consequences of a relationship breakdown, they should act in an even handed and open fashion, not reaching unjustified assumptions about the parties' whereabouts and intentions. They should act on the basis of verified information, doing nothing to prejudice the rights of the parties until a court has dealt with the matter. So, for example, where under the rule in *Greenwich London Borough Council v McGrady* (see above) one of two joint local authority tenants gives notice to quit in due form, so terminating their security, it is *lawful* to accept the notice to quit, but it may be maladministration either to ignore the views of the other joint tenant, or to fail to give that other an opportunity to state his/her case on the matter. This will be particularly true where easy communication with the parties is possible, or where there is the possibility that one party may try to rely on the rule in *McGrady* simply to spite the other. Likewise it is unacceptable for an authority to require

the taking of particular legal steps – steps that the parties are not by law required to take – as a pre-condition for rehousing, for example a requirement that a woman obtain and retain custody of her children, see further *R v Ealing London Borough Council, ex p Sidhu* (1982) 80 LGR 534.

Further reading

Maladministration

Foulkes, *The Local Government Act 1974* (Butterworths) Chap. 3.
Social Welfare Law (Ed. by D.W. Pollard)(Oyez Longman) paras. I.501–I.620.
Reports of the Commission for Local Administration in England (published annually by the Representative Body from 1975 to date, and available from 25 Buckingham Gate, London, SW1E 6LE).
Chinkin, C., 'Local Authority Response to the Local Ombudsman' (1979) JPEL 441.
Chinkin, C., 'The Power of the Local Ombudsman Re-examined' (1980) JPEL 87.
Hoath, D.C., 'Council Tenants' Complaints and the Local Ombudsman' (1978) 128 NLJ 672.
Hughes, D.J., and Jones, S.R., 'Bias in the Allocation and Transfer of Local Authority Housing; A Study of the Reports of the Commission for Local Administration in England' (1979) 1 JSWL 273.
Williams, D.W., 'Social Welfare Consumers and Their Complaints' (1979) 1 JSWL 257.
Markson, H.E., 'Investigating Local Maladministration' (1981) 131 NLJ 844.

Matrimonial homes

Social Welfare Law (Ed. by D.W. Pollard) (Oyez Longman) paras. B791–796.
The Housing of One Parent Families (Housing Services Advisory Group) (Department of the Environment 1978).
Hoath, D.C., *Council Housing* (2nd Edn. 1982, Sweet & Maxwell) Chap. 4.
Murphy, W.T., and Clark, H., *The Family Home* (Sweet & Maxwell, 1983).
Arden, A., and Partington, M., *Housing Law* (Sweet & Maxwell, 1983) Chap. 26.
Witherspoon, S., *A Woman's Place* (Shac, 1985).
Blandy, S., 'Domestic Violence and the Housing Act 1980' (1981) 131 NLJ 520.

Luba, J., 'Domestic Violence and the Housing Act 1980' LAG Bulletin, April 1981, p. 82 and September 1981, p. 211.

Luba, J., 'Joint Secure Tenants' LAG Bulletin, February 1983 p. 26.

Webb, F., 'Notices to Quit by One Joint Tenant' (1983) 45 *The Conveyancer* 194.

Hamilton, R., 'Has the House of Lords Abolished The Domestic Violence Act for Married Women?' *Legal Action* March 1984, p. 25.

Chapter 6

Homelessness

Causes and numbers

Homelessness is one of the most pernicious social problems. If it could be solved many other problems, for example alcoholism, crime and domestic violence, would undoubtedly decline. Unfortunately, homelessness is a complex phenomenon and, as a complex problem, can only be cured by the concerted application of a whole range of determined, *and expensive*, remedial measures. It is not enough simply to say that it is caused by a lack of housing; it is rather caused by a lack of housing in those areas where there is most housing demand. It is no use telling a homeless family in the middle of Newcastle that there are some acceptable empty cottages somewhere in the wilds of Shropshire – people need homes close to their friends, families and in areas where there is some chance of work.

The issue is also complicated in that there is no nationally acceptable definition of homelessness. That provided in the Housing Act 1985 is a minimum standard based on the notions of a person having no accommodation (or being threatened with that condition in a short time) and being able to appeal to a local authority for help. This excludes many who have roofs over their heads but whose living conditions are very poor. These unfortunates include men and women occupying hostels, common lodging houses and resettlement units. Such people have no privacy or security of tenure.

The issue is even more complex in that there is no one single cause of homelessness. People lose their accommodation for many reasons. Among single people the causes range from migration in search of work through the loss of family ties and support to being unable to live in society without constant social and medical support. This last group includes those with severe alcoholic problems and others who find it hard to adjust to a pattern of living outside a rigid organisational framework such as hospital, prison or the armed forces. Homeless families find themselves in that position for a variety of reasons. One common factor in nearly all such cases is poverty. Where a family is

Table A

% by half year	London					Rest of England				
	1978 (1st)	(2nd)	1979 (1st)	(2nd)	1980 (1st)	1978 (1st)	(2nd)	1979 (1st)	(2nd)	1980 (1st)
Living with parents/friends/etc	42	44	45	48	50	36	37	38	41	42
Owner-occupier	5	5	5	5	5	16	15	15	13	13
L.A. tenants	11	10	12	9	11	13	13	14	13	13
H.A. tenants	1	1	1	1	1	1	1	1	1	1
Resident landlord	7	6	7	8	7	3	3	3	3	3
Non-resident Landlord	9	9	9	8	7	11	10	10	10	10
Tied accommodation	6	6	5	6	5	10	10	9	10	9
Squatters	6	5	4	4	5	1	1	1	1	1
Others	14	13	11	11	9	9	11	9	10	8
Total (000s)	7	7	8	8	8	19	19	20	20	21

dependent for most of its income on a wage earner who has a low paid job in an uncertain industry, sudden illness, unemployment or marital break-up can precipitate homelessness. Another common circumstance is that many such families have never had a real home of their own but have frequently been illegal sub-tenants, or service tenants, or living with in-laws.

In John Burnett's *Social History of Housing 1815–1985* (2nd edn) the author reveals that the most common cause of homelessness is a household discovering that it can no longer be housed by parents, relatives or friends, and that this accounts for 50 per cent of all instances of reported homelessness, while domestic violence and eviction from accommodation account for a further 30 per cent between them. Burnett cites the combination of difficult family circumstances and low incomes as the most potent causes of homelessness. Furthermore, the problem is increasing. In 1971 3,918 households were accepted as homeless in London and 4,015 in the rest of England. This rose to 10,840 households in London and 20,970 in the rest of England in 1977. A new method of presenting homelessness statistics was introduced following the passage of the Housing (Homeless Persons) Act 1977, and this showed households accepted according to the type of their most recent accommodation. See Table A.

A further change was then made, presenting the figures to show households accepted by priority need category.

Table B

% by half year	London				Rest of England			
	1980 (2nd)	1981 (1st)	(2nd)	1982 (1st)	1980 (2nd)	1981 (1st)	(2nd)	1982 (1st)
Dependent children	63	61	61	63	69	66	65	64
Pregnancy	16	17	15	11	11	11	10	11
Vulnerability	15	15	16	18	13	13	13	13
Emergency	2	2	2	2	2	3	4	4
No priority	4	4	4	2	5	7	8	8
Total numbers	8820	9060	9410	9020	24350	25790	25750	26680

Another change in presentation techniques shows the figures for England and Wales, again by percentage according to priority need category.

Table C

	1983 %
Dependent children	62
Pregnancy	11
Vulnerability	15
Emergency	3
No Priority	9
Total Numbers	82,755

(Sources: Social Trends 1980, 1984, 1985).

The following points are also worthy of note.

1) In December 1984 there were 7,200 families in bed and breakfast accommodation.

2) The figures represent recorded instances of homelessness, many more instances may not come to the notice of the authorities.

3) It is not possible to know the full extent of homelessness because there are many single homeless people, particularly in London, whose existence and movements are totally unrecorded. John Greve's *Homelessness in London* (1971) estimated there were 11,000 single homeless people in London alone in 1966. The migration of many young people to the capital in search of work and/or excitement has almost certainly greatly increased that number over the last twenty years.

The 1977 Housing (Homeless Persons) Act, now Part III of the 1985 Act, was designed to meet, at least in part, criticisms of the inadequacies of the National Assistance Act 1948, (see the first edition of this work pages 166 to 169), but in practice the new law has proved to be incapable of preventing the rise in the incidence of homelessness. Furthermore it would be hard to think of any legal provisions that have, in recent years, given rise to more litigation in so short a space of time. The result is that the law, far from aiding a homeless person, has become a series of barriers to be surmounted before that person is owed any sort of duty, and even then, as will be seen, the content of that duty may not be very great.

Who are 'the homeless'?

Those persons falling within the Act are defined by section 58, so that a person is homeless if he has no accommodation in England, Wales or Scotland. He has no such accommodation if there is no accommodation which he, together with any person or persons normally residing with him as a member of his family in circumstances in which such residence is reasonable, is entitled to occupy: by having an interest in it or under a court order; by express or implied licence; by virtue of any enactment or rule of law. Such a person is also homeless even where he has accommodation but: cannot secure entry to it; may be subject to violence or threats of likely violence from some person residing in the accommodation if he occupies it; the accommodation is a movable structure vehicle or vessel and there is no place where it can be located for him to reside in it. Persons are 'threatened with homelessness' where it is likely they will become homeless within 28 days.

This defines the class of persons to whom the *various* obligations under the Act can be owed. The persons covered are those having no accommodation, or who will shortly be in that position, in other words those without a roof over their heads. A person will be homeless if he has no accommodation which he has the *right* to occupy (for example as an owner) or is allowed to occupy under some rule of law (for example a statutory tenant), or which he is allowed to occupy by some express or implied licence (for example a person living with relatives). Much here depends on the attitude of individual local authorities. Some follow a liberal interpretation of the Act and classify such people as threatened with homelessness as they have no security of tenure.

However, the case law shows how difficult it can be to decide whether a person has 'no accommodation'. A woman living temporarily in the crisis accommodation provided by a refuge for 'Battered Wives' was held to be homeless in *R v Ealing London Borough Council, ex p Sidhu* (1982) 80 LGR 534, as was a man whose only roof was that put over him nightly in a night shelter, see *R v Waveney District Council, ex p Bowers* [1983] QB 238, [1982] 3 All ER 727. Authorities, under section 75 of the 1985 Act, must consider whether the accommodation is available for occupation by the applicant along with a person who can be reasonably expected to reside with him/her. Thus where an applicant's marriage breaks down and one spouse moves into accommodation provided by the other, but subject to a provision requiring a power of sale over the dwelling to be implemented in the case of cohabitation by the accommodated spouse, and that power is implemented because cohabitation takes place and a child results therefrom, the accommodation is not available for occupation, see *R v Wimborne District Council, ex p Curtis* (1985) 18 HLR 79. A person will have 'no accommodation' if what he has is uninhabitable or incapable of accommodating the number of people living in it, see *R v South Herefordshire Borough Council, ex p Miles* (1984) 17 HLR 82 and *R v Gloucester City Council, ex p Miles* (1985) 17 HLR 292. But a person will *not* have 'no accommodation' merely because the accommodation he does have is inappropriate to the needs of himself and his family. In *Puhlhofer v Hillingdon London Borough Council* [1986] AC 484, [1986] 1 All ER 467 the applicants argued they were homeless because the premises they occupied (a room in a bed and breakfast guest house containing a double bed, single bed, cradle, dressing-table, perambulator and steriliser unit, but having no cooking or washing facilities) were neither large enough to accommodate their family and lacked the basic amenities of family life. The House of Lords rejected this contention, pointing out that the purpose of the homelessness provisions is to be a lifeline for the homeless, and that they are not intended to enable homeless applicants to obtain local authority accommodation which may be legitimately desired by other persons within an authority's area and whose interests must not be prejudiced. Accommodation does not become 'no accommodation' simply because it is statutorily unfit or overcrowded, though, for example, a filthy derelict old shed sheltering a family of some size would be 'no accommodation' simply because it would be incapable of accommodating those persons. It will be seen subsequently that the definition of what constitutes 'accommodation' for the purposes of the legislation, as laid down in the decision in *Puhlhofer*, applies throughout Part III of the 1985 Act, and this will have consequences for all those who are aided. It is also clear that section 22(d) of the Housing Act 1985, which requires that local authorities shall secure that in the selection of tenants they shall give a reasonable preference to homeless persons, is an empty duty in this context. Local authorities are bound to consider the conditions of all those who may legitimately expect housing from them, and this involves considering the relative housing needs of *all* those persons and the availability of suitable housing within an authority's area. Part III of the 1985 Act contains *emergency* provisions, it does not entitle a homeless person to 'short circuit' automatically normal local authority selection and allocation procedures.

Local authorities are also under certain obligations to those who are *threatened* with homelessness which is *likely* to arise within 28 days. Obviously the '28 day rule' should not be rigidly interpreted. If an instance of potential homelessness comes to the attention of the local housing authority they should deal with it as soon as possible. Prompt early action may prevent actual homelessness. [*See Addendum 13.*]

Initial contact with the local authority

When a homeless or potentially homeless person makes contact with the local authority they come under certain duties under section 62 to make inquiries. These arise where the person applies to the authority for accommodation, or for assistance in obtaining accommodation, in circumstances giving them reason to believe he may be homeless or threatened with homelessness. The initial duty is to make such inquiries as are necessary to satisfy themselves as to his condition.

Local housing authorities should have some officer responsible for dealing with these matters. The Act does not lay down any rules for the conduct of inquiries. The Code of Guidance, issued under section 71, see below, urges that they be speedy, but sympathetic. There is no requirement to operate a 24 hours a day, seven days a week service. Co-operation with the social services authority is useful in such circumstances, and progressive authorities have '24 hour-a-day' arrangements.

Once these initial inquiries are made section 62(2) places the authority under a further duty to make inquiries to satisfy themselves as to whether the applicant has priority need, whether he became homeless, or threatened with homelessness, intentionally, and, if they think fit, whether he has a local connection with the district of another local housing authority in England, Wales or Scotland.

There has been litigation as to the content of the inquiry duties. In *R v Hillingdon Homeless Families Panel, ex p Islam* (1981) Times, 9 February Glidewell J held that correct inquiries are those necessary to satisfy the authority about the matter in question. It is for the authority to elicit all the relevant facts and they must generally behave fairly in discharging this function. The onus of making inquiries is on the authority, not the applicant. Once told the applicant is homeless and having been given the source of that information, an authority may not refuse to make inquiries, insisting that the applicant furnishes further confirmation of the facts, see *R v Woodspring District Council, ex p Walters* (1984) 16 HLR 73. An authority is under no duty to make 'CID' type inquiries, *Lally v Kensington and Chelsea Royal Borough* [1980] Times, 27 March, but they must enable the applicant to make his case out, see *R v Wyre Borough Council, ex p Joyce* (1983) 11 HLR 73, and the applicant should ensure the authority is informed of what they otherwise might be unable to find out, see *R v Harrow London Borough Council, ex p Holland* (1982) 4 HLR 108. In conducting its inquiries the authority may accept hearsay, where it is reasonable to do so, and is not obvious 'tittle-tattle', and is under no obligation to put any information received 'chapter-and-verse' to the applicant, though he must be made aware of the substance of evidence discovered so as to counter it where necessary, see *R v Southampton City Council, ex p Ward* (1984) 14 HLR 89, 114. It is not a performance of the obligation to 'rubber stamp' another authority's findings without giving the applicant a chance to explain his case, see *R v South Herefordshire Borough Council, ex p Miles* (1984) 17 HLR 82.

If, under section 63, the local housing authority have reason to believe that an applicant *may be* homeless and have priority need, they must make accommodation available to him pending a decision following their section 62 inquiries, and this duty arises independently of any local connection the applicant may have with the district of another authority.

The duty in section 63 means that no-one who appears to be homeless and also in priority need should ever be left without accommodation pending the completion of inquiries. This accommodation must be continued until inquiries are completed and the authority able to make a final decision.

Whether the section 63 duty is owed depends on whether the applicant is in 'priority need'. 'Priority need' is defined in section 59. A number of persons may have such need: pregnant women, or persons with whom such a woman resides or might reasonably be expected to reside; persons with whom dependent children reside, or might reasonably be expected to; persons vulnerable as a result of old age, mental illness or handicap or physical disability, or other special reasons, or with whom such a vulnerable person resides or might reasonably be expected to; persons homeless or threatened with homelessness as a result of emergencies such as floods, fires or other disasters. The Secretary of State may amend the above list, or add further categories to it, following due consultation with associations representing relevant authorities and such other persons as he considers appropriate.

This definition is far from clear. Though the Code of Guidance gives amplifying guidance, there is too much room for uncertainty and differing interpretation. The Code states: 'The Secretaries of State consider that authorities should treat [as dependent children] all those under the age of sixteen and others under the age of nineteen who are either receiving full-time education or training or are otherwise unable to support themselves'. The Code also states that where appropriate grandchildren, foster and adopted children may all be regarded as dependent. Problems arise in relation to vulnerable persons. The Code suggests that a person has priority need if he is, or his household contains one or more persons, vulnerable for any of the following reasons:

1) Old age, that is being over or nearing normal retiring age;

2) Mental illness or handicap or physical disability, including being deaf, dumb or blind or otherwise substantially disabled;

3) Any other special reason such as being a battered woman *without* a dependent child, or a homeless young person at risk of sexual and/or financial exploitation.

But the advice given in the Code is not legally binding being only a matter for consideration, nor does it go far enough. A man who has just been released from prison or some other sort of institution is undoubtedly vulnerable, yet some local authorities argue that he would not fall within the terms of section 59. Neither is the definition of vulnerability by reason of age sufficiently clear. Some authorities operate policies of not considering persons under the normal retiring age, while there are recorded instances of people over 65 being denied aid as not being vulnerable by reason of age. There is no proper definition given to vulnerability by virtue of mental illness; for example, would this cover a homeless alcoholic? In *R v Waveney District Council, ex p Bowers* [1983] QB 238, [1982] 3 All ER 727 an elderly man who suffered from both alcoholism *and* the consequence of severe head injury was found to be 'vulnerable', and in *R v Bath City Council, ex p Sangermano* (1984) 17 HLR 94 it was said that where a person has mental subnormality, a record of incompetence, and no ability to articulate and communicate, there is evidence of vulnerability. Vulnerability arises where a person is less able to fend for himself so that an injury can befall him in circumstances where a less vulnerable person would be able to cope without ill effects. However, self-imposed disabilities such as drinking problems do not generally constitute vulnerability so as to constitute priority need, and so the homeless alcoholic would probably *not* fall within the terms of section 59.

The duties owed to the homeless

These are contained in section 65. Where the authority are satisfied an applicant has priority need, and are *not* satisfied that he became homeless intentionally, they must, unless they are able to take advantage of the local connection provisions (see below), secure that accommodation becomes available for his occupation. Where satisfied of priority need, but also satisfied there has been intentional homelessness, they must, first, secure that accommodation is made available for his occupation for such period as they consider gives him a reasonable chance of securing accommodation for himself, and, secondly, furnish him with advice and such assistance as they consider appropriate in the circumstances in any attempts he may make to secure occupation for himself. Where not satisfied of priority need they must furnish such advice and assistance as they think appropriate to aid him in his search to secure accommodation. Section 66 lays down the duties owed to those who are *threatened* with homelessness, and these are generally similar to those listed above, save that the object of the exercise here is to ensure that accommodation does not *cease* to be available for occupation by the applicant.

These sections create several classes of persons to whom differing duties are owed.

1) A person who is homeless unintentionally and in priority need, to whom the full duty is owed.

2) A person who is threatened with homelessness, and is in priority need, and who has not become so threatened intentionally, to whom a duty is owed to secure that accommodation does not cease to be available.

3) A person who is homeless, and who has priority need, but who is homeless because of his own intentional act, to whom a duty is owed to make available accommodation for such period as the local authority considers will give him a reasonable opportunity of finding his own accommodation.

4) A person who is homeless but who has no priority need, to whom the only duty owed is to give advice and appropriate assistance.

Much depends on whether the applicant for aid has committed an act of intentional homelessness. Such acts are defined by section 60.

A person is intentionally homeless, or is threatened with homelessness intentionally, where he deliberately does, or fails to do something in consequence of which, or the likely result of which as the case may be, is that he ceases to occupy or will be forced to leave, accommodation which is available for his occupation, and which it would have been reasonable for him to continue to occupy. However, an act or omission in good faith on the part of a person unaware of any relevant fact is not to be treated as deliberate. In determining whether it would have been reasonable for a person to continue to occupy accommodation, regard may be had to the general circumstances prevalent in relation to housing in the district of the authority that person applies to for aid.

This provision has been the subject of considerable litigation, and each of its ingredients has been subjected to judicial attention. Before, however, examining the case law in detail, it should be noted that it is for the authority to satisfy themselves that an applicant falls squarely within all the requirements of section 60 before they can treat him as intentionally homeless.

The first point is that the applicant's condition must have arisen from some deliberate act or omission. This will usually be the act or omission of the applicant, but it may be that of some member of his household in which he has acquiessed, see *Lewis v North Devon District Council* [1981] 1 All ER 27, [1981] 1 WLR 328, and this is especially so where the applicant is a joint tenant with the party at fault and fails to defend possession proceedings brought in consequence of that other's acts, see *R v Cardiff City Council, ex p Thomas* (1983) 9 HLR 64. Failure to control nuisances committed by the members of the applicant's family or lodgers the consequences of which is a grant of possession against the applicant can amount to acquiessence in those acts thus rendering the applicant intentionally homeless, see *R v Salford City Council, ex p Devenport* (1983) 8 HLR 54, and *R v Cardiff City Council, ex p Johns* (1982) 9 HLR 56.

However, in most cases the consequence of intentional homelessness will flow from the applicant's deliberate act or omission. In this context 'deliberate' refers to the *doing* of the act, etc., and not its intended or desired consequences, and, indeed, 'voluntary' is not an inapt synonym, for it is not necessary to show that the applicant did what he did with the intention of getting himself dispossessed. Thus to fail deliberately to pay off mortgage arrears so that the consequence is dispossession is intentional homelessness, see *R v Eastleigh Borough Council, ex p Beattie* [1984] Fam Law 115, 17 HLR 168, and this would also apply to a deliberate refusal to pay rent. However, a failure to pay rent or a mortgage repayment based on a genuine misunderstanding of material facts, such as a belief that the DHSS were making the payment in the applicant's place, would be an act or omission in good faith because of lack of awareness of relevant facts, and so not 'deliberate', see *White v Exeter City Council* [1981] LAG Bulletin 287, and the Code of Guidance which cites those who get into rent arrears being unaware they are entitled to benefits under the Housing Benefits Scheme or other welfare benefits as others who may be regarded as unaware of relevant facts. Likewise where an applicant has taken temporary accommodation *not* knowing he will only be able to occupy it for a short time, he will have been unaware of a relevant fact, though such a person is not allowed to shut his eyes to the self-evident facts of the accommodation he is moving into, see *Krishnan v Hillingdon London Borough Council* [1981] LAG Bulletin 137.

The Code of Guidance argues that a woman who has fled her marital home in consequence of domestic violence should not be treated as intentionally homeless, for it is not reasonable for her to remain. Yet it is tempting to advise a woman in such circumstances to re-obtain her home by seeking an appropriate order under the domestic violence or matrimonial homes legislation, especially where she is the sole or joint tenant of the dwelling. In *R v Wandsworth London Borough Council, ex p Nimako-Boateng* [1984] Fam Law 117, 11 HLR 95 it was said there can be circumstances where the woman should reasonably try to seek to stay in her home and restrain her partner by court order rather than apply to the local authority as homeless. However, this would not be a reasonable course of action where the woman stands little or no chance of gaining an appropriate order. In *Warwick v Warwick* (1981) 1 HLR 139 it was made clear that an order excluding the male spouse from the dwelling would not be granted where the local authority had required such an order as a pre-condition of re-housing, and where it was clear the female spouse had no intention of returning to the dwelling so that the only consequence of the order would be to vacate the dwelling so that the authority could obtain possession. Likewise in *Charles v Charles* [1984] Legal Action (July) p. 81 the court pointed out that when a woman is forced from her home by domestic violence and her partner is then excluded from that dwelling by a court order, to require her to return to the dwelling puts her in a place where the male knows she is and may thus arrive there to further molest and abuse her. In such circumstances a woman fleeing her home should not be regarded as intentionally homeless because she is unwilling to take action under matrimonial etc., legislation.

An applicant living in tied accommodation whose deliberate conduct, as opposed to mere incompetence in the performance of his duties, leads inevitably to dismissal also thereby renders himself intentionally homeless, see *R v Thanet District Council, ex p Reeve* (1982) 6 HLR 31 and *R v Thurrock Borough Council, ex p Williams* (1981) 1 HLR 128.

It must next be shown that the loss of accommodation was the consequence of the applicant's act or omission. As the Code of Guidance in its second edition points out, the courts have established that authorities may look beyond the most immediate cause of homelessness, see *De Falco v Crawley Borough Council* [1980] QB 460, [1980] 1 All ER 913, and *Dyson v Kerrier District Council* [1980] 3 All ER 313, [1980] 1 WLR 1205. If there is a 'chain of causation' flowing unbroken from an initial act of intentional homelessness down to the applicant's current condition, his application will continue to be tainted by the initial act. The chain of causation may be broken by the applicant obtaining some settled accommodation in which he spends a period of time between his initial state of intentional homelessness and his current condition, see *Din v Wandsworth London Borough Council* [1983] 1 AC 657, [1981] 3 All ER 881, but the cases yield few examples of where such a 'break in the chain' has been found. *R v Basingstoke and Deane Borough Council, ex p Bassett* [1984] Fam Law 90, 10 HLR 125 shows that the 'chain of causation' can be broken by some supervening independent cause of homelessness. Where an applicant seeks to rely on having obtained an intervening period of settled accommodation to 'break the chain' what is 'settled' will be a question of fact in each case. Taking a holiday letting will not be enough in this context see *Lambert v Ealing London Borough Council* [1982] 2 All ER 394, [1982] 1 WLR 550, nor will occupying temporary shelter found by relatives in overcrowded circumstances, see *Din v Wandsworth London Borough Council* (supra). Accommodation in a hostel where the rooms have cooking and washing facilities may be 'settled', however, see *R v East Hertfordshire District*

Council, ex p Hunt (1985) 18 HLR 51. Furthermore whether there has been such a break is to be determined objectively, not according to the subjective intentions of the applicant.

The 'cause and effect' nature of the applicant's conduct in relation to his condition must also be established. The authority must be satisfied that it is reasonable to regard the applicant's acts or omissions as having caused his homelessness.

Next it must be demonstrated that occupation of accommodation has ceased in consequence of the applicant's acts or omissions. Though *De Falco v Crawley Borough Council* (see above) made it clear that both the accommodation lost, and the act causing that loss, can occur outside the United Kingdom, authorities should ensure that proper inquiries are made in such cases into the circumstances of the cesser of occupation, see *R v Reigate and Banstead Borough Council, ex p Paris* (1984) 17 HLR 103.

It must then be established that the accommodation lost was available for occupation by the applicant. In this connection the terms of section 75 of the 1985 Act should be noted, for accommodation is 'available' only where it can be occupied by the applicant and by any other person who might reasonably be expected to reside with him. In *Re Islam* [1983] 1 AC 688 it was held that a man who had lost his accommodation – a shared room – because he had brought his wife and children to live with him from overseas was not thereby intentionally homeless. Mr Islam had never actually occupied accommodation available to him *and* those persons who might reasonably be expected to reside with him, and, as such, the intentional homelessness provisions could not apply to the accommodation he had lost. See also *R v Wimborne District Council, ex p Curtis* (supra).

Finally it must be established that it would have been reasonable for the applicant to have continued to occupy the accommodation lost, and in this connection section 60(4) of the 1985 Act allows regard to be had to general circumstances prevailing in relation to housing in the district in determining the reasonableness of the applicant's conduct, though factors other than those mentioned in section 60(4) can also be taken into account in this connection. In his annotations to *The Housing Act 1985* Andrew Arden argues that the factors an authority may consider in coming to a decision on the applicant's conduct include, first, physical factors such as whether there are other people in the area living in worse conditions than the applicant and the general housing conditions and demands of the area, see Code of Guidance para. 2.16. *De Falco v Crawley Borough Council* (supra) and *Tickner v Mole Valley District Council* [1980] LAG Bulletin 187, and issues of overcrowding, unfitness, infestation by vermin and inadequacy of size. See generally *R v Gravesham Borough Council, ex p Winchester* (1986) 18 HLR 207.

Next an authority may consider legal factors affecting the reasonableness of continued occupation. It is not unreasonable to cease to occupy accommodation where an applicant has been told he has no chance of being allowed to stay, for example as an illegal immigrant, see *R v Hillingdon London Borough Council, ex p Wilson* (1983) 12 HLR 61. Nor is it proper for an authority to require an applicant to defend a possession action he has no chance of winning, see *R v Exeter City Council, ex p Gliddon* [1985] 1 All ER 493, 14 HLR 89, *R v Portsmouth City Council, ex p Knight* [1984] Fam Law 304, 12 HLR 60. Nor should an authority consider it necessary for an applicant to stay on either until evicted following a court order, or as a trespasser following the lawful termination of a licence to occupy, see *R v Mole Valley District Council, ex p Minnett* (1983) 12 HLR 48 and *R v Surrey Heath Borough Council, ex p Li* [1985] Fam Law 124, 16 HLR 79. However, the fact that a person is being threatened by creditors may not justify him in ceasing to occupy his accommodation. In such circumstances his proper course of action is to inform the police, see *R v Croydon London Borough Council, ex p Toth* (1986) 'Housing Aid' No. 38, p. 7. An authority may also consider any advice they have given to the applicant before he became homeless and which he has ignored in consequence of which he has ceased to occupy his accommodation, see *Miller v Wandsworth London Borough Council* (1980) Times, 19 March. However, in all these circumstances the authority must direct their mind to the question whether it was reasonable for the applicant to continue to stay in his accommodation, not whether it was reasonable to leave.

A finding of intentional homelessness bars the applicant from making further applications based on the same facts, see *Delahaye v Oswestry Borough Council* (1980) Times, 29 July, though he can re-apply once there is a material change in his circumstances, for example a period spent in settled accommodation (see above). A finding of intentional homelessness against an applicant does not, however, prevent some other member of his household from making an application, provided that person has not acquiessed in the original act of intentional homelessness, see *R v West Dorset District Council, ex p Phillips* (1984) 17 HLR 336. Likewise where a person applies to a local authority and they come to a decision that he is unintentionally homeless, but has no local connection with their area while having such a connection with another authority, they may refer the applicant to that authority who come under a duty to him, notwithstanding their own earlier determination that he was intentionally homeless, see *R v Slough Borough Council, ex p Ealing London Borough Council* [1981] QB 801, [1981] 1 All ER 601.

A person who is homeless, unintentionally, and who has priority need is, in general, owed the full duty under the law; but the authority applied to *may* inquire whether there is a local connection with the district of another authority in England, Wales or Scotland so that they may refer the application to that other authority, see sections 62 and 67 of the 1985 Act. Before such an applicant can be made it must be determined that:

1) Neither the applicant, nor any person who might reasonably be expected to reside with him has a local connection with the district applied to (the 'notifying authority');

2) That the applicant etc., *does* have such a connection with another district (the 'notified authority');

3) That the applicant etc., will *not* run the risk of domestic violence in the notified authority's district, i.e. a risk of violence from a person with whom, but for that risk, he might reasonably be expected to reside, or from a person with whom he formerly resided, or there is a risk of threats of violence from such a person which are likely to be carried out. However, it follows from the decision in *R v Bristol City Council, ex p Browne* [1979] 3 All ER 344, [1979] 1 WLR 1437, that the fact that an applicant has suffered domestic violence in the past does not *necessarily* mean that the person runs the risk of such violence in the future. Each case must be carefully decided in its own facts.

Questions whether the conditions for referral of applications are met are to be determined by agreement between relevant authorities, or, in default of agreement in accordance with arrangements made in directions given by the Secretary of State, see the arbitration provisions of S.I. 1978/69, and the authorities' own Local Authority Agreement 1979, implementing these requirements. *The Agreement on Procedures for Referral of the Homeless* is obtainable from the Association of District Councils, the Association of Metropolitan Authorities and the London Boroughs Association. In *R v Hillingdon London Borough Council, ex p Slough Borough Council* (1980) 130 NLJ 881 certain homeless persons applied for aid, were found homeless, unintentionally so, and in priority need, but were considered to have a local connection with another authority's area. That authority refused to accept this, arbitrators were appointed in accordance with the law and the second authority contended they should consider the issue of intentional homelessness. It was held the arbitrators should consider only the issue of local connection.

What is a 'local connection' is defined in section 61 of the 1985 Act. An applicant may have a connection with an authority's district:

1) because he is, or was, normally resident there of his own choice;

2) because of employment in the district;

3) because of family associations;

4) because of other special circumstances.

But whether such a connection exists is a question of fact. In *Eastleigh Borough Council v Betts* [1983] 2 AC 613, [1983] 2 All ER 1111 the House of Lords held that the onus is on the applicant to show that he has built up and established a real connection with the area of the authority he applied to. He may do this by virtue of a period of residence, or employment, or because of family associations enduring in the area, or because of other special circumstances. When an application is based on residence alone it is not improper for an authority to apply the guideline in the 1979 Local Authority Agreement that to reside in an area for less than six months during the period of twelve months preceding the application is insufficient to establish such a real connection with an area, provided such a guideline is not operated as a rigid rule. During the making of inquiries as to 'local connection' and during the negotiations between authorities the authority first applied to is under a duty to accommodate the applicant, see sections 63(2) and 68(1) of the 1985 Act. Under section 68(2) of the 1985 Act where it is determined that the conditions for referral are satisfied, the notified authority come under the duties imposed by law, otherwise they remain with the notifying authority. It is for the notifying authority to inform the applicant in writing of the outcome and the reasons for the determination, see section 68(3).

It should be noted that the issue is whether the applicant has *no* local connection with the notifying authority's area while having such a connection with the area of the notified authority, *not* whether there is a greater local connection with some other authority's area, see *R v Mr Referee McCall* (1981) 8 HLR 48. Where the applicant has *no* local connection with another authority responsibility remains with the authority first applied to.

In *R v Hillingdon London Borough Council, ex p Streeting* [1980] 3 All ER 413, [1980] 1 WLR 1425, Mrs Streeting was an Ethiopian woman who lived in Ethiopia all her life until 1975 when she bigamously (but innocently) married A, and subsequently bore his child. They lived abroad, from time to time visiting the United Kingdom on leave. In 1979 A died and Mrs Streeting was then living in Athens. She came to the United Kingdom for A's funeral and was given limited permission to stay until November 1979. She was then refused permission to return to Greece, and was frightened to return to Ethiopia. The Home Office classified her as a refugee in November 1979 and Hillingdon LBC gave her temporary accommodation pending inquiries under the Act. The Council concluded that they owed her no duty because, they argued, no duty under the Act was owed to an applicant who has or had no local connection with the area of any housing authority in Great Britain.

This argument was rejected both at first instance and in the Court of Appeal. Lord Denning MR made the point that it is up to the immigration authorities to ensure that large numbers of homeless persons from abroad do not enter this country. Once a person is in this country, and is homeless unintentionally, and has priority need, the duties under the Act are owed to him.

Two riders must be added:

(a) If a person from abroad *deliberately* gives up his accommodation in his own country for no good reason so that he is homeless there, and then comes to this country, then he is to be treated as being intentionally homeless in this country. Merely coming to this country to look for work is not a good reason for giving up a home in another country;

(b) The obligation to the homeless person can be discharged by arranging for accommodation to be provided in the country from which the homeless person has come.

Section 72 allows bodies other than local housing authorities to co-operate in the provision of accommodation for the homeless. Authorities may request other authorities, new town corporations, registered housing associations, or social services authorities for assistance, and these bodies must co-operate in rendering such assistance as is reasonable in the circumstances.

The wording of this provision is so vague as to make it of little value.

The duty to accommodate

The actual duty to accommodate a person who has successfully cleared all the hurdles in the Act is contained in section 65. Section 69 empowers the performance of the duty to accommodate by:

1) The provision of ordinary council housing;

2) Securing that accommodation will be provided by some other person;

3) Giving such advice and assistance as secures that the applicant obtains accommodation from some other person.

The section grants a very wide discretion. The Code of Guidance, paras. A2.1 to A2.15 suggests other ways in which this duty can be discharged such as:

1) granting mortgage assistance to aid house purchase;

2) helping the applicant to obtain a tenancy in the private sector;

3) obtaining accommodation for the applicant from a housing association.

The use of caravans and other interim accommodation such as hostels is recognised reluctantly by the code. There is evidence that authorities, particularly in areas where there is a great deal of housing stress, are using interim accommodation, especially bed and breakfast hotels and other poor quality housing in order to satisfy their obligations under the Act.

In *R v Bristol City Council, ex p Browne* [1979] 3 All ER 344, [1979] 1 WLR 1437 the Queens Bench Divisional Court showed just how wide a discretion is conferred on local authorities by section 6. The applicant and her seven children left the matrimonial home in Tralee, Eire, on medical advice because of the husband's violence. At first the applicant went to a women's hostel in Limerick but when the husband discovered she was there, the hostel arranged for her and the children to go to Bristol. They spent the first night in Bristol in a local hostel but, being unable to stay there any longer, the applicant applied the following day to the Bristol District Council for accommodation as a homeless person. The housing authority commenced inquiries and telephoned the community welfare officer in Tralee who was aware of the husband's violence. He gave an assurance to the housing authority that if the applicant and her children were to return to Tralee he would secure suitable accommodation for them on their arrival. From their inquiries the housing authority concluded that the applicant had become homeless unintentionally and had a priority need and, though she had no connection with Bristol and responsibility for her could not be transferred to any other authority under the Act (because she came from Eire) that the authority had a duty under section 65 to secure accommodation for her. Under section 69 the authority could fulfil that duty by giving the applicant 'such advice and assistance' as would secure that she obtained 'accommodation from some other person'. Since the Tralee welfare officer was willing to secure accommodation for the applicant, the authority considered that they could properly carry out their statutory duty by advising the applicant to return to Tralee and contact the welfare officer there, and by offering to arrange and pay for her journey. The applicant, who did not wish to return to Tralee, applied for judicial review by way of mandamus requiring the authority to provide accommodation for her and the children in Bristol. It was, inter alia, held that:

1) When giving an applicant advice and assistance for the purpose of carrying out their duty within the terms of section 69 a housing authority were not confined to securing that accommodation was obtained from 'some other person' within the authority's area. Accordingly, the

housing authority were entitled to carry out and thereby fulfil their duty by advising and assisting the applicant to obtain accommodation from the welfare officer in Tralee;

2) Even though the welfare officer in Tralee had not specified to the Bristol authority a particular house as being available for the applicant, his offer of accommodation in Tralee was 'accommodation available for occupation' within section 75 since it was sufficient for the housing authority to be satisfied that accommodation would be available if the applicant returned to Tralee.

The accommodation secured for a person under section 69 must comply with section 75 and be available not only for occupation by the applicant but also by any other person who might reasonably be expected to reside with him. But where a person or body, as in *Browne*, promises an authority to find accommodation for a homeless person, then the authority need not be told the exact identity of the proposed accommodation.

Though the duty to accommodate can be discharged in general by making one offer of permanent accommodation, see *R v Westminster City Council, ex p Chambers* (1982) 6 HLR 15, or the offer of a series of temporary housing leading to a permanent dwelling, see *R v East Herefordshire District Council, ex p Hunt* (1985) 18 HLR 51, authorities must behave reasonably in making offers of accommodation, in the sense that an offer must not be perverse or absurd, either as to the premises involved or the time allowed to consider it, see *Parr v Wyre Borough Council* (1982) 2 HLR 71. Accommodation must be habitable, and what is more habitable by the applicant bearing in mind his medical condition, see *R v Ryedale District Council, ex p Smith* (1983) 16 HLR 66. In the light of the decision in *Pulhofer* (supra) it is unlikely that accommodation has to go beyond these requirements and be 'appropriate'. In this context *R v Wandsworth London Borough Council, ex p Lindsay* [1986] Housing Aid No. 38 July, p. 8 should be noted. A young mother, subject to a suspended possession order on her home, was offered a maisonette by the local authority. She alleged that she had been given insufficient time to consider the offer and that the dwelling was not appropriate as it had a balcony constituting a danger to her small son. The court said it could only intervene in relation to the amount of time allowed to consider an offer where the period of consideration allowed was absurdly or perversely inadequate. Furthermore the accommodation was held to be sufficient for the applicant in the light of the *Pulhofer* decision. It may even be that accommodation need not be 'fit' within the meaning of section 604 of the 1985 Act, see *R v Dinefwr Borough Council, ex p Marshall* (1984) 17 HLR 310.

Though, as stated above, making one reasonable offer of

accommodation will generally, at that point of time, satisfy the law's requirements, absolving an authority from the need to do more should the applicant unreasonably refuse the offer, see *R v Hammersmith and Fulham London Borough Council, ex p O' Brian* (1985) 17 HLR 471, that does not mean that the applicant should thereafter be treated as an intentionally homeless person to whom no obligation is owed unless there is an entirely fresh and unconnected incidence of unintentional homelessness. In *R v Ealing London Borough Council, ex p McBain* [1986] 1 All ER 13, [1985] 1 WLR 1351 the Court of Appeal stated that the correct approach is to state that one offer of accommodation unreasonably refused satisfies an authority's obligations *pro tem*, but where the applicant can thereafter show a material change in his circumstances making the previous offer clearly unsuitable as accommodation an authority's obligations are renewed. In judging what is unsuitable regard must be had to the general housing circumstances of the area.

Once, however, the duty to accommodate is owed it is owed indefinitely. In *R v Camden London Borough Council, ex p Waite* (1986) 18 HLR 434, (1986) Times, 12 July it was held that where an applicant is homeless, unintentionally so, and in priority need, the duty to accommodate is owed indefinitely, irrespective of the fact that the applicant previously occupied a dwelling under license in a property with a destined short life which he would have had to vacate at the end of his licence period to allow substantial reconstruction of the building. [*See Addendum 14.*]

Duties of notification

Various duties of notification are imposed by section 64. When certain determinations are made they, and the reasons for them, must be given to the applicant.

These determinations are:

1) whether the person is homeless or threatened with homelessness;

2) whether he has priority need;

3) whether he had become homeless or threatened with homeless intentionally;

4) whether he has a 'local connection' with another housing authority.

Notices must be given in writing, and if not actually received by the applicant, are treated as given only if made available at the offices of the relevant authority for a reasonable period for collection by the applicant or on his behalf.

Offences

Various offences are created by section 74. Where a person, with intent to induce a belief on the part of an authority in connection with their homlessness function as to his, or another's, state of homelessness, threatened homelessness, priority need or unintentional homelessness, knowingly or recklessly makes statements false in material respects, or knowingly withholds information reasonably required by the authority, he commits an offence. Likewise applicants are required to inform authorities of material changes in their circumstances arising before they receive notification of the determinations made on their applications. Authorities are required to explain this obligation to applicants in ordinary language.

Protecting the property of the homeless

Where an authority are under a duty to an applicant under sections 63 (the interim duty to accommodate where there is seeming priority need), 65(2) (the full duty to accommodate), 65(3) (the temporary duty to accommodate an intentionally homeless person who has priority need), 66(2) (the duty in respect of a person threatened with homelessness etc.), or 68 (the duty to accommodate in cases involving the local connection issue), *and* they have reason to believe there is danger of loss or damage to an applicant's personal property by reason of his inability to protect it *and* that no other suitable arrangements have been made, they must take reasonable steps to prevent or mitigate loss or damage to the property in question. A similar *power* exists to protect property where duties under the foregoing provisions are not owed. Authorities are given wide powers to deal with property in such circumstances, including powers of entry. They may decline to take action save upon such conditions as they consider appropriate, for example as to the recovery of charges for having taken action. The duty ceases when the circumstances that gave rise to it cease to apply, and authorities must notify applicants of that fact.

Authorities may also, under section 69(2) of the 1985 Act require persons to whom they owe obligations under sections 63, 65 or 68, to pay reasonable charges for accommodation provided.

Challenging decisions made under the Act and enforcing the duties

When a person feels that the local authority have wrongly determined his application he may follow certain avenues of 'appeal':

1) to a senior officer of the authority who may be able to review the initial decision;

2) to his local councillor;

3) to his MP;

4) to the Commission for Local Administration (see above Chapter 3). This course of action can only be followed where there is maladministration which arises out of failure to fulfil obligations, or unreasonable delay or inefficiency, etc., causing injustice. A failure to follow the provisions of the Code of Guidance could also be a prima facie instance of maladministration.

Recourse to the courts will be rarely available as a remedy since they have shown they wish to leave the day to day administration of the Act to local authorities, and will only involve themselves on points of law.

The general principles of administrative law apply to decisions by authorities. Inter alia authorities must not exceed their powers under the legislation; they must follow correct procedures; they must obey the requirements of the rules of natural justice in dealing with applications fairly; they must not behave perversely by dealing with applicants in a gratuitously oppressive fashion; they must not take into account irrelevant factors, and must consider those that are relevant. In this connection they must 'have regard to' the advice contained in the Code of Guidance issued by the Secretary of State, 2nd edition 1983, but they need not slavishly adhere to it. See further Arden *The Housing Act 1985*, pp. 100–103.

The Act itself specifies no legal channels of appeal, and so any challenge to an authority's decision can in general only be on a point of law, with the burden of proof on the challenger. The challenge will take the form of an application for judicial review under RSC Ord. 53 and section 31 of the Supreme Court Act 1981, and this is the preclusive means of challenge when the actual decision of an authority is being challenged, see *Cocks v Thanet District Council* [1983] 2 AC 286, [1982] 3 All ER 1135. This will cover nearly all potential litigation; though it *might* be possible to rely on the rule in *Thornton v Kirklees Metropolitan Borough Council* [1979] QB 626, [1979] 2 All ER 349 in an extreme case and bring an action for breach of statutory duty, it is hard to think of circumstances in which this could be so. Certainly a plaintiff would have to show that some right in private law had been infringed by the authority he applied to as homeless. See *Mallon v Monklands District Council* 1986 SLT 347 where a lack of accommodation was found to have contributed to psychiatric illness. It is important to be certain that proceedings are correctly commenced, for those begun by writ cannot be treated as if they are an application for judicial review, see *R v Southampton City Council, ex p Ward* (supra). See further Aldous and Alder *Applications for Judicial Review*, p. 103.

Generally a person challenging an authority's decision will desire both interim or 'interlocutory' relief to keep accommodation over his head pending resolution of the issue and a final order enforcing the authority's obligations to him.

Under section 31 of the Supreme Court Act 1981 applications for orders of certiorari, mandamus, etc., must be made to the High Court whose leave must be obtained before the application is made, see section 31(3). See Garner's *Administrative Law* 6th edn., pp. 167 to 187 for detailed disection of procedures. Suffice it to say here that interlocatory relief by way of injunction may be sought to stay an authority's decision pending final settlement of a homelessness dispute. In *De Falco v Crawley Borough Council* (supra) Lord Denning argued that to obtain such relief the applicant should be able to show a strong prima facie case that the authority is in breach of its obligations. This has been disputed by Arden in *The Housing Act 1985* at p. 103, or it may be, as Aldous and Alder point out in *Applications for Judicial Review* at p. 68, that it is harder to obtain an interim mandatory injunction ordering the performance of a positive act than a prohibitory injunction, and an interim mandatory order will often be sought in a homelessness case. With regard to final orders Lord Bridge made it clear in *Cocks v Thanet District Council* (supra) that the courts do not sit to substitute their decisions for those of authorities, though, in practice, on occasions the court's finding that no reasonable authority could have come to the decision actually reached may be enough to settle an issue. Certiorari will be the principal remedy to quash a decision wrong in law, and mandamus will also be appropriately awarded to require a redetermination of issues where, for example, the rules of natural justice have been ignored, or irrelevant factors taken into account. But in any case specific issues of illegality must be pleaded as no order of mandamus will be granted simply to make an authority perform its homelessness obligations generally, see *R v Beverley Borough Council, ex p McPhee* (1978) 122 Sol Jo 760.

The remedies available by way of judicial review are discretionary, and the House of Lords in its decision in *Pulhofer* (supra) clearly indicated that that discretion should be used sparingly in homelessness cases. Review is allowable where an authority has abused its powers by, for example, acting in bad faith, or by committing procedural irregularities, or by behaving unreasonably, that is absurdly or perversely, a point applied by Simon Brown J. in *R v Gravesham Borough Council, ex p Winchester* (1986) 18 HLR 207. Likewise authorities must not fetter their discretion, must consider relevant factors and eschew consideration of irrelevancies. But it is no part of the court's duty to substitute its own views on whether a particular set of facts fits within a particular legal rule for the decision on that by an authority, provided the authority's mechanisms and procedures for making such decisions are fair and reasonable.

Further reading

Books

Arden, A., and Partington, P., *Housing Law* (Sweet & Maxwell, 1983) Chap. 17.
Pollard, D. *Social Welfare Law*, (Oyez Longman) Chapter B3.
Hoath, D. *Homelessness* (Sweet & Maxwell, 1983).
Watchman, P., and Robson, P., *Homelessness and the Law* (The Planing Exchange, 1983).
Austerberry, H., Schott, K., and Watson, S., *Homeless in London 1971–81* (LSE, 1984).
Arden, A., *Homeless Persons – The Housing Act 1985 Part III* (Legal Action Group, 1986).
Malpas, P. (Ed) *The Housing Crisis* (Croom Helm, 1986). Chap. 6
Robson, P., and Watchman, P., *Developments in Homelessness and The Law 1983–85* (The Planning Exchange, 1986).

Reports

Wilkinson, T., *Down and Out* (Quartet Books, 1981).
Womens National Commission, *Homelessness Amongst Women* (Cabinet Office, 1983).
Craig, S., and Schwarz, C., *Down and Out* (Penguin, 1984).

Articles

Wolmar, C., 'The Hostels Debate' *Roof* July/August 1981, p. 16
Jansen, M., and de Smidt, G., 'Young and Homeless' *Roof* May/June 1982, p. 17.
Widdowson, B., 'Tactics in Homelessness Cases' [1982] LAG Bull May, p. 49.
Burrows, L., 'No Respite for the Single Homeless' *Roof* July/August 1982, p. 29.
Hirsch, D., 'Homeless and Jobless' *Roof* September/October 1982, p. 9.
Grosskurth, A., 'When Home is a B & B Hotel' *Roof* January/February 1984, p. 11.

Cowan, R., 'Council Dumps for Homeless Families' *Roof* May/June 1984, p. 12.

Grosskurth, A., 'From Care to Nowhere' *Roof* July/August 1984, p. 11.

Bryan, M., 'Domestic Violence: A Question of Housing' [1984] JSWL 195.

Stearn, J., 'An expensive way of making children ill' *Roof* September/October 1986, p. 11.

Part II
Repairs, housing standards and remedies

Chapter 7

The landlord's obligation to repair and maintain

(Except where expressly stated it may be assumed that the remedies referred to in this chapter apply to both public and private sector tenancies.)

Until recently neither in contract nor tort did the common law give any protection to tenants. The whole attitude of the law was encapsulated in the maxim caveat emptor, or as Erle CJ said in *Robbins v Jones* (1863) 15 CBNS 221 at 239: '. . . fraud apart, there is no law against letting a tumbledown house: and the tenant's remedy is upon his contract, if any'. See *Gordon and Teixeira v Selico and Select Managements Ltd* (1986) 18 HLR 219 for a recent application of this principle. There was no liability in tort whether the damage arose from the landlord's mere neglect or from his careless doing of works of maintenance or installation. In *Otto v Bolton and Norris* [1936] 2 KB 46, [1936] 1 All ER 960 that principle was held to be good law despite *Donoghue v Stevenson*, and it was again applied in *Davis v Foots* [1940] 1 KB 116, [1939] 4 All ER 4 and *Travers v Gloucester Corpn* [1947] KB 71, [1946] 2 All ER 506. Here a local authority let a house with the vent pipe of a gas geyser terminating under the eaves of the house. This dangerous installation led to a build-up of toxic exhaust fumes and as a consequence the tenant's lodger was gassed in the bathroom. The corporation was held not liable in tort.

A growing body of opinion viewed the exemption of lessors from liability in negligence with growing distaste and various attempts were made to end it. For example it was said in *Ball v LCC* [1949] 2 KB 159, [1949] 1 All ER 1056 that a landlord could be liable in *contract* to his tenant for negligent installation work carried out *after* the start of the lease, though non-contracting parties could not sue under this rule. Great changes have now been made in the law, both by statute and by the action of the courts, and it is to these that we must now turn.

Landlord's obligations in tort

a) At common law

Following the decisions in *Cunard v Antifyre Ltd* [1933] 1 KB 551 and
Taylor v Liverpool Corpn [1939] 3 All ER 329 there is no difficulty in
holding a landlord liable in negligence for damage caused *by buildings
retained in his occupation* to persons or to buildings let to a tenant. In
the *Taylor* case the corporation acquired a house with view to
demolishing it. Because there was no other available accommodation
for the tenant he was allowed to stay in the three rooms of the house he
occupied. A brick fell from the chimney stack of the house and hit the
tenant's daughter who was in the back yard of the house at the time.
The corporation had previously been warned of the defective condition
of the chimney. It was held, as the yard did not comprise part of the
demised premises, that the corporation were liable for the injury. In *AC
Billings & Sons Ltd v Riden* [1958] AC 240, [1957] 3 All ER 1 the House
of Lords stated that, irrespective of the lack of a contractual relationship, any person who executes work on premises is under a general duty
to use reasonable care for the safety of those whom he knows, or ought
reasonably to know, may be affected by or lawfully in the vicinity of the
work. Thus a landlord can be liable in tort for dangers he creates *after*
the commencement of the lease. But what of the long established
exemption from tortious liability in respect of dangers existing at the
time of the demise?

In *Rimmer v Liverpool City Council* [1985] QB 1, [1984] 1 All ER
930, the plaintiff was the tenant of a flat owned, designed and built by
the local authority. One internal passageway contained an unprotected
thin glass panel, a cause of complaint by the plaintiff at the start of his
tenancy. The tenant tripped in the passageway, put out his hand to save
himself, and his hand went through the panel, as a result of which he
suffered injury. The Court of Appeal repeated that *the 'bare' landlord
of unfurnished premises, and who has done no work on them, owes no
duty of care to a tenant in respect of the state of the premises when they
were let*, but held that a landlord may owe a duty of care in respect of
being the *designer or builder* of premises. This duty is owed to all
persons who may reasonably be expected to be affected by the design or
construction of the premises, and is a duty to take reasonable care to
ensure such persons do not suffer injury from design or construction
defects (which *may* extend to defects in work of modernisation or conversion etc.) The local authority was in breach of that duty on this
occasion. This is an important decision, having implications for all
authorities and associations who build and/or design dwellings, for
despite the fact that the plaintiff knew the glass panel was dangerous, he

had no chance of removing it and so avoiding the danger. Liability thus arises from the fact of negligent design and/or construction. However, no breach of the duty of care owed occurs in relation to installations in a dwelling where it may reasonably be assumed that the tenant will take adequate steps for the protection of himself and his family, see *Ryan v London Borough of Camden* (1982) 8 HLR 75 where an authority was held not liable to an infant plaintiff injured following contact with uninsulated central heating of a type in common use: the authority could reasonably expect parents to take steps to protect their children in such situations. See also *Sharpe v Manchester Metropolitan District Council* (1977) 5 HLR 71 where the plaintiff took a tenancy of a flat in 1972 and found it infested with cockroaches. The authority tried to eliminate the insects for two years by using emulsified DDT, but failed in their attempts. They were found negligent in that they had failed to treat the service ducts and other spaces in the walls and floor and had used a discredited insecticide. [For periods of limitation in such cases see Arden and Partington, *Housing Law* para. 16–34.]

b) Under statute

Civil liability may also arise under the Defective Premises Act 1972. Section 1 provides (inter alia):

'(1) A person taking on work for or in connection with the provision of a dwelling (whether the dwelling is provided by the erection or by the conversion or enlargement of a building) owes a duty –
   (a) if the building is provided to the order of any person to that person; and
   (b) without prejudice to paragraph (a) above to every person who acquires an interest (whether legal or equitable) in the dwelling; to see that the work which he takes on is done in a workmanlike or, as the case may be, professional manner, with proper materials and so that as regards that work the dwelling will be fit for habitation when completed . . .

(4) A person who –
   (a) in the course of a business which consists of or includes providing or arranging for the provision of dwellings or installation in dwellings; or
   (b) in the exercise of a power of making such provision or arrangements conferred by or by virtue of any enactment; arranges for another to take on work for or in connection with the provision of a dwelling shall be treated for the purposes of this section as included among the persons who have taken on the work'.

So far as public sector dwellings are concerned this provision imposes liability on local authorities and associations, their builders, subcontractors and architects if they fail to build in a professional or workmanlike manner (as the case may be) with proper materials, or fail to ensure that the dwelling is fit for human habitation, a phrase which may be capable of covering such matters as defective design or lay-out. (See Law Com. No. 40, para. 34.) The duty, *which is strict*, is owed to, inter alia, those persons having legal or equitable interests in the dwelling, for example tenants, but *not* their children or visitors. Moreover the duty will only arise in connection with the provision, whether by new construction, conversion or enlargement, of a *dwelling*. The mere enlargement of an existing single dwelling unit would not attract the operation of the law. The provision only applies to dwellings constructed after 1 January 1974, by virtue of section 7(2) of the Act. This provision seems to have been strangely ignored by public sector tenants affected by design or construction defects, though maybe the existence of alternative 'pure' common law remedies in tort, such as the decision in *Rimmer* above, explains this.

Section 3(1) of the Defective Premises Act 1972 provides:

'Where work of construction, repair, maintenance or demolition or any other work is done on or in relation to premises, any duty of care owed, because of the doing of the work, to persons who might reasonably be expected to be affected by the defects in the state of the premises created by the doing of the work shall not be abated by the subsequent disposal of the premises by the person who owed the duty'.

But this statutory displacement of a landlord's immunity in negligence is not without its own problems. First, it only applies, by virtue of section 3(2)(a), to those lettings of premises entered into after the commencement of the Act, 1 January 1974. Second, liability can only arise where there has been a defect created by a positive act classifiable as 'work of construction, repair, maintenance or demolition or any other work done on or in relation to premises'. Thus it seems not *all* 'work' can give rise to liability but only that of the specified kinds, or other 'work' which can be said to be 'done on or in relation to premises' such as, for example, installation of central heating, Nor does this section impose any liability for negligent omissions to do repairs.

Liability for an omission may, however, arise along with other forms of liability under section 4 of the 1972 Act. Section 4(1) provides:

'Where premises are let under a tenancy which puts on the landlord an obligation to the tenant for the maintenance or repair of the premises, the landlord owes to all persons who might reasonably be expected to be affected by defects in the state of the premises a duty to take such care as is reasonable in all the circumstances to see that they are reasonably safe from personal injury or from damage to their property caused by a relevant defect.'

This imposes tortious liability on a landlord towards his tenants, their families and those other persons foreseeably likely to be in the premises, and, by section 6(3) of the Act, he cannot exclude or restrict this duty.

As with section 3, this section also poses problems of interpretation. Liability can only arise in respect of a 'relevant defect'. Such is defined by sub-section (3) as '. . . a defect in the state of the premises existing at or after the material time and arising from, or continuing because of, an act or omission by the landlord which constitutes or would if he had notice of the defect, have constituted a failure by him to carry out his obligation to the tenant for the maintenance or repair of the premises . . .'. Such defects must arise 'at or after the material time', which is further defined by the sub-section as being, in general terms, for tenancies commencing before the Act, the commencement date of the Act (1 January 1974), and in other cases the earliest date on which the tenancy commenced or the tenancy agreement was entered into. Liability arises out of those defects which constitute a breach of the landlord's obligations to repair and maintain. These obligations will include any express covenant to repair given by the landlord and, by virtue of sub-section (5), those implied by statute, such as section 11 of the Landlord and Tenant Act 1985. An even more extended meaning is given to 'obligation' by sub-section (4) which deems for the purposes of the section any *power* a landlord has to repair actually to be an *obligation* to repair. Such powers can arise in many situations. A landlord may have power to enter and do repairs simply because the tenant has defaulted on his own repairing covenants. In such circumstances the Act provides that the landlord, while remaining liable to third parties, shall not actually be liable to the tenant himself. The effect of the decision in *Mint v Good* [1951] 1 KB 517, [1950] 2 All ER 1159 should also be remembered for here Somervell LJ said (at page 522): '. . . in the case of a weekly tenancy, business efficacy will not be effected if the house is allowed to fall into disrepair and no one keeps it in reasonable condition; and it seems to me, therefore, necessary . . . that the . . . landlord should at any rate have the power to keep the place in proper repair . . .'.

Thus an implied power to enter and do repairs would seem to arise in relation to any *weekly* tenancy of a dwelling-house and this will be deemed to the an obligation to repair under sub-section (4).

In *Smith v Bradford Metropolitan Council* (1982) 44 P & CR 171, a local authority tenancy agreement provided that the tenant should give the authority and its officers and workmen reasonable facilities for inspecting the premises let, their state of repair, and to carry out repairs, and the 'premises' in question were defined as the dwelling, and, where the context required, its garage, outbuildings, yards and gardens. The tenant of the dwelling was injured by the defective condition of a rear concrete patio constructed between the house and its garden by a previous tenant. The council knew of the defective condition of this patio, but were they liable for the injury? The Court of Appeal found that their power to enter the premises fell within section 4(4) of the 1972 Act, and was deemed to be an obligation to repair. The context required that the patio be regarded as part of the premises in relation to which the power, and therefore the deemed obligation, to repair existed.

There are a number of subsidiary points to note about this provision. Sub-section (2) provides:

'The said duty is owed if the landlord knows (whether as the result of being notified by the tenant or otherwise) or if he ought in all the circumstances to have known of the relevant defect'.

Thus there is no need for a tenant to give his landlord notice of a defect provided it would be patent on reasonable inspection.

In *Clarke v Taff Ely Borough Council* (1983) 10 HLR 44, Mrs Clarke visited her sister's council house and was injured when the rotten floorboards gave way beneath a table on which she was standing. The house was one of a number of pre-war council houses known to have a potentially dangerous floor construction. The local authority admitted it had never heard of the Defective Premises Act 1972, and their chief housing surveyor agreed that in view of the age of the house, its type and the presence of damp it was foreseeable that rot would occur. Damages of £5,100 were awarded.

Second, a very extended meaning is given to the word 'tenancy' by section 6 of the 1972 Act. The term includes leases and underleases, tenancies at will and sufferance and statutory tenancies. Furthermore section 4(6) itself states:

'This section applies to a right of occupation given by contract or any enactment and not amounting to a tenancy as if the right were a tenancy'.

Thus contractual licenses and restricted contracts under the Rent Act 1977 will both attract the operation of this provision.

Liability under the Occupiers' Liability Act 1957

The common law, as we have already seen in *Taylor v Liverpool Corpn* imposes liability on a landlord for defects on his premises which cause injury to his tenants. Thus if a local authority let the flats in a tower block and retain the common parts, such as the staircases, in their own occupation they will be responsible in tort to persons injured by the defective condition of any of those parts. The Occupiers Liability Act 1957, section 2 also imposes liability in such circumstances, and the 1957 Act adds to the landlord's obligation by stating in section 3(1):

'Where an occupier of premises is bound by contract to permit persons who are strangers to the contract to enter or use the premises, the duty of care which he owes to them as his visitors cannot be restricted or excluded by that contract, but (subject to any provision of the contract to the contrary) shall include the duty to perform his obligations under the contract, whether undertaken for their protection or not, in so far as those obligations go beyond the obligations otherwise involved in that duty'.

The effect of this sub-section is that the landlord cannot by virtue of his contract with his tenants reduce his obligations to their visitors below the standard required by the Act, the 'common duty of care'. Furthermore the tenant's visitors are enabled to claim the benefit of any more onerous obligations inserted in the lease, unless the lease itself specifically excludes this. Whether the landlord can simply exclude the common duty to tenants' visitors simply by posting exclusionary notices, as is allowed generally by section 2(1) of the 1957 Act, is an open question, but the better view of the law is that such an exclusion would not be lawful. (See generally the Unfair Contract Terms Act 1977.) The interested reader is referred to the current editions of the standard works on torts such as Winfield, Street and Clerk and Lindsell for further details.

Landlord's obligations in contract

a) At common law

Before discussing the contractual position it should be stated that contractual remedies will only apply as between contracting parties. Any third party injured by the defective state of a dwelling-house must find his remedy in tort. It should also be noted that it is established by *Batty v Metropolitan Property Realisations Ltd* [1978] QB 554, [1978] 2 All ER 445 that the existence of a contractual remedy will not prevent concurrent liability from arising in tort. That said, a landlord may be liable to his tenant for a breach of an express covenant to repair and maintain a dwelling-house. In such a case the extent of the landlord's liability will depend upon the wording of the covenant. Such express covenants are rare, particularly as many, if not indeed most, leases of small dwelling-houses are created orally on a weekly basis under section 54(2) of the Law of Property Act 1925. The common law has also been unwilling to imply terms into leases. In *Smith v Marrable* (1843) 11 M & W 5, Parke B implied a term into a letting of *furnished* premises that, at the start of the lease, they would be in a habitable condition. The nature of the obligation should be noted: it exists at the start of the lease, and, according to *Sarson v Ròberts* [1895] 2 QB 395, it will not arise if the premises become uninhabitable during the course of the lease. The cases show that what is likely to make a house unfit for habitation in this context are matters likely to affect the health of the incoming tenant, such as infestation by bugs, or defects in the drains, or recent occupation by a person suffering from an easily communicable disease. The meaning given by the common law to 'unfit for human habitation' is therefore different from the meaning the phrase has under the unfit-ness provisions of the Housing Act 1985, which are discussed in the next chapter and the two concepts should not be confused. If furnished pre-mises are 'unfit' at common law the tenant is entitled to quit them by repudiating the tenancy. He may also sue for any loss he has suffered, see: *Wilson v Finch Hatton* (1877) 2 Ex D 336, and *Charsley v Jones* (1889) 53 JP 280. This implied condition is limited to lettings of furnished dwellings. In *Sleafer v Lambeth Borough Council* [1960] 1 QB 43, [1959] 3 All ER 378 it was said that where a landlord lets unfurnished dwellings there will generally be no implied term that they are free of defects.

The law has on occasions implied certain terms into contracts of letting. In *Liverpool City Council v Irwin* [1977] AC 239, [1976] 2 All ER 39 the House of Lords implied a term into a letting of a flat in a high rise block. The facts were that the local authority owned a tower block of flats, access to which was provided by a common staircase and two electrically operated lifts. The tenants also had the use of internal chutes into which to discharge rubbish. Over the years the condition of the block deteriorated, partly as a result of vandalism. Continual defects included: failed lifts; a lack of lighting on the staircases, and blocked rubbish chutes. The tenants refused to pay rent and so the land-lords applied for possession orders on the flats, to which the tenants replied with a counter-claim that (inter alia) the landlords were in breach of the covenant of quiet enjoyment. The House of Lords said that as this was a contract in which the parties had not themselves fully expressed the terms then the court could imply certain terms solely to prevent the contract of letting from becoming inefficacious and absurdly futile. The reasoning that followed was:

1) The tenants had in their leases an implied right or easement to use the stairs, lifts and rubbish chutes as these were necessarily incidental to their occupation of high-rise flats;

2) The landlords must therefore be placed under an implied obligation to take reasonable care to maintain those common areas and facilities;

3) Such an obligation is not, however, absolute because tenants of high-rise blocks must themselves resist vandalism and co-operate in maintaining the common areas in reasonable condition, and

4) The courts have no power to imply such terms in municipal tenancy agreements as they think 'reasonable'. They may only supply such terms as are truly necessary for the functioning of the contract.

It should also be noted that the fact that the landlord is in breach of *his* covenant to repair does not automatically entitle the tenant to treat the lease as at an end, see *Surplice v Farnsworth* (1844) 13 LJ CP 215.

Some comment must be made on what can be termed the 'self-help' remedy created by the decision in *Lee-Parker v Izzet* [1971] 3 All ER 1099, [1971] 1 WLR 1688. Here it was held that, irrespective of the common law rules as to set off, the occupiers of property had a right to recoup themselves out of *future* rent for the cost of repairs to the property, in so far as the repairs fell within the landlord's express or implied covenants, provided that he was in fact in breach of them, and only after due notice and been given to him. The exact limits of this remedy should be noted. A tenant has no right to *withhold* payment of rent to compel his landlord to carry out repairs, and if he does so he will be in breach of his own obligation under the lease. The rule only authorises the deducting of the *proper* cost of repairs from future rent: a tenant is not entitled to expend vast sums on his home and then present his landlord with the bill. The authorities agree that the following steps should be taken before reliance is placed on the rule:

1) The tenant *must* notify the landlord of the disrepair which itself must arise from a breach of the landlord's covenants;

2) At the same time he should obtain at least two builders' estimates as to the likely costs of the repairs and send them to the landlord, warning him at the same time that if repairs are not effected then the tenant will carry out the work and will deduct the cost from future rent;

3) To be absolutely safe, a county court declaration should be obtained authorising this course of action, and

4) having given his landlord time to execute the repairs, the tenant may then proceed to do them himself.

It can be seen that this procedure is neither simple nor rapid. It does, however, have the advantage in that the principle constitutes a defence to a claim for rent, and monies paid on repairs are treated as payments of the rent itself. Some local authorities phrase their tenancy agreements in such a way as to attempt to exclude the operation of the *Lee-Parker* principle, for example: 'The council will not accept responsibility for orders which are given by the tenant direct to statutory undertakings or any other bodies or persons, and any charges arising from such orders will be the tenant's responsibility.' The effect of such wording would not yet seem to have been elucidated in court.

In *Asco Developments Ltd v Lowes* (1978) 248 Estates Gazette 683 the landlords sought summary judgment for arrears of rent under RSC Ord. 14 alleging that there was no defence to the action. The tenants sought to defend on the grounds that the landlords were in breach of their repairing obligations. Megarry V-C held that in certain special circumstances the *Lee-Parker* principle could be applied to monies accrued in rent arrears, and that in the present case the tenants could defend the action. However, the court stated that nothing in the decision should be taken to encourage rent strikes as a means of forcing action on the part of a landlord. It was made quite clear in *Camden Nominees v Forcey* [1940] Ch 352, [1940] 2 All ER 1 that it is no answer to a claim for rent by a landlord for the tenant to say that the landlord has failed to perform his obligations. That case is also authority for the proposition that it is an actionable interference with the contract between a landlord and his tenant for another ternant of that landlord to persuade his fellow tenant not to pay rent in an attempt to force the landlord to perform his obligations. If a tenant is to use the *Lee-Parker* principle in respect of rent arrears, he must specify to the court the sums and costs in question, and must particularise the issues. A judge faced with such issues should act with considerable discretion before allowing the tenant to defend the claim for rent. It would also seem that the fact that the landlords were in voluntary liquidation in the *Asco Developments* case was a factor of great importance to the mind of the judge, and therefore it would be unwise to regard the decision as a major extension of the law. It is, moreover, uncertain whether the *Lee-Parker* principle applies only to the cost of repairs or whether it can be extended to cover other heads of damage.

In *British Anzani (Felixstowe) Ltd v International Marine Management (UK) Ltd* [1980] QB 137, [1979] 2 All ER 1063, Forbes J indicated that *in equity*, as a set off raised by way of defence, unliquidated damages, for example claims for inconvenience and loss of enjoyment, might be recoverable against rent under a tenancy agreement. The tenant must be able to show it would be inequitable in view of the condition of his dwelling to allow the landlord to recover the whole amount of rent claimed. The tenant's contention should be raised as a defence to the landlord's action, and the tenant should make a counter-claim which particularises the nature of the landlord's breach of obligation and the consequent damage. Though it was not *absolutely* necessary that a claim and counter-claim should arise from the same contract, both must stem from very closely connected transactions so that equity can recognise that the tenant's counter-claim goes to the very root of the landlord's claim.

A set off of unliquidated damages is a defence to as much of the plaintiff's claim as is represented by the eventual amount of the award made. If the defendant limits *his* damages to a sum less than that claimed from him then he must pay the balance over and above his counter-claim. But where the defendant's damages are claimed at large and are finally to be decided by the court, and where it is bona fide claimed that they over top the plaintiffs claim, even though they are not yet quantified, then the defendant's set off amounts to a complete defence to the whole of the plaintiff's claim.

It is most unlikely that a court would allow such a measure of equitable relief as would entitle a tenant counter-claiming for unliquidated damages to escape the payment of the whole of a claim for unpaid rent. Any house would have to be in quite awful condition and any rent payable would have to be quite low before these principles could really begin to bring a great deal of relief to tenants. (For damages for breach of covenant to repair see below.) Furthermore this equitable relief is discretionary, and as, 'he who comes to equity must come with clean hands', it is unlikely to be available to a tenant who has been guilty of wrongdoing in relation to the transaction in question. The *British Anzani* case is not likely to be of assistance to rent strikers.

Where a landlord is neglectful of repairing obligations, so that serious deterioration of the dwelling(s) in question is likely, and it can be shown that the landlord is taking no real interest in the property, either to collect rent or to perform obligations, it may be possible to apply to the High Court under section 37(1) of the Supreme Court Act 1981 for the Court to appoint a receiver if it appears just and convenient. The receiver will then manage the property in accordance with the lease until further order, see *Hart v Emelkirk Ltd* [1983] 3 All ER 15, [1983] 1 WLR 1289. However, this remedy may not be sought by *local authority* tenants, see *Parker v Camden London Borough Council* [1985] 2 All ER 141, [1985] 3 WLR 47.

b) Under statute

We have seen how, with some few exceptions, the common law has failed to impose repairing obligations on landlords. Parliament has on a number of occasions attempted to remedy the omission of the common law, but, sadly, the courts have adopted a somewhat restrictive interpretation of the legislation.

As J.I. Reynolds has shown in 'Statutory Covenants of Fitness and Repair: Social Legislation and the Judges' (1974) 37 MLR 377, the restrictive attitude of the common law in relation to landlords' repairing obligations dates from the 1840's – the very period when much evidence was coming to light as to the appalling housing conditions suffered by large numbers of people. Parliament was not slow to act, and the Nuisances Removal, etc (1846) began the great march of public health legislation that was to culminate in the Public Health Act 1875. However, it was not until the 1880's that tenants were given the right to recover damages for a landlord's 'neglect or default in sanitary matters'. Section 12 of the Housing of the Working Classes Act 1885 was designed to remove the anomaly whereby the common law gave protection under *Smith v Marrable* only to tenants of furnished dwellings. The provision was opposed in the House of Lords by Lord Bramwell as an unwarranted interference with the principles of freedom of contract and caveat emptor. That was an ill omen. Though the provision has been retained and refined in subsequent legislation and is presently section 8 of the Landlord and Tenant Act 1985, the attitude of the courts has remained restrictive.

The provision states that in a letting to which it applies there is an implied term of fitness for human habitation at the commencement of the tenancy and that the landlord will keep it so fit throughout its currency.

The principal difficulty with section 8 is that sub-section (3) limits its applicability to contracts of letting where the rent is not more than £80 in relation to Inner London Boroughs or £52 elsewhere in the country, and thus hardly any properties are covered. The courts have 'discovered' other difficulties in the wording of this provision and its ancestors and these have hardened into rules of interpretation which apply not only to section 8 but also to section 11 of the Landlord and Tenant Act 1985. The first point to note is that *Middleton v Hall* (1913) 108 LT 804 and *Ryall v Kidwell & Son* [1914] 3 KB 135 stated that only the tenant can sue. While these decisions have been effectively overruled in tort by section 4 of the Defective Premises Act 1972 (see above) the technical rule remains that privity of contract limits the possibility of suing on the implied covenant only to the contracting parties. Next is should be noted that the landlord cannot be liable under the implied covenant unless the tenant has previously given him notice of the defect. This was decided, in the case of patent defects, by *McCarrick v Liverpool Corpn* [1947] AC 219, [1946] 2 All ER 646, and was applied to latent defects by *O'Brien v Robinson* [1973] AC 912, [1973] 1 All ER

583. It should again be remembered that the tortious remedy under section 4 of the Defective Premises Act 1972 is not made so dependent upon the giving of actual notice. In the case of local authority dwellings, it was held in *Sheldon v West Bromwich Corpn* (1973) 25 P & CR 360 that where a local authority employee knows that premises are defective then his knowledge will be treated as giving the authority notice.

In *McGreal v Wake* (1984) 269 Estates Gazette 1254 though it was stressed that tenants should inform landlords of works necessary to meet breaches of repairing obligations, it can be enough to 'trigger' a landlord's responsibilities if the tenant complains to the local authority and they then serve notice requiring works on the landlord under section 190 of the Housing Act 1985.

The most serious limitation on section 8 was imposed by the Court of Appeal in *Buswell v Goodwin* [1971] 1 All ER 418, [1971] 1 WLR 92. Here a cottage was statutorily unfit and, as the local authority had made a closing order on it, the landlord had commenced possession proceedings against the tenant. He in turn argued that the house was only unfit because the landlord was in breach of his implied contractual obligation under section 8. It can be argued that the standard of repair imported by the implied covenant is absolute, but the Court of Appeal rejected this. Instead, they restricted the ambit of operation of the implied covenant to those cases where a house is capable of being made fit at reasonable expense. The result is that where a house has fallen into an extreme state of disrepair the tenant can no longer rely on the implied covenant. The paradox thus emerges of the tenants of the worst housing receiving the lowest level of legal protection.

We shall now discover that a very similar process of judicial reasoning has emptied much of the meaning from the other statutorily implied covenant, that found under section 11 of the Landlord and Tenant Act 1985.

This provision applies, under section 13 of the Act, to leases of dwelling-houses granted on or after 24 October 1961 for terms of *less* than seven years, so that a lease for a term of seven years is not caught, see *Brikom Investments Ltd v Seaford* [1981] 2 All ER 783, [1981] 1 WLR 863. The obligation is to keep in repair the structure and exterior of the dwelling, including its drains, gutters and external pipes, *and* to keep in repair *and* proper working order the mains services installations, including basins, sinks, baths and sanitary conveniences, but excluding appliances etc., for making use of a mains service, e.g. a refrigerator, *and* to keep in repair and proper working order space and water heating installations. The standard of repair required is determined by having regard to the age, character, prospective life and locality of the dwelling. It is not possible to contract out of this obligation, see section 12 of the Act, save with the consent of the county court.

The policy of Parliament in creating the implied covenant was to prevent unscrupulous landlords from imposing unreasonable repairing obligations on their tenants. It cannot be said, however, that the law has been as successful as it might have been in preventing the occurrence of disrepair and bad housing conditions. Tenants are generally ignorant of their rights, and do not complain about disrepair until it becomes exceptional and intolerable. Alongside this general ignorance and unwillingness to act on the part of tenants there exists the same restrictive judicial attitude as we have seen in relation to the covenant implied under section 8.

This can be seen in decisions as to which matters fall within the scope of the implied covenant. In *Brown v Liverpool Corpn* [1969] 3 All ER 1345, paving flagstones and shallow steps leading to a house were held to be part of its 'exterior', though not its structure. They were necessary for the purpose of gaining access to the house and so fell within the scope of the implied covenant. In *Hopwood v Cannock Chase District Council* [1975] 1 All ER 796, [1975] 1 WLR 373 the slabs in a back yard were held not to fall within the scope of the covenant as the back yard was not the essential means of access to the house. Thus it may be argued that, essential means of access apart, 'exterior' in section 11(1)(a) simply means the outer part of the 'structure' of the dwelling-house and not the contiguous land also included in the lease. So far as the application of the implied covenant to flats is concerned, dicta of the Court of Appeal in *Campden Hill Towers v Gardner* [1977] QB 823, [1977] 1 All ER 739 are most important. The obligation implied by section 11(1)(a) which deals with structural matters, much be taken separately from that implied by section 11(1)(b), which deals with installations. Where the structure is concerned the landlord's obligation extends to anything which can ordinarily be regarded as part of the structure or exterior of the dwelling in question. Thus section 11(1)(a) applies, irrespective of the words of the lease, to the outside walls of a flat (even though they may have been excluded from the demise), the outer sides of horizontal divisions between flats, the outside of the inner party walls of the flat and the structural framework and beams directly supporting the floors, ceilings and walls of a flat. The test to be used in determining the scope of the implied covenant is whether the particular item of disrepair affects the stability or usability of the particular flat in question.

In *Douglas-Scott v Scorgie* [1984] 1 All ER 1086, [1984] 1 WLR 716 the Court of Appeal held that the roof of a building above a top floor flat may be part of the structure and exterior of that flat, irrespective of whether or not it forms part of the demised premises. The question must be determined on a common sense basis, so that where there is an uninhabited attic above a flat the roof above the attic might not be regarded as part of the structure and exterior of the flat. The content of the obligations of public and private sector landlords are the same under this implied covenant, see *Wainwright v Leeds City Council* (1984) 270 Estates Gazette 1289.

So far as section 11(1)(b) is concerned the obligation is merely one to keep in repair and sound working order those relevant installations actually within the physical confines of the flat itself.

The covenant is one to repair, so what is the meaning of the word 'repair'? In *Ravenseft Properties v Davstone (Holdings) Ltd* [1980] QB 12, [1979] 1 All ER 929 a distinction was made between the process of repair and a completely different process which is replacement. Replacement is a process of reconstruction so drastic that at the end of the lease the landlord receives back a wholly different property from that which he demised. 'Repair' on the other hand, according to the decision in *Greg v Planque* [1936] 1 KB 669, simply means making good defects, including renewal where necessary. In other words, simply keeping the property in a condition suitable for the purpose for which it was let. The distinction between these two processes is the scale and degree of the work involved. The fact that work, because of modern statutory requirements or building practices, has to be done to a higher standard than that of the original does not necessarily mean that it cannot be classed as 'repair'. Work will not be classifiable as 'repair' if it results in a reconstruction of the whole, or substantially the whole, of a building.

It is, however, necessary to show disrepair as opposed to a lack of amenity or inefficiency, see *Quick v Taff-Ely Borough Council* [1986] QB 809, [1985] 3 All ER 321. Here a council house built in the early 1970s was thermally inefficient with uninsulated concrete window lintels giving rise to condensation that produced intolerable living conditions. The Court of Appeal accepted that the eradication of a design defect, such as affected the present dwelling, may fall within the ambit of the implied covenant, provided the work required does not amount to substantial reconstruction or improvement, *and* provided the work is necessary to remedy disrepair. To repair is to make good some damage: eradicating a design defect that simply makes a dwelling inefficient or ineffective as a habitation is not automatically therefore repair. In *Quick* the court found the condensation simply made the house function badly or inefficiently, there was no damage or deterioration as such to any components of the structure of the dwelling. The obligation to repair only arises where there is such damage or deterioration, though where this can be shown to exist, discharging the obligation may require eradicating a design defect giving rise to the damage so that to some extent the dwelling is 'improved'. However, substantial reconstruction work will be outside the ambit of a covenant 'to repair'.

Thus if the landlord can show that the work required on any given house is so drastic that it would amount to his getting back, at the end of the term, a substantially different house from that which he let, then that work is outside his obligation to repair. This would seem to be so whether the condition of the property has arisen from either a want to maintenance or faulty design or construction. In *Pembery v Lamdin* [1940] 2 All ER 434 a landlord let certain old premises not constructed with a dampcourse or with waterproofing for the external walls, and covenanted to keep the external part of the let premises in good repair and condition. The tenant claimed that this put the landlord under an obligation to waterproof the outside walls and so render the premises dry. This would have required major construction work both inside and outside the premises. It was held that the obligation on the landlord was only to keep the premises in repair in the condition in which they were demised. In this case he would be required only to point the external brickwork. This, of course, limits the operation of the implied repairing covenant and again produces the paradox that the worse the condition of the property the less is the legal protection enjoyed by the tenant. (However, contrast *Elmcroft Developments Ltd v Tankersley-Sawyer* (1984) 270 Estates Gazette 140 where the court found that replacing an incorrectly laid *and existing* damp proof course in a block of flats was an act of 'repair'.)

It is possible to come to exactly the same conclusion by a different argument, as was shown in *Newham London Borough v Patel* [1979] JPL 303. Here there was general agreement between the parties that Mr Patel's house was in a severely sub-standard condition. The local authority wished to move him to other accommodation and commenced possession proceedings which he resisted, and replied to with a counter-claim for breach of the implied covenant. The Court of Appeal needed little time to dispose of Mr Patel's argument. They looked to section 11(3) which states that the standard of repair required by the covenant is to be determined by having regard to the 'age, character and prospective life of the dwelling-house and the locality in which it is situated'. Mr Patel's house was a poor, old dwelling in bad condition shortly destined for redevelopment. On this basis the court concluded that the prospective life of the dwelling affected the content of the section 11 duty. The local authority could not be required to carry out repairs which the court categorised as 'wholly useless'. The standard of repair thus required under section 11 is far from absolute and will vary according to the factors which the section says have to be taken into account. It would seem that only the stated factors can be considered. The result is that poor, old property, for example that acquired compulsorily and then used on a 'short life' basis, perhaps to accommodate otherwise homeless persons, is effectively outside the protection of the implied covenant.

What damages can be recovered for breach of a covenant to repair? The law was extensively reviewed in *Calabar Properties v Stitcher* [1983] 3 All ER 759, [1984] 1 WLR 287. The fundamental principle is that the object of damages is to restore the tenant to the position he would have been in had there been no breach, a principle that produces different results in different contexts. In relation to periodic lettings of dwellings subject to secure, protected or statutory tenancies the measure of damages will, in general, be as stated in *Hewitt v Rowlands* (1924) 93 LJKB 1080, i.e. the difference in value to the tenant of the premises, from the date of notice of want of repair down to the time of the assessment of damages, between the house in the condition in which it currently is and the condition in which it would be had the landlord, on receipt of notice, fulfilled the obligation to repair; in other words the difference in value to the tenant of the premises in their current condition and the condition in which they should be, bearing in mind their age, character and locality. This sum is, historically, likely to be what the tenant would have to spend in performing the landlord's obligations for him, though it may be a sum computed by reference to a proportion of the periodic rent, plus a sum in respect of inconvenience and discomfort.

Where the dwelling is occupied under a 'long' lease, for example a flat obtained under the 'right to buy', and the landlord retains a repairing obligation which is breached, the appropriate measure of damages will be *either*, where the tenant wishes to sell the dwelling, the difference in the price he received for the dwelling as damaged and the price it would have fetched on the open market had it been repaired, *or*, where the tenant wishes to remain in the dwelling, the cost of taking reasonable alternative accommodation, the cost of redecorating plus some compensation for inconvenience in addition to the cost of repairs.

In such cases it is not enough simply to claim 'damages', the issues must be particularised. 'Special damage' i.e. the precise amount of pecuniary loss suffered by the tenant flowing from the facts must be specifically pleaded. This means that claims for, inter alia, damaged personal property, money spent discharging a landlord's obligations, or remedying damage consequent on a landlord's failure to act, costs of redecorating, costs of eating out should the condition of the dwelling render preparing and eating food there impracticable, the cost of taking alternative accommodation, should this be reasonable, have to be specified. Some general damage, compensation for which will be computed by the court according to the nature of the tenant's interest in the property, must also be generally pleaded, and this include matters such as inconvenience and discomfort, as mentioned above.

Awards of damages vary in such cases, contrast *Taylor v Knowsley Borough Council* (1985) 17 HLR 376 with *Downie v Lambeth London Borough Council* [1986] Legal Action 95, but the trend seems to be for awards to be increasing, and to be in thousands and hundreds of pounds rather than in tens.

It should be remembered that the onus of proof in relation to these matters is on the tenant, see: *Foster v Day* (1968) 208 Estates Gazette 495.

Of course a tenant is not entitled to treat his home in a cavalier and wilful fashion. It was made clear in *Warren v Keen* [1954] 1 QB 15, [1953] 2 All ER 1118 that a tenant is always under some sort of obligation to look after the property he inhabits. In the case of a long lease, say 99 years, the tenant is usually made subject to full repairing covenants.

On the other hand weekly tenants, and that includes the vast majority of public sector tenants, are usually only bound to use the premises in a tenant-like manner. This means taking proper care of the premises, for example cleaning chimneys and windows, replacing electric light bulbs, mending fuses, and unstopping blocked sinks. In *Wycombe Health Authority v Barnett* (1982) 264 Estates Gazette 619 it was stated that in very cold climatic conditions a tenant *may* have to lag water pipes, or use additional heat, or turn off the water supply according to the circumstances, such as the severity of the cold, the duration of contemplated absence from home and the internal condition of the house, in order to behave in a tenant-like manner. The landlord is under no duty under section 11 of the 1985 Act to lag domestic water pipes.

Section 104 of the Housing Act 1985 requires landlords who grant secure tenancies to publish within two years of the commencement of the Act (and thereafter to revise and republish) information, in simple terms, about their secure tenancies. This information must explain inter alia the effect of the implied covenant to repair under section 11 et seq of the Landlord and Tenant Act 1985. All secure tenants must be supplied with a copy of this information.

Under section 96 of the Housing Act 1985 and The Secure Tenancies (Right to Repair) Scheme Regulations S.I. 1985/1493 *secure* tenants are entitled to carry out certain repairs on their homes for which the landlord is responsible (other than repairs to the structure or exterior of flats), and may then recover their costs from their landlords. The tenant must first claim 'the right to repair' stating, in prescribed form, the work to be done, the materials to be used and who is to do the work. The landlord must, within 21 days, accept or refuse the claim. Refusal *must* take place in cases where: the landlord's costs of doing the work would be less than £20; where the specified works do not fall within the landlord's repairing covenant; or where the tenant's specification of materials would not meet the needs of the specified work. Refusal *may* take place: where the landlord's costs would be more than £200; where the landlord intends to do works to fulfil obligations within 28 days of receiving service of the tenant's claim; where the works specified are not reasonably necessary for the tenant's personal comfort or safety, and the landlord intends to do works to fulfil a repairing obligation within the year as part of a programme of works; where the tenant's works would infringe guarantee rights enjoyed by the landlord; where the landlord reasonably requires access to the dwelling in order to inspect the site of the specified works and the tenant has unreasonably failed to provide access. A notice of refusal must particularise the landlord's case. Where none of the above grounds are relied on the landlord must accept the claim, approving works, with or without modifications, and authorising materials to be used. On an accepted claim the landlord will inform the tenant of how much it would cost the landlord to do the work, and what proportion of these costs (between 75 and 100 per cent) the landlord will pay under the regulations. A date for claiming payment will also be set. The landlord's notice must be in prescribed form.

Where the landlord fails to serve notice accepting or refusing the claim, or has refused the claim on grounds either that the landlord will do the work within 28 days or one year, as the case may be, and has failed to do the promised works, the tenant may, where the cost of the works would be not more than £200, serve a default notice on the landlord. The landlord must respond to this within seven days of service either accepting the tenant's claim, or refusing the claim and the default notice. Refusal may take place on grounds similar to those outlined in relation to refusal of claims initially.

Tenants may carry out repair works where their claims have been accepted or where the landlord has failed to respond to a default notice in the specified manner. Payment may be claimed in writing and in specified form from the landlord once the works have been completed, and the landlord has 21 days in which to accept or refuse the claim for payment. Refusal may only take place if certain conditions are not met. Refusal *must* occur where works have not been properly carried out, or the tenant was not entitled to do them. Refusal *may* occur, inter alia, where unauthorised materials have been used or the tenant has unreasonably refused the landlord access to inspect the site of the works.

Where a claim for payment is accepted the amount and style of payment are fixed by the Regulations 22 and 23. It should be noted that, under Regulation 25, where works are carried out under the scheme the landlord's obligations in respect of the relevant lack of repair under repairing covenants are suspended, inter alia, from the acceptance of the tenant's initial claim to service of the tenant's claim for payment. (See further DoE Circular 23/85, and 'Right to Repair' (a guide for public sector landlords) published by the DoE.)

Before concluding this chapter two matters have to be mentioned. The first is to say that is was held in *Proudfoot v Hart* (1890) 25 QBD 42 that where a covenant is one *'to keep in repair'* this imports an initial obligation to put *into* repair, though the standard of repair will vary according to the age, character and locality of the property and the social class of the tenant. Second, something must be said about the remedy of specific performance in relation to repairing covenants. In many cases an award of damages will not be a sufficient remedy for a tenant whose home is in a state of disrepair. He will be more concerned to see the defective premises put into repair. It was thought the remedy of specific performance was not available to a tenant to enable him to force his landlord to perform his repairing obligations. In *Jeune v Queens Cross Properties Ltd* [1974] Ch 97, [1973] 3 All ER 97 it was, however, held that the remedy was available. The law is now contained in section 17 of the Landlord and Tenant Act 1985 which provides:

'(1) In any proceedings in which a tenant of a dwelling alleges a breach on the part of his landlord of a repairing covenant relating to any part of the premises in which the dwelling is comprised, the court may, order specific performance of that covenant, whether or not the breach relates to a part of the premises let to the tenant and notwithstanding any equitable rule restricting the scope of that remedy, whether on the basis of a lack of mutuality or otherwise.

(2) In this section . . .

'repairing covenant' means a covenant to repair, maintain, renew, construct, or replace any property . . .'.

This section applies both to express and implied covenants, so long as the landlord has been given notice of the defect in question. The apparently wide wording of the section should not deceive the reader into believing that any tenant may apply for specific performance of repairing covenants relating to premises demised to other tenants of the same landlord where their dwellings are in the same building. The section is designed to enable tenants to claim specific performance not only of covenants relating to their dwellings, but also of those relating to the common parts of a building containing a number of dwellings. In *Francis v Cowcliffe Ltd* (1976) 33 P & CR 368 the plaintiff's flat on the third floor of a block owned by the defendants was served by a lift. This became inoperable with consequent inconvenience to the plaintiff. The defendants could not install a new lift because they lacked the necessary finance. The provision of lift services was a specific provision of the plaintiff's lease and she applied for specific performance of it. It was held that she was entitled to a decree of specific performance despite the financial difficulties of the defendants, which were of their own making.

Where a covenant to repair relates to the structure of a flat specific performance is available and, it is submitted, would extend, as in *Campden Hill Towers*, to cover the supporting structure, etc., even where that is not comprised in the lease. It must be remembered that the remedy is discretionary. Thus it is unlikely, that a court would order specific performance of a repairing covenant in relation to a dwelling in an extreme state of disrepair with a foreseeably brief life.

Further reading

Social Welfare Law (Ed. by D.W. Pollard) (Oyez Longman) paras. A. 412–A. 415 and A. 423–446.

Arden, A., and Partington, P., *Housing Law* (Sweet & Maxwell, 1983) Chaps. 15 and 16.

Luba, J., *Repairs: Tenants' Rights* (Legal Action Group, 1986) Chaps. 2, 3 and 4.

Martyn, N.C., and Lloyd-Jones, E., *Housing Disrepair* (Longman, 1985) Chaps. 1, 2, 3 and 7.

Cowan, R., 'Living Dangerously' *Roof* March/April 1984, p. 19.

Ormandy, D., 'Legislation to secure fitness for human habitation of leasehold dwelling-houses [1986] JPEL 164.

Reynolds, J.I., 'Statutory Covenants of Fitness and Repair' (1974) 37 MLR 377.

Shotton, T., 'Don't bother us: repair it youself' *Roof* September/October 1983, p. 25.

Smith, P.F., 'Repair and Maintenance in two contexts' [1983] *The Conveyancer* 231.

Waite. A., 'British Anzani and Set-off against Rent: A new departure?' (1982) 132 NLJ 815.

Waite. A., 'Set-off and Distress for Rent' *Legal Action* June 1984, p. 66.

Chapter 8

The individual sub-standard house: problems and remedies

The previous chapter dealt with the repairing obligations imposed by the law on both public and private landlords. However, despite legislative attempts to create minimum standards of housing maintenance, the problem of sub-standard accommodation is still with us. The 1981 House Condition Survey for England showed how the number of dwellings needing repairs costing over £7,000 has risen by 22 per cent in the years since 1976, and that much of this was accounted for by increasing disrepair in the owner-occupied sector, with over half a million such dwellings needing £7,000 or more spent on repairs. In Wales the 1981 survey revealed 1.4 per cent of the public sector housing stock to be unfit, with 9.5 per cent of owner-occupied dwellings also unfit. By 1985 the National Consumer Council could claim that one quarter of England's houses were in need of repairs costing more than £2,500, and that one million dwellings were substandard by virtue of dampness, inadequate natural lighting or poor drainage, see 'The Times' 22 February 1985. By 1986 estimates of £35 billion being needed to carry out repairs and improvements in the private sector of housing were being made, see 'Sunday Times' 15 June 1986. At the same time the average age of the housing stock increases as fewer new dwellings are built: that age is now 55 years, rising by twelve months every two years. Elderly *people* are also particularly likely to be badly affected by substandard housing conditions: some five million homeowners are aged 65 or more, many of them being of limited means, and about two million of them occupy homes needing work costing £2,500 or more.

To deal with these sub-standard dwellings the law has developed a number of different techniques. Area action, be it by way of clearance or improvement, forms the subject matter of the following chapters: our concern here is to examine the means available for dealing with individual properties. Sadly, the law has never quite been able to decide whether housing standards are primarily matters of construction and stability or of health with the result that we have two 'codes' which can both apply to housing, and which can occasionally conflict. Furthermore should any given property fall within the ambit of both codes compliance with the requirements of one will not necessarily satisfy the terms of the other. One of these codes is found in the Housing Act 1985, and the other in the Public Health Act 1936.

The requirements of the Housing Act 1985

In this portion of this chapter all references are, unless otherwise indicated, to the Housing Act 1985.

The standard of fitness

The object of this legislation is to eradicate unfit housing, and in this context the word 'house' includes the yard, gardens and outhouses, etc., belonging to any house, and also any part of a building which is occupied or intended to be occupied as a separate dwelling: see section 623. Thus purpose-built dwelling-houses, flats and converted premises are covered. The standard of fitness is laid down in section 604. By this provision a dwelling is unfit for human habitation only if it is so far defective in relation to certain listed particulars that its condition renders it unsuitable for reasonable occupation. The list of matters to which regard must be had in determining the issue of unfitness is: repair, stability; freedom from damp; internal arrangement; natural lighting; ventilation; water supply; drainage and sanitary conveniences, and the facilities for preparation and cooking of food and for the disposal of waste water. There is *no* legal requirement for a dwelling to have a bathroom, an inside lavatory, a hot water supply, or even an up-to-date system of electrical wiring. Nor does the ministerial guidance on 'unfitness' contained in Ministry of Housing and Local Government Circular No. 69/67 require particularly high standards for any dwelling to be classified as 'fit'. Disrepair in a dwelling must either prevent it functioning in the manner in which it was intended, or be a danger or serious inconvenience to the occupants before action can be taken. A mere lack of internal decoration is not enough, though a lack of exterior painting may lead to such serious disrepair of woodwork as to justify action. Likewise the Circular lays down that evidence of instability is only 'significant if it indicates the probability of further movement which would constitute a threat to the occupants of the house'. Dampness only justifies action where it amounts to a health hazard, and dampness caused by merely temporary condensation or by some small item of disrepair is not of itself a justification for unfitness proceedings. The Circular does suggest that there must be sufficient natural lighting in all living rooms to enable domestic work to be done without artificial light, and that windows should be capable of being opened so that fresh air can circulate readily in the rooms. However, one tap regularly supplying wholesome water is all that is required, and it is also satisfied if the occupants of a dwelling have the exclusive use of a readily accessible water closet which is both properly lit and ventilated.

The duties of local authorities

It is for local housing authorities (district councils and London Boroughs) to decide whether any given house does or does not comply with the statutory standard, though in *Hall v Manchester Corpn* (1915) 84 LJ Ch 732, it was stated that in coming to such a decision they must act in a judicial spirit. Further guidance was given by Atkin LJ in *Morgan v Liverpool Corpn* [1927] 2 KB 131 at 145 where he said the test was: 'If the state of repair of a house is such that by ordinary user damage may naturally be caused to the occupier, either in respect of personal injury to life or limb or injury to health, then the house is not in all respects reasonably fit for human habitation'. By applying that test the House of Lords concluded in *Summers v Salford Corpn* [1943] AC 283, [1943] 1 All ER 68 that a defective sash cord may, in proper circumstances, be enough to render a house unfit. Here the jamming of a bedroom window so that it could not be moved without danger so impaired the ventilation of a bedroom that it constituted an unacceptable interference with ordinary reasonable use.

However, it is obvious that before a local authority can come to any decision as to fitness they must know of the existence of the property in question. Section 605 states it is the duty of the local housing authority, subject to direction by the Secretary of State, to carry out periodic reviews of housing conditions in their area with a view to determining what action to take in respect of, inter alia, the issue of repair notices and slum clearance, etc. Under section 606 authorities must take account of reports of unfit housing made to them by their 'proper officers'. A Justice of the Peace having jurisdiction within an authority's district, or a parish or community council for an area within a district, may also complain in writing to a 'proper officer' that a house is unfit for human habitation. The officer's duty is then to inspect the house and make an appropriate report to the authority. The consideration of information received from the above sources activates the specific duties laid on authorities in respect of unfit housing.

The duty where the house can be made fit at reasonable expense

The duty contained in section 189 relates to those houses capable of being made fit at reasonable expense. Where the authority consider an unfit house is capable of being rendered fit at reasonable expense they must serve a 'repair notice' requiring the execution of specified works within a reasonable time, not being less than twenty-one days, and stating that in their opinion these works will render the dwelling fit.

The notice has to be served on the person 'having control of the house' who is defined by section 398(5) as 'the person who receives the rack rent', and a rack rent is any rent which is *not less* than two-thirds of the net annual value of the house. This rent, according to *Rawlance v Croydon Corpn* [1952] 2 QB 803, [1952] 2 All ER 535, is now effectively the maximum rent recoverable at law; for example a 'fair rent' fixed under the Rent Acts. An estate agent who collects rents on behalf of a landlord would be the relevant person within this definition. However, in *Pollway Nominees Ltd v Croydon London Borough Council* [1986] 2 All ER 849, [1986] 3 WLR 277 the freeholder of a block of long leasehold flats had no right to any habitable part of the block, and received ground rents on the flats which were considerably less than two thirds of the building's full net annual value. It was held the freeholder was not a person 'having control' because the rent received was too low, therefore the notice should not have been served on the freeholder and was a nullity quashable by judicial review. The House of Lords doubted whether a modern purpose built block of flats could be a 'house' for the law's present purposes, though considering that a large old house internally reconstructed as flats for sale on long leases might well continue to be a house. Where a house contains many residential units let on long leases at low ground rents, the 'person having control' is normally all the long lessees collectively as, between them they either receive the rack rents of units they sublet, or would receive those rents if the units were to be so let. In addition section 189(3) gives the local authority a discretion to serve copies of the notice on any other person having an interest in the house, which clearly covers tenants and mortgagees, etc. The repair notice can be challenged under section 191 in the county court within 21 days of service by 'any person aggrieved', a character of notoriously indeterminate legal identity, but here presumably meaning any person whose legal interests in the house in question are affected by the notice. Section 191(2) further allows the judge at that hearing to confirm, quash or vary the notice as he thinks fit, though if he does allow an appeal against a repair notice under section 189 he must, at the local authority's request, actually make a finding as to whether the house can or cannot be rendered fit at reasonable expense. Section 192 gives power to local authorities to buy, either by agreement or compulsorily, any house found on appeal to the court not to be capable of repair at reasonable cost, but only where: 'the court in allowing the appeal has found that the house cannot be rendered fit for human habitation at reasonable expense'. Should the local authority proceed by way of compulsory purchase they must submit their order to the Secretary of State for the Environment within six months of the determination of the appeal, and he cannot confirm it if the owner or a mortgagee, if any, gives a satisfactory undertaking to carry out the works specified in the repair notice. However, on confirmation of the order the local authority may proceed to acquire the house, under section 585 paying the owner its cleared site value. They must then execute all the works specified in the notice and thereafter the house may enter their normal stock of dwellings.

Should the repair notice be ignored the authority *may* themselves carry out the specified works (once it has expired) under section 193. They may recover their necessary costs from the person having control of the house either summarily as a civil debt or in instalments: see section 193(3) and Schedule 10. Furthermore under Schedule 10 they may register their costs as a charge on the property in the Local Land Charges Register. A person aggrieved by the service of a demand for the recovery of such expenses may appeal to the county court under Schedule 10, para. 6. In *Elliott v·Brighton Borough Council*(1981) 79 LGR 506 it was held that section 193 does not oblige an authority to do works not carried out following service of a repairs notice, and that authorities have a general discretion in such cases which they must exercise according to the particular circumstances of the situation.

The duty where the house cannot be made fit at reasonable expense

The principal provision here is section 264 which provides that where the authority are satisfied a house unfit for human habitation is not capable of being rendered fit at reasonable expense, they must serve on the person having control of the house, every other person who is its owner, and all reasonably ascertainable mortgagees, a notice of the time, which must be at least twenty-one days after service of the notice, and the place at which the house, and any offer the person served may wish to submit as to the future of the house and/or the carrying out of works, will be considered.

Thus a 'time and place' notice calls together the local authority and the persons interested in the house to discuss its future. Section 264(3) allows any person served with such a notice to make an offer to the local authority to carry out works on the house. These proposed works together with any other proposals or undertakings as to the future of the house will then be considered at the meeting convened by the notice. For example: an owner may undertake that he will cease to use the property as a dwelling-house, and if this is accepted by the local authority any tenants will, by virtue of section 264(5), lose any Rent Act protection they may have.

An undertaking may take many other forms, such as a proposal to convert two unfit houses into one fit one, as in *Johnson v Leicester Corpn* [1934] 1 KB 638, or to spend a very large sum of money on a house to bring it up to standard as in *Stidworthy and Stidworthy v Brixham UDC* (1935) 2 LJCCR 41. No matter what proposals are put forward at the meeting, by virtue of section 264(2), every person whom on a 'time and place' notice has been served is entitled to be heard, and it was held in *Broadbent v Rotherham Corpn* [1917] 2 Ch 31 that such persons must be given a fair and adequate chance to air their views, for example, furnishing specifications of proposed works. If an undertaking is accepted that premises will not be used as a dwelling-house under section 264(4) then they may become dangerous if they are not made secure against children or vandals, etc. Section 29 of the Local Government (Miscellaneous Provisions) Act 1982 enables a local authority to do such works as they think fit to keep out unauthorised persons and/or to prevent the premises from being a danger to public health. Such action can be taken rapidly as the authority can proceed after giving not less than 48 hours' notice to the owner, or even more expeditiously where immediate steps are required to protect public health.

A local authority are under no obligation to accept any offer made. If they do not accept an undertaking, under section 265 they have a number of alternatives one of which they must choose. Normally they will make a demolition order. Section 268 requires them to serve a copy of this order on every person on whom a 'time and place' notice was served. The order *must* require the premises to be vacated within a specified period, not being less than 28 days from the date on which the order becomes operative, see section 267. *R v Epsom and Ewell Corpn, ex p RB Property Investments (Eastern) Ltd* [1964] 2 All ER 832, [1964] 1 WLR 1060 states that it is mandatory under section 270(1) that the occupier of the house must be informed of the effect of the order and the date by which it requires the building to be vacated. He must be required to quit the building before that date, or before the expiration of 28 days from the service of the notice, whichever is the later. A demolition order removes any Rent Act protection enjoyed by tenants. It is also an offence under section 270(5) for anyone knowingly to occupy or to allow occupation of any premises subject to such an order. Summary conviction leads to a fine and a further fine for every day the offence continues after conviction. The demolition order must also under section 267(1)(b) require the premises to be demolished within six weeks of the expiration of the period allowed for vacation, or from the actual date of vacation, whichever is the later. The local authority may extend this period either under section 267(1)(b), or under section 274 where an owner puts forward proposals to improve and/or reconstruct the house so as to provide one or more fit houses. Such extensions may not be for unreasonable lengths of time, and a seven year extension was held unreasonable in *Pocklington v Melksham UDC* [1964] 2 QB 673, [1964] 2 All ER 862. If there is a failure to comply with a demolition order the local authority are empowered by section 271 to carry out the demolition themselves and to recover their outstanding expenses as a simple contract debt in the local county court from the owner, under section 272. A person aggrieved by the making of a demolition order may appeal against it to the county court. Appeals will be considered more fully below.

Other powers for dealing with houses which cannot be made fit

Demolition may not be a suitable way of dealing with an unfit house which may, for example, be necessary for the support of other houses, or which may have special historical or architectural importance. In such a case the local authority may decide to serve a closing order. The general power to make closing orders is contained in section 265(2) and is limited to situations where:

1) The authority consider it inexpedient to make a demolition order having regard to the effect of the demolition of that house upon any other house or building, or

2) the house has been listed, or has been stated to be of historic or architectural interest by the minister, see section 304. Indeed in this latter situation the *only* order that can be made is a closing order; though in the *former* situation the authority *may* subsequently change their minds and make a demolition order by virtue of section 279. Further provision with respect to such orders is to be found in section 267(2) which permits the local authority to allow the premises to be used for purposes other than as a dwelling-house, and they are not permitted under section 267(3) to withhold their approval unreasonably to such other uses. It is a fineable offence, under section 277, to use the premises knowingly for any purpose other than one approved by the local authority. Under section 276 the making of a closing order takes away any Rent Act security of tenure enjoyed by tenants. Closing orders may also be made by virtue of section 266 in respect of parts of buildings

actually used or suitable for use as dwellings and any underground room which is unfit for human habitation. (Such 'underground rooms' are unfit if their floor surfaces are more than three feet below the adjacent ground surface level, and the average height of the room is not at least seven feet, or the room fails to comply with other local regulations, see sections 280 and 282.) In general the procedure for the making of a closing order is similar to that for making a demolition order and there are the same rights of appeal to the county court under section 269.

Another choice is allowed by section 300(1): 'Where a local authority would under section 265 be required to make a demolition or closing order in respect of a house they may, if it appears to them that the house is or can be rendered capable of providing accommodation which is adequate for the time being, purchase it instead '. This provision only applies to properties that can be 'patched up' to provide temporary shelter on a very short term basis. It was held in *Victoria Square Property Co Ltd v London Borough of Southwark* [1978] 2 All ER 281, [1978] 1 WLR 463 that this does not permit an authority to acquire old, unfit houses with a view to bringing them up to standard so that they can be added to the normal municipal housing stock. Before the power to purchase can be used a copy of the determination to purchase must, by virtue of section 300(2), be served on all persons on whom a 'time and place' notice was served. This again activates the rights of appeal given by section 269. However, in most cases the local authority will be able to proceed to purchase according to section 300(3) either by agreement, or, with ministerial approval, compulsorily. If a compulsory purchase is made then the compensation to be paid according to section 585(1) is: 'the value, at the time when the valuation is made, of the site as a cleared site available for development in accordance with the requirements of the building regulations. See also Chapter 9, below, in relation to clearance procedures.

The appeals procedure

Mention has been made of the procedure available under section 269 which provides that a person aggrieved by a demolition or closing order, or a determination to purchase under section 300, may within twenty-one days of the service of the order appeal to the county court, and on such an appeal the court may confirm, quash or vary the local authority's order, or, if it thinks fit, accept such an undertaking from the appellant as could have been accepted by the authority. Making an appeal suspends the operation of the authority's order until the issue has been disposed of by the courts.

It should, however, be noted that section 269(2) excludes from the definition of 'person aggrieved' any person 'who is in occupation of the premises under a lease or agreement with an unexpired term of three years or less'. Statutory tenants are also probably excluded. Thus in the case of a small dwelling-house only the landlord will normally be able to appeal. Such an appeal, according to *Fletcher v Ilkeston Corpn* (1931) 96 JP 7, may be either or both on questions of law or fact. From the county court an appeal lies to the Court of Appeal. In *Victoria Square Property Co Ltd v London Borough of Southwark* [1978] 2 All ER 281, [1978] 1 WLR 463 the Court of Appeal made it clear that they will only upset the decision of the county court if it can be shown to be wrong in point of law, or if irrelevant considerations have been taken into account, or the relevant ones left unconsidered, or if the decision is totally unreasonable. The considerations which should be considered would seem to include: (i) any need to prevent a loss of residential accommodation in an area; (ii) the desire of a local authority to secure accommodation for persons on their housing waiting list; (iii) the need to prevent over great strain on the general rate fund consequent on the purchase of too much old property, and (iv) the financial implications for the land owner of any decision made. Not all of these considerations will be of equal weight in any given case, and where an owner has deliberately allowed his house to go to rack and ruin the financial implications of subjecting him to a forced sale at site value only may be almost discounted. A prudent local authority should also bear these factors in mind when they are considering any undertaking put forward under section 264.

Subject to this appeal procedure once a demolition or closing order or notice has become operative (which is on the expiration of 21 days from its service, see section 268(2)) no further proceedings can be taken as to any of the matters which could have been raised on an appeal. Professor Garner has, however, argued in *Slum Clearance and Compensation* pp. 28 to 30, that this would not prevent the High Court from issuing an order of certiorari to quash a demolition or closing order if there has been an error of law on the face of the record or some other ultra vires act by the local authority, such as a breach of the rules of natural justice or some improper motive on the part of the members of the authority.

Well maintained payments

Following the service of a demolition order or of a notice of determination to purchase a house 'any person' has a three month period under Schedule 23 to make representations to the authority that the house has been well maintained as a result of work wholly or partly carried out by him or at his expense. Any 'well maintained payment' made to such a person in consequence of his application is now calculated by reference to Schedule 23 para. 4 and S.I. 1982/1112. The amount may be as much as 14 times the rateable value of the house, but it may not exceed the amount by which the full market value exceeds the site value, which may lead to a nil payment as the cleared site value may be quite substantial. Thus if the full market value of a house is £10,000, its cleared site value is £5,000 and its rateable value is £50 *per annum*, then the difference between cleared site and full value is £5,000, and £50 × 14 = £700, and that will be the amount of the well maintained payment. But if the full value is £9,000 and the cleared site value is £8,000 so that their difference is only £1,000 and the property is rated as being worth £100 per annum, then the maximum amount payable by way of a well maintained payment will be only £1,000, for that payment cannot exceed the difference in price between the two stated values for the property.

The mandatory character of the requirements of the legislation

It should now be quite obvious that a local authority faced with evidence of unfitness in respect of an individual house have a number of possible courses of action open to them. What is, however, beyond question is that possession of such evidence activates their statutory duties, and that they come under an obligation to take action. This follows from the decision of the Court of Appeal in *R v Kerrier District Council, ex p Guppy's (Bridport) Ltd* (1976) 32 P & CR 411 that the word 'shall', which occurs in both sections 189 and 264, is imperative. But which duty are the authority to fulfil, that based on repair under section 189 or that based on demolition under section 264? The answer will depend upon whether the house is capable of being made fit at 'reasonable expense', and it is to the definition of this term, that we must now turn.

The question falls to be decided according to sections 206 and 321 which provide:

'In determining for the purposes of this Part of this Act whether premises can be rendered fit for human habitation at a reasonable expense, regard shall be had to the estimated cost of the works necessary to render them so fit and the value which it is estimated that they will have when the works are completed'.

The law requires that those two factors must be considered. But this leaves many questions unanswered such as: are these the only factors to be taken into account, and what is the meaning of the word 'value'? For many years the approach adopted was that suggested by Denning LJ in

Bacon v Grimsby Corpn [1950] 1 KB 272, [1949] 2 All ER 875 which was simply to ask 'is the house worth the cost of the repairs?' Subsequent litigation has given us rather more detailed tests to apply, though sadly the principles laid down have not been entirely consistent. To take the provisions of the sections in order:

a) 'the estimated cost of the works necessary to render them so fit' was considered in *Ellis Copp & Co v Richmond-upon-Thames London Borough Council* (1976) 245 Estates Gazette 931 and would seem to include both the cost of necessary structural works and the cost of making good the decoration of the house after the doing of those works, and

b) 'the value which it is estimated that they will have' has been considered in *Inworth Property Co Ltd v Southwark London Borough Council* (1977) 34 P & CR 186, and said to mean the open market value.

The problem with this latter definition is whether the presence of a sitting tenant, if any, is to be taken into account. In this context the decision of the Court of Appeal in *Dudlow Estates Ltd v Sefton Metropolitan Borough Council* (1978) 249 Estates Gazette 1271 is helpful. The test which it seems should be applied is that of a 'willing buyer and a willing seller'. In other words, the assessment of 'open market value' must be based on a consideration of all the facts and future possibilities about the house, including those about a sitting tenant having Rent Act protection. A greater likelihood of obtaining vacant possession at an early date will increase the value of the property, though it will not probably increase the valuation to the level it would be on a purely vacant possession basis.

Provided these factors are taken into account there is no statutory obligation to consider any others. There are other factors which *may* properly from time to time be considered. There include matters such as the cost of demolition and the present unrepaired value of the property. In any given case, however, the first task is to calculate the cost of the necessary repairs and then to compare these with the estimated repaired value of the house. This value will itself depend on a sliding scale measurement linked to the likelihood of the owner being able to obtain vacant possession. It follows that where the estimated cost of repairs is high and the house in question is occupied by a tenant enjoying Rent Act protection, and who shows no early desire of vacating the property, that the question whether the expense is 'reasonable' is likely to be answered in the negative, and so the property will fall to be dealt with according to section 264. In *Phillips v Newham London Borough Council* (1981) 43 P & CR 54 it was stressed that the courts should be 'realistic' in valuing dwellings as saleable assets, bearing in mind the presence of sitting tenants, so that it is reasonable to compare the value of a dwelling in disrepair, but tenanted by someone having security of tenure, with its value as repaired, but still tenanted, and to compare the figures with the cost of necessary works. A wholly unrealistic and unreasonable valuation of a dwelling may be challenged by way of application for judicial review, even by the sitting tenant, see *R v Ealing London Borough, ex p Richardson* (1982) 4 HLR 125. But challenges must be made expeditiously, *and the* burden of proof is heavy, see *R v Maldon District Council, ex p Fisher* (1986) 18 HLR 197.

Supplementary powers to prevent houses becoming unfit

Obviously there is a danger that an unscrupulous landlord will let his houses run to rack and ruin so that they are incapable of repair at reasonable expense in the hope that the local authority will take action to demolish them. He will then be freed of his tenants and left with valuable cleared sites. The need to prevent such situations was faced by the legislature when it enacted section 190(1)(a). This provides that where an authority are satisfied that a fit house is in substantial disrepair, having regard to its age, character and locality, they may serve a repair notice on the person having control requiring the execution of specified works to bring it up to a reasonable standard, other than internal decoration, within a reasonable time, not less than twenty-one days. The appeal procedure under section 191 applies to such notices, and a 'person aggrieved' may appeal to the county court which may confirm, quash or vary the notice at its discretion. It should be noted that the notice must contain sufficient information to enable its recipient to be able to obtain a competent builder's estimate of the cost of required works. It cannot be vague, but need not say precisely in minute detail what has to be done, a reasonable degree of precision only is required, see *Church of Our Lady of Hal v Camden London Borough Council* (1980) 40 P & CR 472.

It must be noted that this provision grants only a power to local authorities, it does not put them under any duty to act, though the information upon which they may act can come from the usual wide variety of sources. Next it must be remembered that the provision applies to houses that are *in danger of becoming unfit* through disrepair and that there is no power to require the doing of works of mere internal decoration. The power also applies only in those cases where *substantial* repairs are required, and 'substantial' probably means 'large items of repair, or a considerable collection of smaller items'. Finally in the exercise of their power the local authority must have regard to the 'age, character and locality' of the house when deciding what works are necessary to bring it up to a reasonable standard. The nature of this provision was considered in *Hillbank Properties Ltd v Hackney London Borough Council, Talisman Properties Ltd v Hackney London Borough Council* [1978] QB 998, [1978] 3 All ER 343, litigation involving 'one house' property companies, which gives some guidance as to the meaning of 'age, character and locality'. The Court of Appeal in the *Hillbank Properties* case seem to have held that the considerations imported by the phrase 'age, character and locality' include those mentioned by sections 206 and 321, i.e. the estimated cost of the works and the estimated value of the house made fit. The question to be asked under section 190(1)(a) is basically the same as that to be asked under sections 206 and 321: 'is the house worth the cost of repairs?' In determining this question the presence of a sitting tenant cannot be ignored.

Furthermore if there is an appeal against a section 190(1)(a) notice under section 191 then the county court judge may take into account the resources of the owner available to pay for the repairs. In this respect much more can be demanded of a property company, whose 'corporate veil' may be torn so as to reveal the real strength of the finances behind it, than of a poor widow. The *Hillbank* case states that there is no need for local authorities to take this wider range of factors into account when they are taking the administrative decision to issue a section 190(1)(a) notice. All they need to consider is the information they have and then they must be satisfied as to the need for substantial repairs, taking into account the age, character and locality of the property. However, it is submitted that the prudent local authority should pay at least some heed to the other considerations that might arise on an appeal such as the character of the landowner and his past action or inaction in relation to the house in question. It is quite proper for a local authority to serve a section 190(1)(a) notice where they suspect a property owner of allowing disrepair with a view to reaping an unearned reward from the application of the unfitness provisions. Section 190(1)(a) is not to be used as a charter for the worst sort of slum landlord. In *Kenny v Kingston upon Thames Royal London Borough Council* (1985) 17 HLR 344 the Court of Appeal confirmed that in cases where requiring the execution of works will involve the landlord in no financial problems, and where the ultimate value of the building will exceed the repair costs (so that the situation is *not* one in which it would be foolish to require the doing of unjustifiable works) it is proper to consider arguments that the landlord's motives in resorting to inactivity, and the consequences for the tenant in such circumstances, should be taken into account.

Section 190(1)(b) provides that where a local authority are satisfied, following representations made by an occupying tenant, that a house is in such a state of disrepair that, although it is *not* unfit for human habitation, its condition is such as to interfere materially with the personal comfort of the occupying tenant, they may serve on the person having control a repair notice requiring the doing of specified works, other than those of internal decorative repair, within a specified reasonable time. Section 207 defines 'occupying tenant' by reference to Part VII of the Housing Act 1985. This, in section 236(2), defines such a person as someone who is *not* an owner-occupier, but who occupies, or is entitled to occupy, the dwelling as a lessee, or statutory tenant, or as a party to a restricted contract, or in pursuance of agricultural employment.

This provision gives tenants the right to complain to the local authority in those cases where their homes are falling into disrepair serious enough to be a substantial interference with their comfort. The local authority are, however, under no duty to take action in response to such complaints. Should they take action the same considerations will apply to section 190(1)(b) as apply under section 190(1)(a). This provision is intended to overcome the effects of the decision in *National Coal Board v Neath Borough Council* [1976] 2 All ER 478, [1976] 1 WLR 543 (see below). Any proceedings in respect of a house that is a source of substantial discomfort to its occupying tenant, but which is not unfit or otherwise a statutory nuisance, should in future be brought under these powers.

The requirements of the Public Health Act 1936

In this portion of the chapter all section references are, unless otherwise indicated, to the Public Health Act 1936.

The definition of 'statutory nuisance'

The general object of this legislation is the protection of the public health and Part III of the Act is specifically designed to do this by eradication of certain 'statutory nuisances'. By virtue of section 92(1)(a) a dwelling-house may be such a statutory nuisance as the law provides: 'Without prejudice to the exercise by a local authority of any other powers vested in them by or under this Act, the following matters may, subject to the provisions of this Part of this Act be dealt with summarily, and are in this Part of this Act referred to as "statutory nuisances", that is to say:(a) any premises in such a state as to be prejudicial to health or a nuisance. . . .' 'Premises' are defined by section 343 to include messuages, buildings, lands, and easements.

It is thus clear that a dwelling-house can be a statutory nuisance if it is 'prejudicial to health', a term which is itself defined in section 343(1) as 'injurious, or likely to cause injury to health'. 'Health' itself is not statutorily defined. In *Coventry City Council v Cartwright* [1975] 2 All ER 99, [1975] 1 WLR 845, a case arising out of an alleged nuisance caused by the dumping of rubbish, the Divisional Court gave some consideration to whether mental health could be within the protection of the law but reached no concluded opinion on this point. It can be argued that a breakdown in mental health can be caused as a result of a person having to live in a sub-standard house. However, judicial opinion seems to disagree, and to hold that conditions that are 'prejudicial to health' are those which are likely to cause physical illness or disease or to result in an infestation by vermin.

If premises are to be shown to be a statutory nuisance their condition *as a whole* must be so serious that in consequence they are a real risk to health or are a nuisance; a mere lack of internal decorative repair is not enough: see *Springett v Harold* [1954] 1 All ER 568, [1954] 1 WLR 521. Nor is any matter which merely affects the *comfort* of the occupants, even if it amounts to an act of harrassment. The decision in *Betts v Penge UDC* [1942] 2 KB 154, [1942] 2 All ER 61 which held otherwise was said to be wrongly decided by the House of Lords in *Salford City Council v McNally* [1976] AC 379, [1975] 2 All ER 860. It may be enough for conditions to be 'prejudicial to health' if they are such as to cause a person who is already ill to become worse: see the judgment of Kelly CB in *Malton Board of Health v Malton Manure Co* (1879) 4 Ex D 302 at 305.

In *Bennett v Preston District Council* (1983) 'Environmental Health' (April) it was held that defective wiring in a dwelling may be 'prejudicial to health'. Furthermore condensation may also amount to a statutory nuisance, even where the structure is unaffected, see *Dover District Council v Farrar* (1980) 2 HLR 32 and *Greater London Council v Tower Hamlets London Borough Council* (1983) 15 HLR 54, especially where it gives rise to extensive growths of mould and dampness, and arises from a condition arising from the failure of the responsible person to take remedial or preventative action, such as the installation of ventilation, insulation and heating systems. See further *Birmingham District Council v Kelly* (below).

Premises may also come within the statutory definition if they are 'a nuisance'. Does this mean that any common law nuisance is also *ipso facto* a statutory nuisance? The answer is partly 'yes'. For a complainant to prove an allegation based on the 'or a nuisance' limb of the definition he must show that the act or default complained of is either a public or private nuisance, i.e. something causing deleterious affectation to a class of Her Majesty's subjects, *or* a substantial interference with land (or the use and enjoyment thereof) arising outside that land and then proceeding to affect it. So much is clear from the decision in

National Coal Board v Neath Borough Council [1976] 2 All ER 478, [1976] 1 WLR 543 where there were merely minor disrepairs affecting the comfort of the occupiers. However, there is a judicial tradition stretching back to *Malton Board of Health v Malton Manure Co* (1879) 4 Ex D 302, *Great Western Rly Co v Bishop* (1872) LR 7 QB 550, and *Bishop Auckland Local Board v Bishop Auckland Iron and Steel Co* (1882) 10 QBD 138, that situations contemplated as falling within the 'or a nuisance' limb of the definition must have some relation to health. That relation to health is still a requirement of the law. Thus in a case where it is alleged that premises are 'prejudicial to health' it will not matter that only the occupier is affected by the acts, defaults or state of affairs complained of. Where on the other hand it is alleged that the premises are 'a nuisance' the act or default, etc., *must affect persons other than the occupier of the premises.* Furthermore in this latter situation the informant must be able to prove that the nuisance is one that in some way affects or has relevance to his health. It must also be remembered that *R v Newham Justices, ex p Hunt* and *R v Oxted Justices, ex p Franklin* [1976] 1 All ER 839, [1976] 1 WLR 420 established that proceedings brought in respect of a statutory nuisance are criminal in nature and thus the burden of proof on any informant will be correspondingly high. In *Patel v Mehtab* (1980) 5 HLR 80 the court pointed out that the question whether premises are prejudicial to health will turn upon expert evidence, and that the magistrates must pay due heed to the expert testimonies given by one or both sides, and not advance their own lay assessments of the facts over those of expert witnesses.

The procedures for taking action in respect of a statutory nuisance

Both local authorities and private individuals are empowered to take action in respect of statutory nuisances. It will be convenient to consider the powers and duties of local authorities first.

Section 91 places a general duty on local authorities (effectively the district councils and London Boroughs) to inspect their districts to detect statutory nuisances. Sections 93 and 98 thereafter lay down the procedure which a local authority has to follow in the abatement of statutory nuisances, and it would seem from *Cocker v Cardwell* (1869) LR 5 QB 15 that this procedure is mandatory once a local authority decide to act. Where an authority are satisfied of the existence of a statutory nuisance the Act says they 'shall serve' an abatement notice on the person responsible requiring the abatement of the nuisance, and, according to *Bristol Corpn v Sinnott* [1918] 1 Ch 62, giving him a specified reasonable time in which to comply with the notice. However, it was said in *Nottingham Corpn v Newton* [1974] 2 All ER 760, [1974] 1

WLR 923, the first case where a local authority was successfully prosecuted in respect of unfit property also constituting a statutory nuisance, by Lord Widgery CJ that 'shall' in section 93 is not mandatory.
Where a local authority have a choice of remedies between the Public
Health Act 1936 and the Housing Act 1985 the courts will not order
them to use the former in preference to the latter, though as will subsequently be shown the converse is not necessarily so!

The abatement notice is to be served on the person by whose act,
default or sufferance the nuisance arises or continues, or, if he cannot
be found, the owner or occupier of the premises concerned, provided
that where the nuisance arises from any structural defect the notice is to
be served on the owner of the premises. This is apparently so even where
a tenant is in fact responsible, see *Warner v Lambeth London Borough
Council* (1984) 15 HLR 42. Where there is no structural affectation, it
may not always be easy to decide whether the landlord or the tenant
caused the problem, for example, of condensation. In this context
section 343(1) defines the owner as the person who receives the rack rent
of the property either on his own account or as an agent or trustee, or
who would receive it if the premises were let at a rack rent. Should the
abatement notice be disregarded section 94(1) (as amended by section
42 of the Magistrates' Court Act 1952) enables the local authority to lay
an information before a justice of the peace who thereupon must
summon the defaulter to appear before the magistrates. The *Newton*
case again indicates that the local authority have a discretion whether to
proceed under this provision. If at the hearing before the court it is
proved that the alleged nuisance still exists, or although abated, it is
likely to recur then section 94(2) directs that the court 'shall' make a
nuisance order. (See *Coventry City Council v Doyle* [1981] 2 All ER
184, [1981] 1 WLR 1325.) This order may require the defendant to
comply with all or any of the requirements of the abatement notice, or
otherwise to abate the nuisance within a time to be specified in the
order, and to execute any works necessary for these purposes, and/or
prohibit a recurrence of the nuisance and require the defendant to
execute, within a specified time, any works necessary to prevent a
recurrence. In this context the *Newton* case states clearly that the justices *must* issue a nuisance order if the existence or future recurrence of
the nuisance is proved. But, as is clear from the words of the statute,
they have a very considerable discretion as to the *terms* of the order.
When deciding the terms of the order the justices should consider all the
circumstances of the case including the possible gravity of the danger to
the health of the occupants and the imminence of demolition. They may
quite properly require work to be done in phases, allowing for absolutely necessary jobs to be done first, while other tasks can be left till
later, perhaps to be rendered unnecessary by demolition and thus saving expense.

A decision illustrates the ambit of the justices' discretion. In *Lambeth London Borough Council v Stubbs* (1980) 78 LGR 650, the local authority owned an old house the tenants of which were Mr and Mrs Stubbs. The condition of the house constituted a statutory nuisance which was admitted by the council before the justices in proceedings commenced against them by the tenants. The justices refused to adjourn the hearing so that the authority could obtain vacant possession, and instead made a nuisance order requiring the remedying of the most serious defects within 21 days of the vacation of the premises and of the others in 42 days. Shortly thereafter Mr and Mrs Stubbs were rehoused and the house was simply left vacant until it was demolished. The question for the court was whether the action of the council in securing vacant possession was sufficient abatement to comply with the nuisance order. It was held that it was not. Where a house is prejudicial to health simply to move the present occupiers out does not cure the problem, for if other occupiers should move in at a future date their health will then be imperilled. Therefore where the justices make a nuisance order requiring the doing of remedial work, that work must be done; moving the sitting tenant is not enough. See also *Coventry City Council v Doyle* [1981] 2 All ER 184, [1981] 1 WLR 1325, where it was, however, pointed out that different considerations might apply in a case where the premises have been effectively rendered incapable of occupation. Of course where the local authority intend to demolish the property in question within a very short time the court should take that into account when drawing up the order. In such circumstances the local authority should ask the justices to exercise their discretion under section 94(2), to be examined below, to order that the house shall not be used for human habitation. Such an order will remove the need for great expenditure.

In these section 94 proceedings the justices may also fine the defendant up to £200 by virtue of section 99 of and Schedule 2, paragraph 11 to the Control of Pollution Act 1974. Section 94(2) also states:

'Where a nuisance proved to exist is such as to render a building, in the opinion of the court, unfit for human habitation, the nuisance order may prohibit the use of the building for that purpose until a court of summary jurisdiction, being satisfied that it has been rendered fit for human habitation withdraws the prohibition'.

'Unfit for human habitation' in this context does *not* bear its Housing Act meaning, nor is a person displaced from his house as a result of such a prohibition within the rehousing obligations of section 39 of the Land Compensation Act 1973, though he might fall to be dealt with under Part III of the 1985 Act, as having accommodation to which he cannot secure entry. It should also be noted that by virtue of section

94(6) the nuisance order may be addressed to the local authority 'if it appears to the court that the person by whose act or default the nuisance arises, or the owner or occupier of the premises cannot be found'.

Once the nuisance order is issued the penalty for knowingly contravening it, or for failing without reasonable excuse to comply with its term is, under section 95(1) as amended by section 99 of and Schedule 2, paragraph 12 to the Control of Pollution Act 1974, a fine not exceeding £400 and a further fine of up to £50 a day for each day on which the offence continues after conviction. It should also be noted that local authorities may, under section 96, recover their expenses from the person on whom the nuisance order was served. Section 100 allows an authority who are of the opinion that summary proceedings would afford an inadequate remedy to take proceedings in their own name in the High Court for the abatement or prohibition of the nuisance. Local authorities, but *not* private citizens, also have power to deal with nuisances that are likely to recur. If an authority are satisfied that a nuisances is likely to recur on premises they may under section 1(1) of the Public Health (Recurring Nuisances) Act 1961 serve a prohibition notice on the persons on whom an abatement notice can be served. The notice may prohibit a recurrence of the nuisance and may also specify any works necessary to secure this. A failure to comply with the notice is an offence under section 3(1) of the 1961 Act. Section 26 of the 1961 Act also provides a streamlined procedure for dealing with premises comprising statutory nuisances where an authority consider the normal procedure would be too long and drawn out. They may serve notice on the person on whom an abatement notice could have been served of their intention to remedy specific defects. If the addressee does not signify within nine days of service his own intention to do the necessary work they may then proceed to do the works themselves and recover their expenses from him.

The taking of action in respect of statutory nuisances by private citizens

The majority of statutory nuisances will be dealt with by local authorities under the above procedures, but there will be cases where an individual will wish to take action, either because, for example, the local authority is proving dilatory or because it is itself responsible for the nuisance. In these circumstances he can rely on section 99 which provides: 'Complaint of the existence of a statutory nuisance under this Act may be made to a justice of the peace by any person aggrieved by the nuisance, and thereupon the like proceedings shall be had, with the like incidents and consequences as to the making of orders, penalties for disobedience of orders and otherwise, as in the case of a complaint by the local authority, but any such order made in such proceedings may, if the court after giving the local authority an opportunity of being heard thinks fit, direct the authority to abate the nuisance'. Where an individual uses this provision he 'short circuits' the normal procedure and is able to initiate proceedings under section 94 without having first to issue an abatement notice under section 93. In *Warner v Lambeth London Borough Council* (1984) 15 HLR 42 it was held, however, that where an individual takes action under section 99, his information should disclose, in at least summary form, the details that would have been included in an abatement notice as to the capacity in which the defendant is served, and the steps it is alleged he should take to abate the nuisance. In other words the accuser must tell the accused what is required to be done.

It was held in *R v Epping (Waltham Abbey) Justices, ex p Burlinson* [1948] 1 KB 79, [1947] 2 All ER 537 that a private citizen can proceed against a defaulting local authority under section 99, and in *Salford City Council v McNally* it was further held that the fact that the nuisance arose as a result of the authority's exercise of their Housing Act powers was no defence to action taken by one of their tenants deleteriously affected in consequence. In order to use the section 99 procedure an individual must be a 'person aggrieved'. In the present context this includes anyone whose health has actually been injured by the nuisance, or any occupant of the premises or indeed anyone with a legal interest in a house which is permanently affected by the nuisance. In *Gould v Times Square Estates Ltd*, Camberwell Magistrates Court, 1 April 1975, [1975] LAG Bulletin 147, even a squatter in an empty former shop and dwelling accommodation was held able to use section 99 procedure, but the applicability of this provision to trespassers was expressly left undecided in *Coventry City Council v Cartwright*.

In some cases the mere laying of an information by an individual will suffice to bring about remedial action. However, provided the nuisance existed at the date of the laying of the information it seems that the magistrates must order the payment of the reasonable expenses of the 'person aggrieved'. This follows from the fact that the same 'consequences' are required to flow under section 99 proceedings as in the case of proceedings commenced by a local authority, and they, of course, are entitled to their reasonable expenses under section 94(3). The magistrates also have discretion in section 99 proceedings to make a compensation order of up to £1,000 in favour of an occupier under section 35 of the Powers of Criminal Courts Act 1973 as amended by section 60 of the Criminal Law Act 1977.

An individual can also complain under section 322 to the Secretary of State for the Environment that a local authority have not discharged their Public Health Act functions properly. On receipt of such a complaint the Secretary *may* decide to hold a local inquiry to investigate the matter. If he does and finds the complaint justified he may direct the authority to discharge their functions correctly within the time he specifies. If the authority fail to comply the Secretary may apply for an order of mandamus against them or he may transfer their functions to himself.

The relationship between the Housing and Public Health Acts

It cannot be sufficiently stressed that the requirements of the housing and public health 'codes' are separate and equal. Remedial action taken under one will not necessarily satisfy the requirements of the other. Of course action taken to eliminate unfitness in a house will nearly always ensure that it will not be prejudicial to health because in general the standards required by the Housing Act are higher than those under the Public Health Act. This can be illustrated by a simple example: if a house is unfit through dampness caused by the lack of damp-proof course then the Housing Act would require the insertion of such a course to make the house fit and free from damp; if the same house is prejudicial to health because of damp, then the Public Health Act will only require it to be made reasonably free from damp on a periodic basis which may be achieved by lining the walls with damp-proof paper. There are times when the two codes do appear to be in conflict: thus in the *Newton* case the court said local authorities have a discretion as to how best to deal with sub-standard housing: in the *Kerrier* case the unfitness provisions were said to be mandatory, while in the *Salford* case action taken under the Housing Act was said to be no defence to subsequent prosecution under the public health legislation. In fact there is no real conflict between the codes, and the cases can be reconciled. The question always to bear in mind in these situations is: *who* is seeking to do *what* to *whom* by *which* procedures? This question can receive different answers in different circumstances as the following instances will show.

The individual sub-standard house in private ownership

This situation can be illustrated by the facts of the *Kerrier* case. The landlords owned two unfit dwelling-houses, both of which were tenanted. The owners were prepared to make one good house of the two but could not do so without obtaining vacant possession, and had no accommodation for the displaced tenants. The local authority said it had no accommodation either (though it did subsequently rehouse the tenants) and so decided to commence proceedings against the landlords under the Public Health Act in order to require remedial action on the roofs of the houses. The landlords countered this by alleging that the houses were statutorily unfit and that the local authority were therefore in breach of their mandatory duties under the unfitness provisions of the Housing Act 1985 if they failed to proceed under them. The court accepted the landlord's contention. Thus where a *local authority* commence proceedings under the 1936 Act in respect of any house which is a statutory nuisance, the *owner* of the house may allege that they are in dereliction of their duties under the Act of 1985 and may apply for mandamus to compel the performance of whichever of the Housing Act duties is relevant to the house. It is only where it is the local authority seeking to initiate action that the 1985 Act can be used to bar proceedings under the Act of 1936, and even here it must be remembered that mandamus is a discretionary remedy and so a landlord is not guaranteed success if he adopts the style of counter argument developed in the *Kerrier* case. Where the proceedings are between the *tenant* and the *landlord* the local authority's duties have no relevance save insofar as the landlord, having begun separate proceedings against a local authority to compel performances of their duties, might argue that the justices should consider the possible outcome of those proceedings when deciding the content of any nuisance order issued under section 99 of the 1936 Act.

The sub-standard house in local authority ownership

Sections 189 and 264 do not apply to a local authority's own houses *within its own area*, save in the cases where another person also has a relevant interest in the property, for an authority cannot serve a housing order on themselves, see *R v Cardiff City Council, ex p Cross* (1982) 6 HLR 1. Older unfit houses may have been acquired under slum clearance powers, but retained as providing accommodation 'adequate for the time being' under sections 300 and 301 of the 1985 Act. The conception behind these provisions is that such houses should be retained temporarily, and generally only while their occupants are being more appropriately accommodated, but there have been cases where whole areas of unfit houses have been retained in use for many years. The 1985 Act does not aid the occupants of such houses, and, following *Parker v Camden London Borough Council* [1986] Ch 162, [1985] 2 All ER 141, CA, it is inappropriate to apply to the Court under section 37 of the Supreme Court Act 1981 for the appointment of a receiver to manage local authority housing alleged to be ill-managed. However, in such circumstances, provided the existence of a statutory nuisance can be proved, the 1936 Act can be used and any prior action taken under the

1985 Act will be no defence to the local authority.

This was the situation in the *Salford* case. In 1967 Salford Corporation declared certain areas in Lower Broughton, Salford to be clearance areas, and at the same time made compulsory purchase orders on the houses within the areas. However, once the compulsory purchase orders were confirmed the Corporation, realising it could not rehouse all the residents quickly, deferred demolition of the houses for a *minimum* period of *seven* years. By 1974 Mrs McNally's house suffered from an accumulation of refuse, dampness, defective sanitary fittings, unsealed drains, rats, defective windows and/or doors, a leaking roof, defective drainage, and defective plaster work. She commenced proceedings in respect of the statutory nuisance comprised by her house under section 99 of the 1936 Act and succeeded. The House of Lords held that the resolution to defer demolition was no defence to statutory nuisance proceedings. Thus a local authority may not acquire substandard houses and retain them until the occupants can be rehoused without at least ensuring that the houses are not prejudicial to the health of their occupants. It must be remembered that even where an old substandard house is made the subject of a nuisance order the justice's discretion should be so used as to prevent the expenditure of unnecessary sums. The best that can be hoped for is a 'make and mend' operation designed to make the house reasonably bearable as a dwelling. It should be remembered that, after *Saddleworth UDC v Aggregate and Sand Ltd* (1970) 114 Sol Jo 931, a lack of finance does not seem to be a reasonable excuse for not complying with a nuisance order. Local authorities cannot plead poverty in the hope of entirely escaping from the requirements of nuisance orders!

The sub-standard modern council-built house

Evidence is not lacking that bad construction, poor design, unproved building techniques and misguided planning policies have led to the erection of many recent council houses and flats whose inhabitants frequently have to endure extremely unpleasant living conditions. In some modern council properties there are severe problems of damp and condensation which can lead to ruined furniture and clothes and illness in the occupants. In such circumstances housing legislation offers little consolation to the tenant.

The decision in *R v Cardiff City Council, ex p Cross* of course applies to council built as well as council acquired housing. But statutory nuisance proceedings can bring some relief to the tenants of such dwellings. In *Birmingham District Council v Kelly* (1985) 17 HLR 572 the proceedings concerned council built dwellings comprising low rise flats.

The dwellings had defective windows, and were also extensively affected by the growth of mould which was found to be prejudicial to health. The presence of mould was found by the magistrates to be the result of the act, default or sufferance of the local authority because of, inter alia, the poor thermal quality of the flats, the absence of heating provision in the hallways, a gap under the front door of one flat, the poor quality of ventilation in bathrooms and kitchens. In some, but not all of the cases, mould could be attributable, in part, to a condition of some disrepair, though the court found that there was no breach of any obligation laid on the authority as a landlord qua landlord. But that was not enough to prevent inquiry into whether there was liability for the existence of a statutory nuisance, for a landlord may be responsible for the existence of a statutory nuisance that does not also constitute a breach of repairing obligations. The court pointed out that in such circumstances three questions arise: is there a statutory nuisance, is it due to the act, default or sufferance of the local authority, and what steps are necessary to abate it? The court concluded that the answer to the first two questions was 'yes', in that the mould growth was a consequence of condensation attributable to design defects in the flats. But the court pointed out in such circumstances magistrates should use discretion as to the terms of a nuisance order, and that statutory nuisance proceedings should not be used as a means of obtaining for a tenant a benefit which he was aware did not exist when he took the tenancy, and which would over generously favour him in relation to other tenants of the authority. An authority may be required to do works of improvement, but the need for such works must be justified by the evidence and the circumstances. Magistrates should behave reasonably in imposing orders on local authorities, bearing in mind the heavy duties already laid upon them, though they may take together actions brought by a group of tenants living in a block of flats, see *McMahon v Birmingham District Council* [1986] Legal Action 125.

In *Agnew v Waltham Forest London Borough Council* (1984 unreported) 'Housing Aid' January 1985, a flat built at the end of the 1950s was found to be affected by condensation caused by structural defects which were the local authority's responsibility, and they were ordered: to insulate the external walls and roof of the dwelling to current standards; to provide an extractor fan in the bathroom, and to remove all mould growth and make good decorations disturbed.

In *Tusting v Royal Borough of Kensington and Chelsea* (1974) 6 July (unreported) Inner London Crown Court, a tenant alleged that her home in a council block of flats suffered from a defective entrance doorway, split floorboards, dampness and a defective sink and draining board. The Crown Court gave a specific judgment on the problem of dampness caused by condensation which was found to be caused by the inherent coldness of the walls. The court ordered the local authority to alleviate the dampness and condensation within nine months bearing in mind a municipal offer to install central heating and to put interior cladding on the cold walls.

Miscellaneous powers to deal with sub-standard housing

Infested dwellings

Under the Prevention of Damage by Pests Act 1949 both local authorities (London Boroughs and county districts) and private individuals have obligations to secure the eradication of rats and mice. Section 2 of the Act states that, so far as practicable, local authorities are to keep their areas free of such vermin. They must carry out periodic inspection of their areas, destroy rats and mice on their own land and enforce the obligations of private landowners. These obligations are to be found in sections 3 and 4. So far as houses and the land occupied with them are concerned, it is an offence punishable by a fine of up to £5 for the occupier not to give notice to his local authority if he knows that rats and mice are living on or resorting to his land in substantial numbers. Once the local authority know of infestation on private land, whether as a result of the occupier's notice or otherwise, they may serve notice on the occupier, and the owner, of the land requiring, within a specified reasonable time, that the rats and mice on the land should be destroyed and that it should be kept free from such vermin. The local authority may specify reasonable steps to secure this object, including the application of specific treatments to the land and the carrying out of works of structural repair. They may not serve a merely general and unspecific notice; see *Perry v Garner* [1953] 1 QB 335, [1953] 1 All ER 285. They may also specify the times at which any treatment required by the notice is to be carried out.

Other verminous premises

Section 83 of the Public Health Act 1936, as amended by section 35 of the Public Health Act 1961 provides:

'(1) Where a local authority, [county districts] upon consideration of a report from any of their officers, or other information in their possession, are satisfied that any premises —
  (a) are in such a filthy or unwholesome condition as to be prejudicial to health or
  (b) are verminous,

the local authority shall give notice to the owner or occupier of the premises requiring him to take such steps as may be specified in the notice to remedy the condition of the premises by cleansing and disinfecting them, and the notice may require among other things the removal of wallpaper or other covering of the walls, or, in the case of verminous premises, the taking of such steps as many be necessary for destroying or removing vermin'.

The notice may also require, by virtue of sub-section (1A), in the case of premises used for human habitation that they be papered, painted or distempered inside at the choice of the person doing the work. It is an offence to fail to comply with such a notice, and failure to comply may also result in the local authority doing the work and recovering their costs from the defaulter. This provision only applies in extreme cases and does not entitle local authorities to demand a high standard of internal decorative repair from householders. In any proceedings under the provision it is open to the defendant to question the reasonableness of the authority's requirements, or their decision to address the notice to him and not some other affected person.

Dangerous and obstructive buildings

A general power to order the demolition not just of dwelling-houses but of any building classified as 'obstructive' is granted to local authorities by sections 283 to 288 of the Housing Act 1985. The phrase 'obstructive building' is defined as meaning 'a building which, by reason only of its contact with or proximity to, other buildings, is dangerous or injurious to health'. It should also be noted that this provision does *not* apply to any building which is the property of a local authority. The procedure is very similar to that laid down by section 264 of the 1985 Act and involves the service of a 'time and place' notice on the *owner*, i.e. the person entitled to the fee simple, and also any lessee whose unexpired term exceeds three years, giving at least 21 days' notice of the calling of a conference when the future of the property will be considered. If after that conference the authority remain convinced that the property is obstructive they may make a demolition order as to part or the whole of the structure, and require the vacation of the property within two months of the date on which the order becomes operative. Persons aggrieved by the making of the order have 21 days from its date of service to appeal to the county court. In this context 'person aggrieved' does *not* include a tenant with *less* than three years of his term unexpired, and this effectively limits the range of possible appellants to landlords only in the case of most tenanted property. On appeal the court may confirm, quash or vary the order.

The public health legislation also applies to certain buildings classifiable as 'dangerous'. Section 58 of the Public Health Act 1936, as amended by section 24 of the Public Health Act 1961, grants power to local authorities (London Boroughs and district councils) to apply to a court of summary jurisdiction for an order in respect of any building or part of a building that appears to them to be dangerous. If they make out their case the court may make the order requiring the owner (in this context meaning the person receiving the rack rent, or who would receive it if the premises were so let) to execute the works necessary to obviate the danger. The order need not specify how these works are to be done; see *R v Bolton Recorder, ex p McVittie* [1940] 1 KB 290, [1939] 4 All ER 236. This case was one of a pair, the other being *McVittie v Bolton Corpn* [1945] 1 KB 281, [1945] 1 All ER 379. They both arose out of Mr McVittie's abandonment of two adjoining plots of land following a fire which destroyed the buildings on one of them. It took years of action of various sorts to clear the site. Following these cases local authorities should always be careful to specify exactly the land made subject to their order. The cases also establish that the power to demolish a building necessarily extends to all of it including the basement, cellars and foundation.

Failure to comply with such an order enables the local authority to do the work themselves and to recover their reasonable expenses from the defaulter who also makes himself liable to a fine of up to £10. This power is available whether the building is dangerous either to those in the building itself and adjoining buildings, or to persons in the street outside. Emergency powers to deal with dangerous buildings where immediate action appears necessary to the local authority are conferred by section 24 of the Public Health Act 1961. Under this provision notice of the local authority's intention to take immediate preventive action need only be served on the owner and occupier of a building where it is reasonably practicable to do so. Moreover the local authority may recover their reasonable expenses from the owner in respect of their emergency action.

The position in Greater London

Some of the above *public health powers* do *not* apply to the inner London boroughs, The City of London and the Temples, where special legislation applies, though this is generally similar to the powers dealt with above, see *Halsbury's Statutes of England* (3rd Edn) Vol. 20, pp. 185 to 191. (This will be Vol. 26 in the 4th Edn.)

Further reading

Arden, A., and Partington, P., *Housing Law* (Sweet & Maxwell, 1983) Chap. 9–11.

Luba, J., *Repairs: Tenants' Rights* (Legal Action Group, 1986) Chap. 5 and 6.

Martyn, N.C., and Lloyd-Jones, E., *Housing Disrepair* (Longman, 1985) Chap. 5 and 6.

Garner, J.F., *Slum Clearance and Compensation* (Oyez, 1975) pp. 17–35.

Social Welfare Law (Ed. by D.W. Pollard) (Oyez Longman) paras. C. 101–C. 3124, C. 7255–7524.

Franey, R., 'Housing Stress' *Roof* March/April 1982, p. 19.

Haddon, T.B., 'Public Health and Housing Legislation' (1976) 27 NILQ 245.

Hawke, J.N., and Taylor, G.A. 'The Compulsory Repair of Individual, Physically Substandard Housing: The Law in Practice' [1984] JSWL 129.

Hughes, D.J., 'Housing and Public Health – A Continuing Saga' (1977) 28 NILQ 233.

Hughes, D.J., 'Public Health Legislation and the Improvement of Housing Conditions' (1976) NILQ 1.

Hughes D.J., 'What is a Nuisance? – The Public Health Act Revisited' (1976) 27 NILQ 131.

Hughes, D.J., 'Housing Repairs: A Suitable Case for Reform' [1984] JSWL 137.

McQuillan, J., and Finnis, N., 'Ways of Seeing Dampness: When Houses Can't Cope with being Lived In' *Roof*, May 1979, p. 85.

McQuillan, J., Cairns, M., and Ormandy, D., 'Fair Weather Friends' *Roof*, September/October 1981, p. 12.

Ormandy, D., 'Housing Standards' *Roof* January/February 1982, p. 12.

Watkinson, D., 'Legal Remedies for Condensation Damp in the Home' *Legal Action* November 1985, p. 153, and April 1986, p. 49.

Technical Report

Loudon, A.G., *The effects of ventilation and building design factors on the risk of condensation and mould growth in dwellings.* (Building Research Establishment, 1971.)

Chapter 9

Clearance procedures, compulsory purchase and rehousing

The development of the law

Clearance procedures have been part of the law for over a hundred years, the first legislation specifically concerned with such matters being the Artizans' and Labourers Dwellings (or 'Torrens') Act 1868. The word 'slum' is not a legal term of art and the law refers, as we have seen in the previous chapter, to dwellings which are 'unfit for human habitation'. The public mind has become accustomed to referring to the various procedures evolved to deal with areas of unfit housing as 'slum clearance'. The lawyer should be wary of using such non-technical language as there have been considerable differences in the past between the various types of clearance procedures. These differences can be traced through the history of the various Acts relating to the subject. Under the Torrens Act local authorities were empowered to declare premises 'unfit', but rehousing and demolition were not local government responsibilities. It was not until the Artizans' and Labourers' Dwellings Improvement (or 'Cross') Act 1875 that the law provided for both the clearance of an area and its subsequent rebuilding. This Act also introduced alternative grounds for taking action in respect of sub-standard housing: first the 'unfitness' of the houses and, second, the danger to health resulting from the generally bad conditions in the area. The Cross Act also included the first rehousing obligation to be laid on a demolishing authority.

Little use was made of this or subsequent housing legislation until after the First World War when the Acquisition of Land (Assessment of Compensation) Act 1919 and the introduction of exchequer subsidies laid the legal and financial basis for local authorities to acquire substandard houses and provide decent new homes for their inhabitants. Even so the number of houses demolished in the 1920's remained low with only about 2,000 to 5,000 houses each year being made subject to closing and demolition orders, and then usually on an individual basis. Mounting dissatisfaction with the cumbersome and archaic procedures of the law led to radical change in the Housing Act 1930 which introduced many of the procedures still in use today. This legislation introduced a much simpler procedure for area clearance, and also defined 'unfitness' in terms of bad housing conditions. Despite the financial difficulties of the 1930's, a major clearance policy was inaugurated in 1933, and by 1939 houses were being demolished at the rate of about 90,000 a year. Many more were scheduled for demolition.

The Second World War put an end to slum clearance for six years and the desperate shortage of accommodation after the war led to further restriction of demolition until 1953. Another major clearance programme was begun in that year, though it was admitted that in some areas the task of slum clearance could take as long as twenty years. Various changes in the law were also made and these culminated in the Housing Act 1957 which became the principal legislation in this area. By 1959 some 200,000 people a year were being rehoused from unfit houses, but this was not enough to deal with the sub-standard property, and it was also realised that the official estimates of the number of unfit dwellings were far too low. Not only were there many more unfit houses than had been realised, but also substantial numbers of others were declining into unfitness for lack of repair or maintenance. Other houses while not 'unfit' lacked the modern amenities that rising housing expectations demanded.

Major housing surveys carried out under the 1964 Labour Government revealed the existence of 1.8 million unfit dwellings in 1967, together with a further 4.5 million needing repairs or lacking at least one basic amenity. A major change of policy was announced in 1968 when it was decided to switch public investment from new house building into the improvement of older houses. Since then the emphasis in housing policy has been less and less on demolition and rehousing and more and more on rehabilitation, initially of individual houses but now on whole areas. Nevertheless slum clearance continued throughout this period and reached a peak in 1970–71 when some 70,000 houses a year were demolished. Since then there has been a considerable decline in the number of homes demolished. In 1975 the rate of demolition was down to 49,000 a year and over the years 1973 to 1977 the *average* rate fell to about 41,200 *per annum*. In 1977 itself 32,895 unfit houses in clearance areas in England and Wales were demolished. In 1980 in England and Wales, 13,427 houses were comprised in confirmed compulsory purchaser orders. In the financial years 1981/82, 1982/83 and 1983/84 the numbers of dwellings dealt with on an *area* basis were, 19,005, 13,945 and 8,211. (See HMSO *Local Housing Statistics* Nos. 55, 65, 69, 73). Other dwellings were dealt with on an individual basis and, of course, housing authorities have increasingly had to contemplate demolition of some of their houses where repair costs can be prohibitively high. (See 'The Times' 8 and 9 October 1984, inter alia.)

Procedure by way of compulsory purchase

a) Declaring the clearance area

Every local housing authority is under a duty imposed by section 605 of the Housing Act 1985 to inspect its district from time to time with a view to determining what action to take in relation to clearance and redevelopment. It is not only the information so derived that can lead to the declaration of a clearance area. Section 289 of the Housing Act 1985 makes it clear that an authority can act on the basis of official representations, made under section 606 of the Act, or any other information in their possession. What the authority must look for is areas where the houses are unfit for human habitation (as defined by section 604 of the Act; see Chapter 8, above), or are, by reason of their bad arrangement, or the narrowness or bad arrangement of the streets, dangerous or injurious to the health of the inhabitants of the area. They must also be satisfied that the most satisfactory method of dealing with the conditions in the area is demolition of the buildings in it. Clearance area procedure is designed to deal with the areas of poorest housing where rehabilitation is not a practical possibility. Nevertheless before resorting to this procedure the local authority should consider all their housing powers with relation to the area including the possibility of rehabilitation or dealing with the properties on an individual basis.

In this context 'house' has been given a somewhat extended meaning and includes yards, gardens and outhouses appurtenant to houses (Housing Act 1985 s. 623). The courts have also held the following to be 'houses': shops with living rooms over – *Re Bainbridge, South Shields (D'Arcy Street) Compulsory Purchase Order 1937* [1939] 1 KB 500, [1939] 1 All ER 419; garages and stores with dwellings over – *Re Butler, Camberwell (Wingfield Mews), No 2 Clearance Order 1936* [1939] 1 KB 570, [1939] 1 All ER 590; a tenement house, whether with other properties, or comprising by itself a single plot of land made subject to clearance procedure – *Quiltotex Co Ltd v Minister of Housing and Local Government* [1966] 1 QB 704, [1965] 2 All ER 913, and *Annicola Investments Ltd v Minister of Housing and Local Government* [1968] 1 QB 631, [1965] 3 All ER 850.

A clearance area can also be declared in respect of an area where the houses are badly arranged or the streets are narrow or badly arranged. This limb of the provision refers to houses built around central courts and back-to-back dwellings. Back-to-back dwellings provided for working-class people were automatically deemed to be 'unfit' by section 5(1) of the 1957 Housing Act. 'Back-to-back' was not defined by the statute and each case had to be decided on its own facts. In *White v St Marylebone Borough Council* [1915] 3 KB 249 the existence of an air shaft which occupied one-third of the air space between what were otherwise contiguous back-to-back dwellings did not prevent the dwellings from being statutorily prohibited. *Chorley Borough Council v Barratt Developments (North West) Ltd* [1979] 3 All ER 634 shed further light on the meaning of the term 'back-to-back'. A development company developed a system of housebuilding which consisted of four small houses, each having two common inner walls, forming together a single large square block. It was held that these dwellings did not fall within the prohibition against 'back-to-back' houses. The normal popular use of the term refers to terraces of houses where all the dwellings, except those at the ends, have three shared inner walls and only one outside wall. In any case the prohibition in section 5(1) only related to houses provided 'as dwellings for the working classes'. In the instant case it was found that the intending purchasers of the houses could not be described as 'working class' – a phrase which over the years had come to mean, in legal terms, the lower income groups – and neither could it be proved that the development company had any intention of providing 'back-to-back' houses for such people.

Section 5 of the Housing Act 1957 was repealed by Schedule 26 to the Housing Act 1980. For the future local authorities will have to rely on their planning control powers to prevent the erection of 'back-to-back' houses.

A clearance area can only be declared by passing a resolution pursuant to section 289 of the Housing Act 1985. Before any such resolution is passed the authority must satisfy themselves:

1) in so far as suitable accommodation available for the persons who will be displaced by the clearance of the area does not exist, that they can provide or secure the provision of such accommodation in advance of the displacement of the residents, and

2) that their resources are sufficient to carry their resolution into effect.

The effect of these requirements has been considered in the courts. In *Savoury v Secretary of State for Wales* (1974) 31 P & CR 344 a local authority declared a clearance area under section 42 of the 1957 Act and subsequently made a compulsory purchase order on the houses which they submitted for confirmation to the Secretary of State, who confirmed it in due course. The challenge to the order was based, inter alia, on the argument that the 'suitable accommodation' proviso was not satisfied. It was contended that the area in question was a closely knit community where there were many elderly people who relied on their neighbours for help and support which would be taken from them if they were forced to move and were dispersed. This was rejected by the court which ruled that the section itself recognises the inevitability of disruption. The words 'suitable accommodation' do not mean perfectly alternative or identical accommodation. A local authority must have regard to what the displaced residents can be reasonably asked to accept in their new houses. The desirability of rehousing residents, immediately or eventually, close to the site of their old houses should be considered by the local authority, though this is not a factor of overriding importance. The preservation of community spirit should be considered, but this also cannot be an overriding principle as it may not be reasonably practicable to achieve.

In *Eckersley v Secretary of State for the Environment* (1977) 34 P & CR 124, the local authority declared a clearance area in which Mr Eckersley's house was included. They made a compulsory purchase order on the area which was confirmed by the Secretary of State. The appellant sought to quash this order on a number of grounds which included an allegation that the Secretary of State had failed to consider certain material considerations when coming to his decision. These included:

1) whether the local authority's financial resources were sufficient to carry into effect the clearance and redevelopment of the land in question, and

2) the relative costs of clearance and redevelopment compared with the costs of retention and rehabilitation of the houses.

The Court of Appeal found that the first contention was outside the Secretary of State's jurisdiction. The provisos to section 289 of the 1985 Act are solely matters for the local authority alone. An authority must come in good faith and on proper evidence to a decision on these matters before proceeding to declare a clearance area, but that is a matter solely for them and not the Secretary of State. As to allegation (2) the Court held that questions of cost generally are matters for the Secretary of State to consider. There was no evidence that the issue of comparative costs as between demolition and rehabilitation had been considered properly and so the Secretary of State had failed to consider all the issues that should have been considered. The compulsory purchase order was therefore ultra vires and was quashed. In *Ashbridge Investments Ltd v Minister of Housing and Local Government* [1965] 3 All ER 371, [1965] 1 WLR 1320 the Court of Appeal stated that a court should only interfere with the process of clearance, so far as the Secretary of State is concerned, where there is evidence that he has gone beyond the powers granted by the Act or has not complied with its requirements. Furthermore, the court should limit its consideration to the material which was before the Secretary to see whether there has been some legal error made. Fresh evidence can only be admitted in exceptional circumstances.

The local authority must truly intend to demolish the properties when it decides to declare a clearance area and must not intend to use the procedure as a cloak for other housing operations. In *Wahiwala v Secretary of State for the Environment* (1977) 75 LGR 651 a local authority resolved to make a clearance area and made a compulsory purchase order which was subsequently confirmed. It was alleged that the local authority was seeking to acquire the sites of the houses at site value only, whereas they planned to let a housing association rehabilitate some houses once they were acquired. The Court of Appeal found this allegation unfounded, but said that once the compulsory purchase order was confirmed the council came under a duty to demolish the properties. This duty could only be deferred for a limited time, thus making a rehabilitation agreement automatically of no effect. In *Goddard v Minister of Housing and Local Government* [1958] 3 All ER 482, [1958] 1 WLR 1151 the court pronounced upon the meaning of the requirement that an authority must be satisfied that their resources are sufficient to carry their resolution into effect before declaring a clearance area. It was held that it is competent for a local authority to be satisfied of the sufficiency of their resources if they act properly on the advice of their committees. They do not have to have specific figures before them, and, in any case, 'resources' in this context includes credit as well as actual cash in hand.

So as soon as the authority have determined to declare a clearance area they must cause the area to be defined on a map in such a manner as to exclude from the area buildings which are *not* unfit for humans or dangerous or injurious to health. They must then pass the actual resolution declaring the area to be a clearance area, that is to say an area to be cleared of all buildings in compliance with the Housing Act 1985. A copy of this resolution must be sent to the Secretary of State, together with a statement of the number of persons occupying the buildings comprised in the area. Detailed rules as to the drawing up of the necessary plans of clearance areas are to be found in the DoE Circular No. 77/75, Appendix B. A council's resolution declaring a clearance area must correspond in every detail with the map drawn up under these rules. Further guidance is contained in DoE Circular 13/81. This counsels against compulsory action unless there are compelling reasons for taking it, and adds that the necessary authorisation is unlikely to be given in respect of private housing in satisfactory condition, or where voluntary improvement is possible. Authorities should compare demolition and rehabilitation costs. It is also policy to discourage the inclusion of fit dwellings in clearance proceedings. See further below on compulsory purchase procedures. Pursuant to section 289(6) of the

Housing Act 1985, a clearance area is not to be so defined as to include any land which is for the time being included in a general improvement area.

b) The method of dealing with a clearance area

Under section 290(1) of the Housing Act 1985 as soon as may be after declaring a clearance area, the local housing authority must secure its clearance either by purchasing the land and demolishing buildings thereon or by otherwise securing demolition.

Thus a local authority may agree with the affected land owners that they should demolish the buildings. The procedure here is governed by section 292 of the Housing Act 1985 and is dependent upon proper covenants being given that the clearance will be effected. They may themselves decide to acquire the land by agreement and so proceed to clearance. By section 292(2) where a local authority determine to purchase any land comprised in the clearance area they may also purchase any land which is surrounded by the clearance area, the acquisition of which land is reasonably necessary for the purpose of securing a cleared site of convenient shape and dimensions. They may also acquire any adjoining land where this is reasonably necessary for the satisfactory use or development of the cleared area. Such land is known as 'added land'. This does not entitle a local authority to acquire *any* land they desire. This is illustrated by *Coleen Properties v Minister of Housing and Local Government* [1971] 1 All ER 1049, [1971] 1 WLR 433. Here two streets of poor, old houses met at a corner where there was sited a modern block of shops and flats. The local authority declared the streets to be a clearance area and then included the modern building as added land in their compulsory purchase order. The local authority adduced no evidence as to why they needed the added land. The Court of Appeal held that the council's *ipse dixit* was not enough and that they had to prove their real need for the land. What is 'reasonably necessary' is a question of fact in each case and not one of planning policy.

In *Bass Charrington (North) Ltd v Minister of Housing and Local Government* (1970) 22 P & CR 31 it was held that the word 'adjoining' means land which is at least partly contiguous with the land in the clearance area and has continuous boundaries with it. Nor may land be acquired just to create a site of convenient shape and dimensions. Land can only be acquired if it is reasonably necessary, see *Gosling v Secretary of State for the Environment* [1975] JPL 406. The distinction is, of course, somewhat fine and is probably best illustrated by an example: If the clearance area land is merely to be used as a car park the fact that one side is not perfectly straight would not justify acquiring sufficient land to make it so; but if the land is sought for use as a football pitch and the cleared land was *just* insufficient for this purpose, added land might be acquired to enable the development to be carried out.

If a local authority cannot acquire the land by agreement they have compulsory purchase powers in section 290(3) and (4) of the Housing Act 1985. These require that any compulsory purchase order be confirmed by the Secretary of State. (See further DoE Circular 13/81 referred to above.)

Compulsory purchase procedure

Before describing this procedure it must be once more stressed that compulsory purchase is only available to a local authority wishing to demolish sub-standard houses where the houses within an area are actually unfit for human habitation, etc,; where those conditions are best dealt with by demolition; where the necessary accommodation exists to rehouse displaced residents, and where the authority's resources are sufficient to carry out the scheme.

The general procedure authorising the compulsory purchase of land is contained in Schedule 22 to the Housing Act 1985. The order must first of all be in the prescribed form, which is contained in the Housing (Prescribed Forms) Regulations 1972 (S.I. 1972/228, as amended by S.I. 1974/1511 and S.I. 1975/500). The order must describe the land to be acquired by reference to a map, which itself will show the land hatched or coloured according to the rules mentioned earlier in connection with the declaration of the clearance area, so that the unfit houses will be shown as pink, the houses and other buildings included by reason of their bad arrangement will be coloured pink-hatched-grey, and any land to be acquired which is *outside* the clearance area will be coloured grey.

Before submitting the order to the Secretary of State for his confirmation the local authority must first publish in one or more newspapers circulating within their district a notice stating the effect of such an order having been made, and describing the area comprised in the order. They must also state a place where a copy of the order and the map may be seen at all reasonable hours. A similar notice must be served on every owner, lessee, mortgagee and occupier (except tenants for periods of a month or less and statutory tenants) of affected land. This must state the time within which objections (which must be made in writing) to the confirmation of the order can be made. This period must be not less than fourteen days from the service of the notice. It is unnecessary to specify in these notices every single suggestion or instance of unfitness, see *Wyse v Secretary of State for the Environment and Borough of Newcastle-under-Lyme* [1984] JPL 256. If no objections are received then the order may be confirmed. If any are received and are not withdrawn the Secretary of State must hold either a public local inquiry, or afford the objectors an opportunity of being heard by a person appointed by him for that purpose. The date and place of this hearing will be advertised in the local newspapers and the objectors informed. The normal course is to hold a public local inquiry, to which, however, the Inquiries Procedure Rules 1976 (S.I. 1976/746) do not apply. No inquiry will, however, be held if the only objections received relate solely to matters of monetary compensation for the compulsory purchase. Representation is allowed to objectors who may employ a lawyer and/or a surveyor to appear. The inquiry will generally follow the usual compulsory purchase pattern with the authority commencing the proceedings before the Secretary of State's inspector. The objectors will reply and both sides will call, examine and cross-examine witnesses. The normal rules of natural justice will apply, see: *Gill & Co v Secretary of State for the Environment* [1978] JPL 373. All relevant considerations must be taken into account, including a landowner's desire to carry out redevelopment work himself, see *Menachem Schleidler v Secretary of State for the Environment and Gateshead Metropolitan Borough Council* [1983] JPL 383. After the closing speech by the local authority the inspector accompanied by the parties may view the area. It should be noted that it will be the state of the premises at the date of this inspection that will decide whether any given house is finally classified fit or unfit. It is also at this time that the assessment of any well-maintained payments will be made.

Objections are sometimes received based on the ground that given houses are not in fact 'unfit'. In such circumstances the local authority must serve a written notice on the objector stating their reasons for regarding the property as 'unfit'. The objector will then be allowed at least fourteen days to consider the local authority's case before the opening of the inquiry. Such objectors are also entitled to ask the Secretary of State for a written statement of reasons if he ultimately decides that any such house is unfit.

The inspector submits his report to the Secretary of State who, after considering it, may confirm it with or without modifications which can include the exclusion of land from the compulsory purchase order, but which may not authorise the local authority to purchase any more land than was originally included in the order without modification. Where land is excluded, and the compulsory purchase order in respect thereof is refused approval, the clearance area ceases to exist, see *R v Secretary of State for the Environment, ex p Wellingborough Borough Council and Runnymede Borough Council* (1981) 80 LGR 603. Once the order is confirmed the local authority must, according to Schedule 11, paragraph 12 to the Housing Act 1985, publish notice in the local press and also serve notice on the objectors. An administrative undertaking was given in Ministry of Housing and Local Government Circular No. 9/58 that the Secretary of State's letter of decision would include, for the future, the inspector's recommendation and the final decision with the reasons thereof. The letter also will also state that a copy of the inspector's report will be available if a request is made within one month of the date of the letter.

Schedule 11, paragraph 13 to the 1985 Act gives a 'person aggrieved' a six week period to challenge the confirmed order on the grounds that, substantively or procedurally, it goes beyond the powers conferred by the Act. The term 'person aggrieved' is nowadays liberally interpreted to include all persons with genuine legal grievances, but the six weeks time period is rigidly enforced. The statement in Schedule 11, paragraph 13(5) that, apart from the six weeks right of appeal, the order is not to be questioned 'in any legal proceedings whatsoever' is literally construed, see: *Smith v East Elloe RDC* [1956] AC 736, [1956] 1 All ER 855, and *R v Secretary of State for the Environment, ex p Ostler* [1977] QB 122, [1976] 3 All ER 90. It seems that no reason, be it an allegation of bad faith on the part of the local authority, or ignorance on the part of the objector, will persuade the courts to depart from this interpretation of the law.

Schedule 22 para 9 empowers the Secretary of State to make an order in respect of an affected landowner's reasonable costs of opposing an order, which may be deemed to be the acquiring authority's costs. The Secretary of State also has extensive powers, as extended in amendments contained in the Housing and Planning Act 1986, to recover the administrative costs of an inquiry so that authorities are made to bear the costs of clearance inquiries. This must be considered alongside the general strictures on compulsory purchase contained in DoE Circular 13/81 (see above) which makes it clear that it is policy to favour compulsory acquisition only where clear housing gain will result, especially in improvement areas, and where the disposal of the houses after improvement is contemplated.

The acquisition of the land

A copy of the confirmed order has to be served by the local authority on every person on whom they served notice of their intention to submit the order for confirmation, i.e. owners, lessees, mortgagees and long term tenants. This must be done 'so soon as may be' after the confirmation, Schedule 11, paragraph 14(2) to the Housing Act 1985. The local authority may then proceed to acquire the title to the land. This process will be governed by the Compulsory Purchase Act 1965. By section 5(1) of that Act:

'When the acquiring authority require to purchase any of the land subject to compulsory purchase, they shall give notice (hereinafter in this Act referred to as a "notice to treat") to all the persons interested in or having power to sell and convey or release the land, so far as known to the acquiring authority after making diligent inquiry'.

It is obvious that there may therefore be a considerable number of persons who have interests in the land all of which will have to be acquired. In addition to freehold and leasehold estates the courts have held the following to be compensatable interests: an option to acquire the freehold of some fields, *Oppenheimer v Minister of Transport* [1942] 1 KB 242, [1941] 3 All ER 485; an option in a will giving the testatrix's son the option to occupy premises for as long as he wished at a specified rent, which was held to create an equitable lease for life, *Blamires v Bradford Corpn* [1964] Ch 585, [1964] 2 All ER 603.

The notice to treat must be served within three years of the compulsory purchase order becoming operative, see section 4 of the Compulsory Purchase Act 1965. Section 5 also requires that the notice should:

1) give particulars of the land to which it relates;

2) demand particulars of its recipient's estate and interest in the land, and

3) state that the acquiring authority are willing to treat for the purchase of the land, and also as to the compensation to be paid for damage which may be sustained by the execution of the works.

A person served with a notice to treat has, under section 6 f the 1965 Act, 21 days from the time of service to inform the acquiring authority of the particulars of his claim, or to treat with them in respect of it. If he does not do this, or if negotiations as to compensation begin but do not produce agreement, then the question must be referred to the Lands Tribunal for their determination. Once the amount of compensation has been fixed the transfer of the land follows the usual conveyancing pattern. There are minor differences from private transfer by virtue of section 23 of the Compulsory Purchase Act 1965 which provides:

'(1) The costs of all conveyances of the land subject to compulsory purchase shall be borne by the acquiring authority.
(2) The costs shall include all charges and expenses, whether incurred on the part of the seller or on the part of the purchaser,
  (a) of all conveyances and assurances of any of the land, and of any outstanding terms or interests in the land, and
  (b) of declaring, evidencing and verifying the title to the land, terms or interests, and
  (c) of making out and furnishing such abstracts and attested copies as the acquiring authority may require. . . .

(6) Conveyances of the land subject to compulsory purchase may be according to the forms in Schedule 5 to this Act, or as near thereto as the circumstances of the case will admit, or by deed in any other form which the acquiring authority may think fit'.

This provision, along with section 9 of the Act, allows the acquiring authority to deal with the reluctant seller who refuses to co-operate in the transaction. In such circumstances the amount of compensation payable has to be paid into court and the transfer of the title to the interest will be achieved by the authority executing a deed poll.

Entering upon the land

An authority wishing to enter upon the land before completion of the conveyancing procedure may do so by virtue of section 11 of the Compulsory Purchase Act 1965. The acquiring authority must have served a notice to treat before they can proceed under this provision but thereafter they may, by giving not less than fourteen days' notice to owners, lessees and occupiers, enter and take possession of the land specified in the notice. In such circumstances the compensation payable will bear interest from the date of entry until the date of payment. This rate of interest is subject to very regular changes.

General vesting declaration procedure

This procedure, available under the Compulsory Purchase (Vesting Declarations) Act 1981, section 3 is designed to expedite the acquisition process. Where a compulsory purchase order has come into operation, an acquiring authority may execute a general vesting declaration in respect of ail or any of the land they are authorised to acquire. Before making such a declaration the acquiring authority must include in the statutorily required notices of the making or confirmation of the compulsory purchase order certain statements. These are:

1) a statement of the effect of the Act, see S.I. 1982/6 Form 9.

2) a notification to persons entitled to compensation inviting them to give information to the acquiring authority with respect to their names, addresses and the land in question.

These particulars together with the notice of the making or confirmation of the compulsory purchase order must also be registered in the local land charges register. A period of at least two months must then elapse from the first date of publication of the notice before the actual general vesting declaration can be executed, unless all the affected occupiers agree otherwise in writing, thereafter the declaration may be executed. (See sections 4 and 5 of the 1981 Act.) This will begin vesting of the land in the authority. To complete the process further notices must be served on occupiers of affected land (other than those with minor interests) and other persons who have given information in pursuance of the authority's request, stating the effect of the general vesting declaration. In any case the authority must allow 28 days from the end of this last service of notices before the land finally vests in them. (See sections 4 and 6 of the Act.)

The effect of general vesting declaration procedure is that a notice to treat is deemed to be served, and also, that at the end of the period specified in the declaration, the land in question together with the right to enter and take possession vests in the acquiring authority. The former owners are then left solely with a right to compensation. General vesting declaration procedure only applies to the acquisition in general of freehold or long leasehold or other long-term interests. The so called 'minor interests', e.g. periodic tenancies for a year or less, are excluded. In such circumstances where houses are concerned section 584 of the Housing Act 1985 enables the local authority by giving of at least fourteen days' notice, and subject to the payment of compensation, to enter and take possession of the land.

The assessment of compensation

'Compensation' can mean many things to many people affected in different ways by the declaration of a clearance area. The various elements of the total price which the acquiring authority will ultimately have to pay must be considered separately.

The purchase price of the land

Section 579(2) of the Housing Act 1985 provides that in relation to compulsory purchase under section 290 (clearance land) compensation is to be assessed under the Land Compensation Act 1961, subject to the provisions of the 1985 Act. Section 585 further provides the compensation payable for land purchased under section 290 is its cleared site value, though this does not apply to the site of a house or other buildings included in a clearance area solely because they are 'dangerous or injurious to the health of the inhabitants of that area by virtue of its bad arrangement in relation to other buildings or the narrowness or bad arrangements of the streets', unless it is a building constructed or adapted, in whole or in part, for dwelling purposes, and that part which is a dwelling is unfit for human habitation.

Thus the normal rules for assessing the compensation payable in respect of compulsorily acquired land are modified in the case of clearance areas *but only* in relation to the houses and land included by virtue of unfitness. In this case the *only* sum payable *for the land* will be the cleared site value. This 'cleared site value' is a matter of considerable technicality because of the provisions of section 10 of and Schedule 2 to the Land Compensation Act 1961. However, *briefly* the rule is that where the cleared site value would *exceed* the existing market value of the land with the house on it the payment is to be restricted to the value of the site plus the house. If any unfit house is owner-occupied then, according to paragraph 3 of the Schedule, the *minimum* compensation payable will be the gross rateable value, but, to prevent over-compensation this minimum payment will be made *inclusive* of any well maintained or other owner-occupier payments. In those cases where the land, etc. is included solely because of bad arrangements, etc., or for any other reason, for example because it is 'added land' under section 290(2) of the 1985 Act, the ordinary rules for assessing compensation apply.

These rules are contained in section 5 of the Land Compensation Act 1961. The basic rules are:·

1) No allowance may be made on acount of the acquisition being compulsory;

2) The basic value of the land must be assessed on the basis of a willing seller and a willing vendor in the open market;

3) The special suitability or adaptability of the land for any purpose must not be taken into account if that purpose is one to which the land could be applied only in pursuance of statutory powers, or for which there is no market apart from the special needs of a particular purchaser or the requirements of any public authority possessing powers of compulsory acquisition.

4) Where the value of the land is increased by reason of the use thereof or any premises thereon in a manner which could be restrained by any court, or is contrary to law, or is detrimental to the health of the occupants of the premises or to the public health [e.g. if the premises are statutorily overcrowded], the amount of that increase must not be taken into account;

5) Where the land is, and but for the compulsory acquisition would continue to be, devoted to a purpose of such a nature that there is no general demand or market for land for that purpose, the compensation may, if the Lands Tribunal is satisfied that reinstatement in some other place is bona fide intended, be assessed on the basis of the reasonable cost of equivalent reinstatement;

6) The provisions of rule (2) above are not to affect the assessment of compensation for disturbance or any other matter not directly based on the value of the land.

Under section 598 of the 1985 Act, section 4 of the Acquisition of Land Act 1981 applies to the compulsory acquisition of clearance land, whereunder the assessment of compensation there is to be disregarded anything done or undertaken on relevant land with a view to obtaining enhanced compensation.

It must also be remembered that section 50 of the Land Compensation Act 1973 provides that compensation for the compulsory acquisition of an interest in land is not to be reduced because alternative residential accommodation is to be provided for the person entitled to receive compensation.

Well maintained payments

We have already encountered well maintained payments in respect of individual unfit houses in Chapter 8, above, and we must now consider them in relation to houses in clearance areas. Well maintained payments may also be made in respect to 'partially' well maintained houses under Schedule 23, para 5 of the Housing Act 1985, if *either* the exterior or interior has been well maintained, the payment in such cases being one half of the normal amount.

Payments are made to owner occupiers, or, if the house is not owner-occupied, to the person legally responsible for repair. Alternatively payment may be made, wholly or partly, to other persons who satisfy the local authority they have been responsible to a material extent for the property's good maintenance. If it appears equitable to make a payment to such persons the local authority may do so. This latter provision covers tenants provided their entitlement can be made out, though claims by tenants should be notified to their landlords for comments before payments are made, see *Hoggard v Worsbrough UDC* [1962] 2 QB 93, [1962] 1 All ER 468. If rival claims for payment are made each claimant must be given a chance to be heard. See generally section 586 and Schedule 23, paragraph 3 of The Housing Act 1985.

Under Schedule 23, para 7 and 8 of the 1985 Act the following steps are required.

1) Where a house is made subject to a compulsory purchase order as being unfit the local authority must serve notice on every owner, lessee, mortgagee and occupier of the house.

2) This notice must be served not later than that notice which is served explaining the effect of the making of the compulsory purchase order.

3) The notice must state the local authority's opinion of the house, for example whether it is fully or partially well maintained (and if the latter in what respects) or not well maintained at all. The notice must also state the authority's reason for their opinion.

Provision is made for a 'person aggrieved' by a refusal to make a payment or by a decision to make only a partial payment to make written representaions to the Secretary of State challenging the authority's decision. If the Secretary of State considers it appropriate he may cause the house to be inspected by a member of his department, and may then give directions to the local authority to make such payments or further payments as he thinks the case requires.

The meaning of 'well maintained'

Oddly enough the phrase 'well maintained' itself is not defined in the legislation. In *Slum Clearance and Compensation* (4th Edn) Professor Garner says on page 38: 'A good state of decoration, internal and external, would almost certainly entitle a house to be considered under these provisions, and so would the case where money has been spent on (for example) roof repairs and other necessary matters to keep a house weather-tight'. It must be remembered that, by definition, a house which is the subject of a well maintained payment is statutorily unfit and so what is really being looked for is a genuine effort on the part of the person claiming the payment to have kept the property in the best possible state bearing in mind all the problems with which he or she has been faced.

The amount of the payment

Schedule 23, paragraph 4 of the 1985 Act states that amount of a well maintained payment is to be an amount equal to the rateable value multiplied by such a figure as is prescribed from time to time by Statutory Instrument. (See S.I. 1982/1112.) Where a partially well maintained payment is made the computation method used is exactly the same as for a full payment but only half of the resulting sum is paid.

It must also be noted that a well maintained payment may not exceed the amount whereby the full market value of the house exceeds the site value (see Chapter 8, above);

Under section 587 of the Housing Act 1985, Schedule 24, Part I has effect in respect of payments made in relation to owner-occupied houses, and double compensation is generally avoided by section 588 prohibiting well maintained payments under Schedule 23.

Owner-occupier supplements

Where, inter alia, a house has been acquired at *site* value because of, for example, a compulsory purchase order, and

1) at the 'relevant date' (in the case of a house comprised in a clearance area under section 289 this is the date of declaration of the area) and for the preceding two years the house was wholly or partly occupied as a private dwelling, *and*

2) the occupier was a person entitled to an interest in the house or a member of that person's family,

payment is to be made under Schedule 24. Such a payment is also to be made where an interest in the house was acquired by a person *less* than two years before the 'relevant date' where during the lesser period conditions (1) and (2) above were satisfied, *and* the authority are satisfied that before the interest was acquired, the acquirer made all reasonable inquiries to ascertain whether the declaration would be made within two years of the acquisition, and had no reason to believe that it was likely, *and* the person entitled to the interest when it is compulsorily purchased is the acquirer mentioned above, or a member of his family.

The amount of compensation payable is, under Schedule 24, paragraph 4, the full compulsory purchase value (i.e. the market value of the site plus the house) *less* the compensation payable in respect of the interest in connection with the compulsory purchase of the house at site value, i.e. as assessed under section 585 of the 1985 Act, *and also less* a proportion attributable to any part of the house *not* used as a private dwelling. In this context the term 'private dwelling' includes occupation as a private dwelling by the claimant's tenant, see *Hunter v Manchester City Council* [1975] QB 877, [1975] 2 All ER 966.

These provisions allow the making of payments, 'owner-occupiers' supplements', to owner-occupiers of unfit homes who have been driven by housing shortages to purchase substandard dwellings as homes.

So far we have been concerned with payments that go, in general terms, to the owners of certain legally recognised interests in land. In the case of most unfit houses this will mean either the owner-occupier or the landlord, though as we have seen there are times when a tenant can receive a well maintained payment in respect of his home. It is now necessary to consider other payments that may have to be made in respect of unfit houses.

Disturbance payments

These must *not* be confused with disturbance as a head of compensation to be assessed separately under section 5 of the Land Compensation Act 1961, Disturbance as *compensation* is payable to a person whose interest in land has been compulsorily acquired: disturbance as a *payment* is payable to a person whose *occupation* of land is disturbed in consequence of acquisition. Disturbance payments are made according to the provisions of section 37 of the Land Compensation Act 1973, and are payable in respect of displacements occuring on or after 17 October 1972 or 31 July 1974 in the case of displacement following improvements. The following conditions must be satisfied before a payment can be made.

1) The authority must have acted in relation to the land in question either:
    (a) in the exercise of its land acquisition powers, or
    (b) by making or accepting a housing order or undertaking, or serving an improvement notice under Part VII of the Housing Act 1985, or
    (c) by carrying out redevelopment or improvements in respect of land already acquired compulsorily and retained for such purposes, or
    (d) where a housing association, registered under the Housing Associations Act 1985, which has already acquired the land carries out the work of improvement or redevelopment.

2) The person receiving the payment must have been in lawful possession of the land. Thus a mere lodger could not receive a payment under the Act as he has no 'possession' of land. However, a person displaced by reason of compulsory acquisition is entitled to compensation for losses naturally and reasonably flowing therefrom, including those incurred in anticipation of, and prior to, the actual acquisition, see *Prasad v Wolverhampton Borough Council* [1983] Ch 333, [1983] 2 All ER 140, where the occupier vacated a dwelling after the compulsory purchase order, but before notice to treat.

Surrendering a secure tenancy, however, merely extinguishes the interest and is not an 'acquisition' by an authority, and no compensation is accordingly payable, see *R v Islington London Borough Council, ex p Knight* [1984] 1 All ER 154, [1984] 1 WLR 205.

3) The person receiving the payment must:
    (a) have *no* interest in the land for the acquisition of which he is otherwise statutorily entitled to compensation *or*
    (b) have such an interest as is compensatable only under section 585 of the 1985 Act (site value for unfit homes) and which does not

qualify for any supplement under Schedule 24 of the 1985 Act (see above).

4) Where a disturbed occupier is entitled to both a disturbance payment and compensation under section 37 of the Landlord and Tenant Act 1954 he may take only one payment and not both.

Where there is no entitlement to a disturbance payment or to any other form of statutory disturbance an ex gratia payment may be made by the authority concerned under section 37(3) of the Land Compensation Act 1973. Payments can thus be made to lodgers and other mere licensees in deserving cases. Department of the Environment Circular 73/73 urges local authorities to make sympathetic use of this power.

The amount of disturbance payments is governed by section 38 of the 1973 Act. Such a payment must cover:

1) the reasonable moving expenses of the claimant;

2) any loss by reason of disturbance to trade or business (in the case of business premises only), and

3) in the case of a dwelling structurally modified for a disabled person, a reasonable sum to cover the cost of making comparable modifications to his new house, *provided* that in the case of his former home a local authority grant was available to cover the cost of the work.

A disturbance payment carries interest at the rate fixed from time to time under section 32 of the Land Compensation Act 1961 from the date of displacement until payment. Any dispute over the amount of a payment is to be settled by the Lands Tribunal.

Other powers to assist displaced occupiers

The Land Compensation Act 1973, s. 43 allows authorities to pay the reasonable expenses of acquisition of a new dwelling (though *not* the purchase price) to a person displaced from a dwelling in consequence of the exercise of compulsory purchase powers, the making of a housing order or undertaking or the service of an improvement notice under Part VII of the Housing Act 1985, provided that:

1) the dwelling is acquired within one year of the displacement and is comparable with that from which he was reasonably displaced;

2) that the person displaced had no greater interest in his former dwelling than that of a tenant from year to year.

Home loss payments

Department of the Environment Circular No. 73/73, para. 21, states:

'The intention of these special payments is to recognise the personal upset and distress which people suffer when they are compulsorily displaced from their homes . . . either by compulsory purchase, redevelopment or any action under the Housing Acts. The entitlement to a payment is quite separate from and is not dependent on any right to compensation or a disturbance payment'.

Such payments exist under section 29 of the Land Compensation Act 1973, as amended. They are payable to persons who have been in occupation of the dwelling in question, or a substantial part thereof, throughout a period of not less than five years ending with the date of displacement, provided that their occupation arose out of their possessing either an interest in the dwelling, or a statutory tenancy of the dwelling, or a Part VI contract under the Rent Act 1968 in respect of the dwelling, or a right to occupy it under a contract of employment. (Strangely enough the 1973 Act has *not* been amended to take note of the fact that the 1968 Rent Act has been repealed and replaced by the Rent Act 1977 under which the old Part VI contracts are now called 'restricted contracts'.)

A person who is otherwise qualified for a home loss payment will be entitled to receive one if he is displaced from his home as a consequence of any of the following circumstances:

1) the compulsory acquisition of the dwelling;

2) the making, or acceptance, of a housing order or undertaking in respect of the dwelling;

3) the service of an improvement notice under Part VII of the Housing Act 1985 in respect of the dwelling;

4) the carrying out by an authority or registered housing association of works of improvement or redevelopment, etc., in respect of land previously acquired by them.

In this last context it should be noted that a local authority tenant who is displaced from a council-owned house because his landlords wish to demolish and replace dwellings which are unfit is entitled to a home loss payment where his loss is due to redevelopment, see: *R v Corby District Council, ex p McLean* [1975] 2 All ER 568, [1975] 1 WLR 735. Demolition *may* constitute redevelopment for the purpose of this section, even where the proposal is that a third party should erect dwellings on the land, provided the displacement and demolition are essential steps in the redevelopment, see *Greater London Council v Holmes* (1985) 18 HLR 131.

A person who claims a home loss payment as a consequence of the compulsory acquisition of his dwelling will lose his entitlement if he gives up his occupation of the premises on a date before the authority were authorised to acquire them, which would seem to mean the date of confirmation of the compulsory purchase order. Furthermore home loss payments are not payable to persons displaced as a result of their having served plannng blight notices under, for example, section 192 of the Town and Country Planning Act 1971. However, payments are to be made where an authority possessing compulsory purchase powers acquires, by agreement, an interest in a dwelling from any person, *to* any other person displaced from the dwelling in consequence. This protects the rights of tenants where the landlord sells his house by agreement to the local authority.

A claim for a payment must be made in writing, and supported by such reasonable particulars as the local authority may reasonably require. Once the entitlement to a payment is made out the authority have to make the payment not later than three months after the date of the claim, or, if those three months end before the date of displacement, on the date of displacement, see the Land Compensation Act 1973 s. 32 (as amended by the Local Government, Planning and Land Act 1980 s. 114). The amount of the payment will be a sum equal to the rateable value of the dwelling multiplied by three, subject to a maximum of £1,500 and a minimum of £150, see section 30(1) of the 1973 Act. By section 32(6) of the 1973 Act where there are two or more persons entitled to claim a home loss payment in respect of the same dwelling, for example because of joint occupancy, the payment is to be divided equally between them.

Under section 29(3A) of the 1973 Act a person is not 'displaced' from a dwelling in consequence of the acceptance of an undertaking, the service of an improvement notice or the carrying out of any improvement thereto, unless the consequence is *permanent* displacement. In this context improvement includes alteration and enlargement. Can improvement be so drastic as to completely alter the character of a dwelling so that its returning tenant can be said to be permanently displaced because what he returns to is fundamentally different from what he left? The answer can be yes, but it is a question of fact in each case, see *Casale v Islington London Borough Council* (1985) 18 HLR 146.

The fate of the land after acquisition

Under section 291(1) of the Housing Act 1985 the general duty of a local authority who have acquired land for clearance purposes is to see to the vacation and demolition of all buildings as soon as possible. They may do this themselves or they may sell the land subject to a condition that the buildings must be demolished forthwith. This general duty is subject to the power contained in section 301 of the Act which provides for temporary retention of unfit houses in clearance areas, provided the local authority are of the opinion that the houses are or can be rendered capable of providing accommodation which is adequate for the time being. The thinking behind this provision was explained in Ministry of Housing and Local Government Circular No. 55/54: 'In some areas the numbers of unfit houses liable to demolition is so large that it will still be many years before all the houses can be demolished . . . local authorities should be enabled to make those houses which have to be retained for some time more tolerable for the people who will have to live in them until they can be demolished and replaced'.

Accordingly local authorities are given a further power under section 302 of the 1985 Act to do such works as are necessary from time to time to keep the houses up to the standard required by the section. This standard is never very high and does not amount to much more than a requirement of 'patching-up'. Once an authority have decided to clear an area they should proceed to demolish it, *unless* some proper or exceptional requirement *other than* a housing need for short term accommodation capable of being met by using the ability of the dwellings to provide accommodation of a standard adequate for the time being exists, see *R v Birmingham City Council, ex p Sale* (1983) 82 LGR 69, 48 P & CR 270. A local authority is not justified in resolving to postpone demolition and thereafter simply doing nothing to improve the lot of their tenants living in such properties. The passing of such a resolution will not protect an authority should they be found responsible for the existence of a statutory nuisance comprising premises prejudicial to health in the retained houses, see: *Salford City Council v McNally* [1976] AC 379, [1975] 2 All ER 860, and Chapter 8, above.

Rehousing displaced residents

Section 39 of the Land Compensation Act 1973, as amended, provides:

'(1) Where a person is displaced from residential accommodation on any land in consequence of
  (a) the acquisition of the land by an authority possessing compulsory purchase powers;
  (b) the making . . . or acceptance of a housing order . . . or undertaking in respect of a house or building on the land;

(c) where the land has been previously acquired by an authority possessing compulsory purchase powers or appropriated by a local authority and is for the time being held by the authority for the purposes for which it was acquired or appropriated, the carrying out of any improvement to a house or building on the land or of redevelopment on the land;

(d) the service of an improvement notice, within the meaning of Part VII of the Housing Act 1985, in respect of premises in which that accommodation is situated,

and suitable alternative accommodation is not otherwise available to that person, then, subject to the provisions of this section, it shall be the duty of the relevant authority to secure that he will be provided with such other accommodation'.

Within the context of slum clearance, either on an individual or an area basis, this means that local authorities have an obligation to rehouse persons displaced as a result of the making of demolition, closing or clearance orders or the accepting of undertakings under section 264 of the Housing Act 1985. Some local authorities adopt a wider obligation as a matter of administrative practice, and the strictly limited nature of the section 39 obligation should be noted. It does not apply to squatters nor to persons permitted to reside in a house pending its demolition or improvement, such as under a municipally licensed short-life property scheme where, for example, university students are permitted to occupy houses awaiting demolition on a strictly limited time basis. The duty only applies, in general terms, to persons resident in the dwelling on the date when the order, or undertaking, etc., was made or accepted or when notice of its making was published, as the case may be. Moreover, in the case of displacements arising out of the doing of works of improvements the obligation is only owed to persons who are *permanently* displaced.

The greatest restriction on the scope of the obligations is that it confers no right on persons displaced to have priority over other persons on the housing waiting list. In *R v Bristol Corpn, ex p Hendy* [1974] 1 All ER 1047, [1974] 1 WLR 498 the applicant lived in a basement flat where he enjoyed Rent Act security of tenure but which was also statutorily unfit. Mr Hendy had a history of rent arrears with another local authority and Bristol Corporation offered him only temporary accommodation, pending an offer of suitable residential accommodation, on the terms usually offered to prospective municipal tenants. He applied for an order of mandamus to compel the local authority to fulfil their rehousing duty, contending that this was an obligation to provide him with permanent accommodation on terms that gave him a security of tenure equivalent to that which he had enjoyed under his former tenancy. The Court of Appeal refused the order. They concluded that the duty is only to act reasonably and to do the best practicable job in providing a displaced person with other accommodation. A local authority does all that is required by providing such a person with temporary accommodation until a council house is available.

The content of the section 39 duty is not great, though, such as it is, it can be enforced by way of mandamus. Alternatively there may be a remedy by way of an action for breach of statutory duty should a local authority fail to take any action with resultant damage to the plaintiff. In any such actions the exact quantification of loss could prove difficult: see Chapter 6, above.

Rehabilitation of houses in clearance areas

As part of the general change in emphasis from demolition to area improvement, and also because of acute housing shortages in some areas, power is now given to rehabilitate and improve houses within clearance areas which are capable of being improved to the full standard.

Under Schedule 11 of the Housing Act 1985 where a house in a clearance area was purchased under section 290 of the Act by agreement or compulsorily before 2 December 1974, *or* it is subject to a compulsory purchase order made under the section before that date, and confirmed before 2 March 1975, *and* where the house was included in the clearance area because it was unfit for human habitation, *and*, in the opinion of the local housing authority, it is capable of being, and ought to be, improved to 'full standard', the authority may make a rehabilitation order in respect of the house and submit it to the Secretary of State.

The owner of an unfit house within a clearance area may apply to the local authority requesting them to make a rehabilitation order. Whether or not to make such an order is for the local authority to decide, though they must direct themselves properly in law and consider all and only the relevant considerations. In *Elliott v London Borough of Southwark* [1976] 2 All ER 781, [1976] 1 WLR 499, a compulsory purchase order was made and confirmed in respect of certain houses. Following the service of notice to treat some of the affected owners applied for rehabilitation orders on their houses. The council refused the applications, stating that they considered that the land should be cleared and redeveloped for new housing. Local authorities are, of course, under a duty to give their reasons for such a refusal. The owners sought to impugn the decision on the grounds:

1) that the local authority had failed to give an adequate statement of their reasons for refusing the application, and

2) that they had not taken into account the relevant considerations in coming to their decision, in that they had relied solely on the evidence presented at the public local inquiry into the initial compulsory purchase order, and had failed to take account of changes in housing policy and economics since the date of that inquiry.

The Court of Appeal rejected both contentions. The first ground of the appeal was easily dismissed on factual grounds; the statement given contained the salient reason for the authority's decision. As to the second contention the Court held that the local authority were justified in taking the evidence of the inquiry into account, and there was no evidence that they had failed to consider the other relevant issues. The actual factors to be considered in any given situation will vary from case to case, and the courts will not prescribe a list of matters which must be considered. The courts are concerned solely to prevent abuses of discretion and not to substitute their decisions for those of local authorities. Indeed in *A-G, ex rel Rivers-Moore v Portsmouth City Council* (1978) 36 P & CR 416 at 424, Walton J went further and stated that the declaration of a rehabilitation area 'appears to me to be a matter in the discretion of the council. There is no provision made for any challenge to the council's decision in that regard. That being the case I do not see that this court can do anything about it at all, even if it thought the council was being utterly unreasonable in not considering such a solution to the problem'. This should not be read literally, and should be taken rather as authority for the proposition that a court is not there to dispose of municipal decisions merely if it disagrees with them.

Where a local authority resolve to make a rehabilitation order the procedure they must follow is as follows. The order must be made in the prescribed form and must describe the affected properties by reference to a map. Before submitting the order to the Secretary of State for confirmation they must publish notice in one or more local newspapers stating the making and intended application of the order, and giving notice of the time and place where the order and the map can be seen. They must also serve notice on all those persons who were, or who should have been, informed of the making of the original compulsory purchase order, together with any persons having an interest in the property, other than a tenant for a month or less. These notices must state the local authority's reasons for making the order; the effect of the order; that it is to be submitted for confirmation, and the procedure for making objections. If the Secretary of State receives any objections which are not subsequently withdrawn he must hold a public local inquiry, or arrange for the objectors to be heard before his representative. The Secretary may require objectors to state the grounds of their objections in writing, and he may disregard any objection which relates solely to issues of compensation. After considering the report submitted to him following the hearing of objections the Secretary may confirm or amend the order. Following confirmation notice must be published in the local press, and served on objectors. Persons aggrieved by the making of an order have the usual six week right of appeal on a point of law to the High Court. If no such appeal is made the order will come into force and notice of this must be served on all those on whom notice of the original compulsory purchase order was served.

Once the order becomes operative the duty to demolish the properties in question ceases. In its place the local authority come under a duty to take such steps as are necessary to bring them up to the full standard of section 234 of the Housing Act 1985 (see Chapter 10). They must do the work themselves so as to produce one or more full standard dwellings, or, where a house is not vested in them, they must ensure that the houses are so restored. To this end they may accept undertakings from the owner or other persons who have or will have an interest in the houses that the work will be done within an agreed time. Following the coming into effect of a rehabilitation order any affected building previously acquired by the local authority is deemed to have been acquired under either Part II of the Housing Act 1985 or Part VI of the Town and Country Planning Act 1971. Section 593 of the Housing Act 1985 declares that where such a 'deemed acquisition' takes place, the compensation is to be assessed in accordance with either Part II of the 1985 Act or Part VI of the 1971 Act, and this may lead to an increase in the amount of compensation payable. Any affected building *not yet* acquired and in respect of which a notice to treat has *not* been served is freed from the compulsory purchase order, and the clearance area, as from the date when the rehabilitation order becomes effective, see generally Department of the Environment Circular No. 40/75.

Further reading

Arden, A., and Partington, P., *Housing Law* (Sweet & Maxwell, 1983) Chaps. 9 and 23.
Berry, F., *Housing: The Great British Failure* (Charles Knight, 1974) pp. 158–169.
English, J., Madigan, R., and Norman P., *Slum Clearance* (Croom Helm, 1976) Chaps. 1, 2, 3, 6, 7, 8 and 9.
Gee, D., *Slum Clearance* (Shelter).
Jacobs, S., *The Right to a Decent Home* (Routledge and Kegan Paul, 1976).

Social Welfare Law (Ed. by D.W. Pollard) (Oyez Longman) paras. C. 945–C. 1001 and C. 4152–C. 4253.

Articles

Luba, J., 'Financial Compensation for Displaced Tenants' [1985] February *Legal Action*, p. 19.
Shiner, P., 'Demolition of properties in clearance areas' [1983] July LAG Bull 94.
Shiner, P., 'Council "Sin Bin" to be Demolished' *Roof* July/August 1983, p. 6.

Chapter 10

Improvement policies

A response to bad housing conditions based on improvement and area rehabilitation has been preferred housing policy for over a decade. The temptation has been to regard area improvement as a panacea for the ills of decaying inner city areas.

The problem of decaying inner urban areas has been noted for some time. Such localities suffer from multiple deprivation; bad housing is combined with poor educational facilities, a concentration of work opportunities in badly paid unskilled jobs, sickness, a lack of leisure facilities and feelings of social alienation and powerlessness among the inhabitants. The generally bad conditions of housing, education, leisure, employment, social welfare and nourishment in such areas interact to maintain a poor quality of life. Before any real improvement can be expected there has to be a national commitment to raising standards, not just of housing, but of education, employment, health and social welfare for such localities. Housing improvement by itself is not enough. Unfortunately concentration on such individual aspects of the inner urban problem has too often been the hallmark of central policy.

History

Both the Moyne Report Cmd. 4397 (1933) and the Ridley Report Cmd. 6621 (1945) drew attention to the need to prevent housing decline by assisting owners with repair costs, and some limited *powers* of compulsory acquisition in respect of improveable properties were given to local authorities in the Housing Act 1935. The Hobhouse report (1947) recommended powers to bring about compulsory rehabilitation of housing. The Housing Act 1949 introduced grant aiding powers but little initial use was made of them, though reforms contained in the Housing Repairs and Rents Act 1954 led to a greater 'take up' of grants, with 160,000 being made by the end of 1958. In 1960 over 130,000 grants were made and in 1964 the number of houses improved passed

800,000. *Area* improvement, especially as a replacement for clearance policy which was becoming increasingly unpopular, especially as much of the very worst slum housing had by then been demolished, was introduced under the Housing Act 1964; but again little use was made of the powers granted. Reforms introduced by the Act of 1969 led to greater emphasis on improvement, with the rate of improvement rising from 124,000 in 1969, to 233,000 in 1971 and to 454,000 in 1973. However, of these the majority were council owned or owner-occupied dwellings, with little improvement taking place in the private rented sector where the worst houses were to be found. Though between 1969 and 1974 some 1.66 million houses were improved, with 900 general improvement areas declared, many grants were taken up by speculators who used the money to improve houses to make them attractive to middle class purchasers. The consequence was that the original inhabitants of an area could be gradually displaced by these wealthier purchasers, a process known as gentrification.

The Housing Act 1974 was designed, inter alia, to enshrine the policy commitment to improvement, to prevent gentrification and to concentrate resources where they were most required. Concentration of resources on private sector improvement was a principal feature of changes introduced by the Housing Act 1980. Between 1979 and 1984 the yearly totals for all the various grants payable in the private sector rose from 65.4 thousand to 229.6 thousand. At the same time yearly rates for renovation of public sector housing stock rose from 93.2 thousand to 105.4 thousand. [See further Chap. 4 by M. Gibson in *The Housing Crisis* (Ed. Malpass) to which the author acknowledges indebtedness.] Policy continues to concentrate resources on private sector improvement; nevertheless critics of housing policy have continued to argue that those who live in the very worst houses simply cannot afford to participate in the improvement programme, and thus the 'core' of bad housing conditions continues. Furthermore even those householders who can afford to do improvements, given grant aid, are dependent on how much money central government is prepared to devote to the improvement programme, and this is a figure that cannot be guaranteed.

In 1985 the government published *Home Improvements: A New Approach* Cmnd. 9153, a document designed to lead to reductions in public expenditure on improvement and to introduce means testing for grants. In brief the 1985 proposals were as follows:

1) Prime responsibility for housing maintenance and improvements should rest with owners.

2) Public investment is particularly justifiable, however, where either households are living in unhealthy or unsafe housing, or conditions

within an area are such as to discourage individual improvement initiatives or where occupiers are financially unable to meet the cost of requisite works. In consequence public investment should concentrate on aiding those without the capital or income resources to meet the cost of works, and so eligibility for assistance should be determined by an occupier's financial circumstances.

3) *Mandatory* ·grant aid should be given in respect of the worst dwellings for improvement *or* repair work necessary to make a dwelling 'fit' under a new standard of fitness, whereunder a dwelling would be 'fit' where, in the local authority's opinion, it is:

  (a) free of dangerous structural disrepair or instability;
  (b) free of dampness constituting a threat to the occupants;
  (c) adequately naturally lit and ventilated;
  (d) adequately provided with piped wholesome water within the dwelling;
  (e) adequately provided internally with food preparation and cooking facilities, including a sink with a hot and cold water supply;
  (f) provided with a WC suitably internally located for its occupants' exclusive use;
  (g) provided with a fixed bath or shower with a satisfactory hot and cold water supply;
  (h) serviced by an effective drainage system for foul, waste and surface water.

Additionally applicants for grants would have to be eligible for grant aid, and the local authority would have to be convinced of the appropriateness of renovation as a means of dealing with the dwelling.

4) *Discretionary* aid would be available in respect of reasonable repairs and improvements necessary to give dwellings a thirty year life span. The appropriate standard here would be that a dwelling should, after grant aid, be:

  (a) fit for human habitation;
  (b) in reasonable repair
  (c) provided with a wash hand basin with adequate hot and cold water;
  (d) satisfactorily electrically wired and lit;
  (e) adequately provided with heating facilities;
  (f) likely to have a useful life of thirty years.

Aid would be payably in the form of a loan, taken on an interest free but equity shared basis whereby the lender would take a charge on the dwelling proportional to its post-improvement value, the amount to be repaid being that proportion of the dwelling's eventual selling price.

5) Area action should be based on the concept of the *Housing Improvement Area*, declarable by local authorities according to criteria of size, dwelling condition, numbers of local authority dwellings, if any, to be included, the presence of social and environmental problems alongside housing stress, *and probably subject to a power of central governmental veto*. A Housing Improvement Area would act as the focus for co-ordinated area action, but the rules for determining grant assistance would be the same as elsewhere.

These proposals were received critically by many, see for example 'Home Improvement – a New Approach' the response of the Institution of Environmental Health Officers, and *The Housing Crisis* (Ed. Malpass) particularly Chapters 1, 2, 3, 4, and 6. Legislation is still awaited to implement these proposals: in the meantime the following problems continue to bedevil housing renewal policy.

1) The danger that renewal is seen as a cheap alternative to a major national programme of new house building.

2) The fact that grant aid is tied to the concept of the 'eligible expense' on the house. The poor need more help to improve their homes yet they do not receive it; for the poorer the quality of the house the more the householder has to meet from his own pocket. Such out of pocket contributions are way beyond the means of poorer people.

3) The expense and inconvenience of improvement are not reflected in a commensurate increase in the sale value of an improved house.

4) Resistance by private landlords, many of whom derive a substantial income from letting out houses in multiple occupation, and who stand to lose income if their properties are improved and converted into a smaller number of acceptable self-contained units of accommodation.

5) Ignorance and fear on the part of tenants, particularly where many are old or where there is a transient population, leading to a lack of demand for improvement.

6) The complexity and bureaucratic nature of the procedures required to bring about improvement.

7) The fact that areas ripe for improvement from a physical point of view are often socially unready for it because of:
   (a) local disbelief in continued governmental commitment to improvement policies, especially where the declaration of some form of area improvement has been followed by no action at all, which can happen because of the inadequate staff levels of the local authority;
   (b) racial tensions and jealousies;

(c) disinclination on the part of those who stay in such areas to spend any money on their houses, while those who would be prepared to invest are the socially mobile element of the population who are likely to move out to other more favoured localities.

8) The suspicion that improvement policy has become too 'area-orientated' and not enough concerned with improving the lot of those houses and households in the greatest need.

9) Insistence by some local authorities on over-high standards of improvement which daunt some would be improvers.

10) A reaction from inhabitants in improvement areas that the level of improvement and the associated environmental works are cosmetic improvements and irrelevant diversions from the *real* needs of the areas.

11) The high inflation rates of the early 1980s which sent the price of property repairs soaring.

12) The difficulty of finding reputable builders willing to undertake work under an area improvement scheme; a difficulty experienced particularly amongst the immigrant communities.

13) Continued difficulty experienced by local authorities in attracting building society mortgage finance into improvement areas.

14) The lack of a *comprehensive* and effective rehabilitation code.

15) The realisation that the policy of improvement can only work if sufficient resources are allotted to it.

16) The lack of a policy on renewal of public sector housing.

How many unsatisfactory houses are there?

It is impossible to state with certainty how many houses fail to meet acceptable standards. The law has many different standards by which a house can be judged, and different statistical sampling techniques produce different figures. The 1981 House Condition Survey discovered:
   (a) 18.1 million dwellings in England, of which 1.1 million were unfit, largely as a result of disrepair;
   (b) 0.9 million dwellings lacking basic amenities;
   (c) 1 million dwellings requiring repairs costing more than £7,000;
   (d) allowing for overlap between categories the total number of dwellings in poor condition was 2 million, though, on a lower

cost threshold for repairs of £2,500, the number rose to 4.3 million.

The 'Inquiry into the condition of the local authority housing stock in England in 1985' found:

(a) 4.5 million council dwellings of which,
  (i)   115,000 are pre 1919, with 83,000 needing repair work,
  (ii) 977,000 were built between 1919 and 1944, with 794,000 requiring repairs,
  (iii) 1,787,000 were built between 1945 and 1964, with 1,650,000 needing work,
  (iv) 1,530,000 are post 1964 with 1,185,000 needing work;
(b) The average cost of works is £5,000 per house.
(c) The backlog of repair costs is growing at a rate of £900 million p.a. according to the Audit Commission;
(d) In itemised cost terms the repairs needed £2,000 million plus for loadbearing walls, £2,500 million for doors and windows, £2,900 million for heating defects and £1,200 million for kitchen fittings.

Furthermore it must be remembered that, according to tenure and sector, a house in poor condition may be, in legal terms: unfit, but repairable at reasonable cost; unfit but *not* so repairable; fit, but needing substantial repairs; fit but lacking basic amenities; fit, but generally improvable; unfit, in a clearance area, but subject to rehabilitation; a substantial interference with the comfort of its occupying tenant; a statutory nuisance; statutorily overcrowded; fit, possessing all amenities, but needing some repairs under a landlord's obligation to repair, or possibly falling within a secure tenant's 'right to repair'; subject to the housing defects provisions of the 1985 Act, and, of course, many dwellings could fall within one or more classifications. Furthermore many of our housing standards are outmoded. There is an arguable need for a modern, comprehensive and integrated code of housing rehabilitation that takes into account a far wider range of factors, such as for example, housing use patterns and environmental conditions, in laying down requirements designed to secure wholesome and healthful housing for all. [See Hughes: 'Housing Repairs – A Suitable Case for Reform' [1984] JSWL p. 137.] Finally it must be remembered that housing improvement and repair are not 'once for all tasks', and that giving grant aid or taking area action at one point of time does not prevent the need for future expenditure on dwellings. A comprehensive renewal strategy should provide for periodic reviews of past improved dwellings to check whether *further grant aided work is needed*.

House renovation grants

General conditions as to availability

The pattern of grants generally is that they are percentage payments of those costs of improvement, etc., deemed to be eligible. Under Part XV and section 460 of the Housing Act 1985 local authorities (effectively district councils and London Boroughs) are under a duty to provide grants towards the cost of works required for:

1) the provision of dwellings by conversion;

2) the improvement of dwellings;

3) the repair of dwellings;

4) the improvement of houses in multiple occupation;

5) the improvement or repair of the common parts of a building containing one or more flats.

For the purposes of the Act by section 525 a 'dwelling' is a 'building or part of a building occupied or intended to be occupied as a separate dwelling, together with any yard, garden, outhouses . . . belonging to or usually enjoyed with that building or part'. Houses, flats and other buildings, used as residences, and also 'separate' in that they do not share living accommodation such as kitchens, are grant aidable.

Various sorts of grants are payable.

1) An improvement grant – a grant in respect of works required for the provision of a dwelling by the conversion of existing houses or other buildings, or for the improvement of a dwelling.

2) An intermediate grant – a grant in respect of the installation in a dwelling of standard amenities.

3) A special grant – a grant in respect of works required for the installation of standard amenities or the means of escape from fire in a house in multiple occupation.

4) A repair grant – a grant payable in respect of repairs or replacement not associated with improvement.

5) A common parts grant – a grant in respect of works of improvement or repair of common parts in a building containing flats.

In general, under section 462, applications for grants may not be entertained where:

1) the application is for an improvement grant in respect of works of conversion on a house or other building erected after 2 October 1961; or

2) the application is for *any* grant in respect of the improvement or repair of a dwelling provided after 2 October 1961; or

3) the application is for a common parts grant in respect of a building erected after 2 October 1961.

The Secretary of State has power to give directions as to circumstances in which local authorities may entertain such applications, see DoE Circular 21/80.

Other general conditions as to the availability of grants are listed below:

1) An application for a grant must, under section 461:
   (a) specify the premises to which it relates;
   (b) contain particulars of the works in respect of which the grant is sought and give an estimate of their cost, and
   (c) contain such other particulars as are ministerially specified, see DoE Circular 21/80.

2) An authority must not, under section 463 of the 1985 Act as amended by Schedule 3 of the Housing and Planning Act 1986, entertain a grant application, other than for a common parts grant, unless satisfied that the applicant has *either* an owner's interest, that is the fee simple, or a terms of years certain with at least five years unexpired (or alternatively he proposes to acquire such an interest) *or* a tenant's interest, that is a protected tenancy, protected occupancy, statutory tenancy, secure tenancy, a tenancy to which section 1 of the Landlord and Tenant Act 1954 applies with at least five years remaining unexpired, or any other tenancy prescribed by the Secretary of State, in the relevant land. Furthermore authorities may not entertain a tenant's application for an improvement grant in respect of works required to provide a dwelling. Section 463, however, has effect to sections 486 and 494 which relate to certain mandatory grants, see below. Under section 464A of the 1985 Act an application for a common parts grant must not be entertained unless the authority are satisfied, as regards the relevant works, that the applicant is *either*, first, under a duty to carry them out, *or*, second, has a power to do so *and* has a qualifying interest in the building or a dwelling therein, that is the fee simple, a term of years absolute with at least five years unexpired, a tenancy to which section 1 of the Landlord and Tenant Act 1954 applies, a protected tenancy, secure tenancy, protected occupancy, statutory tenancy, and other tenancy prescribed by the Secretary of State. In *either* case a required proportion of the dwellings in the building must be occupied by tenants, this proportion being three quarters, or such other figure prescribed or approved by the Secretary of State. This section was inserted in 1986.

3) A grant application may not be entertained where the relevant works are, or include, works relevant to a previously approved grant application, and the applicant is the person, or the personal representative of the person, who made that application, *save* where the relevant works have not been begun and *either* more than two years have gone by since approval of the previous application, *or* the latter application is made to take advantage of an order varying appropriate percentages for the purposes of determining the amount of grants, see section 461(3) and (4).

4) Authorities may not, under section 465, approve grant applications in respect of relevant works already begun, unless satisfied there were good reasons for anticipating approval.

5) The Secretary of State has power under section 466 to direct that applications for improvement, intermediate or common parts grants may not be approved without his consent.

The percentage of grant payable

Certain expenses of housing improvement and repair work are counted eligible for aid, the grant payable is a specified or 'appropriate' percentage of the eligible expense. Under section 509 of the 1985 Act, 'appropriate percentages' for determining amounts, or maximum amounts of grants, are specified by the Secretary of State with the consent of the Treasury and the approval of the House of Commons. See S.I. 1980/1735. Where a grant is discretionary, that is common parts grants, improvement grants and most special and repair grants, under section 510(b) authorities may fix a grant below the appropriate percentage. If they do so they must give the applicant a written statement of their reasons, as must they also under section 510(a) where *they disapprove a grant* application.

Certificates of future occupation

Applications for grants, other than special grants, may not be entertained unless the application is accompanied by a certificate of *either* owner-occupation or availability for letting under section 464 of the 1985 Act. The former is a certificate stating that the applicant *intends* that, on or before the first anniversary of the 'certified date' (that is the date certified by the authority as that date on which the dwelling first becomes fit for occupation after completion of relevant works, see section 499) and throughout the period of four years ensuing on that anniversary, the dwelling will be the only or main residence of, and will be occupied exclusively by either the applicant himself or a member of his family, or his grandparent or grandchild or his spouse. A similar certificate can be filed by the personal representatives of a deceased person on behalf of beneficiaries. A certificate of availability for letting is one stating that the certifier *intends* that throughout a period of five years beginning with the 'certified date' the dwelling will be let or available for letting as a residence, and not for a holiday, to persons other than members of the certifier's family, *or* the dwelling will be occupied, or available for occupation, by a member of the agricultural population in pursuance of a contract of service, and otherwise than as a tenant. An authority may refuse to entertain a tenant's application for grant aid unless it is accompanied by a certificate of availability for letting from a person who could have made an approvable owner's application.

The payment of grants

The payment of grants, or parts of grants, is conditional on the grant aided work being done to the satisfaction of the local authority. Under section 512(2) of the Housing Act 1985 a local authority may set a time limit of not less than twelve months within which the relevant grant aided works are to be carried out. Section 512(3) empowers them to allow further time for the doing of the work if they are satisfied that the work cannot be, or could not have been, carried out without the doing of additional works. Section 511(2) allows the payment of grants either in whole on the completion of the work or in instalments. Under section 511(3) where a grant is paid in instalments, the aggregate of instalments paid before completion must not at any time exceed:

1) in the case of an intermediate grant the appropriate percentage of the total cost of work so far executed; or

2) in the case of an improvement, special, repair or common parts grant an amount bearing to the total cost of works executed the same proportion as the fixed amount of the grant bears to the eligible expense.

Where an instalment of a grant is paid before the completion of the works, and they are not completed within the time specified, the instalment, and any other sums paid as part of the grant, becomes repayable on the demand of the local authority by the applicant, and carries interest fixed at a 'reasonable' level by the local authority under section 512(4).

Residence conditions

Section 499 of the Housing Act 1985 provides that where an application for an improvement, intermediate or repairs grant is approved, various conditions as to occupation will apply to the dwelling in question during the ensuring five years. In any case where a certificate of owner occupation was given it is a condition of the grant, under section 500, that:

1) throughout the first year of the initial period the dwelling will be occupied exclusively by, or be available for the exclusive occupation of, a 'qualifying person', and

2) if at any time during the subsequent years of the initial period the dwelling is not so occupied, it will at that time be let or available for letting *by* a 'qualifying person' as a residence, and not for a holiday, *to* persons other than members of his family.

'Qualifying persons' are defined by section 500(3) of the 1985 Act as follows:

1) the applicant for the grant;

2) any person deriving title to the dwelling through or under the applicant, for example a purchaser from the applicant;

3) a person who is a member of the applicant's family, or a grandparent or grandchild of the applicant or his spouse;

4) where the estate of a deceased 'qualifying person' is held by personal representatives or trustees, any person beneficially entitled to the estate under the will, intestacy or trust is also a 'qualifying person', and

5) the family, grandparents and grandchildren of such a beneficiary or of his spouse are also qualifying persons.

'Family' is defined by section 520(1) of the Housing Act 1985 as including spouses, sons and daughters, sons-in-law and daughters-in-law, parents and parents-in-law.

In any case where a certificate of availability for letting was given it is a condition of the grant, under section 501, that, *throughout* the initial period:

1) the dwelling will be let or available for letting as a residence, and not for a holiday, *by* a qualifying person *to* persons other than members of the family of that qualifying person; or

2) it will be occupied or available for occupation by a member of the agricultural population in pursuance of a contract of service and otherwise than as a tenant.

In this context 'qualifying person' includes the applicant himself, any person deriving title to the dwelling through or under the applicant *otherwise* than by a conveyance for value, together with the applicant's personal representatives, and beneficiaries, etc.

Thus where an owner-occupied house is grant aided the applicant can sell it without breaking the condition of his grant provided it remains a dwelling. A landlord who applies for grant aid is not given the same freedom.

Other grant conditions

Under section 503 of the 1985 Act, where an application for an improvement, intermediate or repairs grant is approved by a local authority they may impose certain conditions. If a house is comprised in a housing action area or general improvement area they must impose the specified conditions, save that in respect of an owner-occupied dwelling they may dispense with the conditions if they conclude it would be reasonable to do so in the special circumstances of the case. Neither can conditions be imposed where the grant relates to a dwelling:

1) in which a registered or co-operative housing association has an estate or interest; or

2) in respect of which a certificate of owner-occupation has been given *and* which has not at any time during the preceding period of twelve months been wholly or partly let for residential purposes, disregarding for this purpose any letting to the applicant or a member of his family, or a grandparent or grandchild of the applicant or his spouse; or

3) which is occupied or available for occupation by a member of the agricultural population in pursuance of a contract of service and otherwise than as a tenant; or

4) which is occupied by a person who is a protected occupier or statutory tenant under the Rent (Agriculture) Act 1976; or

5) where the application is by a tenant and it is not accompanied by a certificate of availability for letting.

Where conditions can, or must, be imposed, they are, under section 504, as follows:

1) that the dwelling will be let or available for letting on a regulated tenancy or a restricted contract under the Rent Act 1977;

2) that the grant aiding authority may require the owner of the dwelling to certify, within 21 days, that condition (1) above is satisfied;

3) that any tenant if so required will provide the owner with such

information as he may reasonably require to furnish the local authority with the above certificate;

4) where there is no rent registered, or no application or reference for one pending, that steps will be taken to register a rent;

5) where an application or reference for a registered rent has been made that it will be diligently proceeded with and not withdrawn;

6) that no premium shall be required as a condition of the grant, renewal or continuance of the lease or restricted contract as the case may be.

Enforcing the grant conditions

So long as a grant condition remains in force, under section 505 (a period of five years or seven years in the case of houses in housing action areas).

1) it binds any person other than a housing authority or registered housing association, who is for the time being the owner of the grant aided dwelling, and

2) is enforceable against all other persons having any interest in the dwelling.

Where a grant condition is broken the provisions of section 506 of the 1985 Act apply. This *empowers but does not oblige* a local authority to demand certain repayments in cases of breach. Where the grant was on a single dwelling the repayment is a sum equal to the grant with interest. Where the grant related to two or more buildings the sum payable is an amount equal to such part of the grant as relates to the dwelling where the breach has occurred. This also will bear interest. The repayment is due from the *owner* for the time of the dwelling in question. Local authorities are not obliged to demand repayment in respect of breaches of condition, they also have a discretion to demand less than their full entitlement.

Under section 507 of the 1985 Act where grant conditions are in force the owner or mortgagee of the affected dwelling may pay to the local authority the amount of the grant with interest and obtain the extinction of the conditions.

The individual grants

Improvement grants

The payment of improvement grants is controlled by section 470 of the

Housing Act 1985, under which, subject to certain conditions, local authorities may approve applications for such grants in such circumstances as they think fit. In general, under section 468, an application may not be approved unless they are satisfied that on completion of the relevant works the dwelling or dwellings in question will reach the required standard. To reach this standard a dwelling must:

1) have all the standard amenities for the exclusive use of its occupants, that is –
    (a) a fixed bath or shower,
    (b) a hot and cold water supply at a fixed bath or shower,
    (c) a wash hand basin,
    (d) hot and cold water supply at a wash hand basin,
    (e) a sink,
    (f) hot and cold water supply at a sink,
    (g) a water closet,
    (see section 508 of the Housing Act 1985);

2) be in reasonable repair (disregarding internal decoration) having regard to its age, character and locality;

3) conform with such requirements as are specified by the Secretary of State, these are that the dwelling must –
    (i)   be substantially free from damp,
    (ii)   have adequate natural lighting and ventilation,
    (iii) have adequate provision for artificial lighting and sufficient provision of electrical sockets,
    (iv) have adequate drainage facilities,
    (v)   be structurally stable,
    (vi) have satisfactory internal arrangements,
    (vii) have satisfactory facilities for preparing food,
    (viii) have adequate heating facilities,
    (ix) have proper provision for the storage of fuel and refuse,
    (x)   conform with thermal insulation standards.
(This is known as 'the ten point standard,' see DoE Circular No. 21/80, Appendix B, para. 41.)

4) be likely to provide satisfactory housing for a period of thirty years.

Rigid enforcement of the conditions precludes any improvement of property in very poor condition as the maximum grant aid would not meet the expense. Local authorities have discretion under section 468(3), (4) and (5) of the 1985 Act to reduce requirements as to the standard amenities, the requisite standard of repair, the ten point standard and the life expectancy of the building, particularly where they are satisfied than an applicant could not, without undue hardship, finance the cost of the works without the assistance of a grant.

In general under section 469 of the Housing Act 1985 improvement grants may only be approved on dwellings *below* a specified rateble value where the application is accompanied by a certificate of owner-occupation. The specified rateable values are fixed from time to time by the Secretary of State. Section 469(7) lays down that the rateable value restrictions are not to apply to dwellings in housing action areas, nor to applications in respect of a dwelling to be occupied by a disabled person where the relevant works are necessary to meet his particular needs.

An improvement grant may only be used to improve a house, not to repair it. Replacement of electrical wiring, for example, is repair unless carried out as a necessary part of a programme of improvement. Improvement is not renewal but a process of alteration and enlargement, such as providing extensions to give a house a bathroom or an adequate kitchen. Local authorities have a duty under section 471 of the 1985 Act to determine an amount of expense (the 'estimated expense') proper to the carrying out of improvement. Where part of the work is repair and replacement only 50 per cent of its estimated cost can be met by the local authority. The amount of grant payable following this calculation is determined under sections 472 and 473 of the 1985 Act. It will be the *'appropriate percentage'* (fixed from time to time) of the *'eligible expense'*, which is so much of the *'estimated expense'* as does not exceed the *'applicable limit'*. This limit is prescribed from time to time by the Secretary of State. The current limits depend on the geographical location of the dwelling, whether or not it is a listed building and whether or not it is provided by the conversion of a building of three or more storeys. See S.I. 1980/1736 and S.I. 1981/1461.

Intermediate grants

Intermediate grants are paid to secure the provision of standard amenities. Local authorities are required under sections 474, 475 and 479 of the 1985 Act to pay such grants if an application is made in due form. An application must:

1) specify the amenity or amenities to be provided;

2) where only some amenities are to be provided, state whether the dwelling is already provided with the remainder;

3) state, with respect to each amenity to be provided, whether, to the best knowledge of the applicant, the dwelling has been lacking that amenity for a preceding period of not less than twelve months. An application cannot be approved unless the dwelling has been without the amenity in question for a period of not less than twelve months, *or*

unless, though the amenity is present, other relevant works involve unavoidable interference with, or the replacement of, the amenity.

An application for an intermediate grant may not be approved, under section 476, unless the local authority are satisfied that:

1) on completion of the relevant works the dwelling or dwellings in question will be fit for human habitation under section 604 of the Housing Act 1985; or

2) it seems reasonable in the circumstances to approve the application even though the dwelling or dwellings will not reach that standard on completion of the works.

Under section 478 of the 1985 Act where the relevant works in an application for an intermediate grant include works of repair or replacement which, in the opinion of the local authority, go beyond those needed to put the dwelling into reasonable repair, having regard, under section 519, to its age, character, locality and life expectancy, the authority may, with the consent of the applicant, vary the application so that the relevant works:

1) are confined to works *other* than those of repair or replacement, or

2) include only those works of repair and replacement as are necessary for the reasonable repair of the dwelling.

The amount of grant payable is determined by section 480 of the 1985 Act. The local authority must first determine the cost of installing the relevant amenity or amenities and also the proper cost of repairs and replacements. The eligible expense for an intermediate grant is the aggregate of so much of the estimated expense determined in respect of the provision of standard amenities, as does not exceed the total of the sums allowed under section 508 of the 1985 Act *plus* so much of the estimated expense determined in respect of works of repair and replacement subject to expense limits specified from time to time by the Secretary of State, and varying according to the likely condition of the dwelling after completion of the works, the circumstances of the applicant, the location of the dwelling, etc. [See Pollard, *Social Welfare Law* Appendix F7.]

The actual amount of the grant will then be the appropriate percentage of the eligible expense, notification of which must be sent to the applicant under section 482.

Special grants

Special grants are payable in respect of a house in multiple occupation, which is defined by section 525 of the 1985 Act as 'a house which is occupied by persons who do not form a single household, *exclusive* of any part thereof which is occupied as a separate dwelling by persons who do form a single household'. Where, for example, a family occupy part of a house and do not share any 'living accommodation' with the other inhabitants of the house, their home should be distinguished as a separate entity, and, on the basis of being a separate dwelling, qualifies for an intermediate grant in its own right.

Section 487 of the 1985 Act makes the payment of special grants discretionary, save that section 486 makes mandatory grants for:

1) complying with a notice under section 352 of the Housing Act 1985 in so far as it relates to standard amenities, or

2) complying with a notice served under section 366 of the Housing Act 1985 (means of escape from fire).

Under section 484 of the Act of 1985 an application for a special grant must state:

1) the number of households and individuals occupying the house in question.

2) the standard amenities already provided;

3) the existing means of escape from fire.

Save in the cases of mandatory grants, an application cannot be approved, under section 485, unless the local authority are satisfied that the completion of the works will bring the house up to a reasonable standard of repair having regard to its age, character and locality. Any proposed works that would exceed that standard may be struck out of the application by the local authority with the consent of the applicant.

The amount of a special grant is determined by sections 488, 489 and 490 of the 1985 Act. The local authority must first determine the proper expense of:

1) providing standard amenities;

2) providing means of escape from fire; and

3) any works of repair and replacement.

In relation to a mandatory special grant the amount will be the appropriate percentage of the eligible expense determined by aggregating:

1) so much of the cost of providing standard amenities as does not exceed the sum of the amounts specified in section 508(1) of the 1985 Act, allowing for the installation of more than one of any of the standard amenities;

2) the cost of providing means of escape from fire up to a specified amount;

3) the cost of works of repair and replacement up to a specified amount.

The 'specified amounts' are prescribed from time to time by the Secretary of State.

In the case of a discretionary special grant the amount is left to be fixed by the local authority.

Repair grants

Sections 494 and 495 of the 1985 Act give local authorities discretion to make repair grants, but a mandatory repair grant is payable in respect of an application made by a person subject to an order under sections 189 and 190 of the Housing Act 1985 (e.g. a house capable of being made fit at reasonable expense). Nor in such cases need any certificate of future occupation be given. Before exercising their discretion a local authority must, under section 491, be satisfied:

1) that the relevant works are of a substantial and structural character, or that they satisfy other centrally prescribed requirements;

2) that the dwelling is 'old' as defined by the Secretary of State, under section 492, that is erected before 1 January 1919 (S.I. 1982/1205);

3) that in the case of an owner-occupied dwelling situated *outside* a housing action area that it falls, under section 492(2), within prescribed rateable value limits;

4) that, under section 493, on completion of the relevant works the dwelling will attain a reasonable standard of repair having regard to its age, character and locality.

Section 493(2) gives local authorities power to pay repair grants only in respect of those works necessary in their opinion to bring the dwelling up to a reasonable standard.

The amount of a repair grant is determined under sections 496, 497 and 498 of the Housing Act 1985. The local authority must first determine the proper cost of the relevant work. The eligible expense for the purpose of a repair grant must not exceed the sums specified by the Secretary of State. The actual amount of the grant will be:

1) in the case of a mandatory repairs grant the appropriate percentage, as fixed, of the eligible expense, or

2) in other cases a sum to be fixed by the local authority.

The Secretary of State has power under sections 516 and 517 of the 1985 Act to make contributions to grants. The sum, payable annually for twenty years, is equal to the relevant percentage of annual loan charges attributable to the amount of the grant. The relevant percentage may be found specified in orders made by the Secretary of State.

Common parts grants

Sections 498 A to G of the 1985 Act give local authorities discretion to make common parts grants, provided that the relevant building falls within rateable value limits specified by the Secretary of State (save where the building is in a Housing Action Area) and provided they are satisfied that, on completion of the works, the common parts of the building will be in 'reasonable repair'. This is determined under section 519(2) of the Act by having regard to the age, character and locality of the building, the character of the dwellings in it and the period during which they are likely to be residentially, available. Works for which a grant is available are those in connection with the improvement or repair of a building's 'common parts' (i.e. its structure and exterior and common facilities) where the building contains one or more 'flats' (i.e. dwellings which are separate sets of premises divided horizontally from some other part of the building). Works in connection with *providing* a dwelling may not be grant aided under these powers. The authority must determine and estimate the proper costs of the relevant works, and the eligible expense for a grant is so much of that estimated expense as does not exceed the 'prescribed amount' (i.e. a sum prescribed from time to time by the Secretary of State). The actual amount of the grant will be fixed by the authority when they approve the grant application, but it must not exceed the appropriate percentage of the eligible expense. These sections were inserted in 1986.

Defective housing aid

Part XVI of the 1985 Act, replacing The Housing Defects Act 1984, is designed to deal with the consequences of houses of certain public sector housing types with severe inherent structural weaknesses *having passed into private ownership*, frequently under the right to buy provisions. A person is eligible under section 527 of the 1985 Act where he is an individual (other than a trustee or a personal representative), whose dwelling, in which he holds a 'relevant interest', is designated as being defective, and where he satisfies criteria of eligibility. The

Secretary of State may, under section 528, designate classes of buildings defective by reason of design or construction, and whose value is substantially reduced in consequence of these defects becoming known. Designation must describe the qualifying defect, and may be varied or revoked. Local authorities have discretion under section 559 et seq to make local designation schemes, but little use seems to be made of this power. Qualifying 'relevant interests' under section 530 are freeholds, long leaseholds, effectively those granted for more than twenty-one years, provided neither such interest is itself subject to a 'long tenancy'; secure tenancies are not 'long tenancies' for the purposes of the provision. Furthermore certain criteria of eligibility under sections 531 and 532 must be satisfied. Thus a public sector authority (see section 573(1) but *including* local authorities, and registered housing associations other than co-operative associations) must have disposed of a 'relevant interest' in the dwelling and *either*

1) that disposal was made *before* the 'cut-off date' (that is a date specified in the designation) *and* there has been no subsequent disposal for value of a relevant interest in the dwelling by any person since that date; *or*

2) that the person eligible for assistance under section 527 acquired a relevant interest on a disposal occuring within a twelve month period beginning with the cut-off date, *and* he was unaware on the disposal date of the association of the dwelling with the qualifying defect, *and* the price on disposal did not reflect that association, *and* if the cut off date had fallen immediately *after* the disposal date, Condition (1) above would have been satisfied. Furthermore there is no eligibility for assistance when the interest of the applicant is subject to the rights of a protected occupier or statutory tenant under the Rent (Agriculture) Act 1976, nor where the local housing authority conclude that satisfactory remedial work has been done to the dwelling in order to deal with the relevant defect.

An application for aid must, under section 534, be made in writing within a period specified in the designation, but it may not be entertained where an application for other grant aid relevant to the defect has been made, unless that application has been refused, withdrawn, or where the relevant works have been completed. The local housing authority, effectively a district council or London Borough council, must determine *eligibility* for aid. Where no eligibility is found reasons must be given. Where an applicant *is* eligible, they must additionally notify him that he may make a claim under section 537(2), i.e. that aid by way of a reinstatement grant is inappropriate because it would not be reasonable to expect him to secure the carrying out of remedial work, and that repurchase is the appropriate course of action. It is, however, for the authority to determine whether an eligible applicant is to be aided by way of repurchase or reinstatement grant. To qualify for a reinstatement grant: the dwelling must, under section 538, be a *house* that, after reinstatement work, would be likely to provide satisfactory accommodation for at least thirty years *and* which would be mortgageable; the grant must be justifiable having regard to its amount and the likely vacant possession value after reinstatement; the amount of the grant must be unlikely to exceed the aggregate of the price payable on acquisition of the applicant's interest under Part XVI and the sum by way of reimbursement of expenses incidental to repurchase under section 552.

Where an applicant is eligible for aid, under section 540 the authority must give him notice as soon as reasonably practicable stating the form of assistance he is entitled to. Where assistance is to be by way of grant the notice must state: the reasons for the determination; the necessary works and the proper expenditure thereon; an estimate of the amount of grant payable and the condition required under section 542 that the work must be executed to the authority's satisfaction within a specified period. Assistance by way of repurchase is available in all cases where assistance is not by way of grant.

Reinstatement grants cover, under sections 539 and 541, qualifying works, i.e. those works stated in the section 540 notice and 'associated arrangements', i.e. arrangements entered into in connection with relevant works and likely to contribute towards a dwelling's mortgageability. The *amount* of grant payable, under section 543, is the appropriate percentage, as specified by the Secretary of State, of whichever is the *least* of the amount stated in the section 540 notice as the authority's determination of the proper costs of executing qualifying works and making associated arrangements, *or* expenditure actually incurred in doing the works, etc, *or* the sum specified by the Secretary of State as the maximum, allowable expenditure. Under section 545 grants may be paid as single sums or in instalments.

Where assistance is by way of repurchase, Schedule 20 of the 1985 Act applies as to the terms of the repurchase agreement, the price payable and valuation, etc. Where an authority acquire an interest in a defective dwelling by way of repurchase and an individual is an occupier (i.e. a person who occupies it as his only or principal home) of the dwelling throughout the period beginning with the application for assistance and ending immediately before acquisition, and he is a person entitled to assistance by way of repurchase, under section 554 the authority must grant, or arrange for the grant of, a tenancy to him of the dwelling in question, or another appropriately suitable dwelling under section 556 where either the original dwelling may not be safely occupied residentially or the authority intend demolition or other work of reconstruction within a reasonable time of acquisition. But, under section 557 of the 1985 Act, such a grant is not required unless the person aided requests one in writing *before* the service on the person entitled to assistance of the agreement drawn up under Schedule 20 embodying the provisions agreed to be included in the repurchase agreement. [See generally DoE Circulars 28/84 and 14/86.]

Area improvement

The Housing Act 1964 allowed the declaration of 'improvement areas', a concept developed by the 1969 Act as 'general improvement areas'. The 1974 Act created housing action areas, and general improvement areas.

Housing action areas

Housing action areas (HAAs) are areas unsuitable for slum clearance, but where overcrowding and housing stress are acute. The object is that improving action should be fast and concentrated.

Under section 239 of the 1985 Act where a report on an area of housing is submitted to a local authority (that is a district council, a London Borough, and the Common Council of the City of London) by a suitably qualified person (whether or not employed by them) upon their considering it, together with other information, having regard to the physical condition of the housing in and the social conditions of the area, they may resolve to declare the area a HAA and so define it on a map. Such an area can only be declared where the authority are satisfied that within five years their resolution will lead to the improvement of and the proper and effective management and use of housing in the area, and the well being of the residents.

Local authorities are required to have regard to guidance given by the Secretary of State. Such guidance is contained in Department of the Environment Circular No. 14/75. This is especially relevant in relation to the content of the report preceding the resolution. Information should be given about the number of houses in multiple occupation, and hostels in the area, categorised by age, unfitness, lack of amenities, state of repair, rateable value and tenure; the number of households in the area, categorised as above; the presence in an area of significant numbers of persons suffering from social problems such as age, unemployment, ethnic disadvantage, being a single parent, or having a large family; any other special problem of the area, such as harassment, eviction and the numbers of children taken into care; recent changes in housing conditions, improvement grants taken up, planning permission applications and registered rent levels.

The circular also contains guidance on how a local authority should consider the accommodation and social conditions within a potential HAA. Consideration of both is important because the conjunction of bad housing conditions with other social problems and stresses is the indication of the need to declare a HAA. Local authorities should consider the proportion of houses lacking the standard amenities, those that are statutorily unfit or badly laid out, the number of households sharing living and other accommodation, the numbers of households living at a density of more than one and a half persons to a room, the proportion of households in privately rented accommodation, together with the level of 'social problem' households, such as the ill or old, the unemployed or low paid, and the single parent or large families.

Circular No. 14/75 counsels local authorities to consider whether there are sufficient resources to carry through their plan before declaring a HAA. 'Sufficient resources' means the authority's own resources in financial and manpower terms, the resources of local housing associations and the local building industry together with accommodation outside the HAA available to rehouse any persons who may have to be temporarily or permanently displaced. Consideration should be paid to the size of the proposed HAA. There is no 'right' size for a HAA. Much depends upon physical conditions in different localities. The circular suggests an upper limit of 200–300 houses, only to be exceeded for good reason. Circular No. 14/75 states that it is not appropriate to declare a HAA which contains estates or a significant number of houses owned by the local authority.

The procedure for declaring a housing action area

After declaring a HAA the local authority must, under section 240 as amended in 1986:

1) publish in two or more local newspapers notice of the resolution identifying the area and naming a place where a copy of the resolution and the map and report can be inspected during reasonable hours;

2) take such further steps as will secure that the resolution is brought to the notice of affected owners and residents, and ensuring that such persons know where any inquiry or representation regarding the proposed action may be made;

3) send the Secretary of State a copy of the resolution, map and report, together with their proposals to deal with the area;

4) register the declaration as a local land charge.

Under section 241 the Secretary of State may, within 28 days of acknowledging receipt of the proposals, cancel or confirm the resolution, or state that he requires more time to consider it or he may exclude land from the area. Once the Secretary of State makes his decision the local authority must publish it in at least two local newspapers and notify affected owners and residents. Once declared and confirmed an HAA lasts for five years, with the possibility of a further extension of two years, though it may be determined at any time during its currency by a resolution made and published in due form, see sections 239(4), 250 and 251 of the Housing Act 1985.

The consequences of the declaration

Once the HAA is in being the local authority is given a number of powers and duties to enable it to secure its objects.

1) Under section 246 of the Housing Act 1985 they have a duty to bring to the attention of owners and residents details of their proposed action, and information as to the assistance available for the improvement of housing in the area.

2) They may be authorised to acquire land on which is situated living accommodation within the HAA, compulsorily or by agreement, for the purpose of improving the housing and social conditions in the area as a whole, see section 243. An authority may only be authorised to acquire land they presently require, though they do not have to proceed with acquisition should that need disappear by virtue of an owner carrying out voluntary works of improvement, see *Varsani v Secretary of State for the Environment* (1980) 40 P & CR 354.

3) Section 243(3)(a) applies to land acquired and allows the local authority, subject to the consent of the Secretary of State under section 431, to provide housing accommodation by construction, conversion or improvement, and also to improve or repair houses, to manage houses and to provide furniture, fittings and services in relation to housing accommodation. Strict control over the conversion and improvement of dwellings by housing authorities can be maintained by the Secretary of State under section 431 of the 1985 Act which gives him power to prohibit the incurring of expense on conversion and improvement except in accordance with plans he has approved.

4) Section 244 empowers local authorities, in order to improve the amenities of a HAA, to carry out on land belonging to them works other than those to the interior of housing accommodation, or to give assistance to others to carry out such environmental works. Section 245 allows the Secretary of State to make contributions to the carrying out

of such works of sums equal to one half of the annual loan charges referable to expenditure on the works for a period of twenty years subject to an upper limit for any given HAA of £400 × the number of dwelling-houses, houses in multiple occupation and hostels in the area. Under these provisions local authorities may initiate 'enveloping schemes', i.e. programmes of renovation of the *exteriors* of dwellings requiring more than routine maintenance, done on a block or terrace basis to achieve economies of scale, with the *consent* of the dwellings' owners, but at no cost to them. Exchequer contributions are available for such programmes, though those containing anything but small numbers of local authority dwellings are not acceptable to central government, see further DoE Circular 29/82.

5) Under section 247 landlords of houses in HAAs are under a duty to inform the local authority, within seven days, of any notice to quit. In the case of a tenancy due to expire by effluxion time a similar notice must be served at least four weeks before the tenancy expires. Owners of land intending to dispose of such property must given notice to the local authority not less than four weeks nor more than six months before the disposal is carried out. The authority must acknowledge receipt of the notification and state, within four weeks, what action they propose to take. The object of this provision is to enable the local authority to keep a constant check on vacant premises so that, if necessary, they can obtain the property and use it for the benefit of the HAA.

A failure to comply with section 247 is an offence punishable with a fine of up to £400. In *Fawcett v Newcastle-upon-Tyne City Council* (1977) 34 P & CR 83 it was claimed that where a notice to quit was invalid there was no necessity for notification. This was rejected: invalidity is no defence to a prosecution under this provision.

General improvement areas

General improvement areas (GIAs) are declared under section 253 of the Housing Act 1985. The procedure is very similar to that for declaring an HAA, save that ministerial controls are removed. No central approval is required for the declaration of a GIA. A local authority must, under section 254, publish notice of their resolution to declare a GIA in local newspapers, take steps to inform property owners and residents and forward a copy of the resolution to the minister. The difference between the types of improvement areas is that GIAs are restricted to 'predominantly residential areas'. An area including a few shops, offices or factories is not excluded, but the declaration of a GIA is not appropriate within a badly run down area.

Neither may a GIA include any land in a clearance area unless it has already been cleared of buildings, nor any land comprised in a HAA, though a GIA may surround either a clearance area or a HAA, see section 253(2) and (3) of the Housing Act 1985. The general characteristics of a GIA should be those laid down in *Better Homes: The Next Priorities*, Cmnd. 5339. The area should be one of older residential property, free from housing stress, where the physical condition of the property is fundamentally sound and where the houses are capable of providing good living conditions for many years. A GIA should also be an area where house owners are likely to take the initiative in leading the improvement drive. Once declared the GIA is operative until the local authority cancel it, see the Housing Act 1985, s. 258.

The effect of a general improvement area

Local authorities have a number of powers and duties in relation to such areas.

1) Section 257 of the Housing Act 1985 places a duty on local authorities to inform owners and occupiers in the GIA of their proposals to secure the improvement of the amenities of the area and of the assistance available towards the improvement of dwellings.

2) Under section 255 they may acquire land compulsorily or by agreement, and may carry out works on the land or let it or otherwise dispose of it. They may also assist, by making grants or loans or otherwise, in the carrying out of works on land they do not own. They may not use these powers to improve dwellings acquired or provided under other statutory provisions.

3) Section 256 enables them to improve the amenities of a GIA by closing a highway to traffic and carrying out improvements to it such as landscaping.

4) Section 259 allows the Secretary of State to make contributions towards the costs of works carried out by local authorities in GIAs. The sums payable are calculated in a similar way to contributions towards costs incurred in a HAA. [*See Addendum 15.*]

Compulsory improvement

The compulsory improvement powers exist in HAAs and GIAs, and tenants have power to initiate the process in relation to dwellings outside such areas.

Section 210 of the 1985 Act gives local authorities power to serve a 'provisional notice' on the person having control (that is the owner-occupier, or owner or long lessee) of a dwelling within an HAA or GIA if, under section 209 the dwelling:

1) is without one or more of the standard amenities, whether or not it is also in a state of disrepair;

2) was provided before 3 October 1961, and

3) is capable at reasonable expense of improvement to *either* the full or reduced standard. These standards are contained in section 234. The 'full' standard is that a house must: be provided with all standard amenities for its occupants' exclusive use; be in reasonable repair considering its age, character and locality; conform with thermal insulation specifications; be in all other respects fit for human habitation, and be likely to be available as a dwelling for a period of 15 years. The 'reduced' standard is applied where the local housing authority dispense with any of the foregoing requirements and a dwelling satisfies those remaining, save that the requirement as to standard amenities may not be dispensed with where the dwelling is one to which section 352 applies, i.e. in a HMO where the authority has power to require execution of works to render the premises fit for its *number of occupants*.

No notice can be served in respect of a house owned by a local authority, the Commission for the New Towns, the Housing Corporation, a registered housing association, a development corporation, a housing charity trust; nor in respect of a house owned by the Crown or Duchies of Lancaster and Cornwall, except with the consent of those three authorities, see section 232 of the Housing Act 1985. There are further restrictions on the service of notices in respect of *owner-occupied* dwellings. They may not be made subject to notices unless their improvement is necessary for the improvement of an adjacent dwelling which is not owner-occupied, or for which a grant is being given under Part XV of the 1985 Act, see section 210(2).

The provisional notice must specify the works which the local authority consider necessary to bring the house up to standard, and must also state a date, not less than 21 days after service of the notice, time and place at which their proposals, any alternative proposals, temporary or permanent rehousing arrangements, and the views of the occupying tenant (if any) may be discussed. A copy of the notice must be served on any occupying tenant and every other person having an interest in the dwelling (see section 213). All are entitled to be heard when the proposals are discussed, and their views taken into account. Any rehousing arrangements must be formally agreed by the parties in writing. A permanently displaced occupier has rehousing rights under section 39(1)(d) of the Land Compensation Act 1973.

Under section 211 of the 1985 Act the local authority may accept an undertaking from the person having control of the dwelling to bring it up to standard. The undertaking must specify the necessary works and a period, generally nine months, within which they must be done. The local authority must be satisfied as to the housing arrangements for any occupying tenant, who must also consent to the work in writing. Where no such undertaking is accepted or where an undertaking is not fulfilled an improvement notice may be served, under section 214 of the Housing Act 1985, within nine months of the service of the provisional notice where no undertaking has been accepted, or within six months of a failure to fulfil an undertaking. Such a notice cannot be served unless the local authority are satisfied that the dwelling is still subject to area action, that it still lacks one or more standard amenities, and is capable of being brought up to standard at reasonable expense, that it is not owner-occupied, that there are satisfactory housing arrangements for the occupying tenant, and that the occupying tenant has not unreasonably refused to enter into any such arrangements.

The improvement notice must, under section 216 of the 1985 Act, specify the required works, give an estimate of the cost and require execution within a period of twelve months. The notice must be specific as to works, it is not enough to simply require 'provision' of each item in the list of standard amenities, see *Canterbury City Council v Bern* [1981] JPL 749. In *Harrington v Croydon Corpn* [1968] 1 QB 856, [1967] 3 All ER 929 it was held that the works required may include an extension to the dwelling. Section 217 gives a six weeks right to appeal to the county court to the person having control of the dwelling, an occupying tenant or any other person with an interest in the dwelling. There are various grounds of appeal.

1) That the requirements of the notice cannot be met at reasonable expense. What constitutes 'reasonable expense' is not defined in the Act. In *FFF Estates Ltd v Hackney London Borough Council* [1981] QB 503, [1981] 1 All ER 32, the Court of Appeal held that a realistic approach to the value of dwelling-houses as saleable assets in the hands of landlords had to be taken when considering the reasonableness of the expense required to improve them. Regard must be had to the presence of tenants and their rights of continued occupation, and the effect this has on market value. The Court also held that where the occupants of a dwelling shared the use of one or more standard amenities with the occupants of another dwelling, that dwelling was 'without one or more of the standard amenities' within the meaning of section 212 of the 1985 Act. This entitles the local authority to serve

an improvement notice, though it may be contested on the issue of 'reasonable expense'.

2) That the local authority has unreasonably refused to agree to the execution of alternative works.

3) That the dwelling is in a clearance area.

4) That the dwelling no longer lacks standard amenities.

5) That the works specified will not bring the dwelling up to standard.

6) That some other person will derive a benefit from the work, and so ought to pay all or part of the cost.

7) That the improvement notice is invalid for want of formality, though in this case the notice may only be quashed if it has resulted in substantial prejudice to the appellant. In *De Rothschild v Wing RDC* [1967] 1 All ER 597, [1967] 1 WLR 470 it was held that an owner who was ordered to do work he was not legally bound to do was 'substantially prejudiced'.

If the period stipulated in the improvement notice elapses without the work being carried out, or if the person on whom the notice was served notifies the local authority that he is unwilling or unable to do the work, or if they are not satisfied following due inquiry that the work will be completed in the specified time, the local authority may, under section 220 of the Housing Act 1985, do the work themselves, and may, under Schedule 10, recover their reasonable expenses from the person having control of the dwelling.

Section 228 of the 1985 Act enables a person who is under an obligation to carry out improvements by reason of an improvement notice or undertaking to apply for a loan from the local authority to pay for the works. If they are satisfied he is able to repay the loan, that his interest in the dwelling will last for as long as the loan is made, and that the dwelling is adequate security for the loan, they must make it. No loan can be made for any part of the expenditure to be met by an improvement or intermediate grant. Alternatively under section 227 a person having control of a dwelling, who has been served with an improvement notice, may require the local authority, within six months of the notice becoming operative, to purchase his interest. The dwelling will be treated as having been acquired compulsorily under Part II of the Housing Act 1985.

Compulsory improvement outside improvement areas

An occupying tenant of a dwelling which:

1) is not in a GIA or HAA; and

2) is without one or more standard amenities, whether or not it is also in a state of disrepair, and

3) was provided before 3 October 1961,

may write to the local authority requesting them to take action under section 212 of the Housing Act 1985. They must notify the person having control of the dwelling of any representation made. They must take the representations of the tenant into account and decide:

1) whether the representations come from an occupying tenant;

2) whether the dwelling is outside any form of area action, is lacking any standard amenities, and was provided before 3 October 1961;

3) whether the dwelling is capable at reasonable expense of improvement;

4) whether, having regard to all the circumstances, the dwelling ought to be improved, and whether it is unlikely to be improved unless they use their compulsory powers.

They must then decide either:

1) to serve on the person having control of the dwelling a provisional notice, in which case the compulsory improvement procedure described above begins, or

2) to notify the occupying tenant that they do not intend to serve such a notice, giving him their written reasons for the decision.

The phrase 'occupying tenant' is defined by section 236(2) as meaning a person who is *not* an owner-occupier, but who occupies a dwelling by virtue of a lease, statutory tenancy, restricted contract or because of agricultural employment. (See generally *FFF Estates Ltd v Hackney London Borough Council,* above.)

Further reading

Cullingworth, J.B., *Essays on Housing Policy* (Allen and Unwin, 1979) Chap. 5.
Hadden, T., *Compulsory Repair and Improvement* (Centre for Socio-Legal Studies, Wolfson College, Oxford, 1978).
Monck, E., and Lomas, G., *Housing Action Areas: Success and Failure* (Centre for Environment Studies, 1980).
Paris, C., and Blackaby, B., *Not Much Improvement* (Heinneman, 1979).
Rowland, J., *Community Decay* (Penguin, 1973).

Arden, A., and Partington, P., *Housing Law* (Sweet & Maxwell, 1983) Chap. 14.

Malpas, P. (Ed), *The Housing Crisis* (Croom Helm, 1986) Chaps. 1–4, 6.

Home Improvements: A New Approach Cmnd. 9153.

Niner, P., and Forrest, R., *Housing Action Area Policy and Progress: The Residents' Perspective* University of Birmingham (CURBS 1982).

Social Welfare Law (Ed. by D.W. Pollard) (Oyez Longman) paras. C. 3126–C. 3160, C. 4445–C. 4734 and F. 2601–F. 2976.

Karn, V., and Whittle, B., 'Birmingham's Urban Cosmetics', *Roof* November 1978, pp. 163–164.

Paris, C., 'Housing Action Areas' *Roof*, January 1977, pp. 9–14.

Wintour, J., and Franey, R., 'Are Improvement Grants Tied Up in the Town Halls?', *Roof* May 1978, pp. 81–83.

Wintour, J., and Van Dyke, S., 'Housing Action Areas: But Where's the Action', *Roof* July 1977, pp. 105–113.

'Housing in Housing Action Areas', *Roof* September 1979, pp. 151–153.

Hughes, D., 'Housing Repairs – A Suitable Case for Reform' (1984) JSWL p. 137.

Short, J.R., and Bassett, K.A., 'Housing policy and the inner city in the 1970s' Institute of British Geographers 'Transactions' NS Vol. 16, (1981), pp. 293–312.

Perry, J., and Gibson, M., 'Pause for Renewal' *Roof* July/August 1981, p. 23.

Sills, A., Taylor, G. and Golding, P., 'Where the Money Goes' *Roof* July/August 1983, p. 23.

Perry, J., 'What Boom?' *Roof* November/December 1983, p. 25.

Fielding, N., 'The Next Step in the Improvement Grant Fox-Trot' *Roof* July/August 1984, p. 19.

Chapter 11

Multi-occupancy and overcrowding

Introduction

Multi-occupation and overcrowding occur together in sufficient cases to convey an impression that they are always associated evils. In fact, as has been shown by David Smith and Anne Whalley in *Racial Minorities and Public Housing* (PEP Broadsheet No. 556) p. 99, the problem of overcrowding is not restricted to multi-occupied dwellings, nor even primarily associated with them. Nor should it be assumed that conditions in all multi-occupied houses are necessarily bad. Nevertheless it is the case that a combination of poor amenities and overcrowding is nowadays most often found in multi-occupied houses. This must always be born in mind even though it must also be remembered that not every multi-occupied house is overcrowded, and that overcrowding can occur even in a single small one-family dwelling-house.

Multi-occupation and overcrowding can arise for totally different reasons in different areas of varying housing types. In the past the typically overcrowded house was the small 'two-up-and-two-down' house situated in industrial towns and cities. Frequently such houses stood together in yards, courts or terraces and shared lavatories and water supplies with other similar houses. They were overcrowded either because of the sexual composition of the families occupying them, with brothers and sisters frequently having to share bedrooms until the eldest ones left home to get married, or because the houses were simply too small to be able to accommodate properly the large families occupying them. The law relating to overcrowding was developed primarily to deal with situations of the above kind. In our own day the nature of the problem has altered. Anyone who is familiar with the urban geography of the nation will be aware that one of the great unanswered problems of housing policy is what to do with the very large Victorian and Edwardian houses found in inner suburban areas.

These large, old and once proud houses are obviously ripe for conversion into multi-occupation. Where the conversion is sympathetically and well done the result is the provision of much useful accommodation. However, unscrupulous owners have indulged far too often in unsatisfactory divisions, failing to provide proper cooking and sanitary facilities, and frequently resorting to overcrowding the individual units of accommodation provided as a way of extracting the maximum financial return from their properties. The result has been the production of squalor. It is in properties such as these that multi-occupation and over-crowding occur together. [See further Cullingworth, *Essays on Housing Policy* p. 65.]

Local authorities have many powers available to combat such unsatisfactory housing conditions. These powers confer a great deal of discretion on authorities, and their use is, in any case, subject to two major constraints:

1) a lack of staff and other resources necessary to implement the powers fully;

2) the fact that an energetic use of the available powers usually means a reduction of overcrowding and the closing of houses which cannot be brought up to the required legal standards, leading to increased demands upon the already limited stock of municipal housing.

An authority making the fullest use of its powers to combat both over-crowding and multi-occupation would have to accept either an increase in its housing waiting list or a cut back in its clearance programme. Few authorities are prepared to accept such consequences. So the problems continue, frequently exacerbated by administrative systems which separate public health supervision of multi-occupied houses and housing management and allocation into distinct departments with little liaison between the two. It must also be admitted that the law relating to these issues has traditionally been negative in its approach to the problems. There has been little articulation in the past of a legal policy to encourage good quality conversions. However, as we have seen the amendments to the law relating to special grants for houses in multiple occupation made by the Housing Act 1980 did go some way to rectifying this omission. The existence of purely negative powers of control has encouraged local authorities to take little action because these powers, by their very nature, offer little or no way of transforming the worst multi-occupied properties into acceptable accommodation. They can, of course, prevent the use of such properties for accommodation purposes but this only leads to increased housing demand being placed on the already overstretched public sector of housing.

The size of the problem

In 1983 The Shelter National Housing Aid Trust bulletin reported the existence of over 120,000 houses in multiple occupation (HMOs) in England, of which it was claimed 85 per cent needed remedial action under housing legislation. In 1986 The Department of the Environment concluded there were 127,000 HMOs in England and Wales lacking the legal requirements relating to fire escapes. The DoE estimated in 1986 there were 334,000 HMOs, including houses subdivided as flats and flatlets and bedsitters, lodging houses, hostels, bed and breakfast establishments and houses shared by students; some 2 million people were *estimated* as living in these properties. In addition to problems associated with lack of effective means of escape from fire, it appears 110,000 HMOs need major repairs, 96,000 are lacking basic amenities, 77,000 are managed unsatisfactorily and 53,000 are overcrowded; some houses fall into more than one category. The most serious issue in relation to HMOs remains the risk of fire in such properties; between 1978 and 1981 some 550 people died in fires in HMOs, and the risk of death or injury caused by fire in such dwellings is some ten times greater than in a self contained dwelling. [See also 'Councils Fiddle as Hostels Burn' *Roof* January/February 1985; 'Fire Emphasises Need for HMO Bill' *Roof* July/August 1984; 'HMOs Still A Fire Risk' *Legal Action* January 1984; 'Death in a Classic HMO' *London Housing* January 1984; 'Another HMO Fire Tragedy' *London Housing* February 1983; 'Legal Protection Against Fire' LAG Bulletin, December 1982, and *Roof* (Notes) May/June 1986, p. 5.] The most salient facts are that 43 per cent of HMOs are in London; some 2 million people, 4 per cent of the population, live in HMOs, 55 per cent of which justify action.

The supervision of multi-occupation by planning control

Under planning law 'development' may not in general be carried out without a grant of planning permission from the local planning authority. Can local authorities use their planning powers to prevent the inception of undesirable multi-occupation developments? Section 22(1) of the Town and Country Planning Act 1971 defines development as:

'the carrying out of building, engineering, mining or other operations in, on, over or under land, or the making of any material change in the use of any buildings or other land'.

Section 22(2)(a) excludes from this definition:

'the carrying out of works for the maintenance, improvement or other alteration of any building, being works which affect only the interior of the building or which do not materially affect the external appearance of the building'.

But section 22(3)(a) goes on to provide:

'For the avoidance of doubt it is hereby declared for the purposes of this section – the use as two or more separate dwelling-houses of any building previously used as a single dwelling-house involves a material change in the use of the building and of each part thereof which is so used'.

Unfortunately doubt in this area of the law has not been avoided, and it is not entirely certain whether a change from single residential to multi-occupied use inevitably constitutes an act of development by virtue of being either a material change of use or by falling within section 22(3)(a) above, and so requiring planning permission. In *Ealing Corpn v Ryan* [1965] 2 QB 486, [1965] 1 All ER 137 a local planning authority alleged that unauthorised development had taken place in that the use of a house had changed from being a single dwelling to use as two or more separate dwellings. The house was found to contain several families who all shared a common kitchen, and presumably the lavatory and bathroom also. It was held that on such facts the house had not been divided into *separate* dwellings. Cases decided on the doctrine of sharing in relation to the Rent Acts were followed. Thus a house may be occupied by two or more persons living separately under one roof, without their occupying 'separate dwellings', provided they are sharing certain common living accommodation, which, following *Goodrich v Paisner* [1957] AC 65, [1956] 2 All ER 176, certainly includes kitchens. Multiple occupation by itself therefore is insufficient to bring section 22(3)(a) of the Town and Country Planning Act 1971 into operation. That provision is designed to deal with the situation where the new dwellings can be regarded as truly separate, self-contained and independent, in which circumstances the existence or absence of any form of physical reconstruction will be a factor of great importance.

But multi-occupation of a dwelling-house may still constitute development even though there has been no conversion into separate dwellings for the conversion may amount to a material change of use under section 22(1) of the 1971 Act. In *Birmingham Corpn v Minister of Housing and Local Government and Habib Ullah* [1964] 1 QB 178, [1963] 3 All ER 668 three former singly-occupied houses were let in parts to a number of occupants each paying a weekly rent. The local planning authority alleged unauthorised development, which the minister refused to accept as he considered that there was no change of use: the houses remained solely in residential use. The Divisional Court held otherwise, and pointed out that there had been a change of use in that the houses, which had previously been used as single family accommodation, were being used for gain by their owner letting them out as rooms. The material change of use is constituted by the real change from family/residential to commercial/residential use.

It had been argued from *Duffy v Pilling* (1977) 33 P & CR 85 that where a single person owns or rents a house and lives there with lodgers, generally providing meals for them but sometimes allowing them to provide for themselves, there is no change of use unless there is some form of physical division between the parts each person occupies. This decision is generally agreed to be most unsatisfactory, and the better view of the law is that a material change of use occurs as soon as a predominantly single family use alters into a predominantly non-family use. Once the lodgers predominate then a change of use has taken place. Certainly in *Lipson v Secretary of State for the Environment* (1977) 33 P & CR 95 a change of use of premises from self-contained flats to individual bed-sitters was found to be a material change of use. The test that emerges from the decisions is to ask a simple question of fact in each case: 'who has control over the property?' If control is in the hands of one person who has a small number of others living with him there is no material change of use. On the other hand if the effective control of the property has been 'parcelled out' amongst a number of individuals, the best evidence of which is a physical partitioning of the premises, then a multi-occupancy will have arisen and will constitute a material change of use for which planning permission will be required. See also *Panayi v Secretary of State for the Environment* [1985] JPL 783, where the use of four self-contained flats as a hostel to house homeless families was held to constitute a material change of use.

It is questionable how far a local authority may go in using its planning powers in order to prevent the spread of undesirable multi-occupation. An outright policy of refusing any application for planning permission to convert premises to multi-occupation would undoubtedly be an illegal fetter on discretion. Nor would it appear generally proper for a local authority to take into account the character of the person applying for planning permission. Even an applicant who had a long history of abuse in relation to his tenants, for example convictions for harassment, etc., under the Protection from Eviction Act 1977, or of mismanagement in relation to other multi-occupied properties owned by him, could not be refused planning permission merely because of his misdeeds as they are matters relevant to other areas of law and do not raise real issues of planning as such. Neither could an authority impose restrictive conditions designed to regulate future behaviour on a grant of permission to such a person for the whole thrust of the cases is that a planning condition must always relate fairly to the physical development, and not to the subsequent use by the developer of his powers of letting and management.

In *Mixnam's Properties Ltd v Chertsey UDC* [1965] AC 735, [1964] 2

All ER 627 a local authority attempted to use powers conferred by the Caravan Sites and Control of Development Act 1960 to impose requirements on a site owner that would have required them to give caravan occupiers, inter alia, security of tenure equivalent to that enjoyed by tenants protected by the Rent Acts. It was held that the authority had no power to impose such requirements. On the basis of ministerial decisions on planning appeals the proper factors to be taken into account by a local planning authority in these situations include: the density of housing; the possibility of overcrowding; the amenities of the neighbourhood; any prevailing shortage of accommodation in the locality; the suitability of the premises for conversion; architectural considerations and, occasionally, the problems that might arise from an increase in the number of cars that incoming residents might wish to park in the area. All these are, of course, proper land use considerations.

Planning control is ineffective with regard to controlling the spread of HMOs because it is often ignored, and planning officers are too occupied to undertake enforcement action.

The supervision of multi-occupation under the Housing Acts

The Housing Act 1985, Part XI is the principal legislation, consolidating previous enactments, though regular attempts are made by parliamentary pressure groups to *reform* the law, and increase controls over HMOs, see Baroness Vickers's Housing (Multiple Occupation) Bill 1986.

The definition of multi-occupation

The Housing Act 1985 s. 345 provides that a multi-occupancy arises when a house 'is occupied by persons who do not form a single household'. Unfortunately the word 'household' is itself not defined by law and this has given rise to litigation. In *Wolkind v Ali* [1975] 1 All ER 193, [1975] 1 WLR 170 Mr Ali occupied certain premises which he used as a lodging house. Under their statutory powers the local authority served on him a notice prescribing the number of persons who could lawfully sleep in certain rooms. These restrictions were observed by Mr Ali until he was joined by his large family from abroad. Thereafter the premises were occupied solely by the family. Mr Ali was subsequently charged with exceeding the prescribed numbers of persons allowed to sleep in certain rooms in the house. The Divisional Court held that Mr Ali was not guilty of the offence with which he was charged. The local authority's multi-occupancy powers did not apply to this house as it was being used only by a single household.

On the other hand it was held in *Okereke v Brent London Borough Council* [1967] 1 QB 42, [1966] 1 All ER 150 that, once a property is divided between separate households, it makes no difference whether the multiple occupation arises from a physical division of the building or not. Here a house built originally for occupation by one family had been converted into separate self-contained dwellings. The basement and ground floor were each occupied by one family and the first floor by two or more families, who shared a bathroom, water closet and kitchen. The second floor was unoccupied and unfit for occupation. It was held that the house as a whole was multi occupied.

Thus where there is a clear division of control over a house between two or more households the multi-occupancy powers apply. Likewise (as has been argued previously in relation to the cases that have arisen as a result of the use of planning control with regard to multi-occupation) where a person lives in or occupies a house, and there caters for lodgers on a *substantial* scale, and shares control with them, as a commercial enterprise, a multiple occupation of that property arises.

But what of the situation where persons live together freely and communally in a house? In *Simmons v Pizzey* [1979] AC 37, [1977] 2 All ER 432 Mrs Pizzey occupied a property in a London surburb as a refuge for 'battered women'. The local authority fixed, under statutory powers, a maximum number of persons who might lawfully occupy the house, and Mrs Pizzey was subsequently charged with a failure to comply with the authority's direction. Her defence was that the house was not multi-occupied as all the residents lived there communally as one household. The House of Lords rejected this argument and laid down a number of tests to be applied in deciding whether a group of persons do or do not form a single household.

1) The number of persons occupying the property, and the place of its location, must be considered. Where, for example, 30 or more persons occupy a surburban house they can hardly be regarded as forming a single household.

2) The length of time for which each person occupies the property must be considered. A fluctuating and constantly altering population is a clear indication that the property is multi-occupied.

3) The intention of the owner of the property has to be taken into account. Mrs Pizzey, for example, never intended to set up a permanent community of women. Her intention was to provide a place of refuge for women who had been maltreated by their husbands. Some of the women simply needed time to get away from their homes to let the

domestic violence spend itself, while others had no intention of ever returning to their husbands but wished to go to friends, relatives or to set up their own new homes.

This approach to the definition of 'household' was followed by the Court of Appeal in *Silbers v Southwark London Borough Council* (1977) 122 Sol Jo 128. Here a common lodging house was used for accommodating some 70 women, some of whom were alcoholics while others were mentally disturbed. They stayed there for varying periods or indefinitely. It was held that such a fluctuating group of residents could not be regarded as forming a single household. It is not necessary for persons to have exclusive possession of different parts of the property for them to form individual households and for a multi-occupancy to arise. Indeed it seems from dicta in *Milford Properties v London Borough of Hammersmith* (1978) JPL 76 that a multi-occupancy can arise even where some of the occupiers are in the premises unlawfully, for example as unlawful sub-tenants. In *Hackney London Borough v Ezedinma* [1981] 3 All ER 438 the court stressed that what constitutes a household is a question of fact and degree. Thus groups of students each of whom has a separate tenancy of a room in a house may nevertheless group together to form 'households'. On the other hand, various homeless families may be so accommodated in a house as to occupy it *not* as a single household, thus constituting it a HMO, see *R v Hackney London Borough Council, ex p Thrasyvoulou* (1986) Times, 30 May, (1986) 18 HLR 370. Many so called 'hotels' are occupied on this basis.

Local authority powers

Management orders

By virtue of section 369 of the Housing Act 1985 the Secretary of State has power to make a code to ensure proper standards of management in HMOs. This code is contained in the Housing (Management of Houses in Multiple Occupation) Regulations 1962 (S.I. 1962/668). Where it appears to a local authority that a multi-occupied house is in an unsatis-factory state as a consequence of failure to maintain proper standards of management they may by order under section 370 of the 1985 Act apply the management code to that house. Orders under this provision come into force on the date on which they are made, though within seven days from their making the local authority must serve a copy of the order on the owner of the house, and on every person whom they know to be a lessee of the house, and also post a copy of the order in some conspicuous place in the house where it is accessible to the inhabitants. Such orders are local land charges. Persons on whom copies of the order have been served have, under section 371, a period of 21 days (or such longer period that the local authority may by writing allow) from the service of the copy to appeal against the order, on the ground that it is unnecessary, to the magistrates. Should an appeal be made the court is to take into account the state of the house, both at the time of the making of the order as well as at the time when the appeal was instituted: merely temporary improvements are thus to be disregarded. Once a management order is made its remains operative until revoked by the local authority on the application of any person having an estate or interest in the house. Should an authority refuse such an application, or fail to notify an applicant of their decision within 35 days, there is a further right of appeal to the magistrates' court, who may revoke the order if they feel there has been a substantial change in the circumstances since it was made and that it is in other respects just to order a revocation.

A management order imposes certain duties on 'the manager' of the house in question. He is defined in the management regulations as a person who, being an owner or lessee of a house, receives rents or other payments from tenants of parts of the house or who are lodgers therein, and also any person who receives such payments on behalf of an owner or lessee as a trustee or agent. The actual duties of the manager are:

1) To maintain in good repair and proper, clean working order all means of water supply and drainage;

2) To maintain and keep in proper order and repair installations for the supply of gas and electricity, and for lighting and heating the common parts;

3) To keep safe and unobstructed, clean and in good order all common parts and facilities;

4) To make certain that at the commencement of a period of letting the rooms, facilities and service installations are clean and in good repair and order;

5) To maintain all means of ventilation in good order;

6) To maintain proper means of escape from fire;

7) To maintain in correct order all outbuildings, yards, forecourts or gardens in common use, together with any boundary walls and fences thereto;

8) To make available an adequate supply of rubbish bins, and not to allow refuse and litter to accumulate in the premises;

9) To take reasonable precautions to prevent injury to the occupants as a result of any structural defects, and

10) To display within the premises a printed copy of the regulations, and also a notice giving the manager's name and address.

The regulations also require that the local authority maintain a register of the names and addresses of managers of HMOs subject to the management code. Persons served with copies of the management order are also required to give the local authority details of their interest in the house, of its occupation, and also of any agents or trustees. They may also be required to supply details of any other person with an interest in the house, and the name and address of the manager. It should also be remembered that the regulations require the occupants of multi-occupied houses to co-operate with managers and not to hinder them.

Under section 369(5) of the 1985 Act it is an offence *knowingly* to contravene management regulations, and an offence of *strict* liability where there are relevant defects in premises to fail without reasonable excuse to comply with the regulations, see *City of Westminster v Mavroghenis* (1983) 11 HLR 56.

Powers to require the doing of further works

If in the opinion of a local authority a HMO is defective because of neglect in complying with the management regulations or other failure to observe proper standards of management or maintenance corresponding to those in the regulations, they may serve a notice under the Housing Act 1985 s. 372 on the manager specifying the works necessary to make good the defects and requiring their execution. The notice must allow at least 21 days for the doing of the works, though this period may be extended from time to time with the written permission of the authority. Information of the service of the notice must also be served on all other persons who are known to the local authority to be owners, lessees or mortgagees of the house. Following the service of the notice the person on whom it has been served has, under section 373, a period of 21 days (or such longer period as the local authority may allow) to appeal against the notice to the magistrates' courts. The grounds on which such an appeal is made are:

1) that the condition of the house did not justify the local authority in requiring the execution of the specified works;

2) that there has been some material error, defect or informality in, or in connection with, the notice;

3) that the authority have refused unreasonably to approve the execution of alternative works, or that the works required are otherwise unreasonable in character or extent or are unnecessary;

4) that the time allowed for the doing of the works is not reasonably sufficient, or

5) some person other than the appellant is wholly or partly responsible for the state of affairs, or will benefit from the doing of the works, and therefore ought to bear the whole or part of the cost of the works.

The appeal powers can be productive of delay in implementing remedial action; delays of between fifteen and eighteen months are not unknown.

Further powers to require the doing of works are conferred by section 352 of the 1985 Act. If a local authority, having regard to the number of individuals or households accommodated in a multi-occupied house, consider that it is so far defective with regard to a number of listed particulars that it is not reasonably suitable for occupation by the individuals or households, they may serve a notice specifying the works which, in their opinion, are necessary to make the premises reasonably suitable for occupation, and requiring the execution of those works. The particulars the local authority may consider are: natural and artificial lighting; ventilation; water supply; personal washing facilities; drainage and sanitary conveniences; facilities for the storage, preparation and cooking of food, and for the disposal of waste water, and installations for space heating or for the use of space heating appliances. The notice must allow at least 21 days for the doing of the works, but this period may be extended by written permission. The notice is to be served either:

1) On the person having control of the house, i.e. the person who receives the rack rent of the property, or who would receive it if it were so let, or

2) On any person to whom the house is let at a rack rent, or an agent or trustee for such a person, and who receives rent or other payments from tenants or lodgers in the house.

Where a section 352 notice is served the local authority must also inform any other person who is known to them to be an owner, lessee or mortgagee of the property of the service. The notice may be withdrawn in writing if the local authority are satisfied that the level of occupation of the house has been reduced, and will remain reduced, to such a level as to render the doing of the works unnecessary.

The issue of fire precautions in relation to HMOs has already been mentioned. Under section 365 of the 1985 Act where a local authority consider a HMO is not adequately supplied with means of escape from fire they may exercise their powers, and *must* do so if the house falls within a description of houses specified by order by the Secretary of State, see S.I. 1981/1576, making mandatory the exercise of powers in relation to HMOs of at least three storeys (excluding those below principal entrance floor level) having a combined floor area of all storeys in excess of 500 square metres. Before taking action, authorities must consult with relevant fire authorities, see generally DoE Circular 25/82 which also gives guidance on other relevant legislation, though in practice liaison between the various authorities is often poor.

The powers are quite extensive. The local authority may serve a notice on any person on whom they may serve notice under section 352 of the 1985 Act specifying the works required to provide the necessary means of escape from fire, and also requiring the execution of that work within a period of not less than 21 days from the service of the notice. This period may be extended from time to time. The fact of service must also be communicated to all other persons known by the local authority to be owners, lessees or mortgagees of the house, see section 366.

Where it appears that the means of escape from fire would be adequate if part of the house ceased to be used for human habitation, the local authority may under section 368 secure that. Alternatively they may secure the closure of part of the house while serving notice specifying those works necessary to supply the rest of the house with adequate fire escapes. In the execution of these powers they may accept undertakings from owners or mortgagees that part or parts of houses will not be used for human habitation without the consent of the local authority. It is an offence to use, or to permit the use of, any part of a house subject to a closing undertaking. Where such an undertaking is not accepted, or if one accepted is found to be broken, the local authority may make a closing order on the relevant part of the house. That part of the house closed will lose any protection under the Rent Act 1977, but displaced residents will fall within the rehousing obligations under section 39 of the Land Compensation Act 1973. Where a closing order is made it must be determined *provided* the local authority are satisfied that the means of escape from fire are adequate (owing to a change of circumstances) and will remain so if the closed part of the house is made available for human habitation.

The term 'means of escape from fire' was given a wide meaning in *Horgan v Birmingham Corpn* (1964) 108 Sol Jo 991 to include not just fire escapes as such but also ancillary matters such as screens operating to keep escape routes clear of smoke. [See also DoE Circular 25/82.]

A person on whom a notice is served under either section 352 or sections 365 and 367 of the 1985 Act may, within 21 days of service (or within such longer period as the local authority allow in writing) appeal against the notice to the county court. The grounds on which an appeal can be made are *similar* to those relating to appeals made under section 373 which have been discussed above. If a notice under sections 352, 366, or 372 is not complied with, or if the person on whom it was served informs the local authority in writing that he is not able to do the works, section 375 of the 1985 Act allows the authority to do the work themselves. They may then recover their reasonable expenses under Schedule 10 of the Act from the person on whom the notice was served, or where an agent or trustee was served, in whole or in part from the person on whose behalf the agent or trustee was acting. Recovery may be by action in the county court. It should also be noted that a *wilful failure* to comply with a notice issued under sections 352, 366, or 372 of the 1985 Act is, by virtue of section 376(1) of the Housing Act 1985, an offence punishable by a fine. By virtue of section 376(2) of the Housing Act 1985, where a person is initially convicted of the offence created by section 376(1) of the Act, he commits a further new offence if he then wilfully fails to leave the work undone. Furthermore this provision lays down that the obligation to do works created by a notice served under sections 352, 366, or 372 of the Act is a continuing one, despite any expiration of the time limits set by the notice, thus a failure to comply with the *continuing* obligation itself constitutes a continuing offence. This meaning of 'wilful failure' was stated in *Honig v Islington London Borough* [1972] Crim LR 126 to include voluntary omissions to act, irrespective of motive. It appears that the only allowable reasons for not acting are force majeure, accident or impossibility.

Section 377 of the 1985 Act applies where any person, being an occupier, or owner of premises, and having received notice of intended action under sections 352, 366, or 372 of the Act prevents the carrying into effect of the proposals. A magistrates' court may order such a person to allow the doing of what is necessary. If he fails to comply with their order he is liable on summary conviction to a fine, and to a further fine for every day on which his failure continues.

Power to prevent overcrowding in multi-occupied houses

Where a notice, or further notice, under section 352 of the 1985 Act *could be* served the local authority may use their powers under section 354 of the Act to make a direction fixing the highest number of individuals or households or both who may occupy the house in its existing condition. At least seven days before making such a direction the local authority must serve on the owner and every known lessee notice of their intention, and also post a copy of this notice in the house in some place where it is accessible to the occupants. A right solely to make representations is given to those on whom such a notice is served. The direction once given makes it the duty under section 355 of 'the occupier', who is any person entitled or authorised to permit individuals to take up residence in the house, to keep the number of persons in the house within the permitted number. In *Hackney London Borough v Ezedinma* [1981] 3 All ER 438 a managing estate agent was held to fall within this definition as he had been authorised by the owner of the house to let out its rooms. Copies of the direction must be served, within seven days of its making, on the owner and known lessees of the house, and also posted within the house in some place where the occupants can have access to it. It is an offence under section 355(2) knowingly to fail to comply with a direction.

A section 354 direction can only be issued at a time when the house to which it applies is multi-occupied, and further multiple occupation of the premises at the time of the alleged offence is an essential requirement for liability. However, it seems from *Simmons v Pizzey* [1979] AC 37, [1977] 2 All ER 432 that once a direction is validly given a temporary cessation of multiple occupation does not end the direction but merely suspends its operation; it will revive and be applicable as soon as the house is again multi-occupied. There is no right to appeal against the giving of a section 354 direction as such. However, local authorities have power under section 357 to revoke or vary such directions, following changes of circumstances affecting the house, or the execution of works there, on the application of anyone having an estate or interest in the house. An unreasonable refusal to exercise this power can form the subject of an appeal to the county court.

A further power to control overcrowding is given by section 358 of the Housing Act 1985. Where it appears to a local authority that an excessive number of persons, having regard to the number of rooms available, is being, or is likely to be, accommodated in a house in multiple occupation they may serve on the occupier, or on the person having control or management of the house, or on both, an 'overcrowding notice'. This notice must state, under section 359, in relation to every room on the premises what the authority considers to be the maximum number of persons who can suitably sleep therein, if any. Special maxima may be included in the notice where some or all of the persons occupying the room are below such an age as is specified.

The local authority may require a number of courses of action from persons on whom such notice is served. The first such course, under section 360, is that he must refrain from:

1) knowingly permitting any room to be occupied as sleeping accommodation otherwise than in accordance with the notice, or

2) knowingly permitting persons to occupy the premises as sleeping

accommodation in such numbers that it is not possible to avoid persons of opposite sexes not living together as husband and wife, and over the age of twelve, sleeping in the same room, it being assumed that the persons who occupy the premises as sleeping accommodation sleep only in rooms for which the notice sets a maximum, and that the maximum for each room is not exceeded.

The *alternative* course of action, under section 361, is that the person on whom the notice is served must refrain from:

1) knowingly permitting any *new* resident to occupy a room as sleeping accommodation otherwise than in accordance with the notice, or from

2) knowingly permitting a new resident to occupy part of the premises for sleeping if that is not possible without persons of opposite sexes, and not living as man and wife, sleeping in the same room.

Not less than seven days before serving such a notice, under section 358(2), the local authority must:

1) inform the occupier of the premises, and any person appearing to have the control and management thereof, in writing of their intention to serve the notice, and

2) ensure, so far as reasonably possible, that every other person living in the house is informed of their intention.

Those informed must be given an opportunity of making representations regarding the proposal to serve a notice. A person aggrieved by an overcrowding notice may, under section 362, appeal against it to the county court within 21 days of service, and the court may confirm, quash or vary the order. Once an order is in force it is an offence to contravene it.

Such a notice may, under section 363, be revoked or varied at any time by the local authority on the application of any person having an estate or interest in the house. If they refuse such an application, or fail to notify the applicant of their decision, the applicant may again appeal to the county court.

During the currency of an overcrowding notice, under section 364, the local authority may give notice requiring the occupier to furnish them with written particulars as to:

1) the number of individuals on a specified date using the premises as sleeping accommodation;

2) the number of families or households to whom the individuals belong;

3) their names, and the names of the heads of families and households;

4) the rooms used by those individuals and families or households respectively.

It is an offence to fail to supply such particulars or to file a false return.

Supplementary powers

Local authorities have a number of supplementary powers to aid them in the exercise of their powers over multi-occupied houses. Under the Housing Act 1985, s. 395(1) an authorised officer may enter any house, after giving 24 hours' notice in writing of his intention to both the occupier and the owner, if the latter is known, in order to determine whether multi-occupation powers should be exercised. By virtue of section 356 of the 1985 Act at any time after a section 354 Direction is in force a local authority may serve a further notice on the occupier of the house in question requiring him to give a written statement of:

1) the number of individuals living in the house (or part of it) on a specified date;

2) the number of families or households to which those individuals belong;

3) the names of the individuals, and of the heads of families or households, and

4) the rooms used by those individuals and families or households respectively.

A failure to reply, or the making of a false reply, is an offence.

The Housing Act 1985, section 395(2) empowers local authorities to enter houses for the purpose of ascertaining whether there has been a contravention of any regulation or direction made under sections 346, 355, 358, 368, 369, 376 of the Act, and in such a case notice need not be given in advance.

Tenements

Sections 352(6) and 374 of the 1985 Act extend local authorities' powers under sections 352(1) (relating to fitness) and sections 369 to 373 (relating to management) to cover blocks of tenement buildings, i.e. any building:

1) which is not a house but comprises separate dwellings, two or more of which do not have lavatories and personal washing facilities accessible only to those living in the dwelling, or

2) which is not a house but comprises separate dwellings two or more of which are occupied by persons who do not form a single household.

In a tenement block of this sort the individual occupiers share lavatories and bathrooms, etc., but have their own individual cooking facilities in their houses. Moreover they will be tenants and not mere licensees or lodgers. These provisions extend the power to apply the management code, and also to require the doing of certain works, but *not* to check overcrowding, to such premises.

Registration

Section 346 of the 1985 Act grants powers to local authorities to register houses in multiple-occupation and tenements within their areas. A scheme has to be submitted for central approval, and local authorities are under an obligation both to publicise their intention to submit a scheme and also its confirmation. A scheme made empowers a local authority to seek particulars for registration from any person with an estate or interest in the house or living in it, and may also make it the duty of certain prescribed persons to notify the local authority that a house appears to be registrable. Occupiers of the house, its owners, lessees, mortgagees, those who receive its rents, and its managers may also be required to give information to the local authority under the Local Government (Miscellaneous Provisions) Act 1976, s. 16. This provision imposes a fine for non-compliance with, or the wrongful supply of false information in answer to, their request. Section 350(1), (2) of the Housing Act 1985, makes it an offence to fail to provide a local authority with information in connection with their registration enquiries. The 1985 Act, however, allows the insertion of *regulatory* or control provisions in a registration scheme under section 347 where a house is occupied by *more* than two households, or by one household and four individuals. Thus a local authority may under section 348 refuse to register a house: (a) on the ground that it is unsuitable and incapable of being made suitable for occupation; (b) because the person having control, or intended as the manager is not 'fit and proper'. They may also require the execution of works as a condition of registration. Written statements of reasons for refusing to register a house must be given, and there is a period of 21 days thereafter in which an appeal can be made to the county court, who may confirm, reverse or vary the decision of the local authority. It is an offence under section 346(6) of the Housing Act 1985 to contravene or to fail to comply with any provision of a registration scheme. Under section 347(1) of the 1985 Act registration schemes may contain control provisions for *preventing* a house from being multi-occupied, *unless* the house is registered, *and* the number of households or persons occupying it does not exceed its registered number. Control provisions may also under section 347(2) prohibit persons from *permitting* others to take up residence in a house, but may not prohibit a person from taking up or remaining in residence in the house.

Control orders

To deal with HMOs in the worst condition housing authorities· may make 'control orders' allowing them to take over the management of houses for up to five years and act as if they were the owners. It is a proper use of this power to make an order to ensure the continuance in use and operation of a house, see *R v Southwark London Borough, ex p Lewis Levy Ltd* (1983) 267 Estates Gazette 1040. Under section 379 of the 1985 Act an order can be made:

1) if a notice has been served under sections 352 or 372 (i.e. requiring execution of works) or if a direction has been given under section 354 (limits on numbers of occupants) or an order under section 370 is in force (application of the management code); or

2) if it appears to the local authority that the state or condition of the house is such as to call for the taking of any such action, *and*

3) if it also appears to the authority that the state of the house is such that it is necessary to make a control order to protect the safety, welfare or health of the persons living in the house.

Control orders are designed to deal with the most squalid conditions and so there is no lengthy procedure as to their making. Such an order comes into force when made, and as soon as practicable thereafter the local authority must enter the premises and take such immediate steps as are necessary to protect the residents' health, welfare and safety. A copy of the order has to be posted in the house where it is accessible to the residents, and copies must also be served on every person who, before the order, was the manager of the house, or had control of it, or was an owner, lessee or mortgagee of the house. These copies of the order must be accompanied by a notice setting out rights of appeal against the order under section 384 of the 1985 Act (see below).

The effect of a control order

A control order transfers full possession and control of the house to the local authority and cancels any orders, notices or directions already made under the management provisions of the Act, but without prejudice to any liabilities incurred thereunder. It is possible to exclude from control, by virtue of section 380 of the Housing Act 1985, any part of the house which is occupied by an owner or tenant of the whole house. Such an excluded part will be subject under section 387(3) to the authority's right of entry for the purposes of survey, or to execute any works in any part of the house which is subject to the order. The authority may grant, under section 381(2) of the Act, weekly or monthly tenancies within the property, but rights and obligations of existing residents are protected by section 382, and this extends to any protection enjoyed by virtue of the Rent Acts. Section 385 lays an initial double duty on the local authority once they have control:

1) to maintain proper standards of management and take any action which would have been necessary under the management provisions of the Act, and

2) to keep the house insured against fire.

Thereafter section 386 requires them to prepare a scheme and to serve a copy on the dispossessed proprietor and on all other owners, lessees and mortgagees of the house, not later than eight weeks from the making of the control order. The scheme must, under Schedule 13 Part I, provide for the execution of, and payment for, works involving capital expenditure needed to satisfy the 1985 Act, or any other housing or public health legislation. The scheme must also state what the authority consider to be the highest number of individuals who should be allowed from time to time to reside in the house. The scheme must also include an estimate of the balance of the moneys that will accrue to the local authority in the form of rents, etc., from the residents, after they have paid the dispossessed proprietor his compensation, and disbursed all other payments, other than those in respect of the management powers under the Act, i.e. capital expenditure. Throughout the life of the control order the authority must also keep half yearly accounts under Schedule 13, paragraph 4. They must balance the capital expenditure against the surplus balances (revenue) arising from the rents, etc., referred to above. Any excess of capital expenditure over the revenue surplus carries interest, while an excess of the surplus over expenditure reduces the interest. The cost of expenditure and the interest thereon constitute a charge on the premises and all estates and interests therein.

During the currency of a control order section 389 of the Housing Act 1985 requires the local authority to pay to the 'dispossessed proprietor' (i.e. the person who would have otherwise been entitled to the rents from the property) compensation at an annual rate of an amount equal to one half of the gross rateable value as at the date when the control order came into force multiplied by a figure specified by the Secretary of State.

Appeals

Any person having an estate or interest in the house, or otherwise pre-judiced by the making of a control order, may appeal against its making to the county court under section 384. A similar right of appeal exists under Schedule 13 against the local authority's scheme. However, the period for an appeal runs out in both cases six weeks after a copy of the scheme has been served.

Control orders expire after five years, unless they are revoked earlier by the local authority, Housing Act 1985, s. 392. A person may apply for early revocation, giving reasons therefor, and if this application is rejected, or ignored for six weeks, he may apply to the county court for the order to be revoked. An unsuccessful appeal precludes further applications to the court for a period of six months.

A local authority has power under Schedule 13 Part IV to make a compulsory purchase order on a property subject to a control order. Where the authority makes the compulsory purchase order within 28 days of making the control order they need not prepare or serve a management scheme until after the decision of the Secretary of State to reject or confirm the compulsory purchase order. Provision is made for the satisfaction of the financial obligations of both the local authority and the owner: he is to receive any surplus revenue balance in the hands of the local authority; they may recover their capital expenditure on works necessary under the Act, from the revenue balance derived from rents received from the house or from the compulsory purchase compensation.

Common lodging houses

Common lodging houses fall within the powers of local authorities by virtue of Part XII of the Housing Act 1985 which lays down certain standards to ensure a basic, though not very high, level of cleanliness and repair within such premises. A common lodging house, by virtue of section 401 of the 1985 Act, is: 'a house (other than a public assistance institution) provided for the purpose of accommodating by night poor persons, not being members of the same family, who resort there and are allowed to occupy one common room for the purpose of sleeping or eating, and includes, where part only of a house is so used, the part so used'. The definition appears to *exclude* from its operation reception facilities provided by the Social Services Secretary, and also accom-modation provided under the National Assistance Act 1948, such premises surely being 'public assistance' institutions. The section covers dwelling-houses, and also purpose-built common lodging houses, *but not premises not built as houses*, e.g. a purpose-built hotel.

Once a house is found to be within the definition it is immaterial that its owner calls it a 'hostel' or 'guest house', nor does it matter whether the accommodation is let for a week, for a night or some other period of less than a week, see *People's Hostels Ltd v Turley* [1939] 1 KB 149, [1938] 4 All ER 72. However, in order to constitute a common lodging house there must be common sleeping or eating accommodation – see *LCC v Hankins* [1914] 1 KB 490 – though the mere division of a large room into smaller cubicles by the erection of screens will not prevent that room being treated as common sleeping accommodation – see *Logsdon v Trotter* [1900] 1 QB 617. A common lodging house need not necessarily be run for commercial reasons, even charitable institutions can be controlled by the law, *Logsdon v Booth* [1900] 1 QB 401. A common lodging house can be a house in multiple occupation, and also falls within the statutory nuisance and fitness for human habitation powers of local authorities. See *R v Southwark London Borough, ex p Lewis Levy Ltd* (1983) 267 Estates Gazette 1040, and *R v Camden London Borough Council, ex p Rowton (Camden Town) Ltd* (1983) 10 HLR 28.

Under sections 402 and 408 of the 1985 Act it is an offence for a person to keep a common lodging house unless he is registered in that capacity with the local authority. Local authorities must, under section 404, register keepers unless they are satisfied that:

1) an applicant for registration is unfit to be a keeper; or

2) the premises are unsuitable for use as a common lodging house, having regard to the sanitation, water supply, means of escape from fire, etc.; or

3) the use of the premises as a common lodging house would cause inconvenience or annoyance to persons in the neighbourhood.

A refusal to register must be given in writing and accompanied by reasons, and a person aggrieved by such a refusal may appeal to the justices, see section 405 of the 1985 Act. The period of registration may be for up to thirteen months. Despite these provisions many common lodging houses are unregistered because many 'keepers' do not realise that they should apply for registration.

The keeper's duties. By section 407 of the 1985 Act the keeper or his duly registered deputy must be on duty between 9.00 pm and 6.00 am as well as maintain general management over the house and its inmates. The keeper must supply to the local authority, on their request, a list of persons who occupied the house during the day or night preceding the request. Keepers must also allow the local authority's duly authorised officers to have free access to all parts of their houses.

Supervisory powers of local authorities

Under section 39 of the Public Health (Control of Disease) Act 1984 common lodging house keepers must notify the local authority of any person in their houses suffering from 'infectious diseases' (see Pollard: *Social Welfare Law* paras. C5835–C5836). Where local authority officers have reasonable grounds to believe a person in a common lodging house is suffering from a 'notifiable' disease (i.e. Cholera, Plague, Relapsing Fever, Smallpox and Typhus) they may be authorised by the justices to enter the house and ascertain the facts, see section 40 of the 1984 Act. Under section 41 of that Act persons suffering from 'notifiable' diseases may be removed to hospital, and section 42 authorises the closure of common loging houses affected by 'notifiable' diseases. Local authorities have power under section 406 of the 1985 Act to make byelaws:

1) for fixing the maximum number of persons allowed to use a common lodging house, and to provide for the separation of the sexes;

2) for promoting cleanliness and ventilation;

3) to provide for precautions against the spread of infection in common lodging houses, and

4) generally to secure the well ordering of such premises.

Model byelaws have been issued by the Department of Health and Social Security. (See Pollard, *Social Welfare Law*, paras. C5837–5838.)

Local authorities, however, do not always enforce the standards of the Act because some keepers, if proceeded against, would simply close down their houses, thus imposing an increased number of homeless persons on the authorities. Nevertheless by section 408 of the Act any person who:

1) contravenes or fails to comply with any provision of Part XII, or

2) fails in his duty as a keeper to maintain the premises in a fit state to be used as a common lodging house, or

3) deliberately misleads the local authority in relation to an application for registration,

commits an offence. Where a keeper is convicted of such an offence, or contravening a byelaw relating to common lodging houses, the court may cancel his registration and may disqualify him from registration for such period as it thinks fit, see section 409 of the Act.

Overcrowding

We have already seen how, historically, overcrowding was a problem principally associated with areas of poor court and terrace houses, but that today it can also occur in multi-occupied premises. Our present concern is with overcrowding in separate dwelling-houses.

Local authority powers with regard to overcrowding are found in Part X of the 1985 Act, but this is derived from much older legislation, and its standards have been criticised as out of date. In England and Wales in 1977 some 5 per cent of households were overcrowded according to the 'room standard' (see below). Though Scots law is outside this work's scope it should be noted that in Scotland overcrowding in 1977 affected over 8 per cent of households, and was particularly prevalent in Glasgow. Under sections 324 and 343 of the Act overcrowding powers apply in relation to 'dwellings', i.e. *premises* used or suitable for use as a *separate* dwelling. This would seem apt to include caravans, see *DPP v Carrick District Council* (unreported, Truro Magistrates Court, 'Housing Aid' January 1985 No. 31, p. 5).

The definition of overcrowding

A dwelling is overcrowded when the number of persons sleeping in it contravenes *either* section 325 (room standard) or section 326 (space standard). Under the former, standards are contravened when the number of persons sleeping in a dwelling and the number of rooms available for sleeping is such that two persons of opposite sexes and not living together as man and wife must sleep in the same room. Children under ten are left out of account in the calculation, and rooms are available for sleeping if they are locally used *either* as bedrooms or living rooms. Under the latter standard a contravention occurs when the numbers sleeping in a dwelling exceed the permitted number having regard to numbers and floor areas of rooms in the dwelling available for sleeping. The permitted number for a dwelling is whichever is the *lesser* of *either* the number specified in Table I below, or the aggregate for all rooms available for sleeping in the dwelling of numbers of persons specified in Table II in relation to each room of the floor area specified in that table.

Table I

Number of rooms	Number of persons
1	2
2	3
3	5
4	7.5
5 or more	2 for each room

Table II

Floor area of room	Number of persons
110 square feet or more	2
90–110 square feet	1.5
70–90 square feet	1
50–70 square feet	0.5
Under 50 square feet	NIL

A child under one and a half years is not reckoned in these calculations, and a child between one and a half and ten counts as half a unit.

Rules for the measurement of rooms in order to obtain the permitted number are found in the Housing Act (Overcrowding and Miscellaneous Forms) Regulations 1937 (S.R. & O. 1937 No. 80) reg. 4, the principal effect of which is to *exclude* from the measured floor area any part of the floor over which the ceiling height is less than five feet.

It should be noted that *all* persons who use the house as their home should be counted when deciding whether there is overcrowding, and not just those who are sleeping there at any given time. If this were not so the law could be ignored by persons sleeping on a shift or 'Box and Cox' basis. In *Zaitzeff v Olmi* (1952) 102 LJO 416 (county court) a daughter away at a boarding school was held to be living at home for the purposes of the permitted number standard. It should also be noted that the only rooms that can be taken into account when deciding the issue of overcrowding are those normally used in the locality either as living rooms or bedrooms, Housing Act 1985, section 326(2)(b).

Section 330 of the Act permits local authorities to license an occupier to exceed the permitted number standard, but only up to the number specified in the licence and only for a period of up to twelve months. Within that period the licence may be revoked by the authority giving the occupier one month's notice. Licences may be granted to take account of seasonal increases of population in a district, for example to allow for the accommodation of migratory agricultural workers or holiday makers, or in other 'exceptional circumstances', an undefined phrase that might cover the sheltering of wives and children driven from the homes by matrimonial disputes or other persons rendered homeless by disaster.

Offences

These are principally defined by sections 327 and 331 of the Housing Act 1985, and can be committed by the occupier of a dwelling-house and by the landlord where the property is let. The occupier who causes or permits overcrowding commits a summary offence for which he may be fined, save where he acts under license of the local authority granted under section 330 (see above), or where his case falls within either section 328 or 329. Under the former where a dwelling becomes overcrowded solely by virtue of a child attaining the age of ten, then the occupier commits no offence *provided* he applies, or has so applied before the relevant birthday, to the local housing authority for suitable alternative accommodation, *and provided that all the persons* sleeping in the dwelling are those who were living there when the child reached the relevant age and who live there continuously afterwards, or are the children of those persons. But the exemption ceases to apply if either suitable alternative accommodation is offered to the occupier and he fails to accept it or he otherwise fails to take reasonable steps to secure the removal of persons who are not members of his family from the house. A mere visit by a member of the occupier's family who normally lives elsewhere which causes temporary overcrowding is not an offence, and this circumstance is excluded from criminal liability by section 329 of the 1985 Act.

Section 342 of the Act defines 'suitable alternative accommodation' as a dwelling-house as to which the following conditions are satisfied, that is to say –

1) the house must be a house in which the occupier and his family can live without causing it to be overcrowded;

2) the local authority must certify the house to be suitable to the needs of the occupier and his family as respects security of tenure and proximity to place of work and otherwise and to be suitable in relation to his means; and

3) where the dwelling is a local authority house, they certify it as suitable to the needs of the occupier and his family. In this context a two bedroom dwelling provides accommodation for four people, three bedrooms accommodate five people and four bedrooms seven.

So far as a *landlord* is concerned, he will commit an offence under section 331 and be deemed to have caused or permitted overcrowding if:

1) after receiving notice from the local authority that his house is overcrowded he fails to take reasonable steps to abate the overcrowding, or

2) he let the house having reasonable cause to believe that it would become overcrowded, or if he failed to make inquiries of the proposed occupier as to the number, age and sex of persons who would be allowed to sleep in the house.

To aid the landlord in the abatement of overcrowding section 101 of the Rent Act 1977 takes away any security of tenure enjoyed by a tenant in a house which is so overcrowded that the occupier is guilty of an offence.

But to prevent families from being dispossessed and made homeless, Ministry of Health Circular No. 17/49 makes certain recommendations. First, occupiers whose houses have become overcrowded merely by the natural increase of children, and who have not deliberately aggravated the situation by taking in additional persons, such as lodgers, should be encouraged to apply for suitable alternative accommodation to the local authority, thus terminating their own criminal liability and so escaping from dispossession under section 101 of the 1977 Act. Second, local authorities have been advised to use their powers to license overcrowding under the Act so as to prevent criminal liability falling on an occupier. A landlord is under a duty by virtue of section 333 of the Housing Act 1985 to inform the local authority within seven days of overcrowding within any of his houses that has come to his knowledge.

In order to inform occupiers of their rights, section 332 of the 1985 Act requires that a summary of Part X of the Act shall be contained in any rent book or similar document given to the tenant, together with a statement of the permitted number of persons in relation to the house. A local authority are under an obligation to inform either the occupier or the landlord, if either apply, of the permitted number of persons in relation to the house in question. With regard to tenancies where rent is payable weekly a landlord is under an obligation to supply his tenant with a rent book by virtue of section 4 of the Landlord and Tenant Act 1985.

Enforcement and remedial powers and duties of local authorities

The Housing Act 1985, section 339 makes it the duty of the local authority to enforce the duties relating to overcrowding, and only they may prosecute. Where the local authority itself is responsible as landlord for overcrowding they can themselves be prosecuted by another person but only with the consent of the Attorney-General. To aid them in discharging their obligations a local authority may serve notice on an occupier requiring him to give them within fourteen days a written statement of the number, ages and sexes of the persons sleeping in the house. Failing to comply with this request or deliberately making a false return will involve the occupier in criminal liability, for which he can be fined on summary conviction, see Housing Act 1985 section 335.

Section 338 grants a power to the local authority to commence possession proceedings in respect of a privately rented overcrowded house. If they notify an occupier in writing that overcrowding exists and require him to abate it within fourteen days, and if he takes no action, or having taken action allows overcrowding to recur, within three months, then they may apply to the county court for possession to be given to the landlord. According to Jenkins LJ in *Zbytniewski v Broughton* [1956] 2 QB 673 at 688, [1956] 3 All ER 348 at 356: 'the position crystallises at the end of the period of three months, and, provided the house is still overcrowded at the date when the complaint is made to the court . . ., then the order for possession must go'. Any expenses incurred by the local authority under this power may be recovered by them summarily as a civil debt from the landlord. Tenants displaced in consequence of the use of this power do not fall within the scope of the local authority's rehousing obligations under the Land Compensation Act 1973.

Local authorities are also under a general duty under section 334 of the 1985 Act to investigate overcrowding within their areas of which they become aware, to make a report to the Secretary of State of their findings, and of the number of new houses needed to relieve the overcrowding. The Secretary of State may direct an authority to make such an investigation and report.

Further reading

Arden, A., and Partington, M., *Housing Law* (Sweet & Maxwell, 1983) Chap. 12.

Garner, J.F., *Alteration or Conversion of Houses* (Oyez Longman) (4th edn., 1975) pp. 15–20.

Smith, D., *Racial Disadvantage in Britain* (Penguin, 1977) pp. 230–242 and 270–274.

Smith, D., and Whalley, A., *Racial Minorities and Public Housing* (PEP Broadsheet No. 556) pp. 99–106.

Kirby, K., and Sopp, L., *Houses in Multiple Occupation in England and Wales* HMSO (1986).

Social Welfare Law (Ed. by D.W. Pollard) (Oyez Longman) paras. C. 5500–C. 6089 and C. 6400–C. 6444.

Summers, D., 'Overcrowding: The Human Cost' *Roof* May/June 1981, pp. 16–17/23.

Grosskurth, A., 'Lives on the line' *Roof* November/December 1984, pp. 11–14.

Wolmar, C., 'Overcrowding in Southall', *Roof* July/August 1980, pp.117–118.

Index